Israeli Peacemaking Since 1967

Examining the Israeli–Arab conflict as an "intractable conflict," *Israeli Peacemaking Since 1967* seeks to determine just which factors, or combination of factors, impacted upon Israel's positions in past peacemaking efforts, possibly accounting for breakthroughs or failures to reach agreement.

From the rejection of King Hussein's little known overtures immediately after the Six-Day War, through President Sadat's futile efforts to avoid war in the early 1970s, to repeated third-party mediated talks with Syria, factors including deep-seated mistrust, leadership style, and domestic political spoilers contributed to failures even as public opinion and international circumstances may have been favorable. How these and other factors intervened, changed, or were handled, allowing for the few breakthroughs (with Egypt and Jordan) or the near breakthrough of the Annapolis process with the Palestinians, provides not only an understanding of the past but possible keys for future Israeli–Arab peace efforts.

Employing extensive use of archival material, as well as interviews and thorough research of available sources, this book provides insight on just which factors, or combination of factors, account for the few successful but far more numerous failed efforts to resolve the conflict – a framework useful for examining the Israeli–Arab conflict today and intractable conflicts in general.

Galia Golan is a leading Israeli political scientist, Darwin Professor of Soviet and East European Studies Emerita, formerly head of the Political Science Department at the Hebrew University, Jerusalem, currently Head of the M.A. and Conflict Resolution Programs at the Interdisciplinary Center, Herzliya (IDC), and the author of ten books, many of which address the Arab–Israeli conflict. She has also co-edited a volume with Walid Salem, *Non-State Actors in the Middle East: Factors for Peace and Democracy* (Routledge, 2013).

UCLA Center for Middle East Development (CMED)
Series Editors
Steven Spiegel, UCLA
Elizabeth Matthews, California State University, San Marcos

The UCLA Center for Middle East Development (CMED) series on Middle East security and cooperation is designed to present a variety of perspectives on a specific topic, such as democracy in the Middle East, dynamics of Israeli–Palestinian relations, Gulf security, and the gender factor in the Middle East. The uniqueness of the series is that the authors write from the viewpoint of a variety of countries so that no matter what the issue, articles appear from many different states, both within and beyond the region. No existing series provides a comparable multinational collection of authors in each volume. Thus, the series presents a combination of writers from countries who, for political reasons, do not always publish in the same volume. The series features a number of sub-themes under a single heading, covering security, social, political, and economic factors affecting the Middle East.

1 **The Struggle over Democracy in the Middle East**
Regional Politics and External Policies
Edited by Nathan J. Brown and Emad El-Din Shahin

2 **Women in the Middle East and North Africa**
Agents of Change
Edited by Fatima Sadiqi and Moha Ennaji

3 **The Israel-Palestine Conflict**
Parallel Discourses
Edited by Elizabeth Matthews

4 **Gender and Violence in the Middle East**
Edited by Moha Ennaji and Fatima Sadiqi

5 **Non-State Actors in the Middle East**
Factors for Peace and Democracy
Galia Golan and Walid Salem

6 **Regional Security Dialogue in the Middle East**
Changes, Challenges and Opportunities
Edited by Chen Kane and Egle Murauskaite

7 **Israeli Peacemaking Since 1967**
Factors Behind the Breakthroughs and Failure
Galia Golan

Israeli Peacemaking Since 1967

Factors Behind the Breakthroughs and Failures

Galia Golan

Routledge
Taylor & Francis Group

LONDON AND NEW YORK

First published 2015
by Routledge
2 Park Square, Milton Park, Abingdon, Oxon OX14 4RN

and by Routledge
711 Third Avenue, New York, NY 10017

Routledge is an imprint of the Taylor & Francis Group, an informa business

© 2015 Galia Golan

The right of Galia Golan to be identified as author of this work has been asserted by her in accordance with sections 77 and 78 of the Copyright, Designs and Patents Act 1988.

All rights reserved. No part of this book may be reprinted or reproduced or utilised in any form or by any electronic, mechanical, or other means, now known or hereafter invented, including photocopying and recording, or in any information storage or retrieval system, without permission in writing from the publishers.

Trademark notice: Product or corporate names may be trademarks or registered trademarks, and are used only for identification and explanation without intent to infringe.

British Library Cataloguing in Publication Data
A catalogue record for this book is available from the British Library

Library of Congress Cataloging in Publication Data
Golan, Galia.
Israeli peacemaking since 1967 : factors behind the breakthroughs and failures / Galia Golan.
pages cm. -- (UCLA Center for Middle East development series)
Includes bibliographical references and index.
1. Arab-Israeli conflict--Diplomatic history. 2. Arab-Israeli conflict--Peace. I. Title.
DS119.7.G617 2014
327.5694017'4927--dc23
2014002663

ISBN: 978-1-138-78434-5 (hbk)
ISBN: 978-1-138-78435-2 (pbk)
ISBN: 978-1-315-76622-5 (ebk)

Typeset in Times New Roman
by Taylor & Francis Books

To my grandchildren, in the hope that they will soon see the advent of a final breakthrough to peace.

Contents

	List of Maps	viii
	Preface	ix
1	Introduction	1
2	1967–1968 Failure	10
3	Breakthrough with Egypt	29
4	Failure on the Syrian Track	57
5	Jordan Again: Failures and Breakthrough	94
6	Oslo I: Breakthrough and Failure	118
7	Oslo II: Barak and Camp David	142
8	Olmert's Near Breakthroughs: Annapolis Process and Syrian Talks	166
9	Conclusions	201
	Bibliography	218
	Index	228

List of Maps

1.1	Israel and the Occupied Territories, 1967	7
2.1	Expansion of Jerusalem	12
2.2	The Alon Plan	15
3.1	Israeli–Egyptian Interim Agreement 1975	37
4.1	Israeli–Syrian borders	66
5.1	Israeli–Jordanian Peace Treaty 1994	110
7.1	Israeli Proposal Camp David 2000	147
7.2	Clinton Parameters (approximation)	158
8.1	Olmert Proposal 2008 (approximation)	180
8.2	Abu Mazen Proposal 2008 (approximation)	181

Preface

Curiosity is as good a reason as any to write a book. And, indeed, that was the reason for most of the books I have written, as distinct from the posing of an hypothesis to be proven or disproven. In the case of the present book, my curiosity was sparked by two events – actually, people. The first was a graduate student and friend, Itay Mizrav, who told me of a "fascinating" M.A. seminar he was taking with Professor Eli Podeh on "Missed Opportunities" in the Arab–Israeli conflict. The second was a passing comment by Professor Zaki Shalom at a conference abroad to the effect that King Hussein had made a peace offer to Israel in the summer of 1967. The latter revelation actually angered me since I remembered hastening to see the Occupied Territories (especially Bethlehem, Jericho, etc.) immediately after the 1967 war since at the time we fully expected that Israel would be returning the territories, in exchange for peace. Moshe Dayan, then minister of defense, had actually said the government was waiting for a phone call – a comment made more cynically, I now know, than sincerely at the time. There were, of course, those who knew about the Jordanian initiative, but the general public and even many of my academic colleagues were not aware of this. So, my curiosity having been sparked by these two comments, I began researching past Israeli negotiations with the purpose not only of finding out what had transpired, but, more importantly for me, why – if peace had been offered, or perhaps been possible, at various times since 1967, why were we still struggling with the conflict? Thus, my interest was to try to determine just what accounted for – and perhaps still accounts for – the failure to reach peace or, conversely, the few successes that did occur. More specifically, I was interested in understanding what motivated or shaped Israeli positions at each (potential) cross-road. This has not been of merely academic interest to me, though I believe my findings will be of some academic value. Rather, it has been important to me personally, as an Israeli, to understand what lay behind the contribution – or lack of contribution – of my own government to the breakthroughs or failures in the attempts at resolution of the conflict over the years. This is of particular importance to me and many other Israelis who believe that resolution of the conflict is essential to the well-being and future of Israel no less than it is to that of the Palestinians or our other neighbors. It is my hope that identifying, to the extent possible, those factors that affected past efforts at peacemaking can inform and improve future efforts.

A number of people assisted me in the preparation of this book, most notably my two assistants, Eddo Bar and Lavi Melman, who were extraordinarily helpful with the research. Their resourcefulness, thoroughness, and dedication were indispensable. I am particularly indebted to Shaul Arieli for the use of his maps and also his explanations and comments; similarly, Uri Bar Josef was of great assistance. I enjoyed numerous stimulating conversations with Ambassador Dan Kurtzer on the topic and, additionally, a number of people consented to extensive interviews, preferring anonymity. I am grateful to them as well. The Lauder School of Government, Diplomacy and Strategy at the Interdisciplinary Center, Herzliya, generously provided research funds, and the fantastic staff of the IDC Library were most helpful in ferreting out material for me. Gila Svirsky was kind enough to provide transliteration of the Hebrew titles for the references, though we have left proper nouns (names, labels) in their familiar form. In general, I am grateful to friends, colleagues, and family with whom I discussed many of the often depressing things I discovered researching this book – in particular, the fact that there need not have been so many failures. Everyone's patience is greatly appreciated, including that of the excellent people at Routledge and the UCLA series in which this book appears.

1 Introduction

The Arab–Israeli conflict, as a prolonged, periodically violent, and unresolved conflict generally falls into the category of "intractable" conflicts. While not necessarily unresolvable, such conflicts are characterized by the difficulty to transform them – that is, to achieve a breakthrough to peaceful resolution. Therefore, a search for just which factors – in their presence or absence – can make a difference with regard to a breakthrough is of utmost importance. Concomitantly, an understanding of those factors that impede or actually cause failure are no less important. The identification of such factors, the context in which they appear, or their very absence at any given time, as well as the inter-relationship and interaction between them may provide keys to eventual resolution of the conflict.

The factors themselves are linked to the various characteristics of intractable conflict, beyond, of course, from the dominant characteristic of intractability. There is a quite a long list of additional characteristics, suggested most notably by Louis Kriesberg and also Peter Coleman, the earliest researchers of the phenomenon. Kriesberg's explanation of intractable conflict notes such characteristics as deep-seated identity issues, repeated cycles of violence, perception of the conflict by the protagonists as destructive, internalized longstanding grievances (serving as reasons for continuing the conflict), and institutionalization of the conflict.[1] Characteristics are dynamic (changing over time) and often linked to one another, but Kriesberg ties them to four core components: identities, grievances, goals, and means. Identities are the ways in which the protagonists view themselves as a collective or in relationship to their adversaries and the way their adversaries view them. These may stand in a negative relationship to one another, full expression of one perceived as negating the other in a zero-sum relationship. Herb Kelman calls these "monolithic identities."[2] Thus, identity issues may be perceived as existential threats, particularly in ethno-national conflicts.[3] Grievances are generally connected to the issue of justice or the perception of wrongs that have been done by one side to the other. Goals are a component when one side perceives the goals of the other side as damaging or costly or uncompromising. Goals, too, may be perceived as a zero-sum matter. Finally, it is characteristic of intractable conflict that coercion is perceived as the only effective means, creating a culture of violence in which force or violence, often reciprocated, contribute to a conflict's destructiveness and persistence, according to Kriesberg.

Peter Coleman's approach from political psychology includes some 57 possible characteristics, many of which are more detailed aspects of some of Kriesberg's categories or components.[4] Notable additions are: "tainted infrastructure: compromised institutions, laws, and social norms for conflict regulation," "multiple and varied stakeholders," "intragroup divisions and factions," "hub issues: grievances embedded with broad beliefs, ideologies, and basic assumptions," "pervasiveness: conflict spreads into functional aspects of life (education, cultural systems, etc.) and transforms them into tools of conflict," and many more. The long list might also include history (past trauma), ideology, simple thirst for power, or repeated misperceptions, betrayal of trust, and emotions such as frustration, fear, hate, sense of loss, loyalty, anger, disgust. Like Kriesberg, Coleman sees the many characteristics as dynamic, particularly with regard to salience but also in connection with each other. There can be tipping points at which increasing intensity of a conflict goes beyond a threshold into a situation of no constraints.[5] At the same time, both thinking and emotions harden, with a feeling that there is no solution. If religion (which reflects faith rather than reason or empirical evidence) is added, contrary views may be perceived as threatening, thereby hardening thinking and emotions.[6]

Moving into the realm of emotions, Daniel Bar-tal sums up many of the above-mentioned characteristics as part of an "Ethos of Conflict" that develops in an intractable conflict. This is a situation in which the conflict has become a central, unifying factor in society with "frozen" beliefs regarding: the justice of one's goals, security concerns (threats and dangers), de-legitimization (and dehumanization) of the adversary, a positive collective self-image, sense of victimization (due to acts of the adversary), perceived need for unity, the value of patriotism, and peace (as a goal – i.e., belief that one is peace-loving). The dominant emotion behind these beliefs is fear, leading to anger and hate.[7] These emotions may be directly connected with the element of trust, or rather mistrust of the other side. Trust in the context of conflict has been defined most often as reliance on or belief that the other side will do what it has committed to do, or expectations of reciprocity.[8] A certain risk or gamble is implied, distrust or the absence of trust rendering the risk factor greater. At play is the credibility of the commitment of the other side to honor an agreement. Where credibility is absent or low, there is an unwillingness to make judgments or (to risk) actions such as compromises based on the commitments of the other side. Misperception may be one direct result.[9]

Obviously the attributes ascribed to intractable conflict are factors that operate toward rendering the conflict intractable and as such can be said to constitute barriers to resolution. Amongst other things, the dynamics of the psychological factors "inhibit de-escalation of a conflict and peaceful resolution" "because adhering to their goals results in delegitimization, distrust, and hatred" of the adversary.[10] In more concrete terms, these factors, individually or in combination, may thwart efforts to reach agreement, operating at the elite (decision-making) level or within the society at large, affecting public opinion, which may, in turn, affect decision-making. Overcoming these barriers may be only one task, for at the extremes they will have produced outright opposition in the form of veto-players or spoilers with whom would-be peacemakers must contend.[11] Spoilers' efforts to undermine a peace process or agreement may be motivated by concern over a threat to their worldview, their interests, or their power. Thus they range from those ideologically opposed to those who may lose out or believe that they will lose from a particular agreement. Steven Stedman speaks of three types of spoilers: the greedy spoiler (seeking better conditions on a cost/benefit basis); total spoilers whose goals are uncompromising and incompatible with the proposed agreement; and the limited spoiler who has modest goals. While all three may be committed more or less to their goals, only the total spoiler remains unchanging. Both Coleman and Miriam Ellman suggest that religiously motivated spoilers might be included in this group. Other categorization might describe spoilers as those who perceive transformation of the conflict as undermining their rights, privileges, resources, or security.[12] Just as there are many methods that spoilers may employ, including violence, there are also many circumstances in which they may operate (outside the process, within, etc.). For example, Ellman specifically deals with critical coalition partners, while others refer to unintentional spoilers whose actions – or lack of action – weaken trust without explicitly intending such an outcome.[13] An additional category has been suggested of "devious spoilers" – that is, those who actually enter negotiations or a peace process with no intention of reaching agreement, possibly because they simply do not believe that their adversary is capable of compromise on issues essential to the other side.[14]

Thus there are numerous factors constituting barriers that may impede resolution of an intractable conflict or its transformation, preventing a significant breakthrough in relations between the protagonists. The persistence of such barriers, including the existence of spoilers, may turn a potential breakthrough or actual peace process into a failure. Yet, there are many suggested ways of overcoming the barriers, coping with the different factors and managing spoilers. In general, one might simply say that a significant weakening of, or changes in any or some of, the above factors could make a difference. In the domestic realm, as suggested by Kriesberg, changes may occur in public opinion or public support, possibly (but not necessarily) as the result of other domestic changes or events, such as socio-economic developments (e.g., recession, globalization); a dramatic or traumatic event (which Ronald Krebs maintains can even be war[15]); leadership change (what Ellman refers to as change in agency[16]); power shifts; demography (immigration, generational change); perceived costs of continued conflict; "war weariness"; reduction or satisfaction of grievances; changes in relative weight of domestic groups (such as peace groups, or those who profit from the conflict) or the weakening of spoilers; new technology and weapons development presenting an intolerable threat or changing the nature of the threat; change in the image of the enemy;

the appearance of a new, threatening enemy; change in the conceptualization of national (collective) identity; ideological change.[17] Changes in one protagonist may trigger change in the other – for example, revision of the adversary's goals, strength, or composition, satisfaction of some of its grievances; Coleman refers to good signs or confidence-building measures from the other side that allay fears for the future.

William Zartman would put it more simply as the perception, by both sides, of having reached a mutually hurting stalemate coupled with the appearance of an opportunity. The latter may come from outside and, indeed, outside factors may play an important role in combating intractability: regional developments (threatening instability or power shifts and interests, alliances), power shifts in the international arena, global norms, third-party involvement (pressure, mediation, tradeoffs, proposals, guarantees). Finally, overcoming barriers must include dealing with spoilers, whether they work inside or outside (e.g., from the diaspora) or third parties altogether. Stedman suggests three ways in which spoilers may be "managed": inducement, socialization, and coercion. The first would involve addressing the grievances or fears of the spoilers; others might call this inclusion. The second would entail incentives and persuasion to abide by accepted norms of behavior, and the third would threaten punishment (penalties). The punishment need not be direct or military, but rather could rely on arguments such as the spoiler's potential losses since the train would leave the station with or without them.

Within almost each of these factors that may lead to change or overcoming barriers, there are sub-categories, variations, and, in some cases, methodologies for ensuring them. Coleman, in particular, focuses on the more long-term, psychological, and epistemological methods for breaking down the barriers, while everything from peace education, peace journalism, track two endeavors, grass roots activism, citizen diplomacy, and more are part of conflict resolution repertoires important for transforming intractable conflicts.[18] Some of these are geared to the public at large, others to elites and decision-makers, or all together. Similarly, not necessarily all the characteristic of intractable conflict nor all the factors for changing them apply to the general public as well as the leadership, though the Ethos of Conflict presumably does apply to both, to one degree or another. In any case, the roles of both the public and the leadership must be considered in analyzing a breakthrough or failure.

As an intractable conflict, the Arab–Israeli conflict has demonstrated or experienced most if not all the characteristics mentioned. Indeed, it has been cited as an example of such a conflict by Coleman, Kriesberg, Bar-tal, and others, serving as a model for understanding intractable conflict perhaps even more frequently than Northern Ireland or Cyprus amongst other intractable conflicts. While various characteristics, such as its centuries-long history of persecution and the Holocaust, or its relatively recent creation as a Jewish state in the midst of an Arab/Muslim region, or its particular political system and mix of religion with nationalism may all be specific to Israel, they nevertheless fit the multifaceted paradigm of intractability (and the Ethos of

Conflict) within the categories of history, identity, ideology, grievances, and the like. Of importance to this study is how these and other attributes of intractability served to block or prevent a breakthrough, or led to a failure, or, conversely, which of them underwent a change (and why), enabling a breakthrough.

A breakthrough refers to transformation of the conflict to a peace process – that is, the opening of steps or talks leading to negotiations and possibly actual conflict resolution (success). This may entail reacting to or initiating some stimulus, such as taking advantage of an opportunity that arises or creating an opportunity. Whatever the circumstances, the phenomenon is a breakthrough leading to peace or at least significant transformation of the conflict that might lead to peace. A failure then would be the failure to take advantage of an opportunity that might lead to a breakthrough, or failure might be an actual peace process (negotiations, partial agreements) that is ended without achieving resolution of the conflict. A set of steps, such as the Oslo Accords, might constitute both a breakthrough and a failure. Of interest is just what factors may account for the breakthrough and/or the failure.

It may be impossible to know with certainty exactly what caused a breakthrough or what changes took place that moved matters toward resolution or what characteristics of intractable conflict might account for the failure. Nor does it seem possible to quantify confidently the role or relative value of each factor, particularly, as pointed out by both Kriesberg and Coleman, because there is usually an interplay of factors, with some more dominant, some less salient (even unconscious), perhaps testable only at a given time. Archival material, memoires, interviews all contribute to our understanding, but much is still highly subjective (and partial) as well as open to interpretation. For example, the myriad accounts of the Camp David 2000 talks, even by participants, are testimony to these difficulties. In addition, ideally one would try to determine such factors as they may have operated on both sides of a conflict. And insofar as the interdependence of factors on both sides is essential to the analysis, this shall be attempted. The main, more modest endeavor, however, shall be to try to determine just what factors were operative on the Israeli side of the conflict.

The instances that will be analyzed with regard to breakthroughs and failures are the following:

Breakthroughs:

- Egypt 1975–1979;
- Jordan 1994;
- Oslo 1993–1996.

Failures:

- Jordan 1967–1968;
- Syria 1991–2000;
- Oslo–Camp David 1996–2000.

Near breakthroughs:

- Annapolis Process (Palestine, Syria).

There have been many attempts at resolving the Arab–Israeli conflict altogether or in its parts (bilateral peace agreements) since 1948. Most of them, obviously, failed, though there have been notable breakthroughs even in some of the cases that ultimately failed, in addition to the two successful achievements of peace agreements (Israel–Egypt; Israel–Jordan). While there were a number of attempts in the first decade of Israel's existence, some of which have been at least partially analyzed,[19] the choice of 1967 for the timeframe is due to a number of reasons. Although before and after 1967 most of the core issues and problems were ostensibly the same (land, refugees, water, Israel's legitimacy and security), the 1967 war changed the nature or salience of the issues facing the protagonists, as well as many of the parameters of any eventual agreement. Prior to 1967 the conflict was viewed (particularly in the international community) as a conflict between states, with the addition of a serious humanitarian refugee problem. Moreover, despite certain territorial interests and even discussions on such matters between Israel and Egypt or Israel and Jordan, the conflict appeared to be of a zero-sum nature (i.e., acceptance or rejection of Israel's existence by its neighbors). It may be argued, in addition, that failure to deal with the Palestinians as a national rather than a purely refugee issue only served to delay the zero-sum battle over Palestine.

1967 ushered in a new era in the conflict. In addition to significant developments within Israel, major changes emerged with the 1967 Israeli occupation of Syrian, Egyptian, and Jordanian lands beyond the 1949 Armistice Lines. These lands had a complicated history. When the Ottoman Empire was divided up after World War I, the British were given a mandate over Palestine. In 1922 they gave the territory in the eastern part of the Mandate to the Hashemite Kingdom forming the country of Transjordan. The area to the west of the Jordan River remained the Palestine Mandate under the British. When the British gave up the mandate in 1947, the United Nations adopted the partition of Palestine (UNGA Resolution 181) into a "Jewish state" and an "Arab state", minus Jerusalem, which was to be under international control. As a result of the 1948 Arab–Israeli war, both Israel and Jordan captured and incorporated into their countries parts of Jerusalem and lands that were to have been part of the Arab state according to the Partition Plan. The part annexed by Jordan (in 1950) was what is known as the West Bank (of the Jordan River), although only Britain and Pakistan recognized the annexation (excluding East Jerusalem). Israel's borders, including the lands beyond the Partition Plan lines, were never recognized or made official by Israel; rather, they were a *de facto* (temporary) border determined by the 1949 Armistice Agreements. Israel's border with Syria theoretically was the international border drawn between Syria and the Mandate by France and Britain in 1923, but the Armistice Agreements of 1949 between Israel and Syria left a long swatch of land, beneath and beyond the Golan (Syrian) Heights, disputed and demilitarized.[20] Between 1949 and 1967 certain parts of this changed hands and both countries took over much of the demilitarized area, resulting in a Syrian presence in the northeastern corner of the Sea of Galilee, slightly west of the international border, when the 1967 war broke out. Sinai was a part of Egypt (since 1906); but the Gaza Strip, part of the former British Mandate (and due to be part of the Arab state called for in the Partition Plan), had been held by Egypt as a separate enclave under military rule since the 1949 Armistice Agreements. With the 1967 war some 1.5 million Palestinians came under Israeli control (in Jordan's West Bank, including East Jerusalem, and Egypt's Gaza Strip).[21]

The significance of the 1967 changes were, first, that Israel now held bargaining chips – namely, additional territories that might enable a land for peace deal: a return of the lands to the previous sovereigns (Syria, Egypt, and Jordan) in exchange for peace, without touching on the territorial integrity of Israel within its *de facto* borders, the 1949 Armistice lines, referred to today as

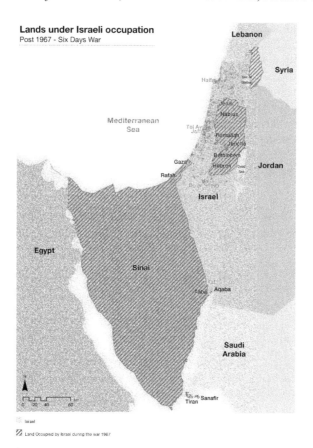

Map 1.1 Israel and the Occupied Territories, 1967
Source: Shaul Arieli

the green line or Israel proper. Indeed, this was the principle inherent in United Nations Security Council Resolution 242 adopted a few months after the war and accepted by Israel and, ultimately, the neighboring states. Second, the primary thrust of the Palestinian issue was henceforth no longer one solely of refugees but of national self-determination for a people under foreign occupation. This was not initially grasped (UNSC Resolution 242 continued the "refugee only" approach), although it was to emerge with the transformation of the Palestine Liberation Organization (PLO) into a gradually recognized national liberation movement after 1969.[22] Moreover, the new situation would affect the chances for peace between Israel and the Palestinians only once the link was made between the demand for self-determination from foreign occupation, on the one hand, and the lands occupied in 1967, on the other – namely, the creation of a Palestinian state next to rather than instead of the state of Israel. This linkage (limiting the locale for a Palestinian state to the West Bank and Gaza Strip) was long debated within the PLO (and urged by the Soviets) throughout most of the 1970s and 1980s; but it was accepted by the PLO only in 1988, as we shall see. It was at this point, made possible by the 1967 war, that an alternative to the zero-sum relationship between Israeli and Palestinian goals emerged.

Thus the 1967 war was to have a profound effect on the conflict. It precipitated significant changes in many aspects of the conflict, unleashing processes and developments within the protagonists themselves, including Israel, while also introducing possibilities and, arguably, opportunities for resolution. Indeed since 1967 the government of Israel found itself in numerous peacemaking efforts (not necessarily initiated or sought by Israel), resulting in the breakthroughs, failures, and near breakthrough listed above. The following chapters will seek to identify and understand the factors that accounted for these results.

Notes

1 Louis Kriesberg, "Nature, Dynamics and Phases of Intractability," in Chester Crocker, Fen Osler Hampson, and Pamela Aall (Eds), *Grasping the Nettle* (Washington, DC: United States Institute of Peace [USIP], 2005): 65–68.
2 Herb Kelman, "Reconciliation as Identity Change: A Social-Psychological perspective," paper cited in Peter Coleman, "Conflict, Complexity, and Change: A Meta-framework for Addressing Protracted, Intractable Conflicts – III," *Peace and Conflict: Journal of Peace Psychology*, 12(4), 2006: 330.
3 Nadim Rouhana and Daniel Bar-Tal, "Psychological Dynamics of Intractable Ethnonational Conflicts," *American Psychologist*, 53(7), 1998: 761–770.
4 Peter Coleman, *The Five Percent* (New York, NY: PBS, 2011): 32–33.
5 Peter Coleman, "Paradigmatic Framing of Protracted, Intractable Conflict: Toward a Meta-framework – II," *Peace and Conflict: Journal of Peace Psychology*, 10(3), 2004: 107–235.
6 *Ibid*, and Robin Vallacher, Peter Coleman, Andrzej Nowak, and Lan Bui-Wrzosinska, "Rethinking Intractable Conflict: The Perspective of Dynamical Systems," *American Psychologist*, 65(4), 2010: 262–278.
7 Daniel Bar-Tal, Eran Halperin, Keren Sharvit, and Anat Zafran, "Ethos of Conflict: The Concept and Its Measurement," *Peace and Conflict: Journal of Peace Psychology*, 18(1), 2012: 40–61; Daniel Bar-Tal, "Why Does Fear Override

Hope in Societies Engulfed in Intractable Conflict, as It Does in Israeli Society," *Political Psychology*, 22(3), 2001; Rafi Nets-Zehngut and Daniel Bar-Tal, "The Intractable Israeli-Palestinian Conflict and Possible Pathways to Peace," in J. Kuriansky (Ed.), *Beyond Bullets and Bombs: Grassroots Peacebuilding between Israelis and Palestinians*, (Westport, CT: Praeger, 2007): 3–13; Daniel Bar-Tal, Erin Halperin, and Neta Oren, "Socio-Psychological Barriers to Peace-making," *Social Issues and Policy Review*, 4(1), 2010: 63–109.
8 Michal Shamir and Tammy Sagiv-Schifter, "Conflict Identity and Tolerance: Israel in the Al-Aqsa Intifada," *Political Psychology*, 27(4), 2006: 569–595; Deborah Welch Larson "Trust and Missed Opportunities in International Relations," *Political Psychology*, 18(3), 1997: 701–734; Andrew Kydd, *Trust and Mistrust in International Relations*, (Princeton, NJ: Princeton University Press, 2005).
9 Barbara Walter, "The Critical Barrier to Civil War Settlement," *International Organization*, 51(3), 1997: 335–364; Russell Hardin, "Trusting Persons, Trusting Institutions," in R. J. Zeckhauser (Ed.), *Strategy and Choice* (Cambridge. MA: MIT University Press, 1991); Robert Jervis, *Perception and Misperception in International Politics* (Princeton, NJ: Princeton University Press, 1976); Deborah Welch Larson, 1997.
10 Rafi Nets-Zehngut and Daniel Bar-Tal, citing Nadim Rouhana and Daniel Bar-Tal, "Psychological Dynamics of Intractable Conflicts," *American Psychologist*, 53, 1998: 761–770; and Daniel Bar-Tal, "From Intractable Conflict through Conflict Resolution to Reconciliation: Psychological Analysis," *Political Psychology*, 21(2), 2002: 351–365.
11 Stephen Stedman, "Spoiler Problems in Peace Processes," in Paul Stern and Daniel Druckman (Eds), *International Conflict Resolution After the Cold War* (Washington, DC: National Academies Press, 2000): 178–224; Miriam Ellman, "Israel Democracy: Barriers to Making Peace," in Miriam Ellman, Oded Haklai, and Hendrik Spruyt, *Democracy and Conflict Resolution: The Dilemmas of Israeli Peacemaking* (Syracuse, NY: Syracuse University Press, 2013).
12 Edward Newman and Oliver Richmond, *Challenges to Peacebuilding: Managing Spoilers during Conflict Resolution* (Tokyo: UN University Press, 2006): 18.
13 Roger MacGinty, "Northern Ireland and Accidental Spoiling," in Edward Newman and Oliver Richmond (Eds), *Challenges to Peacebuilding: Managing Spoilers during Conflict Resolution* (Tokyo: UN University Press, 2006): 153–172.
14 Newman and Richmond, 2006: 18.
15 Ronald Krebs, "Can War Be an Engine of Liberalism?," unpublished paper for APSA, 2 September 2011.
16 Miriam Ellman *et al.*, 2013.
17 See Louis Kriesberg and Bruce Dalton, *Constructive Conflicts* (Lanham, MD: Rowman and Littlefield Publishers, 2011): 177–213.
18 Peter Coleman, *The Five Percent*: 32–33, 111–183. See also Bruce Dayton and Louis Kriesberg (Ed.), *Conflict Transformation and Peacebuilding* (New York, NY: Routledge, 2009); Paul Stern and Daniel Druckman, 2000.
19 There is much to be said about these earlier attempts and proposals believed by some to have, perhaps, provided a basis for agreement. An analysis of their failure is interesting but beyond the scope of this book. The most comprehensive if concentrated accounts may be found Benny Morris, *Righteous Victims* (New York, NY: Alfred Knopf, 1999).
20 The disputed areas were, in part, the result of the shifting positions of Israeli and Syrian forces at the close of the 1948 war. Syria's sovereignty over the Golan (Syrian) Heights, however, was not disputed.
21 Almost all of the 150,000 Syrian residents of the Golan Heights fled eastward in Syria during the war. The residents of four small Druze towns remained.
22 After Fatah, under Arafat, assumed the leadership of the movement.

2 1967–1968 Failure

The 1967 war could have precipitated a breakthrough, at least from the Israeli point of view. An opportunity for peace had emerged due to, first, changes on the ground – namely, the "bargaining card" now acquired in the form of the occupied territories beyond the 1949 Armistice lines; second, an incentive had been created for the Arab states – namely, the return of their territory; and, third, Israel was now in a strengthened position thanks to its demonstrated military superiority. Moreover, while Israel could and did expect international pressure to withdraw, as had occurred following the 1956 war, particularly from Washington, its international situation was relatively good. As distinct from 1956, the Israeli attack on 5 June 1967 was generally viewed as one forced upon the country by Egyptian moves, and in many circles Israel was perceived as the heroic victim more or less abandoned by the world to face three Arab armies alone. Even if this attitude was not universal, Israel was not generally perceived as an aggressor, thus granting the country somewhat more leeway or bargaining power (e.g., to demand peace agreements in exchange for land) than in 1956.

The United States, at least according to President Johnson's comments to Israel, was not entirely happy that Israel had preempted the war, but it was optimistic that a breakthrough for peace might now be possible.[1] American policy objectives in the region were traditionally focused on stability and the avoidance of polarization so that Washington could pursue its interests with both Israel and the Arab states.[2] Following Soviet entry into the region in the mid-1950s, primarily through an increasingly positive relationship with Egypt, the US had the added goal of preventing any broadening of the Soviets' positions there as well as trying to reduce their existing positions. This meant not only seeking to improve relations with Egypt, but also efforts to sustain the pro-western King in Jordan, without harming relations with Israel – to which the US had become increasingly committed in the 1960s. Given this commitment and that of the Soviets to Egypt and, more recently, Syria, the ongoing Arab–Israeli conflict had become more dangerous for the super powers.[3] US–Soviet confrontation had been avoided during the June war, and a modicum of cooperation had been achieved regarding a cease-fire, as both super powers refrained from direct involvement. Nonetheless, the dangers inherent in the conflict had become quite clear. Egypt's defeat in the war provided Moscow with an opportunity to secure long-sought bases and personnel deployment in Egypt (directed against NATO in the Mediterranean) in exchange for a massive rearming of the country. Nonetheless, Moscow, like the US, had an interest in preventing another violent outbreak and was willing to work with the Americans on a plan for possible resolution of the conflict, or at least greater containment. In order to remain a major player in post-war developments, the Soviets not only "represented" Egypt politically, but also pressed for international rather than local, bilateral negotiations favored by Israel and the US. For Moscow, the task was to secure a return of the territories to the Arab states; for the US it was to promote a settlement of the conflict – the two were not contradictory. Thus, despite the super power competition, the post-war meeting between US and Soviet leaders at Glassboro, New Jersey, on 23–25 June 1967 promised an international environment that might be conducive to a breakthrough.

At the domestic level, inside Israel, the public response to the stunning victory in the war was a general euphoria, pride, and delight with the possession of the newly acquired territories. At the same time, there was a general sense that merely returning these territories would now, finally, bring recognition and peace to the country.[4] The euphoria did, however, also include those for whom the possibility of now achieving the (nationalist or religious) dream of "Greater Israel" (the "Land of Israel," or *Eretz Israel* in Biblical times) was more important than peace – a segment of the population that was to become more powerful (though not necessarily more numerous) in the future.[5] On the whole, though, the unexpected six-day, three-front victory seemed to overcome the entrenched sense of victimhood; the victory went a long way toward eliminating the public's fears of the Arab states and the pre-war apparitions of a second Holocaust.[6] Indeed, a predominant view was one of contempt for Arab military capabilities (or lack thereof), accompanied by a sense of Israeli military invincibility. Conceivably, this could outweigh the historic insecurities and entrenched sense of victimhood. Moreover, public self-confidence was matched by confidence in the national unity government created on the eve of the war – a government which could, therefore, most likely lead the public in whatever direction it chose.

Changed circumstances; domestic and international conditions appeared auspicious for a breakthrough. Why then the failure?

After the war, on 18 and 19 June 1967 and throughout the following weeks, expecting international pressure but also cognizant of the opportunity to achieve some agreements, the Israeli government set its positions regarding the territories conquered in the war.[7] With regard to the West Bank, there was, in fact, no decision taken because of significant differences within the government. These were not, however, differences between left and right due to the pre-war addition of the Menachem Begin, leader of the right-wing Gahal Party[8] (including Herut, today's Likud) to the coalition. Nor were they even differences over relinquishing all of the territory – none of the 20 members of the government favored relinquishing *all* of the territory, though there were some who saw the danger in holding onto all but a small part of it due to the demographic issue, and most opposed annexation (which would have meant providing citizenship to the 1.2 million Palestinians there). Rather, the differences and discussions were within the left, born of political and even personal rivalries but also based on different visions and possible arrangements.[9] The main differences focused on the partner with whom to talk, the local Palestinians, or the Jordanians. The basic understanding agreed within the government was that the Jordan River would constitute Israel's border, meaning Israeli control of the Jordan–Rift Valley, no matter what arrangement would be decided for the rest of the West Bank. Thus, a number of ideas were proposed, from autonomy for the local population but under continued Israeli rule; or independence for major parts of the area, possibly limited in power but, in any case, territorially surrounded by Israel; or some kind of settlement with Jordan along new lines of demarcation.[10] Another understanding within the government from the outset was that Jerusalem would be united under Israeli sovereignty. The Jordanian built wall dividing east from west Jerusalem was physically dismantled; the city was united within days of the military move into East Jerusalem. Retention of East Jerusalem was included in the 19 June government decision and on 25 June there was a government decision to extend Israeli law to East Jerusalem, enacted into law on 27 June along with a major expansion of the city's borders into the West Bank.

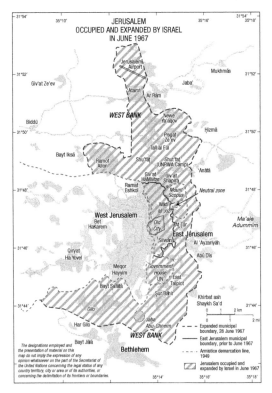

Map 2.1 Expansion of Jerusalem
Source: Jan de Jong, Foundation for Middle East Peace

As the political leadership debated options, talks were opened with local influential Palestinians regarding autonomy or limited statehood. Specifically, there was an idea of a Palestinian state in certain areas of the West Bank, as an enclave completely surrounded territorially by Israel. Israel would maintain control of all borders, foreign policy (one version allowed this to be independently Palestinian), security (e.g., a police force but not a local army), and it would settle the areas not included in the "state."[11] There were proposals of autonomy for the whole area within the borders of the West Bank, exclusive of East Jerusalem, but the autonomy plan presented on 27 July 1967 (the first Alon Plan) was actually the same as the idea for a state – namely, areas within the West Bank (surrounded by Israel) to be autonomous and the rest settled by Israelis. Both the ideas of this type of state and of autonomy were discussed, often simultaneously, with local Palestinians throughout 1967; but by the beginning of 1968 autonomy was gaining greater attention (and support by Eshkol). In all of these plans, various proposals were made for moving the refugees to other areas or countries. However, neither the limited state nor the autonomy idea found support amongst the Palestinians consulted. Some were still loyal to Jordan, almost all were unwilling to act independently of the Arab states, there was no willingness to accord Israel control of East Jerusalem, and there was no united Palestinian leadership capable of taking such a decision in any case (although at one point Israel initiated indirect contact with the PLO – though at this time the PLO itself was not a particularly representative or effective organization).[12] On the whole, the limitations proposed by Israel for the state or an autonomous area left any willing Palestinian leader with little to try to interest the Palestinian population. At the same time, the United States was pressing Israel to deal with Jordan, out of Washington's interest in preserving the King's rule and preventing any kind of Soviet inroad into this pro-western country.

Defense Minister Moshe Dayan, despite the fact that he favored the Palestinian option, had declared immediately after the war that Israel was waiting for a phone call, meaning (presumably) waiting for an Arab state to discuss peace in exchange for return of its territory. Actually, the phone call did come, from King Hussein. It came first in the form of talks with the Americans, including a private conversation with President Johnson, on 28 June 1967, followed by the opening of a secret meeting with the Israelis on 2 July 1967 in London. These direct and also indirect talks (primarily through the Americans) continued in starts and stops for over a year. Initially Israel would not state its conditions for peace (because it had not decided on a policy yet), and King Hussein would not make a clear commitment on peace without hearing Israel's terms. According to Hussein's biographer Nigel Ashton, the King did express his willingness "to enter into formal peace negotiations provided he knew in advance that all of the substantive issues, including the status of the occupied territories, would be open for serious discussion."[13]

The King did convey his proposal for a settlement to the Americans, declaring that he was willing to make a separate peace agreement. He would demand "return to the 4 June 1967 lines, including Jordanian control of the Old City of Jerusalem ... some border rectification, accompanied by over-flight rights and port facilities in Israel."[14] Israel basically put off an additional meeting until the fall, while trying to decide between the Palestinian and the Jordanian options. There was skepticism in the government regarding the King's intention to make peace, and the King himself appeared to backtrack at the end of July. He accused the Americans of moving toward a hardline Israeli position (which he believed consisted of an Israeli intention of holding onto territory and also East Jerusalem), saying he would prefer to obtain general Arab backing for a peace deal.[15] The Americans thought he was simply trying to improve his bargaining position; but, in any case, Hussein was willing to resume talks with Israel following the August Arab summit in Khartoum, which, he explained, had adopted a moderate position (and provided him Egyptian agreement for talks for a settlement but not a separate peace agreement with Israel). Once UN Resolution 242 was passed in November, with its call for peace and also assurance of "territorial integrity" (an Arab demand), Hussein was willing to continue for a separate deal.[16] However, return of territory to Jordan was not on the Israeli agenda at this time. According to a telegram to the State Department from the US delegation to the UN, Eban had clarified that "If Hussein said he was [sic] ready to negotiate tomorrow, majority of Israeli people would support such move. However, Jordan cannot get back to June 4 situation. Emphasis in Jordanian settlement, however, would not be on territory [as would be the case with Egypt, see below] but on security. Possibility exists for a free port, economic integration of Jordan. Eban also mentioned possibility of a demilitarization of West Bank with some kind of Israeli military presence."[17] In the early discussions for a United Nations Security Council resolution, Israeli diplomats suggested to the US (possibly disingenuously given the clear position during the 18–19 June government discussions) that the status of Jerusalem might be "negotiable."[18] In any case, during discussions around the formulation of a Security Council resolution, Israeli positions appeared to harden, viewed by the Americans (and Jordan) as indicative of Israel's interest in remaining in the West Bank and East Jerusalem.[19]

As Israel's positions became clearer in the form of the second Alon Plan (presented to Hussein at a September 1968 meeting in London but generally known since early 1968) – namely, holding onto the Jordan Rift Valley and other parts of the West Bank, as well as East Jerusalem – prospects for an agreement were virtually nil (as accurately assessed by Foreign Minister Abba Eban and Dayan even earlier).[20]

The King was adamant about "territorial integrity" – in other words, return to the pre-June situation of Jordanian sovereignty over the West Bank and especially East Jerusalem. While cognizant that peace with Jordan was possible, the Israeli leadership was not willing to budge on these two demands, and so peace with Jordan was rejected in favor of holding onto parts of the territory.[21] Officially (and in conversations with the Americans), Israel attributed

1967–1968 Failure 15

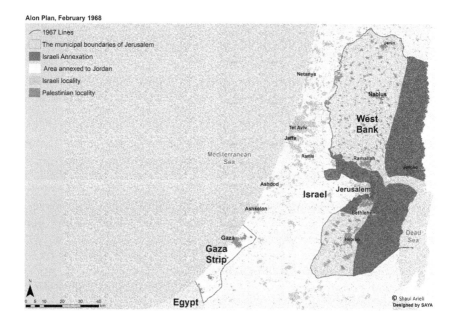

Map 2.2 The Alon Plan
Source: Shaul Arieli

the stalemate to Arab unwillingness to deal directly with Israel, although, in fact, King Hussein had been holding direct talks with Israel since 2 July (and before 1967). While further contacts and secret talks with Jordan were to occur often over the ensuing years, this Jordanian initiative/Israeli refusal marked the failure of the first post-1967 peace effort between the two countries.

Examining this failure from the point of view of intractable conflict, one explanation may be that despite the changed military situation on the ground (i.e., Israel's now proven might and the strength of its bargaining position), Israeli leaders' ingrained – and apparently unchanged – security concerns dominated. One might call them "insecurity" concerns, the result of an internalized mistrust of the enemy (or possibly of non-Jews as such), nurtured by the conscious or unconscious impact of the Holocaust and past oppression, but also by the Arabs' past steadfast refusal to accept Israel within the region.[22] This touched on a matter of legitimacy, which prompted Israel's demand for direct negotiations with the Arabs as a sign of recognition of the state. Ultimately the matter of legitimacy was connected with national identity – namely, Israelis' collective perception of Israel as unaccepted, a victim to enemy hostility (perceived as unchanged), and unjust rejection of the Jews' historic, national, and, for some, religious bond to the Land of Israel, part of which had now been recovered. Indeed, in his first talks with King Hussein on 2 July 1967, Israeli negotiator Yaacov Herzog (head of the Prime Minister's Office) delivered a long lecture on this need for the Arabs to recognize Israel's claim and right to be where it was – namely, the Jewish link to the Land of Israel. While the ruling party (the Labor Alignment, later called Labor Party[23]) was willing to give up Israel's "justified" possession (i.e., as Biblical Land of Israel) of the newly acquired land for the sake of peace, not all of the land could be relinquished inasmuch as "peace" was not to be trusted.[24] In fact, the starting point and unanimous position at the beginning of the post-war talks in June 1967 was that the Arabs would not make peace with Israel, and if they did, they could not be trusted.[25] Therefore, any peace agreement must contain the elements of preparation for winning if not preventing the next war. The demand to hold onto the Jordan Rift Valley, which separates the west bank from the east bank of the Jordan River and the rest of Jordan, was viewed by the Israeli leadership as necessary to prevent the entry of an army, particularly a third army (e.g., Iraqi) into the West Bank and from there posing a threat to Israel.[26] There had actually been an agreement between Jordan and Israel prior to 1967 barring the entry into the West Bank of heavy armor, and it had, in fact, been violated in the 1967 war. There had also been Fatah terrorist attacks conducted against Israel from Jordanian territory prior to the war. That these had occurred in a situation in which the two countries were in a state of war, not peace, apparently made no difference to the thinking of both the civilian and military members of the Israeli leadership. Actually, together with the fact that Jordan had joined the war despite Israeli assurances on 5 June that it would not be attacked, these violations of the modicum of trust that had built up over the years between Israel and King Hussein may have contributed to the persistence of the internalized view of the enemy, even Jordan, as immutably hostile.[27] Ever mistrustful, Israeli leaders sought to prevent a repetition should there be a return of territory to Jordan. This could be done only, presumably, by maintaining control over the eastern border of the West Bank, even if this meant that peace with Jordan would be sacrificed. Such a sacrifice (an "either/or decision") was not the way it was perceived initially; those in the leadership who believed that peace with Jordan was a possibility apparently also believed that Jordan could be persuaded to accept Israel's terms. Some in the government (and the Americans) were less sanguine about this possibility, but to no avail. Neither Israel's proven military strength (and the Arabs' weakness) nor Jordan's explanations that in a time of peace there would be no need for such security concerns[28] could overcome Israelis' mistrust, fear, and identity that were linked with a sense of victimhood and isolation. Israel's demand for the Jordan Rift Valley remained one of the two "deal breakers" with Jordan.[29]

The demand to hold onto all of Jerusalem was of a somewhat different nature. The issue of Jerusalem was neither framed nor motivated by military security concerns. Rather, it was solely connected to identity and legitimacy-related concerns. Jerusalem was the physical as well as symbolic embodiment of Israeli claims to be in the region, based on history and religion. In this way, Jerusalem was different from the rest of the territories taken in the war. It held not insignificant emotional value even for much of the majority, secular public of Israel. Attachment to the city had been strengthened over the years by the simple denial (by Jordan) of entry to East Jerusalem, its old city, the Jewish quarter and Jewish religious sites. It was not only the religious public in Israel who abhorred the presence of a wall across the middle of the city. In fact, whatever the nature of attachment, there were those in the government who were careful to avoid an explicit religious claim for Israeli control. Aware of the importance of Jerusalem to the Muslim (and Christian) world, Moshe Dayan, for example, sought to avoid even the appearance of a religious conflict. Thus, he had ordered the removal of the Israeli flag placed victoriously by Israeli soldiers over the Al Aksa mosque when East Jerusalem was taken in the June war.

There was a security element to the Jerusalem issue. Prior to the war, West Jerusalem had been surrounded by Jordan on three sides, with what was called the Jerusalem corridor jutting like a finger into the West Bank (and completely under siege during the 1948 war). In addition, the Jordanian Legion had been stationed in the heart of Jerusalem, on the walls of the Old City from which it had occasionally fired upon West Jerusalem until 1967. Indeed, in the Israeli government discussion on East Jerusalem at the end of June, there were proposals to expand the city well into the heart of the West Bank as a means of gaining surrounding areas for future protection of the city.[30] However, this expansion also had the purpose of ensuring an Israeli hold on as much of the West Bank as possible, in view of the expectation that much of this territory might be returned to Jordan. In general, there had been many within the military as well as the political leadership, among them Moshe Dayan, who had been concerned about Israel's 1949–1967 *de facto* eastern (and northern) borders and welcomed at least some adjustments such as those that might be provided by a greatly expanded Jerusalem.[31] These considerations, like those regarding the Jordan Rift Valley, were born of a period that had been without a peace agreement; but these same considerations persisted even into ostensible preparations for peace.

One of the considerations in the territorial decision on expanded Jerusalem was the issue, raised also by Moshe Dayan, of the risk in expanding to the point of absorbing too many Palestinians. Some 70,000 were, in fact, added to Israel with the municipal borders finally chosen for Jerusalem (in the government and Knesset decisions of 25–27 June 1967); but this apparently was a compromise designed to limit the Palestinian presence in Jerusalem to no more than roughly one quarter (later set at 28 percent) of the city's population. Beyond that, heavily populated areas of the West Bank could, apparently, be returned to Jordan, relieving Israel of both the burden and threat of an additional approximately 700,000 Palestinians.[32] While the core issue in the Arab–Israeli conflict was, in fact, the clash between Jewish self-determination and the indigenous Palestinian population, Israel's leaders at the time viewed the Arab states, rather than the Palestinians, as the existential threat to the country, so long as Palestinian numbers inside Israel were kept in check. This is the reason that the Labor Party on the whole preferred what was called the

"Jordanian option," to return (most of) the West Bank to Jordan.[33] Yet, the willingness to relinquish at least part of the West Bank – what became known as the "land for peace" policy – was not only a matter of security consideration but one linked to a basic value or tenet dear to the leadership, and to the Israeli public as well: maintaining the Jewish nature of Israel – namely, a Jewish majority among the citizens of the state. This demographic consideration was to become paramount many years later, even outweighing security concerns.[34]

Nonetheless, Israel's adamant refusal to concede King Hussein's demand for a return of East Jerusalem as a condition for peace went well beyond security consideration or arguments. Indeed, in the negotiations with Jordan, it was the Jerusalem issue that dominated the discussions and provoked the greatest resistance on both sides. Israel was willing to offer the Jordanians certain access or religious rights in the city, but there was to be no challenge to Israeli sovereignty over all of the (now expanded) city. Since the only security concern over the city, that of a Jordanian military presence in East Jerusalem, was one that could have been allayed by an agreement on demilitarization, one can only conclude that some other, presumably emotional, identity-related considerations were the basis for Israel's preference of Jerusalem without peace rather than peace without Jerusalem. In 1947 the decision had been opposite, in a sense: Ben Gurion and his party, Mapai, accepted the partition resolution despite the plan's internationalization of Jerusalem; but its later counterpart, Ahdut Avoda, along with Herut (the forerunner of the Likud) opposed the plan because of its exclusion of Jerusalem from the Jewish state. It was also Ahdut Avoda, now part of the Labor Alignment, that had championed Israeli expansion eastward over the intervening years. These political positions were supported in the 1967 government not only by the members of the former Ahdut Avoda, but also, mainly, by the right-wing Gahal Party, which included Herut, under Menachem Begin. This party had been brought into the government for the sake of national unity in the tense days prior to the June war. Gahal clearly had an ideological (nationalist) as well as nationalist-historic interest in holding onto as much of the newly acquired land as possible. For Herut, these were "liberated" territories, possibly even a step toward the eventual achievement of the party's aspiration for "both banks of the Jordan, East and West," as expressed in its party anthem. The National Religious Party (Mafdal), also in the government coalition, added a religious element to this aspiration, as many of the party's adherents believed the "liberation" of these "God given lands" to be a step toward ultimate redemption for the Jewish people. Such identity-related sentiments, of both Herut and Mafdal, were thus strengthened as a result of the war. While neither party was a critical or even strong component of the Labor Alignment-led coalition (as distinct from their power in later years), they did add their nationalist/religious claims to the post-war deliberations, providing at least a contributing factor for the failure to reach a breakthrough. Yet, it was not these members of the government who held the key to Israel's intransigence over Jerusalem. It was the secular, even former military, members of Mapai who held fast to this decision. The quotes below provide a sample of the emotional/historic, nationalist, and even religious attachment to Jerusalem, as expressed by two quintessential secularist Israelis, coupled with the symbolic and physical link between the city and Israel's legitimacy – that is, the right of the Jewish state to be where it was physically:

> For some two thousand years the Temple Mount was forbidden to the Jews. Until you came – you, the paratroopers – and returned it to the bosom of the nation ... . Endless words of longing have expressed the deep yearning for Jerusalem that beats within the Jewish heart. You have been given the great privilege of completing the circle, of returning to the nation its capital and its holy center ... Jerusalem is yours forever.[35]
> (Commander Motta Gur to his brigade upon their recapture of Jerusalem's Old City and holy sites; later chief of staff, later still, a member of Labor governments)

> We have returned to all that is holy in our land. We have returned never to be parted from it again.[36]
> (Defense Minister Moshe Dayan upon reaching the Western Wall and, years later, in connection with 1978 Camp David talks on Jerusalem)

> In order to arrange that [all of] Jerusalem not be our capital, it was not enough for the UN Security Council and Assembly to pass resolutions to that effect. They would need to rewrite the Bible, and nullify 3,000 years of our faith, our hopes, our yearnings and our prayers.[37]

These sentiments were clearly echoed within the Israeli public. The war itself had produced an intense patriotism which now turned into often extreme nationalism, rapidly joined in certain circles to religious nationalism and messianic sentiments. One study of generally secular young people indicated a new feeling of connectedness with both the Jewish people as a whole and the land to which the Jews (Israel) had now returned.[38] This is not to say that it was public opinion that determined or even played a role in the debates and decisions of the government regarding the West Bank and Jerusalem. There is no indication that this was a factor. But the political leadership certainly knew that it had general support for the decisions it, in fact, took even if the specifics were not initially part of the public discourse. Beyond the new confidence in the government (as distinct from the lack of confidence in Eshkol and his government prior to the creation of the national unity government before the war), the public in general shared the emotional, historically based attachment to Jerusalem and the West Bank. Indeed, one survey indicated 89 percent in favor of holding onto at least part of them, some 90 percent opposing a return of the Old City of Jerusalem even as part of a peace agreement.[39]

These historic, religious, or emotional factors were far less – if at all – relevant when it came to the government's decisions on the other two areas occupied in 1967: Syria's Golan Heights and Egypt's Sinai Desert. At least the price to be considered was, apparently, less burdened by such sentiments. This may explain the 19 June 1967 Israeli government decision to agree to withdraw all the way to the international border with Syria, which would mean returning the Golan Heights subject to certain security demands, and with regard to Egypt, to return all of the Sinai to Egypt, but without the Gaza Strip. Out of demographic concerns, it was decided that the Gaza Strip would be occupied rather than annexed until the roughly 400,000 Palestinian refugees there could be relocated (to the West Bank or outside).[40] However, the Israeli decision to return Sinai (and the Golan Heights) did not refer to all of Sinai, for in addition to Gaza the decision noted security needs, which would later be spelled out. These included access to Sharm el-Sheikh at the southern-most tip of the Sinai peninsula and other security-related issues that would ultimately constitute a deal-breaker with Egypt.[41] The same would prove to be the case regarding Syria.

As in the case of Jordan, so too with regard to Egypt (and Syria), Eshkol said in the 18–19 June 1967 discussions. "Like Begin," he did not believe that peace was enough since it would not be quiet even with a peace agreement, and "we know who we are dealing with."[42] Therefore, the 19 June decision to return Sinai and the Golan Heights spoke of withdrawal to the international borders and "the security needs of Israel," and included demands for various security measures such as demilitarization as well as other matters – for example, use of the Suez Canal and protection of water sources on the Golan. But it is somewhat surprising that the major area to be kept, ostensibly for security reasons, was the Gaza Strip. Areas of greater security threat (e.g., the Golan Heights) were, at least in principle, to be returned. It is true that in the past (pre-1956) there had been terrorist attacks from Gaza, and Israel had also entertained a more general concern over a potential attack route via the Strip, facilitated by the large concentration of Palestinians there. But regarding the areas Israel was willing to relinquish, there had been pre-1967 violations of demilitarization understandings, in both the Sinai and in the demilitarized zone with Syria, as well as interference in Israeli shipping by Egypt and attacks from the Golan Heights and terrorist intrusions from Syrian-based Palestinians. Indeed, it was such intrusions that actually had led to the 1967 war. So with regard to Sinai and the Golan, one might have expected similar security considerations or demands as those raised with Jordan regarding the Jordan Rift Valley. While some of these were discussed, and Sharm el-Sheikh was, indeed, demanded, the 19 June 1967 decision to keep Gaza suggests that the major consideration was not always security but rather the ideological view of an historic right to all of Mandate Palestine, or the religious/nationalist view of Gaza as part of the Biblical Land of Israel.

The public, unaware of the 19 June decisions (which were, in fact, kept secret), harbored different sentiments on these territories. One study, immediately after the war, found that some 85 percent of Israelis opposed a return of the Golan (in a 1968 study, this was 93 percent) – far more than the 71 percent who did not want a return of any part of the West Bank, and 52 percent opposed a return of Sinai.[43] These findings presumably reflected the initial enthusiasm of the public in response to the surprising new acquisitions, though the attachment to the Golan long remained relatively more important in the eyes of the public than the other areas, presumably because of the strategic position overlooking Israeli territory (a security concern) regarding the Golan and perhaps also because of the beauty of the area. In any case, public opinion does not seem to have played a role in the government's decision to return the Golan, and Sinai, to the international borders.

Given these Israeli decisions, one might speculate that breakthroughs might have been possible with Syria and Egypt. It remains unclear if Israel's June decisions were, in fact, ever conveyed to these two countries. There are unconfirmed reports that Dean Rusk passed the proposal to the Egyptians, and in September Abba Eban told the Americans at the UN that Israel had "passed a message" to Egypt but, apparently, Egypt was not willing to make peace and unlikely to give up Gaza or agree to anything less than return of all of Sinai, including Sharm el-Sheikh.[44] So far as can be determined, however, the decision was not, in fact, passed to the Egyptians.[45] The Syrians too were unlikely to agree to the international border since by the eve of the June war they had gradually taken territory in the demilitarized zone and a bit west of the 1923 line. (The difference between this 4 June 1967 line and the international border of 1923 would later become a major issue, as we shall see below.) Moreover, the Syrian regime at the time was particularly militant regarding Israel altogether.

Israel's willingness to give up almost all of the Sinai and the Golan in exchange for peace, but not all of the West Bank or East Jerusalem (or Gaza) would attest to the over-riding importance of nationalist, identity-related, historic, and even religious factors. The strength of these factors apparently remained unchanged, or insufficiently changed, by the results of the war. Even Israel's demonstrated military might, the newfound confidence on the part of the public, a strong national unity government, international favor, and the opportunity of peace with its eastern neighbor did not make the difference for the Israeli leadership when faced with the issues of historic Palestine/*Eretz Israel*, and especially Jerusalem.

This initial period of potential breakthrough was short lived. Israel's 19 June 1967 positions had already hardened over the summer;[46] settlement building had even begun on the Golan. The Americans had become aware of this change and expressed concern to the Israelis, even as they publicly supported Israel's positions. Washington was particularly concerned over the Jerusalem question and urged Israel to take up Jordan's offer.[47] The Americans argued that there was a possibility for a breakthrough and this would be in Israel's interests and those of the US. They added the importance of preventing arms deliveries from the Soviet Union to Jordan, implying US interest in the

King's regime and preventing further Soviet inroads in the region. Signs of US concern over Israeli recalcitrance continued throughout the remainder of Johnson's presidency.

The Khartoum Conference at the end of August merely hardened Israeli positions further. At that meeting the Arab League resolved that there would be no recognition, no negotiations, no peace with Israel. What many failed to note was that Syria's leaders had refused even to attend, out of opposition to Egypt's pressure for political rather than military moves against Israel – a position reflected in the resolution's support for international diplomatic efforts for the return of the territories; and the PLO had left the meeting, refusing to sign, presumably because the only territories referred to in the resolution were those taken in the 1967 war (Palestinian rights were mentioned only cursorily, later in the resolution).[48]

For Israel the three no's, as they were referred to upon endless occasions over the next 25 years, brought back the only briefly relieved existential anxieties. This represented a misunderstanding of the Khartoum decision; Hussein was to characterize the Khartoum decision, as, indeed, it was perceived in the Arab world, as an achievement of the moderate camp led by himself and Nasser.[49] But for Israelis, including apparently most of the leadership, Khartoum was understood as evidence that the war had changed nothing; legitimacy and therefore safety were still denied and once again Israel, it was felt, was a victim of undeserved hatred and rejection. Even Egyptian and Jordanian agreement to United Nations Security Council Resolution 242 in November 1967 did nothing to relieve these concerns. Despite even the most negative interpretation of the Khartoum resolution, by accepting UNSC Resolution 242, Egypt and Jordan agreed to the principle of peace with Israel ("the need to work for a just and lasting peace in which every state in the area can live in security .... Termination of all claims or states of belligerency and respect for and acknowledgment of the sovereignty, territorial integrity and political independence of every state in the area and their [sic] right to live in peace within secure and recognized boundaries free from threats or acts of force.") These were the very principles that had caused Syria and the PLO to refuse to accept Resolution 242.[50] The price for Israel: "the inadmissibility of acquisition of territory by war" and "Withdrawal of Israeli armed forces from territories occupied in the recent conflict." The latter formulation was compromise wording sought by Israel and achieved with US and British help, for it carried no clear specification of the extent of the Israeli withdrawal (though the implication was clear given the reference to "the recent conflict.")

In any case, the Khartoum resolution served as justification (though as we have seen, not the reason) for a hardening of Israeli positions. Ignoring what could be seen as the moderate side of the government 19 June decisions, Jerusalem began to speak of withdrawal only within the context of a final peace accord and only to lines in keeping with Israel's security needs as well as historic rights, in time enunciated as "no return to the 4 June 1967 lines."[51] This included not only second thoughts regarding Syria, but even that Sinai was no longer to be totally returned, if indeed that had ever been the intention.[52] An Egyptian proposal for a non-belligerency pact (with demilitarization of Sinai and Israeli use of the Canal) was rejected, as Eban explained to the Americans at the UN in September 1967 that he was "not sure UAR [the United Arab Republic] understands clearly [the] relationship between end of belligerency and territorial problems ... . Eban gave [the] impression that Israel has tried to and will try again to make it clear to [the] Egyptians that they could get [a] substantial part of territory back in return for what Eban called a 'juridical definition of relations' between Israel and Egyptians." Peace was the issue with UAR, not primarily territorial problems. Israel must have a relationship on a "contractual basis", which includes recognition of Israeli sovereignty and "total non-belligerency."[53] The building of settlements in the occupied territories began officially in September 1967 (though even leading members of the Labor-Alignment had already joined the movement for "Greater Israel" created during the summer and some settlement activity had begun on the Golan as well). This is not to say that the principle of returning (some) territories for peace was abandoned. Talks with Jordan continued throughout 1968, but by that time, with Israel finally decided on the Jordanian option, the Alon Plan made it official that Israel intended to hold on to the Jordan Rift Valley and East Jerusalem, even at the risk of losing an opportunity for peace.

Factors such as the poor decision-making process due to rivalries and differences of opinion within the Israeli government may have played a role in the impression made upon the Arab (and US) leaders, but they do not appear to have played a role with regard to the actual failure to reach a breakthrough. The differences of opinion were over issues such as the autonomy or limited statehood for the Palestinians (ideas which, in any case, were rejected by the local Palestinians) or returning part of the West Bank to Jordan. The real debates were not between the left and the right in the government but within the dominant leftist camp. Most importantly, there were no problems within the Israeli government over the two deal breakers for Jordan – namely, continued Israel control of the Jordan Rift Valley and East Jerusalem. The flawed decision-making process was responsible for the delay in engaging Jordan, but from the outset both Jordan and Israel (along with the Americans) knew that a deal with Jordan would stand or fall over the territorial issue and especially Jerusalem, no matter when the talks would actually take place. Similarly, public opinion does not appear to have been a factor – one way or another – in the government's deliberations, for public opinion generally supported holding onto all the territories, including the areas the government was ready to return. Yigal Alon once suggested that the Jordanian option as distinct from the Palestinian option was the result of American pressure, and, indeed, there was an American preference for Jordan.[54] However, the actual shift to this option appears to have been the result of the internal discussions, as well as the limited nature of the proposal put to the Palestinians. The United States, increasingly preoccupied with Vietnam at the time, did not apply pressure beyond moderate efforts at persuasion and did not play as large a role in the whole matter as it gradually did after 1968 (under Nixon and Kissinger).

The characterization of the 4 June 1967 lines as "Auschwitz lines" by the generally dovish Abba Eban[55] may sum up the underlying factors in the eyes both of the Israeli public and the left as well as the right wing of politicians at the time. Jewish history, entrenched mistrust of the enemies, deeply embedded fear, were all part of the "security" concern that had become part of Israeli identity and sense of victimhood. However, the immensely frequent and consistent references to Israel's "rights" to these lands, all of them,[56] attest to the connected factor of the need for recognition of Israel's "legitimacy" as well an increasingly strong ideology of nationalism, patriotism, and outright chauvinism coupled, in some circles, with religious messianism. It is impossible to know if underlying these factors there was also a motivation simply for power in the form of territory. The geographic as well as historic, ideological, and even psychological circumstances would provide ample cover for such aspirations, but they were also weighty elements in themselves, sufficient even to account for the failure. The post-1967 situation – namely, the startling victory in the war with its demonstration of Israeli power (in the eyes of the Israeli public as well as the leadership), a strong government enjoying enormous public support, plus the peace offers of King Hussein and some signs of a possibility with Egypt – created the potential for a breakthrough. These even occasioned a series of direct and indirect efforts to transform the conflict, but the net result was failure. It was to be a long time before a real breakthrough would occur.

Notes

1 Foreign Relations of the United States (FRUS), 1964–1968, XIX, Arab–Israeli Crisis and War 1967, Doc. 488, "Memorandum of Conversation" between President Johnson and Foreign Minister Abba Eban, 24 October 1967.
2 For American policy, see Stephen Spiegel, *The Other Arab-Israeli Conflict* (Chicago, IL: University of Chicago Press, 1985); Kenneth Stein, *Heroic Diplomacy* (New York, NY: Routledge, 1999).
3 For Soviet policy, see Galia Golan, *Soviet Policies in the Middle East: From World War II to Gorbachev* (Cambridge, MA: Cambridge University Press, 1990).
4 Poll, in Jacob Shamir and Michal Shamir, *The Anatomy of Public Opinion* (Ann Arbor, MI: University of Michigan Press, 2000): 168–169, citing Gutman poll at the end of June 1967 which has a high of over 80 percent unwilling to return the West Bank.
5 Holding onto the land was never to outweigh Jewish majority or even peace as a preferred value amongst Israelis (see Shamir and Shamir, 2000; Michal Shamir and Asher Arian, "Competing Values and Policy Choices: Israeli Public Opinion on Foreign and Security Affairs," *British Journal of Political Science*, 24(2), 1994: 249–271).
6 During the waiting period, graves had been prepared for thousands of casualties and the public (though not the Israel Defense Forces) expected house to house fighting. The IDF was far more confident and, of course, better informed about

the relative strength and likely outcomes. Interviews in kibbutzim after the war indicated that young soldiers going into battle had had thoughts of the Holocaust. Shapira, Avraham (Ed.), *Siah Lohamim: [Soldiers' Conversations]* (Kevutzat HaverimTze'irim Meha-tenu'ah Ha-kibutzit, 1968).
7 Israel State Archives (ISA) (Hebrew), Documents 1–6: a-8164/7; a-8164/8; a-8164/9, and a-7634/5 (Government Publications, Periodic History, Stenographic Minutes of Meetings of the Government, 18 and 19 June 1967 April–June 1967, including Six Day War).
8 Herut and the Liberal Party joined to form Gahal in 1965.
9 For example, particularly, but not only, between Prime Minister Eshkol and Moshe Dayan (from Ben Gurion's breakaway party, Rafi), who had been appointed to replace Eshkol as defense minister just before the war. Traditionally the prime minister held the defense portfolio as well.
10 Aside from the archival protocols of these discussions, other accounts may be found in Avi Raz, *The Bride and The Dowry* (New Haven, CT: Yale University Press, 2012); Reuven Pedatzur, *Nitzahon Ha-mevukha: Mediniyut Memshelet Eshkol Ba-shtachim Le-ahar Milhemet Sheshet Ha-yamim [Embarrassing Victory: The Eshkol Government Policy in the Territories After the Six Day War]* (Tel Aviv: Yad Tabenkin, 1996); and Tom Segev, *1967: Israel, the War, and the Year that Transformed the Middle East* (New York, NY: Metropolitan Books, 2007). Positions were also conveyed to the Americans, see, for example, ISA, a-7634/5 "Decision of the Government," 19 June 1967, or discussions recorded in FRUS, XIX, Arab–Israeli Conflict and War, 1967 – for example, Doc. 290, "Telegram from the Embassy in Israel to the Department of State," 15 June 1967 and Doc. 369, "Memorandum of Conversation," 15 July 1967 (Eban in Washington).
11 At one point, Dayan suggested a confederation between Israel and a Palestinian state in the West Bank, but quickly abandoned the idea (Pedatzur, 1996: 80).
12 Segev, 2007: 518 on the PLO; Fatah joined the PLO only in 1968, assuming the leadership in 1969.
13 Nigel Ashton, *King Hussein of Jordan* (New Haven, CT: Yale University Press, 2008): 124. The King told British Foreign Secretary George Brown, immediately after his meeting with the Americans, that he would make a separate peace if a common Arab effort failed (Aston, quoting British document).
14 As conveyed via the US Ambassador to Jordan (FRUS XIX, Doc. 370, Memorandum of a Meeting of the "Inner Circle of the Control Group" – Katzenbach, Eugene Rostow, Battle, Kohler, and Wriggins, plus Walsh and Burns) (Johnson Library, National Security File, Middle East Crisis, Vol. VIII) Washington, 16 July 1967; FRUS, XIX, Doc. 331, "Memorandum of Conversation," 28 June 1967; see also FRUS, XIX, Doc. 360, "Telegram from the Department of State to the Mission to the United Nations," 13 July 1967).
15 FRUS, XIX, Doc. 393, "Telegram from the Embassy in Jordan to the Department of State," 28 July 1967.See also, Samir Mutawi, *Jordan in the 1967 War* (Cambridge, MA: Cambridge University Press, 1987): 175; Segev, 2007: 511. Mutawi, Segev and Avi Shlaim, *Lion of Jordan* (London: Allen Lane, 2007) all have details of the 2 July 1967 discussions between King Hussein and Yaacov Herzog, as well as later meetings.
16 Segev, 2007: 567 (e.g., Eshkol's comments to his party's Political Committee, 3 June 1968). "Territorial integrity" was the most the Arabs could get in the resolution instead of an explicit demand for Israeli withdrawal from *all the* territories occupied in the 1967 war.
17 FRUS, XIX, Doc. 449, "Telegram of the Mission of the United States to the Department of State," 26 September 1967.
18 FRUS, XIX, Doc. 505, "Telegram from the Department of State to the Embassy in Israel," 5 November 1967, referring to earlier Israeli comments on Jerusalem.

19 *Ibid.*
20 Pedatzur, 1996: 103 (Eban); Amos Shifris, *Yisrael Galili* (Ramat Efal: Yad Tabenkin, 2010) [Hebrew]: 334 (Dayan); also, Nathan Yanai, *Moshe Dayan: Al Tahalich Ha-shalom ve Atida shel Israel*, [*Moshe Dayan: On the Peace Process and the Future of Israel*] (Tel Aviv: Ministry of Defense, 1988): 104.
21 Eshkol acknowledged this on 3 June 1968 (ISA 7921/A-13), as did Rabin (FRUS, 1964–1968, XX, Arab–Israeli Dispute 1967–1968, Doc. 185, "Memorandum of Conversation" (with US State Department – Under Secretary of State Rostov and others including Dayan), 4 June 1968. Jordanian Foreign Minister Zaid Rifai, who accompanied the King in most of his talks with Israel, said later that Hussein had taken a very daring and risky step and had been "shocked when the Israeli response was that they were willing to sign a peace treaty with Jordan but only if Jordan agreed to cede parts of the West Bank and all of Arab East Jerusalem" (Shlaim, 2007: 282 (interview). Shlaim has detailed accounts of subsequent Jordanian–Israeli talks).
22 See, Yechiel Klar, Noa Schori-Eyal, and Yonat Klar, "The 'Never Again' State of Israel: The Emergence of the Holocaust as a Core Feature of Israeli Identity and its Four Incongruent Voices," *Journal of Social Issues*, 69(1), 2013: 125–143 on experiments inspired by Zygmund Bauman. See also Bauman's interview, "The Golden Compass," in *Haaretz*, 15 February 2013 (that logic guiding Israel is the idea that "Jews are constantly facing a looming Holocaust … [leading] to insularity and isolationism").
23 In 1965, Mapai, the leading party of the labor movement, joined with Ahdut Avoda to create the Labor Alignment for the 1965 elections. In 1968 the breakoff group Rafi joined them to create the Labor Party for the 1968 elections. In 1969 Mapam joined and the name Labor Alignment was restored.
24 Also illustrative of the lack of trust was Yigal Alon's supporting argument (expressed on 30 July 1967) for holding onto the West Bank that "we must always take into consideration the chance that the Jordanian regime may be changed": Yigal Alon, *Be-hatira Le-shalom* [*In Search of Peace*], Tel Aviv: Hakibbutz Hameuchad, 1989: 28.
25 ISA, a-8164/7, Documents 1 & 2, Protocol – Government Meeting, 18 June 1967; Hagai Tzoref, *Levi Eshkol: Rosh Ha-memshala Ha-shlishi: Mivhar Te'udot Mi-pirkei Ha-yav-1895–1969* [*Levi Eshkol: the Third Prime Minister: Selections of Documents from his Life*] (Jerusalem: State Archive, 2002): 580. Only one member of the government mentioned that King Hussein had made some moderate comments a few days before (Minister of Police Eliyahu Sasson, Doc. 2).
26 There were other Israeli territorial demands but these were in the nature of minor adjustments – for example, the Latrun area that King Hussein appears to have been willing to consider (FRUS 1964–1968, XX, Arab–Israeli Dispute, 1967–1968, Doc. 221, "Telegram from the Embassy in Jordan to the Department of State," 20 July 1968).
27 This sentiment was expressed by Yigal Alon (Alon, 1989: 28) though he ultimately was willing to agree to the Jordanian option, February 1968, but only with significant parts of the West Bank in Israeli hands. (Alon, 1989: 27–30) If Israel felt its trust betrayed by Jordan, King Hussein is said to have himself felt betrayed before the war by the Israeli military incursion into Jordan at Samu against Fatah operatives in November 1966 (Ashton, 2008: 190; Shlaim, 2007: 262).
28 FRUS XIX, Doc. 331, "Memorandum of Conversation" (between King Hussein and President Johnson), 28 June 1967.
29 In August 1968, King Hussein told the US that in order to accommodate Israeli concerns he would not place the Jordanian army in the West Bank if there were a peace agreement, needing no more than minimum forces to preserve public order. He was also willing to consider border "rectifications" (probably in the Latrun

area), but there was no sign that these would include Israel military control or sovereignty over the Jordan Rift Valley, and he opposed Israeli retention of East Jerusalem (FRUS, XX, Doc. 227, "Telegram from the Embassy in Jordan to the Department of State," 3 August 1968).
30 Dayan argued against a very broad expansion proposed by General Rehavam Zehevi (Gandhi) on the grounds that such a large annexation would include too many Palestinians (Pedatzur, 1996: 117–118).
31 Such "adjustments" had, in fact, been made on the ground, unofficially, many times over the years, most notably by actions of Ariel Sharon's commando 101 unit.
32 Statistics vary on the number of West Bank residents at the time of the war, with some estimates, including students and others temporarily abroad, as high as 800,000, while Israeli figures from September 1967 were a little less than 600,000 (Israel Central Bureau of Statistics (CBS), 31, XII, 1967).
33 Although there were some who spoke of the need to placate Palestinian demands by creating a state for the Palestinians in most of the West Bank and Jordan.
34 Shamir and Shamir, 2000; Michal Shamir and Asher Arian, "Competing Values and Policy Choices: Israeli Public Opinion on Foreign and Security Affairs," *British Journal of Political Science*, 24(2), 1994: 249–271.
35 See www.sixdaywar.org/content/ReunificationJerusalem.asp (CAMERA Committee for the Accuracy of Reporting on the Middle East in America).
36 Cited in Jerold Auerbach, *Are We One: Jewish Identity in the US and Israel* (New Brunswick, NJ: Rutgers University Press, 2001): 97.
37 Moshe Dayan, *Breakthrough* (London: Weidenfeld and Nicholson, 1981): 176.
38 Segev, 2007: 557.
39 Segev, 2007: 551.
40 Segev, 2007: 522–544 regarding the Gaza refugee issue. Land was purchased outside for voluntary relocation; it is not clear if relocation to the West Bank was to be voluntary or forced.
41 ISA, *The Peace Plan of the Government of Israel: Israel Policy Determinations Regarding the Future of the Territories Occupied in the Six-Day War, 18–19 June 1967*, "Decision," (Hebrew), 19 June 2012; www.archive.gov.il/nr/rdon/yres/A8EE926E-9A1B-4281-AOIC-F6C93349AB15/O/haclata31101968.pdf.
42 Tzoref, 2002: 580.
43 Segev, 2007: 551. A January 1968 survey had 91 percent opposed to returning all or some of the West Bank (up from the June 1967 poll), but the next month this fell to 75 percent and over the years gradually declined further; Asher Arian, *Security Threatened* (Cambridge, MA: Cambridge University Press, 1995): 102.
44 Egyptian Foreign Minister Fawzi met with US Secretary of State Dean Rusk on 21 June 1967, but there is no mention of an Israeli offer in the record of the conversation. (FRUS XIX, Doc. 327, "Telegram from the Mission to the United Nations to the Department of State," 27 July 1969). Samir Mutawi (1987: 180) claims the offer was conveyed to the Arab states but they did not respond because Jordan was not included. Abba Eban's 25 September 1967 remark in FRUS, XIX, Doc. 449, "Telegram of the Mission of the United States to the United Nations to the Department of State," 26 September 1967.
45 Avi Raz, "The Generous Peace Offer that Was Never Offered: The Israeli Cabinet Resolution of June 19, 1967," *Diplomatic History*, 37(1), 2013: 85–108 has a detailed study of the fate of the decision and the myth of its having been rejected if even presented to the Arab states.
46 Pedatzur, 1996: 69–70; FRUS, XIX, Doc. 425, "Telegram from the Embassy in Israel to the Department of State," 21 August 1969 (from US Embassy in Tel Aviv) cited expansionist public comments by Israeli politicians, but also continued Arab reluctance to make peace; "Memorandum from Special Consultant to the President, McGeorge Bundy," on 31 July 1967 also referred to a hardening of the Israeli

position, though this is at a time of the Jordanian retreat from its earlier willingness to talk before there was a joint Arab decision (FRUS XIX, Doc. 399).
47 FRUS, XIX, Doc. 411, "Telegram from the Department of State to Embassy in Israel," 9 August 1967 and Doc. 425, 21 August 1967.
48 Avraham Sela, *The Decline of the Arab Israeli Conflict* (Albany, NY: SUNY University Press, 1998).
49 Shlaim, 2007 (citing King Hussein): 366–68; Sela, 1998: 98–109; Pedatzur, 1996: 142.
50 For the PLO, in addition to the recognition of Israel implied in Resolution 242, the resolution referred to the Palestinian issue only as one of a refugee problem rather than one of national rights; Galia Golan, *The Soviet Union and the Palestinian Liberation Movement* (New York, NY: Praeger, 1980).
51 The secretary of the Prime Minister's Office, Adi Yaffe, wrote to the Israeli ambassador in Washington, Avraham Harman, in late 1967: "it doesn't seem like the decisions made by the government in June still hold, as the days pass, the idea of maintaining control over the territories, for security and historical purposes, grew stronger" (cited in Pedatzur, 1996: 70) On 31 October 1968, the government officially revoked the June 1967 decisions (www.archive.gov.il/nr/rdon/yres/A8EE926E-9A1B-4281-AOIC-F6C93349AB15/O/haclata31101968.pdf).
52 Shifris, 2010: 335 (quoting Alon in 27 September 1968 talk with Rifai).
53 FRUS, XIX, Doc. 434, "Telegram from the United States Interest Section of the Spanish Embassy in the UAR to the Department of State," 11 September 1967; Doc. 449, "Telegram from the Mission to the United Nations to the Department of State," 26 September 1967; Doc. 466, "Telegram from the Department of State to the United States Interest Section of the Spanish Embassy in the UAR," 12 October 1967.
54 Eshkol said that the Jordanian option was result of US pressure (Shifris, 2010: 33; see also Pedatzur, 1996: 100).
55 "We have openly said that the map will never again be the same as on June 4, 1967. For us, this is a matter of security and of principles. The June map is for us equivalent to insecurity and danger. I do not exaggerate when I say that it has for us something of a memory of Auschwitz. We shudder when we think of what would have awaited us in the circumstances of June, 1967, if we had been defeated; with Syrians on the mountain and we in the valley, with the Jordanian army in sight of the sea, with the Egyptians who hold our throat in their hands in Gaza. This is a situation which will never be repeated in history" (to *Der Spiegel*, 5 November 1969); Yitzhak Tabenkin, (kibbutz founder and labor movement leader): "the borders prior to June 5th brought a Holocaust upon us, a Holocaust worse than the Nazi Holocaust. After the Nazi Holocaust, enough Jews were left to re-build the people and establish the State, however, if the State were destroyed now, a future revival of the Jewish People would be doubtful": Arieh Naor, *Greater Israel: Theology and Policy* (Haifa: University of Haifa Press and Zmora-Bitan, 2001): 324.
56 A study of Israeli attitudes to the occupied territories found consistent sentiment within the Labor Party leadership (as well as in parties to its right) that these territories historically and rightfully belong exclusively to the Jewish people, even if, for pragmatic, demographic reasons – namely, the need to maintain a Jewish majority in Israel – parts might be relinquished; Tamir Magal, Neta Oren, Daniel Bar-Tal, and Eran Halperin, "Psychological Legitimization – Views of the Israeli Occupation by Jews in Israel," in D. Bar-Tal and I. Schnell (Eds), *The Impacts of Lasting Occupation: Lessons from Israeli Society* (New York, NY: Oxford University Press, 2013): 122–185.

3 Breakthrough with Egypt

The first successful breakthrough came with Egypt: the peace agreement signed in 1979 which had built on the post-1973 war accords – the 1974 disengagement of forces and the 1975 Interim Accord. However, these ultimately successful steps had actually been preceded by two failed attempts at a breakthrough in the early 1970s. A brief look at these failures may help to elucidate those factors which finally did determine the later success.

The Israeli retreat from the 19 June 1967 decision regarding Sinai, in addition to the decision to annex the Gaza Strip, most likely precluded an agreement with Egypt in the early post-1967 war period, although there is no evidence that Egypt ever received the Israeli proposal. In any case, Israel generally dismissed various attempts by Nasser to (indirectly) talk about the end of belligerency, rather than peace. Since these Egyptian offers were usually, though not always, accompanied by demands for Israeli withdrawal from all the territories, not just Sinai, and without a promise of peace, they were not accorded serious consideration by Israel. The government's position remained firmly that only direct negotiations for a peace agreement would be acceptable. Towards the end of the War of Attrition (which had been launched by Egypt in early 1969), both Israel and Egypt appeared to soften their positions, apparently in response to US (and Soviet) efforts to end the war. In a speech on 26 May 1970, Golda Meir, now prime minister, accepted what was called the Rhodes formula – that is, the services of a third party for negotiations as called for in United Nations Security Council Resolution 242.[1] Speculation attributes this Israeli concession to the need for American F-4 aircraft being negotiated with the US at the time.[2] Nasser, for his part, was apparently responding to Soviet pressures (and his losses in the War of Attrition); in his May Day speech of 1970, Nasser spoke of the need to explore a political solution. It is impossible to know if these Israeli and Egyptian positions would have led to a breakthrough had Nasser not died in September 1970; he had not abandoned his refusal to negotiate directly or sign a peace agreement with Israel, and Israel, for its part, was adamant that there would be no return to the 4 June 1967 lines, despite having accepted UNSC Resolution 242 in all its parts with the August 1970 ceasefire.

The more promising opportunity, and failure, came only once the leadership of Egypt changed and Anwar Sadat came to power after Nasser's death. It was presumably this leadership change that led Moshe Dayan to propose to the Israeli government towards the end of 1970 (and later to the Americans) that an effort be made for an agreement whereby Israel would withdraw its forces to a point some 20 miles east of the Suez Canal. This would allow for the Egyptians to open the Canal and rebuild their cities on the western banks of the Canal, presumably reducing a future interest in going to war. The cabinet rejected the proposal, but Sadat presented an almost identical one two months later. His initiative, made in a 4 February 1971 speech to the Egyptian National Assembly – and elaborated upon a few months later – called for an Egyptian force to be allowed on the eastern bank plus a timetable for full implementation of UNSC Resolution 242 (i.e., total Israeli withdrawal).[3] Concentrating exclusively on the territories lost in 1967, he supported the international efforts, specifically the Jarring mission, for peace. Shortly thereafter (7 March 1971), he agreed to a plan proposed by Jarring for Egyptian peace with Israel in exchange for withdrawal from Sinai, including demilitarized zones, UN peace-keepers for Sharm el-Sheikh, and freedom of navigation.[4] Early 1973, even as he was planning military action, Sadat abandoned the partial withdrawal idea in favor of a peace agreement with Israel in exchange for a return of Egyptian territory. In talks with the Americans, the parameters of the proposal were detailed, but the final status was not entirely clear; the Egyptians insisted – and the Americans concluded the same – that Sadat had offered Israel a bilateral peace agreement.[5] These peace offers reflected Sadat's concentrated effort to regain the Sinai as part of a broad policy designed primarily to relieve Egypt of its military burden in order to improve the country's economy. Never a fan of the Soviets, Sadat disentangled the regime from both the Soviets' military presence and political supporters with the hope of winning American support that would, in turn, limit American backing of Israel and press the latter to agree to a deal – as well, presumably, as promote US assistance to Egypt's economy.[6]

The bare facts are that Israel's responses to both the 1971 Suez Canal withdrawal proposal (the partial accord) and Jarring's broader peace proposal were delayed, much to the annoyance of the Americans, and ultimately negative, with the stipulation that Israel would not return to the 4 June 1967 borders. In the wake of a secret Soviet proposal put to the Americans in August 1971 and conveyed to Israel in November, Meir was ready to agree to the original partial accord proposal, with some caveats and some concessions,[7] but again not what would be a second stage: an overall peace settlement. With regard to the partial accord proposals, the specific issues revolved around the depth of the withdrawal, and the transfer (or not) of Egyptian personnel to the eastern side of the Canal (civilian or military or none, and when), but there was also an Israeli demand that the withdrawal be reciprocated by a non-belligerency pledge by Egypt (reduced later to a demand for an extended cease-fire), while Egypt added a link between the partial agreement and subsequent implementation of UNSC Resolution 242 (i.e., full withdrawal). The latter was at the core of Israel's rejection of the Egyptian response to Jarring's proposal – namely, that Egypt's agreement to peace with Israel was predicated on Israeli withdrawal from the Sinai (and also Gaza), to be followed by similar agreements with the other two states plus resolution of the refugee issue. While, in 1971, Israel was willing to have the Americans pursue talks with Egypt (and the Soviets) regarding a peace settlement (termed "proximity talks"), it made it clear to the US that Israel would not agree to any proposal based on the idea of a return to the 4 June 1967 borders. Israel's response in 1973 was basically the same.

Two factors played a major role in the Israeli rejection of the 1971 and 1973 proposals: security and mistrust. The two were linked but much of the haggling (with the Americans) revolved around specific security considerations. Even before the 1967 war, as early as the mid-1950s, Israel had strong concerns over access to Sharm el-Sheikh and the freedom of Israeli shipping, as well as flights in the area. Egypt had periodically interfered with Israeli access, and, consequently, one of the objectives in the 1956 Israeli attack in Sinai had been to gain control of a land link to Sharm el-Sheikh. Beyond that there were interests in the major passes (Gidi and Mitla) in the Sinai, along with the intention of keeping Gaza. Thus, in keeping with its decision after the Six Day War to determine the borders according to Israel's security needs, the Israeli cabinet agreed on 31 March 1971 that "a secure border for Israel requires changes in the former international frontier, including retention of the Gaza Strip, continued Israeli control at Sharm el-Sheikh and a territorial link to the State of Israel. Continued control does not signify a presence but rather concrete military control, though the Israeli position regarding the legal form of such control has yet to be formulated."[8] In 1971 Prime Minister Golda Meir told then ambassador to the US Yitzhak Rabin to inform the Americans that "Israel's policy aims toward a considerable change in her border with Egypt. That means a change of sovereignty, not just an Israeli presence. We do not employ the term 'annexation' because of its negative connotation."[9] This position appeared to change somewhat in 1973, at least in speaking with the Americans. Following Sadat's security advisor Hafez Ismail's February visit to Washington (in which the possibility of an international force for Sharm el-Sheikh was raised by the Egyptians), Nixon suggested to Meir that what the Egyptians wanted was sovereignty, what Israel wanted was security, so perhaps there could be agreement, to which Meir agreed in principle. The implication was some Israeli military presence in Sharm el-Sheikh. What concerned Meir, and presumably the government, both in 1971 and in 1973, was that Washington might be promoting the 1969 Rogers plan, which basically called for full withdrawal with only minor border adjustments. This amounted to "insecure borders" in Meir's eyes, and her agreement to proximity talks was premised on US "shelving" of the Rogers Plan.[10]

The apparently purely security-dictated positions of Israel were predicated on a basic mistrust of the enemy, Egypt in this case. Golda Meir later wrote: "The Arab leaders pretend that their real objective is limited to reaching the lines of 4 June 1967, but we know their true objective: the total subjugation of the State of Israel." And "I have never doubted for an instant that the true aim of the Arab states has always been, and still is, the total destruction of the State of Israel [or that] ... even if we had gone back far beyond the 1967 lines to some miniature enclave, they would not still have tried to eradicate it and us."[11] The three no's of Khartoum were well entrenched in the minds of Israelis, including, of course, that of Golda Meir, leaving little room for trust. To this was added the more recent violation of the agreement ending the War of Attrition, when Egypt moved Soviet-supplied SAM 3 missiles up to the banks of the Suez Canal. In her conversation with President Nixon and Kissinger on 1 March 1973, Meir expressed doubts regarding Egypt's true intentions, asking: "What does Egypt really want? They tell their friends that Israel must go back to the '67 borders and deal with the Palestinians," which, in Meir's eyes meant they were not really talking about peace with Israel but placing impossible demands. Rabin, too, reacted with skepticism when Kissinger provided him a summary of the talks with Ismail. Rabin seemed less worried about the territorial aspect than the apparent sequential linkage of withdrawal to be followed by resolution of the Palestinian issue, meaning that peace would not be achieved by the withdrawal. The "core" issue would remain and that was one that had ramifications for Israel's legitimacy in the region.[12] Thus, Rabin's reaction was also evidence of an underlying mistrust based on the suspicion or conviction that the Arabs simply would not make peace with Israel.[13] There appeared also to be an element of disdain within the Israeli leadership for the Egyptians, reflected both by an arrogant dismissal of their military capabilities but also a more specific contempt for Sadat, as clearly evident in mocking comments made by Abba Eban to the Americans in May 1973.[14] Indeed, before the war of 1973 there was a general, not just Israeli, tendency to underestimate Sadat and to deride his many declarations of intentions to go to war.

Israeli mistrust, however, extended also to the US, both in the form of concern that the Rogers Plan was still operative and that the US might agree to a deal with the Soviets that would premise a return to the 4 June lines. This mistrust was expressed directly by Meir to Rabin and could also be seen in her demand to Nixon in 1971 that the US not present itself as representing Israeli positions in the proximity talks, nor make "a deal contrary to Israel's wishes ... [nor] exert pressure on Israel to concede to positions reached in any such discussions."[15] Moreover, Meir was chronically concerned about what she perceived as the fragility of America's arms supply commitment to Israel.[16]

Mistrust of the American administration had some basis, for Washington (particularly Nixon and the State Department, as distinct from Kissinger), often expressed dissatisfaction with what they perceived as Israeli intransigence. Discussions of Israeli arms requests (specifically aircraft) were often colored by at least implied linkage to greater Israeli flexibility regarding negotiations for a settlement. The underlying difference in the US and Israeli views, however, was a fundamental disparity regarding just what could be regarded as a breakthrough. For the US, Arab willingness to make peace with Israel constituted a breakthrough; but, in Israeli eyes, linking this to full withdrawal was tantamount to no breakthrough at all since this was out of the question for Jerusalem. Indeed, this was explained in great detail in a later article by Meir's advisor Mordecai Gazit.[17] Even the partial agreement proposal was rejected because of a link to future withdrawal. What was seen by the US (and the Soviets) as an Arab concession – to make peace with Israel in the 1949–1967 borders (i.e., accept Israel) – was perceived by Israeli leaders as an impossible (unacceptable) demand, especially if accompanied by a demand regarding the refugees, which Israel also interpreted as an impossible demand and therefore a sign of a continued Arab hardline.[18]

It may be the case that in 1971 the Israeli leadership (particularly, but not only, Prime Minister Golda Meir) did not believe Sadat was making a genuine peace proposal, though Dayan's pronouncement at the time that he preferred "Sharm el-Sheikh without peace rather than peace without Sharm el-Sheikh" suggests at least some understanding. Be that as it may, there is clearer evidence that in 1973 Israeli leaders did realize that Egypt was offering peace. Israeli historian Uri Bar-Joseph has published archival material demonstrating that the Ismail proposals were rejected out of a preference for holding onto the territories – that is, a rejection of a return to the 1967 border with Egypt.[19] A discussion on 18 April 1973 between Golda Meir, Minister of Defense Moshe Dayan, Minister without Portfolio (and closest advisor to Meir) Yisrael Galili, the chief of staff, the head of military intelligence, and the head of the Mossad dealt with increasing signs of Egyptian and Syrian preparations for war. All but the head of military intelligence (Eli Zeira) agreed that the signs indeed pointed to the likelihood of war. The discussion then turned to the question of whether or not to inform the government (full cabinet) and the public about the approaching danger of war. Bar-Joseph brings the following quote of Yisrael Galili:

> All this system [of Egyptian war threats] is the outcome of the fact that we are not ready to return the former [1967] line. Apparently, if you take what Hafiz [Ismail] had said ... the starting point is that they are ready for peace and a system of agreements and international guarantees etc. – all these on condition that we fully return to the former border.[20]

Nonetheless, the discussion did not revolve around the Egyptian proposal, but rather focused on what and to whom the danger of war should be revealed. Galili again clarified:

> There is a possibility to avoid this disaster [the war], if we are ready to enter a series of discussions on the basis of returning to the former border.[21]

The decision was to tell the government of the impending danger, but Dayan recommended:

> I would not suggest ... that it would be brought to the cabinet in the context of whether we are ready even to go to war in order to avoid returning to the green [1967 border] line.[22]

While the government was to be informed, the public was not, despite the fact that the Israeli press, like the international press, carried reports of Arab threats and even preparations for war. In any case, there does not seem to have been any concern that the Israeli public might prefer the Egyptian offer – if they were to know of it. Surveys at the time indicated that over 90 percent of the public were unwilling to give up Sharm el-Sheikh, though the percentage was much less (still over 50 percent) regarding all or part of Sinai.[23] One may conclude that Meir and her advisors assumed the public would support their opposition to returning territory, though their only expressed concern related to the reaction of the government, not public opinion.

Meir was also worried about telling the Americans about the signs of war lest this bring pressure on Israel to pursue the Egyptian proposals. This concern echoed an earlier admission of Meir during the discussions over peace with Jordan in 1967–1968 when she said that she feared that King Hussein might say he was willing to sign a peace agreement, and Israel would have to give in to his demands.[24] Then, as in 1973 (and 1971), Meir's considerations were based on security factors, although Rabin suggested to Kissinger that the fact that 1973 was an election year might account for more bellicose positions on the part of Israeli politicians.[25] Rabin was referring to Dayan, who he said would be challenging Meir; but there was also the challenge from the opposition party, Gahal, which presented any sign of government flexibility as weakness. However, it was also the case that Meir had a deep mistrust of the Arabs or agreements with them, possibly as a result of Jordanian King Abdulla's abandonment of the non-belligerency pact she had initialed with him and his 1951 assassination, most likely because of it. Years later she was to comment that you cannot make a peace agreement with an Arab leader because he would be assassinated, implying that there was no chance that such an agreement would last.[26]

Meir's concerns over American pressure were not totally unfounded, as already noted, but American positions, specifically those of Kissinger, may actually have been a contributing factor in the Israeli rejection of the 1973 initiative. The State Department under William Rogers was convinced that the Egyptians' initiative was "a great breakthrough," and President Nixon himself believed Israel was unduly intransigent.[27] However, in a conversation with Nixon, Kissinger characterized Rogers' opinion of the initiative as "total nonsense," and conveyed more than skepticism in his conversations with Rabin both before and after Ismail's February visit, putting off the next US meeting with the Egyptian to May.[28]

This did not convey a message of urgency, or pressure, to the Israelis. Moreover, Kissinger returned to the idea of a partial accord even after it had been dropped by the Egyptians in favor of a peace agreement. And it may have been with this in mind that Meir suggested to visiting German Chancellor Willy Brandt that he act as a go-between for a partial deal with Egypt.[29] In the ongoing discussions with the Soviets, Kissinger basically avoided Brezhnev's urgings to work out something toward a settlement, due to the likelihood of war, before and at the June 1973 summit. This is not to say that Kissinger wanted war;[30] there is evidence that he did not believe at this time that Sadat would go to war. But his strategy for the Arab–Israeli conflict was designed to remove the Soviets from the region, and this precluded reaching a settlement together with Moscow or even so long as the Soviets played a role. Therefore, he adopted a step-by-step approach rather than seeking an overall settlement (the opposite approach of his rival Rogers).[31] Kissinger appears to have preferred a drawn-out procedure during which the Arabs would despair of the Soviets' gaining their territories back for them and thus eject them, as Sadat was in the process of doing.[32] A simpler, additional, explanation may be that Kissinger was well aware that a peace agreement could not be achieved in view of Israel's refusal to return the territories. Whatever lay behind Kissinger's step-by-step strategy, the message Israel received directly from him was that he, Kissinger, "would seek ways of preventing American-Soviet negotiations on Brezhnev's proposals" should Israel reject such proposals – since they were most likely to be based on the 4 June 1967 lines.[33]

Yet, despite the failures of Sadat's 1971 and 1973 initiatives, after the October 1973 Yom Kippur war a breakthrough did occur – actually two breakthroughs: the Interim Accord of 1975 and the ultimate breakthrough of the 1979 Israeli–Egyptian Peace Agreement. While Labor Party leaders were to maintain that the 1975 agreement negotiated by their government paved the way for, and thus was crucial to, the final peace agreement, the negotiations for the Interim Accord were ultimately limited to the task of further military disengagement. The 1975 accord was initiated by the Americans as a post-1973 war second disengagement of forces, in a period of heightened tension due to uncertainty regarding the renewal of the previous agreements. Rabin, however, had come to office with the express purpose of pursuing peace agreements and he clearly preferred that any further agreements be a political step toward peace.[34] While this was a general interest, Rabin's focus was on Egypt. Presumably, as a military man, Rabin believed – and stated – that it was more important to deal with the surrounding states, whose military power could conceivably constitute a strategic threat to Israel, as distinct from the Palestinians' terrorist tactics.[35] But Rabin viewed Syria as more extreme than Egypt and, therefore, "not a realistic" partner for peace at the time; nor was there room for another disengagement of forces on the Golan (Israel did withdraw from a small area, Kuneitra, in the earlier post-war disengagement with Syria)[36] And while talks had been started with Jordan, any move on that front would ultimately require, according to Rabin (like Meir), a turn to the Israeli electorate.[37] A second agreement with Egypt would respond to the American interest in showing progress on the Middle East front (strengthening Washington's budding relationship with Sadat to the detriment of Moscow), as well as possibly ease some of Israel's isolation. Rabin spoke of the fact that most of the countries in the world were supporting the Arabs and even the Palestine Liberation Organization (PLO), a fact that behooved Israel to show flexibility.[38] There was also an Israeli interest in preventing a resumption of the December 1973 Geneva Conference with its emphasis on a comprehensive agreement and Soviet-backed Arab demands for full withdrawal. At the same time, Rabin wanted Egyptian commitments to abide by, and extend, the commitments to maintain the early post-war troop disengagement's suspension of hostilities.

Because of the limited nature of both the disengagement and the 1974–1975 talks – namely, the absence of a link to a peace treaty – the negotiations focused primarily on security-related issues. These issues were mainly the depth of the withdrawal, Egyptian presence in evacuated areas, monitoring and early warning stations, but also the duration of the agreement.[39] The return of the oil fields to Egypt was also negotiated, though not the topic of particular controversy (belying a purely economic basis for Israel's positions even as Jerusalem sought future imports from these fields). Yet, as in the pre-war talks and, in fact, Rabin's original goal[40] for a second agreement with Egypt, Israel sought a political *quid pro quo* for its withdrawal in the form of a non-belligerency pact – which Egypt refused. There was, however, agreement finally on a "non-use of force" clause, along with clauses negating the use of military means, to remain in effect until superseded by another agreement.

Most importantly, the Interim Accord pledged continued efforts to reach a peace agreement within the Geneva Conference framework as called for in UNSC Resolution 338 (passed to bring an end to the Yom Kippur War). While that resolution itself notes UNSC 242, Resolution 242 was strikingly missing from the Interim Accord – since Israel objected (as it had in 1971) to linkage that might imply full withdrawal. The reference to Geneva did, however, imply a comprehensive framework as distinct from Egypt acting alone in the future, although neither Egypt nor Israel was interested in a resumption of Geneva since the conference would not only include the Soviets but also tie progress on one track to progress on all tracks.[41]

The real story of the Interim Accord was the role of the United States, or, actually, the US pressure on Israel. For some this was the main factor that made this agreement possible.[42] An agreement was important to the US in order to stabilize the situation – namely, to forestall an outbreak of new hostilities (linked to pressure from Syria as well). There was also the problem of the oil embargo and also the risk of Soviet recuperation in the region.[43] The log-jam in the Kissinger-mediated negotiations was Israeli withdrawal – to the Gidi and Mitla passes or beyond them and the early warning stations that Israel had in those areas (this included, therefore, the issue of what forces would enter the evacuated area). While Rabin relented somewhat on the withdrawal lines, the stalemate remained, leading President Ford to declare a

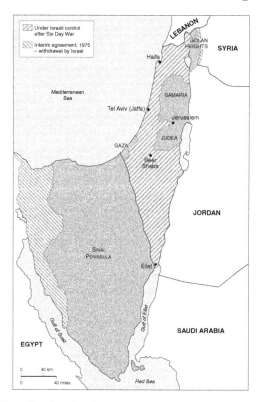

Map 3.1 Israeli–Egyptian Interim Agreement 1975
Source: Washington Institute for Near East Policy, http://mfa.gov.il/MFA/AboutIsrael/
Maps/Pages/Sinai%20Interim%20Agreement-%201975.aspx

"reassessment" of American policy toward Israel which turned into a six-month hiatus in any new military contracts with Israel and a cancellation of a scheduled visit by Shimon Peres. In the end, Rabin conceded on withdrawal from the passes in exchange for American responsibility for the early warning stations and certain political as well as economic commitments to Israel. Similar to his concession on "non-use of force" instead of an end of the state of belligerency, Rabin's concession on the withdrawal was attributed (by him) to his determination to reach an agreement, rather than to US pressure. The American lever, aside from the suspension of talks on new arms agreements, had been to threaten a return to the Geneva conference, something Israel disdained because the conference carried the risk of an imposed settlement due to Soviet pressure or, more likely, would end in nothing since the Arab states attending would be demanding full Israeli withdrawal. Yet, Rabin believed that the American threat to return to Geneva was an empty one since Kissinger had no desire to bring the Soviets into negotiations.

Rabin justified his concession on the passes with the remark that "a line" in the "great wastes" of the Sinai Desert was meaningless (as distinct from the situation of "populated areas in the Israeli heartland");[44] yet, in fact, in the course of the negotiations he had resisted withdrawal to this line on the grounds that Israel needed "defensible borders." Presumably American control of the early warning stations, plus a demilitarized buffer zone (monitored by the UN), could substitute for such borders. These security considerations were influenced by another factor; Rabin spoke to Kissinger of his commitment to reach an agreement for personal as well as national reasons given the danger of a new war if agreement were not reached: his sense of responsibility for the lives of every Israeli soldier, and the fact that his own son and son-in-law were both serving in tank units in the Sinai.[45] The personality of his opponent, Sadat, was also a factor for Rabin. Approaching the talks, Rabin studied Sadat, seeking information about his character and his views. This would suggest a degree of open-mindedness and objectivity, but underlying mistrust was also still evident. He believed that Sadat himself was "fickle," referring at one point to the fact that Sadat had abandoned King Hussein in favor of the PLO at the recent Arab League conference in Rabat, and so "if Sadat was capable of breaking an agreement with a fellow Arab leader, how was he likely to treat an agreement with Israel if other Arab states placed him under pressure."[46]

Still deeper mistrust was evident in Rabin's declaration to the Americans that "no Arab ruler is prepared to make true peace and normalization of relations with Israel."[47] For that reason Israel could not, he said, "go back to the 4 June 1967 lines" which borders he characterized as having been "the cause" of the 1967 war, adding: "We need defensible borders, and those are not the same as 4 June lines."[48] As he explained to President Ford, "when we talk of peace, I mean by this our existence as a Jewish state, with boundaries we can defend with our defenses ... the Arabs stress total Israeli withdrawal to the pre-June 1967 lines, which we consider practically indefensible."[49] Thus, Israel's positions were once again predicated on the assumption that peace would not be lasting, and, therefore, Israel needed to be prepared, as it were, for the next war. Yet, Rabin did allow that there could be change in the future; he spoke of partial agreements and stages "that will secure a lowering of military activity and create conditions enabling us to test the intentions of each Arab country, to see whether or not it seeks peace."[50] He told Ford that "there is an accumulation of suspicion that must be cleared on the way to peace ... . In order to change attitudes in the area it would take a very long time."[51] But he also believed that it might be possible to secure Egyptian adherence to the agreement if Egypt had sufficient interest in it – in a business sense, for example to protect the Sinai oil fields.[52] Ultimately, Rabin also believed the interim agreement would bring Egypt closer to the US, lead to Egyptian loss of Soviet weaponry, and drive a wedge between Egypt and Syria – all of which would leave Sadat with no alternative but a political solution with Israel.[53] But during the impasse in the Interim Agreement talks, he told the Americans: "in terms of the readiness of Israel for a final peace and the needs of Israeli security, the 1967 lines with respect to Egypt and

Syria do not allow for security arrangements which are required for a small country of three million people against a composition of states who total 60-to-65 million ... we have not sensed an Arab readiness to come close to the essentials of peace as we see them from our point of view."[54]

Some domestic factors played a role with regard to Rabin's decisions. At the time, he spoke of the open "wounds of war" of the Israeli people and his sense of responsibility to the people. However, he also mentioned, at least as an arguing point with the Americans, that there were those ("of my countrymen") who felt that if war were inevitable, it would be preferable to have it break out on the present lines rather than the eastern side of the passes to which Egypt demanded Israel withdraw.[55] These "countrymen" apparently included members of the military establishment in Israel, for Rabin spoke of "skeptics" whom the chief of staff found it difficult to convince with regard to the terms of the agreement. The implication is that he engaged the chief of staff to help neutralize these opponents. In political circles, three members of Rabin's own party, most prominent among them Moshe Dayan, voted against the Interim Accord in the Knesset on 1 September 1975, along with a few members from other parties that were partners in Rabin's government coalition.

Aside from the ruling coalition, there were many more potential spoilers within the Knesset. While almost the entire Knesset supported Rabin's resistance to the Americans during the reassessment, the final accord precipitated a fierce debate, with just 70 of the 120 Knesset voting in favor, 43 against, and 7 abstentions.[56] Moreover, the opposition right-wing party, and especially the settler movement Gush Emunim, had staged a vociferous campaign during the negotiations, even vilifying Kissinger personally as an enemy of Israel for his shuttle diplomacy. This public rejected the very idea of any withdrawal from any territory. It could be argued that the public demonstrations against an agreement might have strengthened Rabin's hand in his test of wills with Kissinger, perhaps proving how hard it would be for the prime minister to agree to the American/Egyptian demands. At one point, Rabin conveyed this to Sadat in a letter he asked Kissinger to deliver, saying that in order to convince the Israeli people of the need to make these difficult decisions, he needed to see "that the act of withdrawal marks the real beginning of progress towards peace by deeds and words that demonstrate the intention of peace."[57] But, in fact, Rabin was furious over the Gush Emunim treatment of Kissinger, which appeared to make it more, not less difficult to deal with the Americans. During the "reassessment" Rabin himself employed public opinion, more constructively presumably from his and Israel's point of view. He sought to strengthen his hand by a public campaign in the United States, enlisting the Jewish diaspora, which culminated in a letter from 76 senators calling for support for Israel and satisfaction of its defense requirements.[58] One cannot accurately gauge the value of this role played by the diaspora, since the White House did not go back on its positions or end the reassessment because of their actions. The administration did, however, attach some importance to the campaign, as evidenced by meetings the White House held with leaders of

American Jewry and also with Senator Javits, who had initiated the letter.[59] It is conceivable, though there is no direct evidence, that the letter and lobbying contributed to American willingness to seek the creative solutions finally reached to achieve Israeli agreement in the end.[60]

Rabin was keenly aware of the responsibility upon him and even the political price he might have to pay were he not to succeed in working out an agreement, particularly if the security situation were to deteriorate.[61] This concern was linked to what Rabin correctly noted as a serious decline in public trust of the country's leaders as a result of the 1973 war, as we shall discuss below. Rabin also took care to gain some military, economic, and political commitments from the Americans, including a US promise not to talk with the PLO unless it recognized Israel's right to exist and accepted Resolution 242. These were spelled out in a Memorandum of Understanding, separate from the Israeli–Egyptian agreement.[62] They do not appear to have been the subject of major differences between Rabin and Kissinger, nor were they an integral part of the negotiations over the Interim Accord.

In all there were quite a number of factors, sometimes contradictory, that led to the breakthrough of the Interim Accord, from the limited military nature of the agreement (it did not deal with 4 June 1967 lines or the critical Sharm el-Sheikh issue, although it did deal with the important passes) to heavy American pressure. The instability of the post-Yom Kippur War period played a role, along with the interest of Sadat in a further Israeli withdrawal. Undoubtedly a decisive factor was Rabin's leadership and determination; but, judging from his memoirs, quite a number of factors, including domestic and even some of a more personal nature, operated as well on his decision-making. The underlying mistrust of the Arabs, including Sadat, remained but Rabin sought to compensate for this in the design of the agreement. To some degree this may have justified the concessions that he made; he insisted these concessions were not due to American pressure but, rather, amply suited to Israel's security needs for the future as well as the present.

Far more complex, and significant, was the breakthrough for peace with Egypt, with a total withdrawal to the 4 June 1967 lines, undertaken by the leader of the right-wing Likud[63] Prime Minister Menachem Begin who came to power in 1977. Many of the circumstances and factors that paved the way for this breakthrough had played a role in the achievement of the Interim Accord; but their impact was to be far greater when it came to a total withdrawal in exchange for peace with Egypt. Moreover, still more factors were to enter the picture.

In a delayed reaction to the Yom Kippur War, Israeli elections in the spring of 1977 brought about a total transformation of the country's politics, ejecting Labor and installing a government of the right wing (Likud Party) for the first time in the state and pre-state history. Now prime minister, Likud leader Menachem Begin sought a meeting with Sadat, dispatching Moshe Dayan (now Begin's foreign minister) for secret talks with Egyptian officials in Morocco, in addition to indirect contacts through Rumanian President Nicolai

Ceausescu.[64] Just months before, Jimmy Carter had assumed power in the United States and almost immediately initiated steps for a resumption of the Geneva Conference. Sadat, who was amenable to Begin's wish for a meeting, increasingly despaired that a renewed Geneva conference would actually ever take place or achieve anything;[65] moreover, he became apprehensive of the Americans after Washington's acquiescence to Israeli demands regarding a statement Washington had issued with the Soviets in connection with Geneva. In preparation for a renewed Geneva conference, the US and USSR had issued a joint statement on 1 October 1977 reiterating Resolution 242 but adding the Palestinians' "legitimate rights."[66] Alarmed, Israel dispatched Dayan to Washington with a working paper that basically voided the Soviet–American statement. The US announced its acceptance of Israel's working paper, a move that may have persuaded Sadat that the Americans were still bowing to Israel interests. In view of these developments and, perhaps even more, a wish to deal separately with Israel rather than be limited by a more collective Arab approach, Sadat announced his willingness to go to Jerusalem to address the Israeli parliament, which he did on 20 November 1977.

This extraordinary act on the part of the Egyptian leader ushered in a period of nonetheless difficult negotiations, prompting the Americans to step in. With the direct involvement of President Carter, the US mediated a framework agreement at Camp David one year later. The talks at Camp David were fraught with difficulty, particularly over issues such as the Israeli settlements in the Sinai and the air fields, but most of all Sadat's demand for linkage with some kind of solution for the Palestinians on the West Bank.[67] Ultimately, with further American involvement, the Egyptian–Israeli Peace Agreement of March 1979 was achieved over the vociferous objections of many of Begin's supporters. The Sinai settlements were to be completely evacuated and there was linkage of sorts – though not as a precondition – to an autonomy arrangement for the West Bank and Gaza, which included Jordan as well as local Palestinians. Sadat had initially called for the return of Gaza to Egypt but subsequently related to it as part of Palestinian autonomy. While he sought Egyptian participation in the interim UN force for the West Bank autonomy period, once Israel rejected this Sadat did not make an issue of it.[68] The matter of Jerusalem was not so amicably resolved: each of the two leaders sent a letter to President Carter with each country's (contradictory) position regarding Jerusalem (Sadat: "Arab Jerusalem as an integral part of the West Bank"; Begin: "Jerusalem is one city, indivisible, Capital of the State of Israel").[69]

Obviously a major factor for the transformation in Israeli–Egyptian relations and the achievement of peace was the change of leadership – Sadat in Egypt and then Israeli successors to Golda Meir in Israel, first Rabin and then Begin. As already noted, Israeli leaders and others were far from impressed by Sadat when he came to power in 1970; but the 1973 war and subsequent negotiations for the Interim Accord led to a far more serious appraisal of the man. Nonetheless, while the leadership change in Egypt was an essential factor in the breakthrough, on its own it was not enough – as already evidenced by the failure of the 1971 and 1973 Egyptian initiatives. On the Israeli side the leadership change was critical, though not necessarily the change from Meir to Rabin. While Rabin was more flexible than his predecessor, it is not at all clear how Rabin would have dealt with anything more than the limited military disengagement of the Interim Accord. It is not certain that he would have been willing to relinquish Sharm el-Sheikh, for example; he was as skeptical about the wisdom of returning to the 1967 lines as Meir.[70] Nevertheless, Rabin had commented once to the Americans that he cared little about Sharm el-Sheikh, saying: "we just want to be there until we see a commitment to peace that is solid."[71] Menachem Begin's attitude to these lines, however, was somewhat different and based on other considerations, as shall see below. Additionally, there was also a leadership change in the US, bringing in a president and a security advisor with a different view of the protagonists to the conflict.

Before examining the role of these leadership changes in achieving the breakthrough, another perhaps crucial factor must be examined – namely, the altered context as a result of the Yom Kippur War. It has been said that the war was a critical factor for Egypt, for the early victories against the ostensibly invincible Israeli army facilitated Sadat's efforts to move toward what would ultimately be a separate peace agreement with Israel.[72] With Egypt's honor now restored, Sadat was able to negotiate with Israel on a more equal basis. Yet, inasmuch as Sadat had been willing to negotiate even before the war, this may not have been as critical a factor for the post-war talks as claimed. Nonetheless, Sadat himself did refer to "new facts" created by the war, as the Egyptian people were no longer seen as a "'lifeless body'."[73]

Certainly for Israel, the war played a key role. The Yom Kippur War was traumatic for Israelis. The surprise of the attack, the unpreparedness of the army, the losses of the first few days, the false assurances given the public by the leadership with regard to these matters in the first few days, as well as the very large number of wounded and killed all led to a serious blow to Israeli morale and an unprecedented loss of public trust in the country's leaders. Popular protests led to the creation of a government commission of inquiry, the Agranat Commission; but the report of the inquiry only led to further mistrust and disillusionment. The more immediate result was the resignation of Golda Meir and her government (even though the commission did not hold the civilian echelon responsible for the failures); the delayed result was the removal of Labor from power altogether in the 1977 elections.[74]

The fall of the long-touted Bar Lev line of Israeli defenses at the Canal, the failure of the Israel Defense Forces' (IDF's) first counter-offensive, along with the rapid advance of the Syrians in the north, struck at Israelis' confidence, indeed the arrogance, vis à vis the Arab armies that had been so pervasive since the startling victories of 1967. Moreover, the "strategic depth" and "defensible borders" that the territories presumably provided had actually weakened Israel's ability to counter attack given the time and effort it took to get Israeli reservists and supplies to the Canal. Similarly, the settlements on the Golan – also once popularly perceived as contributing to security – actually had to be evacuated at the outbreak of the war. Thus, the view of the territories as a security asset suffered a blow, apparently creating some readiness for territorial compromise at least on the Egyptian front, with the added incentive of avoiding another war after the terrible losses suffered. This new reality may have been reflected in Rabin's decisions for the Interim Accord; it was also apparent in Israeli public opinion. Just one month after the Yom Kippur War, public opinion against returning any or all of the territories dropped significantly in what was to become a gradual decline in opposition. More specifically, opposition to returning any or all of the West Bank, the Gaza Strip, and, most of all, Sinai fell sharply.[75] Strangely, in contradiction to the views on the whole Sinai in the same studies, there was only a much smaller decline in what was still strong opposition to giving up Sharm el-Sheikh (and the Golan).[76]

Thus, on the background of the Yom Kippur War, it was a far less confident, still angry and somewhat confused public that brought the right wing to power for the first time in Israel's short history. As the opinion polls suggest, the public had not turned massively to the right; rather, the electorate was divided, with many seeking to punish Labor by voting for a newly created center party, the Democratic Party for Change (DASH). This party then opted to reject Labor, joining the Likud in creating a coalition government led by Menachem Begin.[77]

Begin's response to the post-war situation was similar to Rabin's in that he saw the importance of achieving a more stable situation vis à vis the countries that had invaded – namely, Egypt and Syria. Yet his policies regarding the occupied territories and possible peace agreements were motivated by quite different considerations than those of Rabin or the Labor Party. And it was this difference that made the leadership change to Begin a significant factor in the achievement of the peace agreement with Egypt. For Begin the key was *Eretz Israel* (Land of Israel) – the "sacred" land of greater Israel that belonged to the Jews by historical, even religious right. Labor, too, believed that Israel had a right to these lands, as evidenced by both leadership statements and party platforms after 1967.[78] However, Labor, without relinquishing this claim, was willing to give up some of this land for pragmatic purposes to be determined primarily by security criteria. As Rabin had said: "Our right to the land is unshakeable. That is not the crux of the argument. ... In my view the Jordan is the defense line of Israel."[79] For Begin, "no part of Judea and Samaria [the Biblical names for the areas of the West Bank] can be given away."[80] But *Eretz Israel* included the West Bank, Gaza, and Jerusalem – not Sinai, not the Golan. Therefore, Begin could and did agree in June 1967, while a member of the unity government, to return the Sinai to Egypt and the Golan to Syria. Later it could be said that returning Sinai fulfilled Resolution 242 (in the Israeli interpretation that "territories" not "the territories" had to be relinquished), leaving the West Bank and Gaza in Israeli hands – which according to Begin were "liberated" lands and therefore not part of the "occupied" land referred to in Resolution 242. Nonetheless, Begin was still wary of any reference to the resolution, as evidenced by his resignation from the unity government in 1970 over this issue. But beyond rhetoric or tactics, Begin believed that peace with Egypt (and Syria) would weaken Jordan (which he did not recognize as a legitimate state) as well as the Palestinians, the real challengers to Israel's hold on the West Bank.[81]

Begin's underlying interest in weakening the Palestinians in the effort to keep the West Bank leads us to another important factor at play: the leadership change in the United States that brought Jimmy Carter to power. Carter, and his national security advisor Zbigniew Brzezinski, favored a comprehensive agreement (as distinct from Kissinger's step-by-step approach) through a revived Geneva Conference which would require dealing with the West Bank as well. Still more disturbingly in Begin's eyes, the US president also began to speak of Palestinian rights and the need for a Palestinian "homeland."[82] This worrisome development, coming as it did when the PLO had gained widespread international support, particularly at the UN,[83] was all the more reason for Begin to pursue what appeared to be an Egyptian interest in reaching a separate agreement.

If all of these underlying factors – leadership changes in Egypt (Sadat) and the US (Carter), the war and the fall of Labor in Israel, Likud ideology, and, to some degree, the growing international popularity of the PLO – led Begin to seek talks with Egypt (which he did through secret meetings with the Egyptians in Morocco and intermediaries, primarily Rumania), still other factors contributed significantly to the ultimate breakthrough of the 1979 agreement. Many would likely maintain that the single most important factor was Sadat's historic trip to Jerusalem. Indeed, it is impossible to know if peace would have been achieved without this gesture, for Sadat's dramatic visit affected what was possibly the most important obstacle to peace for Israelis: the psychological barrier. Indeed, this was Sadat's intention in the symbolic act of coming to the controversial city of Jerusalem and speaking at the Knesset, seat of the unrecognized capital of Israel. There could be no more genuine signal of peaceful intent than the willingness of an Egyptian leader to take the risk (political as well as physical) of such a trip. The visit itself went a long way toward overcoming the deep-seated mistrust and fears of the Israeli public, generated by the years of war, hostility, propaganda, and incitement. But for the Israeli political and military elites, the more reassuring aspect may have been Sadat's speech in the Knesset.[84] Though he repeated the usual demands for Israeli withdrawal from all the territories occupied in 1967, including "Arab Jerusalem," and the need to create a Palestinian state, Sadat addressed Israel's most visceral need for Arab recognition of Israel's legitimacy as part of the region. Though Begin himself maintained that he was in no need of anyone to recognize what was Israel's right – to exist[85] – the idea that the Arab world would never accept the state of Israel was basic to the mistrust and insecurity that had characterized Israeli policies since 1948. It was this that Sadat addressed in his speech when he advocated several times "an Israel that lives in the region with her Arab neighbors in security and safety," adding "In all sincerity I tell you we welcome you among us with full security and safety." ... "Yes, today I tell you, and I declare it to the whole world, that we accept to live with you in permanent peace based on justice." And: "As we really and truly seek peace we really and truly welcome you to live among us in peace and security."[86]

As transformative as the visit and the speech were, however, the ensuing talks were difficult even to the point of near failure. The Sinai did not carry with it the problems of ideology, religion, and history that the West Bank (or Jerusalem) did, and Begin was indeed interested in reaching a peace agreement with Egypt. But Begin's objective of a deal that would enhance, rather than hurt, his more central goal of holding onto the West Bank (*"Eretz Israel"*), coupled with his ideological loyalty to the settlement project as a whole,[87] proved to be critical issues. Moreover, the absence of trust, despite Sadat's visit and declarations, prompted Israeli security demands for keeping the military airfields in Sinai, along with early warning stations, limits on Egyptian forces, and demilitarization. Therefore, still more factors were brought into play to enable the final success.

The contributions in the negotiations of a number of participants from both the Israeli and Egyptian side (Aharon Barak, Ezer Weizman, Osama el Baz, Boutros Boutros Ghali, and others whose stories may never be fully known[88]) played a role, as did Ariel Sharon's phone call to Begin expressing a willingness to forego the settlements in Sinai. But the most important personal contribution may be that of Carter. After a year of unsuccessful talks, Carter invited Begin and Sadat to Camp David to work out a Framework Agreement addressing all the issues of a final peace accord. It was, in fact, not only American mediation providing over 20 drafts but also Carter's personal persuasion and persistence that produced solutions to the controversial issues. Carter managed to keep the negotiations going despite Israeli and Egyptian threats to leave, packed bags and all. Without his direct involvement it is most likely that no agreement would have emerged from Camp David, though some of Carter's "solutions" were based on ambiguities and misunderstandings that later proved problematic, most notably the period of a freeze of settlement building in the West Bank.[89]

Nonetheless, a willingness to tolerate a lack of clarity, including language differences and even contradictory positions (viz. the letters on Jerusalem) was actually a factor that facilitated the final breakthrough. For example, Begin provided a note with his own semantics, using the name "Judea and Samaria" rather than the "West Bank," the "Arabs of *Eretz Israel*" instead of the "Palestinians." Actually crucial was the ambiguity regarding the linkage demanded by Sadat between the peace accord and the autonomy plan for the Palestinians in the West Bank and Gaza. Originally Begin's own idea, the autonomy plan adopted at Camp David left the final status of the area (after a five-year period of autonomy) open ended, without any prior claim to Israeli sovereignty (though the Likud Party platform of 1977 said clearly "between the sea and the Jordan, there will be Jewish sovereignty alone. Any plan that involves surrendering parts of Western *Eretz Israel* militates against our right to the Land").[90] This also meant, however, that there was no commitment to an Israeli withdrawal. More significantly, perhaps, there was also no clear or direct linkage in the form of conditionality or otherwise between the autonomy plan and the 1979 peace agreement with Egypt. Instead of actual linkage, both "agreements" were simply presented in parallel. It is more than conceivable that Begin had no intention of implementing the autonomy plan; indeed, when Dayan and Weizman later understood this they actually resigned from the autonomy talks team and later from the government.[91] For Begin, the final version of the autonomy plan, ultimately forced upon him by the Americans (due to Egyptian insistence), was no more than a face-saving device to enable Sadat to make a separate peace with Israel. Having reportedly told US Secretary of State Cyrus Vance that he would "never preside over the transfer of one inch of the Land of Israel to anyone else's sovereignty," he is said to have replied, when asked by Secretary Vance what would be the fate of the West Bank once the allotted five-year autonomy period ended, "By the end of the five-year period I may not be around."[92] Presumably with the same vague future in mind, he was willing to include a phrase about "the legitimate rights of the Palestinians," stating later, according to one account, that it had little meaning in reality.[93]

While willing to find a way to resolve some issues by means of semantics, ambiguity,[94] or separate understandings, Begin's approach reflected basic mistrust and suspicion. Even Ezer Weisman, who trusted Sadat's intentions, told an interviewer at the time of the signing of the Peace Agreement that he had told Sadat: "Do you really imagine that because of [your visit] we can place all our trust in your hands? Today you are president, tomorrow not. Israel's existence cannot be dependent on you."[95] And, referring later to these talks, Elyakim Rubinstein, also a member of the delegation, attributed the distrust to "an inherited suspicion in Israelis ... derived from Jewish history and psychology" that plays a major role in Israeli decision-making.[96]

Begin, like Golda Meir in the past, was suspicious of both American[97] and Egyptian intentions regarding demands for future withdrawals, specifically from the West Bank or Jerusalem. In addition to the separate letters regarding Jerusalem, Begin was most cautious with regard to any mention of Resolution 242. According to Carter's aide, William Quandt, "First, the text said that 'the results of the negotiations' should be based on all the principles of UN Resolution 242, and the principles, including withdrawal, were then enumerated. Begin argued that the wording should be changed to read 'the negotiations' should be based on 242, not 'the results of the negotiations.' By this he meant that any party could raise the points mentioned in 242 during the negotiations, but that the final agreement need not reflect these principles."[98] Nor, Begin insisted, should the principles be listed, including "withdrawal." While the Americans understood this as a "watering down" to merely a vague reference to Resolution 242, for Begin it was a reflection of his sensitivity (actually opposition) to Resolution 242 and his suspicions regarding the real intentions of Carter and Sadat (namely, withdrawal on all fronts).[99] Regarding the Egyptians, Begin's concern was that Sadat's comments in the Knesset notwithstanding, Egypt's loyalty to its Arab brothers would take precedence over the agreement with Israel.[100] This concern was the reason for Begin's insistence upon the inclusion in article VI of the final peace agreement of the phrase that "in the event of a conflict between the obligations of the Parties under the present Treaty and any of the other obligations, the obligations under this Treaty will be binding and implemented."[101]

There was one other factor that most observers believe played a role in the achievement of peace with Egypt.[102] Beginning with the negative public response to the Yom Kippur War, the anti-government demonstrations and the Agranat Commission, all of which led to the resignation of the Meir government, public opinion appears to have now become a consideration for Israeli decision-makers. The public was clearly touched by Sadat's visit; and surveys of opinion regarding the territories were but one reflection of this (opposition to returning the Sinai plummeted from 39 percent in 1976 to just 16 percent during November to December 1977[103]), while expectations were high regarding a possible peace with Egypt. As intended by Sadat, psychological barriers were apparently surmounted for the most part as the public expected a positive outcome to the post-visit talks. This sentiment was clearly expressed when the subsequent talks began to break down. A group of some 348 reserve officers and soldiers published an open letter of concern:

> Citizens that also serve as soldiers and officers in the reserve forces are sending this letter to you. The following words are not written with a light heart. However at this time when new horizons of peace and cooperation are for the first time being proposed to the State of Israel, we feel obliged to call upon you to prevent taking any steps that could cause endless problems to our people and our state.
>
> We are writing this with deep anxiety, as a government that prefers the existence of the State of Israel within the borders of "Greater Israel" to its existence in peace with good neighborliness, will be difficult for us to accept. A government that prefers existence of settlements beyond the Green Line to elimination of this historic conflict with creation of normalization of relationships in our region will evoke questions regarding the path we are taking. A government policy that will cause a continuation of control over roughly million Arabs will hurt the Jewish-democratic character of the state, and will make it difficult for us to identify with the path of the State of Israel.
>
> We are aware of the security needs of the State of Israel and the difficulties facing the path to peace. But we know that true security will only be reached with the arrival of peace. The power of the IDF is in the identification of its soldiers with the path of the State of Israel.[104]

Coming from army reservists, most of whom were officers and, in some cases, high officers, the letter evoked a massive response, culminating in Israel's unprecedently large political demonstration of 100,000 people in Tel Aviv on the eve of Begin's departure for Camp David. Indeed, Begin later wrote Israeli writer Amos Oz that he was not able to shake off the impression of the "100,000 rally," and according to one account, Begin believed that he could not return empty handed in view of this public outpouring.[105] There was also pressure from within the government coalition, for the center party DASH threatened to bolt if peace with Sadat were not achieved. Public opinion remained strongly in favor following Camp David as well, with some 75 percent support for the Framework Agreement achieved there, and even 70 percent supporting removal of the settlements.[106]

There were, however, also potential spoilers. As in the period of Rabin's negotiations for the Interim Accord, these came from the right, primarily from the settler population and the extreme right. However, Begin, unlike Rabin, could not simply ignore (or chastise) them since most, in fact, came not only from his coalition (namely, the National Religious Party, NRP), but also from among his own party. These included leading figures such as Yitzhak Shamir, Moshe Arens, and Shmuel Katz (who resigned as minister of information in protest after Camp David). Some, like Arens – at the time Israeli ambassador to Washington – opposed the agreement out of security considerations (still clinging to the idea of Sinai as a buffer zone). He was said to believe that Begin's concessions (regarding security matters such as the airfields and early warning stations) had been due, in part, to the pressure of the peace demonstration.[107] Others, like Shamir, opposed relinquishing any territory, viewing Sinai as part of the Biblical Land of Israel. Indeed, for the most part, objections were based on ideological and, for the NRP, religious considerations.

One participant in the talks later asserted that these potential spoilers were ineffectual in part because the press was not allowed to cover the Camp David talks, so pressure from these circles could not find its way into the talks. Rubinstein actually believed that "the peace would not have been obtained if the media had been allowed to cover the [meeting]."[108] Begin did, however, respond somewhat to objectors from among his supporters by conditioning the Framework Agreement of Camp David upon a Knesset vote regarding the evacuation of the Sinai settlements. But he managed to undermine these same opponents by ultimately demanding a vote on the agreement as a whole, not the specific clauses.[109] Another way in which he sought to deal with potential spoilers was to explain, repeatedly, that he had made no commitment to withdraw from the West Bank nor had even used that term (rather than Judea and Samaria) or the word "Palestinians."[110] On the whole, however, even his stature among right-wing members of the Knesset (MKs), based primarily on his role in the pre-state underground struggle for independence, was insufficient to gain the support of his whole coalition or even his own party. In the Knesset vote on the Camp David agreement, only 9 MKs from

Begin's 21 member Herut faction of the Likud voted in favor (7 voted against, 5 abstained), and only 5 of the NRP's 12 MKs voted in favor (3 voted against, and 4 abstained). In addition, 4 of the opposition Labor Party MKs voted against the Camp David agreement, while 3 abstained. Although Shimon Peres, head of the opposition in the Knesset, voted in favor, he frequently expressed his belief that Labor could have made a better agreement – namely, saved the settlements.[111]

When it came to the vote on the Peace Treaty itself, Begin still had to placate objectors. It is possible that his resumption of settlement building, and his insistence to the Americans that he had not agreed to more than a brief freeze, were designed for that purpose. He also had to face noisy Gush Emunim demonstrators – whose demonstrations continued throughout the actual withdrawals, especially during the evacuation of the northern Sinai settlements. Begin may actually have used this opposition to bolster his bargaining position in the final and, once again, difficult discussions with the Americans and Egyptians on the treaty. Once again, though, the potential spoilers were far too weak to block the final agreement. Despite a stormy debate, the Knesset easily approved the peace treaty in a 95 to 18 vote with two abstentions and three not participating. Nonetheless, two ministers in Begin's government, among them Ariel Sharon, actually voted against, while Shamir (later Begin's successor) was among the two abstentions.

Thus, a number of factors combined to transform Israel's intractable conflict with Egypt. Changes in the leadership of both countries were critical; changes in the context (the impact of the 1973 war) and changes in the external environment (Carter's positions, preparations for renewed collective efforts) were contributing factors. And it clearly helped that the issue of Sinai was not burdened – at least in the view of Begin – with historic–religious attachments. In the negotiations themselves, the role played by the Americans was critical, and public opinion may also have contributed at least in part to the agreement. Potential spoilers were far too few to have an effect even if they came from the ranks of Begin's own supporters. However, it is not certain that any of these factors, singly or even together, would have been sufficient for the final breakthrough had Sadat's dramatic visit not dissipated most if not all of the psychological barriers. Most significantly for the outcome, neither Begin's lingering mistrust nor his ideological attachment to the settlements was allowed to prevent a final peace deal.[112] Indeed, this was the major difference in the role played by the mistrust factor in 1979 as compared with the 1967–1968 and 1973 efforts. Then Labor leaders were willing to forego peace with Jordan, and later with Egypt, due to an unwillingness to relinquish land that they perceived as necessary for Israel's security, but a perception of security that was based on their mistrust of Arab willingness to accept Israel's legitimacy in the region. It is possible that Begin's mistrust was mitigated somewhat by Sadat's visit and proclamations of acceptance of Israel. These did affect the Israeli public. It seems more likely that the risks involved were outweighed in Begin's eyes by the political gain; he was ultimately willing to make the

50 Breakthrough with Egypt

territorial sacrifice of Sinai, mistrust notwithstanding, out of his ideologically motivated interest in preserving *Eretz Israel* (the West Bank and Gaza) and the conviction that this agreement would serve that purpose.

Notes

1 There remained differences of interpretation over the role of the third party, UN special representative Gunnar Jarring. Israel maintained that his task was to act as go between for the two sides but not to propose solutions as a mediator.
2 Lawrence Whetten, *The Canal War* (Cambridge, MA: MIT Press, 1974): 101.
3 Anwar Sadat Archives (University of Maryland), Presidential Speeches, "Announcement of Peace Initiative," 4 February 1971, and "Excerpts from a Speech by President Sadat Further Defining the Peace Initiative," 1 May 1971 (http://sadat.umd.edu/archives/speeches.htm).
4 "The United Arab Republic Reply to Ambassador Jarring's Aide Memoire, February 15, 1971," document in in J. N. Moore (Ed.). *The Arab–Israeli Conflict, Readings and Documents* (Princeton, NJ: Princeton University Press, 1977): 1151–1153 read: "When Israel gives these commitments [per Resolution 242] the UAR will be ready to enter a peace agreement with Israel" (1153); Whetten, 1975: 147; Steven Spiegel, *The Other Israeli–Arab Conflict* (Chicago, IL: Chicago University Press, 1985): 204.
5 FRUS XXV, Arab–Israeli Crisis and War 1973, Doc. 26, "Memorandum for the President's Files by the President's Deputy Assistant for National Security (Scowcroft)," 23 February 1973. Hafez Ismail spoke of resolving the "international" aspect (i.e., returning the territories of the Arab states in exchange for peace), and then the "core" problem, that of the Jews and Palestinians (to which "Egypt was not a party"), could be worked out between the Jews and Palestinians. There was also talk of linkage to agreements with Syria and Jordan leading to "full peace." The Egyptians also spoke of a referendum for the Gaza inhabitants regarding their future, though Ismail told the US that Israel would probably have to withdraw first so the Gazans could decide freely.
6 This is all clearly spelled out in Ismail's conversations with the Americans and may be found in Sadat's speeches and autobiography. Sadat expelled the Soviet forces in July 1972 after earlier steps to free himself of Nasser's pro-Soviet colleagues (notably former Vice-President Ali Sabry) and Nasser's socialist-leaning economic policies. For the troubled relations with Moscow, see Galia Golan, *Yom Kippur and After: The Soviet Union and the Middle East Crisis,* (Cambridge, MA: Cambridge University Press, 1977): 21–73.
7 Israeli concessions, for example, withdrawal as far back as the passes, agreement to uniformed Egyptian personnel on the eastern side of the Canal.
8 Yitzhak Rabin, *The Rabin Memoirs* (Berkeley, CA: University of California Press, 1996): 211.
9 Rabin, 1996: 210.
10 Rabin, 1996: 191–218, and FRUS, 1969–1976, XXV, Arab–Israeli Crisis and War, 1973, Doc. 33, "Memorandum From Harold H. Saunders of the National Security Council Staff to the President's Assistant for National Security Affairs (Kissinger)," 1 March 1973.
11 Golda Meir, *My Life* (New York, NY: Putnam and Sons, 1975): 365, 364.
12 Just prior to Ismail's February 1973 visit, Rabin told Kissinger: "The most uncompromising formula was the one Sadat gave to Jarring in February 1970 [*1971*]. It cleverly distinguished between an agreement between Israel and Egypt, the essence of which is total withdrawal, but without committing Egypt on the

issues that are really necessary for peace. Their basic strategy is to distinguish between the two phases of the struggle – Nasser called it land and people. Eliminating the consequences of aggression is one part of it. ... Their objectives are to weaken the link between the US and Israel" (FRUS XXV, Doc. 23, "Memorandum of Conversation," 22 February 1973). See also, Yitzhak Rabin, *Pinkas Sherut [Service Diary]* (Tel Aviv: Sifriat Maariv, 1979): 330.
13 Rabin was at odds with Golda in the 1971 discussions and, possibly, supported the partial accord idea; but this later comment suggests that his problem may not have been her rejection of Sadat's proposals but the manner in which she handled the whole issue (Rabin, 1996: 194–196). In his autobiography in Hebrew he says that the government in Jerusalem was too inflexible and should have offered a plan of its own, given the difference he perceived between Sadat and his predecessor Nasser (Rabin, *Service File*, 330–334, 344–346).
14 FRUS XXV, Doc. 55, "Memorandum of Conversation," 12 May 1973 – "Sadat is not bright, but he can think a few steps ahead." Eban conversation with Kissinger.
15 Rabin, 1996: 209, 211.
16 Meir discusses this concern in *My Life*, 1975: 386–387; but does not mention the Egyptian proposals of 1971 or 1973.
17 Mordecai Gazit (head of the Prime Minister's Office at the time), "Egypt and Israel – Was There a Peace Opportunity Missed in 1971?," *Journal of Contemporary History*, 32, 1997: 97–115.
18 This might explain Rabin's comment to Kissinger on Ismail's comments in 1973: "It's the toughest Egyptian position we have ever had," FRUS XXV, Doc. 31, "Memorandum of Conversation," 27 February 1973.
19 Uri Bar-Joseph, "Last Chance to Avoid War: Sadat's Peace Initiative of 1973 and Its Failure," *Journal of Contemporary History*, 41(3), 2006: 545–556.
20 Bar-Josef, 2006: 553, citing a stenographic protocol of a discussion in the prime minister's residence on 18 April 1973. Transcript made by Hanoch Bartov at the meeting, published later in Hanoch Bartov, *Dado: 48 Shana Ve-od 20 Yom [Dado: 48 Years and 20 Days More]* (Tel Aviv: Sifriat Maariv, 2002).
21 *Ibid.*
22 *Ibid.*
23 Asher Arian, *Security Threatened: Surveying Israeli Opinion on Peace and War* (Cambridge, MA: Cambridge University Press, 1995): 102 (surveys of the Gutman Institute from February 1968 to 1978). The percentages at the end of 1972 (no available figures for early 1973) indicated 96 percent opposed to giving up all or part of the Golan, 78 percent the Gaza Strip, 69 percent all or part of the West Bank.
24 Tom Segev, *1967: Israel, the War, and the Year that Transformed the Middle East* (New York, NY: Metropolitan Books, 2007): 566, citing discussion of the Labor Party's Political Committee.
25 FRUS XXV, Doc 23, 22 February 1973.
26 Yigal Alon had made a similar comment in a reference to Abdullah during the post-1967 discussions; Yigal Alon, *Be-hatira Le-shalom [In Search of Peace]* (Tel Aviv: Hakibbutz Hameuchad, 1989): 38.
27 FRUS XXV, Doc. 24, "Conversation between President Nixon and his Assistant for National Security Affairs (Kissinger)," 23 February 1973.
28 *Ibid*; FRUS XXV, Doc. 31, "Memorandum of Conversation," 27 February 1973.
29 Israel State Archives, "Publication Commemorating the Fortieth Anniversary of the Historic Visit to Israel of Chancellor Willy Brandt of West Germany, June 1973," 9 June 2013.
30 Though there are those who claim that Kissinger did believe that a war would restore Egypt's honor and thus pave the way for an American engineered settlement. Some former Soviet officials have claimed there was Egyptian, US, and even

Israeli "collusion" regarding preparations for a limited war: former Middle East expert, later prime minister of Russia, Yevgeny Primakov – (Yevgeny Primakov, *Russia and the Arabs* (New York, NY: Basic Books, 2009): 141; former KGB chief in Egypt Vasili Mitrokhin – Christopher Andrew and Vasilij Mitrochin, *The World Was Going Our Way: The KGB and the Battle for the Third World* (New York, NY: Basic Books, 2005): 154–155; and former Soviet ambassador to Egypt V. M. Vinogradov – V. M. Vinogradov, *Diplomatiia: Liudi i Sobitiia. Iz Zapisok Posla* [*Diplomat: People and Events. From the Ambassador's Notes*] (Moskva: Rosspen, 1998): 238–245.

31 Spiegel, 1985: 166–218.
32 As he put it, "Our strategy during this period was ... try to create a need for an American role before we give it ... we tried to create such frustrations that the Arabs would leave the Soviet Union and come to us. We didn't want the impression that Soviet pressure produces results – that had to be us. The Soviets could give only arms." This was the policy before the war and the origin of the step-by-step approach, at least insofar as the Egyptians were concerned. Kissinger explained that the policy was changed in 1974 at least with regard to Egypt, though the step by step approach remained (FRUS, 1969–1976, Arab Israeli Dispute, XXVI, Doc. 95, "Memorandum of Conversation," 12 August 1974).
33 Rabin, 1996: 205.
34 See interview Rabin gave the Israeli paper *Davar*, 16 September 1974 (Israel Ministry of Foreign Affairs (MFA), Rabin Speeches, 1974–1977).
35 Rabin interview to *Yedioth Aharonoth*, 26 July 1974.
36 Israel Army Radio, 10 August 1974 (MFA), Rabin Speeches, Volume 3: 1974–1977.
37 The efforts with Jordan are discussed below. Golda Meir, just before her resignation, Protocol, Twenty-First Session of the Eighth Knesset, Sunday, 10 March 1974; Rabin speech to the Knesset, 3 June 1974 (MFA, Volume 3: 1974–1977). Even if elections were not Rabin's preference, his coalition (which included the National Religious Party) would most likely have collapsed had he made concessions on the West Bank.
38 Rabin interview, Israel Television, 20 September 1974 (MFA).
39 Israel wanted the agreement open ended; Sadat wanted it renewable on a regular basis so that it did not look like a final agreement (i.e., no further withdrawals). Details of the talks may be found in the Foreign Relations of the US (FRUS), Vol. XXVI, *Arab–Israeli Dispute 1969–1976*; Rabin, 1996; William Quandt, *Camp David: Peacemaking and Politics* (Washington, DC: The Brookings Institution, 1986). Sadat gives these talks almost no mention in his autobiography (Anwar el-Sadat, *In Search of Identity* (New York, NY: Harper & Row, 1978).
40 Rabin speech to the Knesset, 3 June 1974 (MFA, Rabin Speeches, Vol. 3: 1974–1977).
41 Israel's official position on Resolution 242 (despite its particular interpretation of some of the clauses) was not entirely clear. The Roger's Initiative for ending the War of Attrition in August 1970 included a reference to the resolution and specified Israeli withdrawal on all fronts; it was therefore opposed by the right-wing party Gahal. Its leader, Menachem Begin, took the party out of the government, maintaining that this Israeli agreement to Resolution 242 in all its parts constituted willingness to give up territory.
42 Yaacov Bar-Siman-Tov, "Peace Policy as Domestic and Foreign Policy: The Israeli Case," in Sasson Soffer (Ed.), *Peacemaking in a Divided Society, Israel After Rabin* (London: Frank Cass, 2001): 27–54.
43 For sample of US concerns, see FRUS XXVI, Doc. 123, "Memorandum of Conversation," 9 December 1973; Doc. 126, "Minutes of Washington Special Actions Group Meeting," 14 January 1974; FRUS XXVI, Doc. 189, "Memorandum of Conversation" (with 20 leaders of US Jewry, in New York), 15 June 1975.
44 Rabin, 1996: 272.

Breakthrough with Egypt 53

45 Rabin spoke of this not as an example of why he might compromise, but, rather, he said this when he was refusing to compromise – to show Kissinger how hard it was for him to take the firm stand.
46 Rabin, 1996: 250.
47 Rabin, 1996: 263.
48 Rabin, 1996: 263.
49 FRUS, XXVI *Arab–Israeli Dispute*, Doc. 183, "Memorandum of Conversation," 11 June 1975.
50 MFA, Rabin Speeches, Vol. 3: 1974–1977.
51 FRUS, XXVI *Arab–Israeli Dispute*, Doc. 183, "Memorandum of Conversation," 11 June 1975.
52 Rabin, 1996: 251, 274.
53 Rabin, 1996: 250.
54 FRUS, XXVI *Arab–Israeli Dispute*, Doc. 183, "Memorandum of Conversation," 11 June 1975.
55 Rabin, 1996: 242, 245.
56 In March 1975, some 92 members had supported Rabin's stand, and only four had opposed, while six abstained.
57 FRUS, XXVI *Arab–Israeli Dispute*, Doc. 144, "Memorandum from the President's Deputy Assistant for National Security (Scowcroft) to the President," 13 March 1975.
58 FRUS, XXVI *Arab–Israeli Dispute*, Doc. 180, "Memorandum of Conversation," 9 June 1975. Kissinger told the President that Javitz with Ambassador Dinitz had initiated the letter.
59 FRUS XXVI, Doc. 189, "Memorandum of Conversation," 15 June 1975 (meeting with Jewish leaders); FRUS XXVI, Doc. 201, "Memorandum of Conversation," 27 June 1975 (meeting with Javitz). See also FRUS XXVI, Doc. 181, "Briefing Memorandum from Assistant Secretary of State for Congressional Relations (McCloskey) to Secretary of State Kissinger," undated. In a scathing attack on both Kissinger and what he perceived as US bias toward Israel, George Ball (former US undersecretary of state) maintained that the letter did lead to what he claimed were serious US concessions to Israel in the 1975 agreement (George Ball, "Israeli–American Relations," *Foreign Affairs*, 58(2), 1979: 240–241).
60 An Israeli proposal was that American (not Egyptian) personnel man the early warning stations in the areas that Israel would evacuate. Washington opposed stationing such a large number of personnel there; the compromise was that the stations would fly the US flag but be manned by Egyptian and Israeli personnel.
61 Rabin, 1996: 271–272.
62 "Agreements Published by the Foreign Affairs Committee of the US Senate Regarding the Interim Agreement of 1975," in Binyamin Neuberger, *Mediniyut Hutz Shel Yisrael: Kovetz Mismakhim*, I (*Foreign Policy of Israel*) (Tel Aviv: The Open University, 2004): 336–340.
63 In the many internal shifts in Israel political parties, the Likud, dominated by Herut with Begin at its head, replaced Gahal in 1973.
64 The secret channel with the Egyptians via the Moroccans had been set up in Golda Meir's time after the Yom Kippur war. Austrian Bruno Kreisky was another intermediary for the meeting.
65 At one point Sadat even suggested a broader conference be held in East Jerusalem to resolve the Arab–Israeli conflict (including all the permanent members of the Security Council. Sadat, 1978: 307–308; Ismail Fahmy, *Negotiating for Peace in the Middle East* (London: Croom-Helm, 1983): 255, 259–264 (Fahmy claimed the idea of a broader conference actually was his); Moshe Dayan, *Breakthrough* (London: Weidenfeld and Nicholson, 1981): 87; William Quandt, *Peace Process* (Washington, DC: The Brookings Institution, 1993): 270.

54 Breakthrough with Egypt

66 Later, Begin actually accepted this wording, as we shall see below.
67 Quite thorough coverage may be found in William Quandt, *Camp David: Peacemaking and Politics* (Washington, DC: The Brookings Institution, 1986). Also, Moshe Dayan, 1981; Ezer Weizman, *Battle for Peace* (New York, NY: Bantam Books, 1981); Jimmy Carter, *Keeping the Faith: Memoires of a President* (New York, NY: Bantam Books, 1982); Aryeh Naor, *Begin Ba-shilton: 'edut Ishit* [*Begin in Power: Personal Evidence*] (Tel Aviv: Yedioth Sfarim, 1993).
68 For Sadat's initial demand for Gaza, see Quandt, 1986: Appendix D, 358 ("Egyptian Proposal at Camp David").
69 Quandt, 1986: 385–386 (documents of Appendix G to the Framework Agreement). The autonomy plan was later adopted almost word for word (excluding a role for Jordan) in the form of the 1993 Oslo Accords.
70 See his comment, above, during the talks for the Interim Accord (Rabin, 1996: 263).
71 FRUS, XXVI, Doc. 183, "Memorandum of Conversation," 11 June 1975.
72 For example, Benny Morris, *Righteous Victims* (New York, NY: Alfred Knopf, 1999): 667.
73 Sadat, 1978: 304, and in his speech at the Knesset ("Documents Related to the Peace Process between Israel and Her Neighbors," www.knesset.gov.il).
74 Corruption was also a factor in the overall rejection of Labor.
75 Arian, 1995: 102. On Sinai, percentages fell from 69 to 36 percent just one month after the war and continued to decline steadily; on the West Bank – from 82 to 58 percent, with minor fluctuations but an overall decline following in the studies up to 1978. Arian's study does not indicate opinion on Jerusalem prior to 1975; but in the period between 1975 and 1978 the percentages against giving up any part of Jerusalem ranged between 71 and 87 percent; in 1993 they were 83 percent.
76 From 94 to 86 percent opposing return (Arian, 1995: 102).
77 The party DASH (Democratic Movement for Change) consisted of past military, academic, and other leaders usually identified with Labor previously.
78 See Tamir Magal, Neta Oren, Daniel Bar-Tal, Eran Halperin, "Psychological Legitimization – Views of the Israeli Occupation by Jews in Israel," in D. Bar-Tal and I. Schnell (Eds), *The Impacts of Lasting Occupation: Lessons from Israeli Society* (New York, NY: Oxford University Press, 2013): 122–185. The Zionist proposal to the Paris Peace Conference 1919 included all of the area of the west bank plus the east bank of the Jordan River up to the outskirts of Amman: map in Mark Tessler, *A History of the Israeli–Palestinian Conflict* (Bloomington, IN: Indiana University Press, 1994): 163. The Herut Party anthem referred to both banks of the Jordan.
79 Cabinet Communique on settlements in the West Bank, 26 July 1974, and Statement in the Knesset by Prime Minister Rabin, 31 July 1974, Vol. 3: 1974–1977 (MFA). One analyst called this the difference between redeemers and custodians; between liberate and a bargaining chip (Amnon Sella, "Custodians and Redeemers: Israeli Leaders' Perceptions of Peace, 1967–79," in S. Lustick (Ed.), *Arab–Israeli Relations*, VII (New York, NY: Garlan, 1994): 248–263); another explains it as the difference between proprietary versus egalitarian (non-exclusive) rights. (Haim Gans, *A Just Zionism: On the Morality of the Jewish State* (Oxford, UK: Oxford University Press, 2008)).
80 *Ibid.*
81 Naor, 1993: 99,106. It has been claimed that Begin viewed the Palestinians as a potential national minority in Israel that might even be given citizenship; the PLO was viewed not as a national liberation movement but as a "murder organization … a political tool of the Arab States": Likud Party platform, 1977, cited by Colin Shindler, *Israel, Likud and the Zionist Dream* (New York, NY: I. B. Tauris, 1995): 89.
82 16 March 1977 speech in Clinton, Massachusetts.

83 Note Arafat's appearance there and the 1975 "Zionism Is Racism" General Assembly resolution.
84 Demonstrative of their skepticism, chief of staff Mota Gur was not alone in viewing Sadat's offer to visit as a cover for war preparations (*Yedioth Aharonoth*, 14 November 1977, interview of Gur); both he and acting Defense Minister Yigal Yadin actually urged Begin to mobilize two armored divisions. Naor, 1993: 145; Shlomo Gazit, "Israel–Egypt: What Went Wrong? Nothing," in Edwin Corr, Joseph Ginat, Shaul Gabbay (Eds), *The Search for Israeli–Arab Peace*, (Brighton, UK: Sussex Academic Press, 2007): 105–106.
85 Begin said this in a conversation with Carter, over the Kissinger promise to Rabin that the US would not negotiate with the PLO unless the organization recognized Israel's right to exist (and accepted Resolution 242): Yehuda Avner, *The Prime Ministers* (London: The Toby Press, 2010): 426, and a second time, 440. Eric Silver, *Begin: A Biography* (London: Weidenfeld and Nicholson, 1984): 167 has the full quote in which Begin added "God gave us that right 4,000 years ago." Begin also said this in presenting his government to the Knesset on 20 June 1977; but he clarified that he did want mutual recognition of "sovereignty."
86 Knesset, "Documents ... " (www.knesset.gov.il).
87 He had once declared his intention of setting up a home in the Neot Sinai settlement.
88 Boutros Boutros Ghali said in his memoirs that the major roles in the talks were played by Carter, Aharon Barak, and Osama el-Baz. Boutros Boutros-Ghali, *Egypt's Road to Jerusalem* (New York, NY: Random House, 1997): 143.
89 There was subsequent serious disagreement between Begin and the Americans, with Begin insisting he had meant it to be only three months and the US claiming Begin had agreed to a freeze for the entire period of the autonomy negotiations. Quandt, 1986: 248; 263–264; for further details, see Carter, 1982: 397 and Morris, 1999: 479.
90 Shindler, 1995: 85; Likud Platform for the Ninth Knesset (1977), Likud Archives, Tel Aviv.
91 Dayan, 1981: 303–305; Weizman, 1981: 384. For the demise of the post-1979 autonomy talks, see Yaacov Bar-Siman-Tov, *Israel and the Peace Process* (New York, NY: SUNY Press, 1994): 195–202.
92 Quoted by Silver, 1984: 203 based on his interview with Vance; also cited by Avner, 2010: 496 based on interviews and his own notes.
93 Weizman, 1981: 373. Begin accepted this previously rejected phrase (known as Carter's Aswan formula) in order to avoid any mention of an eventual state as demanded by Sadat (Dayan, 1981: 110, 174).
94 Begin was considered a stickler for detail at Camp David, and the presence of the legal advisor to the government, Barak, is often cited as evidence of this. Indeed, Begin was far more demanding than Sadat regarding detail and formulations, but it was actually such insistence that led to varied, even contradictory formulations open to (mis)interpretation between the three parties later.
95 *Maariv*, 24 March 1978. This is notably reminiscent of Yigal Allon's comment in 1967 with regard to King Hussein (see Chapter 2).
96 Elyakim Rubinstein, *Darkei Shalom* [*Paths of Peace*] (Tel Aviv: Ministry of Defense, 1992): 93.
97 Though Meir maintained that Begin was more confident about having his way with the Americans (Meir, 1975: 322–333). Presenting his new government to the Knesset on 20 June 1977, Begin reportedly asserted that the US needed Israel more than Israel needed the US (Silver, 1984: 167, who was present at the speech), though in the official record of the speech Begin merely implied this.
98 Quandt, 1986: 246.
99 Begin also resisted the mention of Resolution 242's reference to "the inadmissibility of acquisition of territory by war," which Aharon Barak and Osama el

56 Breakthrough with Egypt

Baz agreed to drop in exchange for Begin's agreement to the "legitimate rights of the Palestinians" phrase. Instead, an annex was added containing the entire text of Resolution 242 (Silver, 1984: 197).
100 Naor, 1993: 186–187; Quandt, 1986: 304–311, regarding this and Begin's suspicions over Sadat's addition of the words "comprehensive peace."
101 MFA, *Israel–Egypt Peace Treaty*, 26 March 1979.
102 For example, Morris, 1999: 461; Shindler, 1995: 92.
103 Arian, 1995: 102.
104 Translation mine, to be found on www.peacenow.co.il. Peace Now, Israel's longest lasting and only mass peace movement, resulted from this letter.
105 Mordecai Bar-On, *Shalom Achshav: Lediyukna Shel Tnu'ah* [*Peace Now: Portrait of a Movement*] (Tel Aviv: Kibbutz Meuchad, 1985): 31–32, attributes this widely cited comment to Weizman, though in his own book Weizman says categorically that while he was "charmed" by Peace Now, no cabinet decision was influenced by its protests (Weizman, 1981: 306).
106 Bar-Siman-Tov, 1994: 150–152.
107 Morris, 1999: 463.
108 Rubinstein, 1992: 99–100.
109 Morris and Shindler discuss the differences within the Likud.
110 Shindler, 1995: 96–97. See also Morris, 1999: 474.
111 Comments to the Labor Party and the author; Shimon Peres, *Battling for Peace* (New York, NY: Random House, 1995): 255.
112 At Camp David Weizman feared that "Begin's ideology would outweigh the dictates of immediate reality" and put it to him that the issue was "settlements or peace"(Weizman, 1981: 370).

4 Failure on the Syrian Track

During the negotiations for the 1975 Interim Accord with Egypt, as already noted, Yitzhak Rabin had this to say in response to American pressure: "no Arab ruler is prepared to make true peace and normalization of relations with Israel."[1] He explained that the Arabs demand full withdrawal to the 4 June 1967 borders, which Israel cannot do, for security reasons. Indeed, Rabin was not the Israeli leader but, rather, Begin who agreed to do just this in exchange for peace with Egypt. In 1992, however, it was Rabin who was challenged to do it for peace with a second Arab state: Syria. Few, if any, believed that peace could be achieved with Syria without full withdrawal from the Golan Heights – no less than what had been accorded Egypt. And in 1974 Rabin had said very clearly that he saw "no possibility of our giving up the Golan Heights .... . Even under a peace treaty, the Golan Heights must be within Israel's jurisdiction."[2] Therefore, the major questions to be addressed are: was the Rabin of 1992 the same as the Rabin of 1974–1975? Or did he believe that peace was possible with Syria, and was he willing to pay the price in territory? And, ultimately, was Rabin's attitude the key – or obstacle – to achieving a breakthrough, as distinct from the Syrian side of the negotiations?

There have been a number of attempts to answer these questions, most authoritatively in the quite detailed accounts of the negotiations provided by direct participants in the 1992–1995 talks.[3] These, along with other observers, differ regarding the positions or intentions of President Hafiz al-Assad of Syria; but it is agreed that the potential for a breakthrough may be traced to Syria's agreement to participate in the Madrid Conference of 1991.[4] The conference itself was the result of an outside factor – namely, a commitment the United States had made to the Arab countries, and specifically Syria, in order to build a coalition against Iraq after its invasion of Kuwait in August 1990. Saddam Hussein had proclaimed that he would withdraw from Kuwait when Israel would withdraw from the occupied territories. While this was a basically demagogic pronouncement, Washington nonetheless understood the connection in the minds of its would-be allies in the region and, therefore, spoke of what might be termed "sequential linkage."[5] President Bush promised the Arabs and Gorbachev (the Soviets still had a Friendship Pact with Iraq) that following the Kuwait crisis, an effort would be made to resolve the Arab–Israeli conflict in order to ensure stability in the region. Washington did, indeed, have an interest in such stability, and so it organized the Madrid Conference under the co-sponsorship of the US and the Soviet Union as a step in that direction. Syria still resisted participating, but agreed after US Secretary of State Baker assured Assad that Washington would provide guarantees and even peacekeepers should a deal be made on the Golan.[6] Assad's underlying motivation, however, was apparently his interest in improved relations with the United States given the loss of his Soviet backers and the "new world order" of the post-Soviet era, as well as economic problems at home. And improved relations with the United States dictated at least some effort at peacemaking with Israel. Whether Assad's motives for attending the Madrid Conference were purely US focused or, perhaps, the "strategic decision for peace" that the Syrians were later to claim they had made became a major question.[7]

Israel, for its part, was even more reluctant to attend Madrid given its customary apprehensions about dealing with the Arabs collectively rather than bilaterally. Moreover, Likud Prime Minister Yitzhak Shamir, whose major concern related rather to the West Bank and the Palestinian issue, maintained that Israel had fulfilled Resolution 242 by withdrawing from Sinai and need do nothing more. However, promoting the Madrid meeting, Baker conveyed to Shamir Arab willingness to negotiate with Israel, including Syrian agreement to the idea of confidence-raising measures. He also provided certain assurances as incentives for Israeli participation, among them the same suggestion given Assad of US guarantees and troops on the Golan.[8] Baker also reiterated the 1 September 1975 commitment made by President Ford to Rabin in conjunction with the Interim Agreement, that in forming its position on borders, the US would give "great weight to Israel's position that any peace agreement with Syria must be predicated on Israel remaining on the Golan Heights" (the Hebrew translation reads "in the Golan Heights," which was the more common way in Israel of referring to the Golan).[9]

The Madrid Conference of October 1991 opened what was to become a series of bilateral negotiations (Israel and Syria, Israel and Lebanon, Israel and a Jordanian–Palestinian delegation[10]), alongside multilateral negotiations (which Syria refused to attend) that included countries from within and outside the region, on topics of refugees, arms control, water, environment, and economic development. Thus began the bilateral talks between Israel and Syria, both directly and via the intermediary of the United States, that were to continue off and on for the next nine years. Shamir made repeated statements of opposition to any territorial changes, including with regard to the Golan, and he later admitted that he had intended only to drag out the post-Madrid talks.[11] Nonetheless, in early 1992 he reportedly authorized a secret "non-official emissary" to convey to Damascus that Israel did not rule out the possibility of some territorial concessions in the Golan.[12] Roughly the same time, 6 March 1992, Syria's chief negotiator in the bilateral talks said "we are willing to make peace with Israel with all the attributes of that peace and we hope that you in your turn ... [will] implement withdrawal from the territories that you occupied in 1967."[13] Promising as it may have been, this public statement called for "comprehensive peace," and went on explicitly to demand full withdrawal from all the territories, thereby including withdrawal from the West Bank which was clearly a non-starter for Shamir.[14] Actually, these basically preliminary talks in Washington were best described as difficult, and they were rapidly superseded by the elections in Israel (June 1992) and in the US (6 November 1992), leading to a whole new set of negotiations and perhaps greater potential for a breakthrough.

There were a number of factors that might have worked toward a genuine breakthrough, the most important of which may well have been the leadership change in Israel. The Rabin of 1992 does appear to have changed from the Rabin of 1974. In presenting his government to the Israeli Knesset on 13 July 1992, Rabin spoke at length of what he viewed as both an opportunity and a need for peace – as distinct from a "peace process." Indeed, in what was almost a retort to his 1975 position, he said clearly that the basis for ending the Arab–Israeli conflict would be "recognition by the Arab states and the Palestinians of Israel as a sovereign state with the right to live within peace and security. *We believe wholeheartedly that this is possible, that it is imperative, and that it will happen* [emphasis mine]."

His widow, Leah Rabin, was later to say that the change in Rabin was the result of the Intifada, leading him as early as 1989 to the conclusion that the occupation must end, though she does not mention the change with regard to the Arab states.[15] The Palestinian issue was indeed the focus of Rabin's "inaugural" speech (and of his election campaign), and the Intifada was a key factor in the move toward the Oslo Accords, as we shall see below. Yet, Rabin himself indicated the major factor behind his broader conception of peace: the change in the external environment. This was the collapse of the Soviet Union and the end of the Cold War or, as he put it: "Walls of enmity have fallen, borders have been erased, great powers have crumbled and ideologies collapsed ... we must join the international campaign for peace, reconciliation and cooperation that is currently sweeping the globe. Otherwise we will be left behind, all alone."[16] He may also have been considering a related element of the momentous changes known as the "new world order," notably the emergence of the United States – Israel's unofficial ally – as the sole super power. This was a factor that might not only strengthen Israel's bargaining position but also provide incentive, even need, for the Arab world to turn to the United States (as the recent Gulf War had just demonstrated), thereby possibly altering Arab positions vis à vis Israel. Further, the regional environment now contained the additional element of a still broader spread of radical Islamism, threatening many of the regimes and possibly creating greater concern among Arab leaders than their conflict with Israel. This too might operate as a factor for new policies regarding Israel and chances for peace.

These changes in the world and regional environment created what Rabin was to call a "window of opportunity"; but this term implied also a time limit. That time limit was connected to a negative phenomenon also emerging, that of potential nuclearization of the region. Rabin asserted in the same speech: "Israel has long since readied itself to face threat of nuclear arms. Nevertheless, the situation obliges us to give further thought to the urgent need for an end to the Arab-Israeli conflict and for peace with our neighbors."[17] Describing this as a "strategic imperative," Rabin, according to US negotiator Dennis Ross believed that Israel would never be in a stronger position both militarily and because of US policies in the region. However, according to Ross's summary of Rabin's comments to him privately, "within a decade, if Israel did not capitalize on the current favorable conditions, it could face dangers from Iran or possibly a resurgent Iraq ... each of which might acquire unconventional military capabilities. It was necessary to transform the Middle East before that could happen."[18] Former head of army intelligence Uri Sagie also mentions Rabin's determination "to achieve agreements with our neighbors before the Iranians got the bomb."[19] And close Rabin associate Eitan Haber has added a Rabin concern over the future resilience of the Israeli public given the exodus of tens of thousands of Tel Aviv residents during the SCUD attacks of the Iraq War. Indeed, Rabin contrasted this behavior with the staunch response of Tel Aviv to Egyptian bombing in 1948, commenting to Haber: "how much longer can people take it?"[20]

There were signs that the change occurring in Rabin's thinking about the possibilities for peace included some new thinking about Syria as well. In June 1988, for example, Rabin had clearly said that Syria was not a partner for peace; but in late 1991 he referred positively to the Syrians' consistent adherence to the 1974 disengagement agreement, saying that Israel could talk with Damascus, and in the 1992 election campaign he actually said that there was some "limited room for territorial compromise" on the Golan.[21] Nonetheless, the Labor Party platform for the 1992 elections had said "Israel views the Golan as an area of importance to its peace and security ... in any peace agreement and security arrangements with Syria, Israeli security and settlement presence and control will continue."[22] Rabin's preference clearly was to deal first with the Palestinian issue,[23] changing this position only a month after his election.

One might explain Rabin's decision to deal with Syria on the grounds that, as in the case of Egypt, he saw the strategic threat to Israel of war with a well-armed state, Syria, as distinct from the non-existential dangers posed by the Palestinians. Additionally, as he was to say later to both the Americans and the Israeli public, the Syrians had a clear address in the form of a leader capable of making hard decisions.[24] Yet, neither of those factors had been any less relevant before the elections, when Rabin nonetheless prioritized the Palestinian track. It would appear that the reason for his decision to move on the Syrian track first may be traced to the Americans. In late July 1992, Baker once again traveled to Jerusalem, bringing a message from Assad that the Syrian leader was seriously interested in peace with Israel.[25] Baker added that the US was willing to help in achieving and securing such an agreement. Itamar Rabinovich, the person whom Rabin chose to conduct the negotiations, reports that Rabin remained nonetheless skeptical of Assad's intentions but was willing to explore that track. According to Rabinovich, Rabin was also impressed by the Americans' willingness to become involved – especially because Jerusalem needed to repair the relationship with Washington that had suffered under Shamir.[26]

Thus, a further external factor that contributed to the potential for a breakthrough was the position and role of Washington. The leadership change in the US, and with it the change of some of the persons dealing with the post-Madrid talks, may not have occasioned a significant shift for Washington since both the previous and the new president, Clinton, were interested in pursuing an Arab–Israeli agreement and believed the Syrian track to be more promising. The thinking in the Clinton administration followed the lines of what they believed to be Rabin's preference, on the basis of the strategic threat that Syria – as distinct from the Palestinians – could pose to Israel. In addition, according to Ross, the US estimate was that Syrian peace with Israel would create a "circle of peace" enabling the remaining parties, such as Jordan and Lebanon, to make a similar peace with Israel. It would also weaken and bring pressure on the Palestine Liberation Organization, influence the Gulf states (among which US ally Saudi Arabia was now at odds with the PLO due to the organization's support for Saddam Hussein), and "insulate Israel from more distant threats from Iraq and Iran."[27] In fact, aside from the brief period of the Carter administration, Washington had generally favored the Arab states over the Palestinians when dealing with the conflict, and in this post-Soviet, post-Gulf War period improved US relations with Syria were still very much on Washington's agenda for the stabilization of the region. While the State Department had not yet taken Syria off its list of states supporting terrorism (because of the continued presence of various groups in Damascus), the PLO was on the list as a terrorist organization itself and something of anathema to American lawmakers and public.

Domestic Israeli factors were also important to the possibility of a breakthrough. With regard to Israeli public opinion, it could be argued, and it may have become Rabin's position at some point, that it would be easier for the government to give up the Golan than the West Bank – and to remove the settlements there. The ideological–religious factor did not apply to the Golan, and the settlers there were from circles close to the labor movement and the left, possibly willing to evacuate for the sake of peace. Yet, it was public opinion, and especially among these same Labor-associated Golan settlers, that constituted a major concern for Rabin. He felt a particular commitment to the Golan settlers, who might feel that he had betrayed them. Indeed, many did and joined right-wing activists (in part from West Bank settlements) using the term "traitor" in demonstrations organized once Rabin spoke of talks with Syria and the possibility of some settlement evacuation.[28] With regard to the general public, opinion polls in June 1992 (before the elections) indicated some 71 percent opposed to giving back any part of the Golan, 22 percent willing to give back some, 7 percent willing to give back all.[29] After Rabin spoke of the various conditions he would demand in exchange for possible territorial concessions on the Golan, a September 1992 poll found that if the option of returning a small part were presented, only 49 percent of the public opposed returning any part while 33 percent were willing to return a small part.[30] Still, only 6 percent were willing to return all of the Golan when polled in September 1992. Within the Labor Party itself, there were probably more supporters of retaining the Golan than favoring compromise, at least among Rabin's camp. In the longstanding internal rivalry within the Labor Party, Rabin's camp was, in fact, identified with what was known as the "activists," formerly associated with Ahdut Avoda and its kibbutz movement, while the Peres camp was considered "dovish." Thus, it was his own camp that Rabin would have to sway, though he would not have a similar problem with the military, which, as he once told Dennis Ross, was fully behind him.[31] It was partially from Rabin's camp in Labor that a movement emerged specifically around the Golan issue, ultimately leaving the Labor Party in 1996 to create a new, centrist party.[32] Thus, opposition from within his own party was to be a crucial barrier since Rabin's coalition government had only a two member majority of the Knesset, along with five (mainly Arab) non-coalition members. And within his coalition, the religious party, Shas, with its six members of Knesset (MKs) was often relatively hawkish (and, indeed, did bolt the coalition when the Oslo Accords were signed the following year). Thus, negative public opinion and potential spoilers were factors that might militate against a breakthrough, possibly even becoming the determining factor, at least for Rabin, as negotiations with Syria proceeded.

Anticipating the opposition, Rabin's presentation of his peace plans regarding Syria, in a speech to a special session of the Knesset on 9 September 1992 before leaving for Washington, was very circumspect, emphasizing the exploratory nature of the talks with regard to Syria's intentions.[33] He was also circumspect with regard to his own intentions. While he had authorized Rabinovich to open the Washington talks in August with a statement that Resolution 242 in all its parts applied to the Golan, in his Knesset speech Rabin said this resolution had many interpretations, and he made no commitment to any territorial withdrawal, though he said that might be what Syria would expect. He even spoke of the possibility of an interim agreement. But in an effort to neutralize potential spoilers from the Likud, Rabin quoted something Begin had declared in the 1981 Knesset debate on the bill extending Israeli law to the Golan: "'From a political perspective, I [Begin] declare in the presence of every member of the cabinet sitting here, that at the moment the Syrian president says he is prepared to conduct negotiations with Israel towards a peace treaty, the negotiations for a peace treaty with Israel will commence at that exact moment, and no obstacles will stand in our way.'"[34]

Rabin sought to overcome domestic opposition in two ways. The first was an effort throughout the entire period of the negotiations to elicit from Syria some kind of confidence-building measures or gesture, similar, for example, to Sadat's dramatic visit, that he might use to persuade the public and opponents in Israel that Damascus was serious. The second was a decision to hold a referendum in Israel should an agreement with Syria actually be reached. Rabin explained to President Clinton during a March 1993 trip to Washington that without the first, specifically a meeting between the two leaders, it was unlikely that peace could be concluded, and that the second, the referendum, was necessary inasmuch as the Golan issue had not been raised in the Israeli elections and, therefore, he did not feel that he had a mandate to make a decision on his own. Both Rabinovich and Uri Sagie (chief of IDF intelligence at the time and present in much of this negotiation) maintain that Rabin's concern over public reaction was a major, if not the major, factor for Rabin regarding the Syrian talks. Sagie would even list this as the cause of the ultimate failure, though Rabin's view of leadership was more one of leading than following the public.[35] Rabinovich mentions two other factors holding Rabin back – namely, concern over the possible trauma of trying to evacuate the settlers who had been living on the Golan for almost 30 years, and the more security-related concern over "the value of a piece of paper" (i.e., a treaty versus a physical presence on the Golan Heights).[36] The latter had particular resonance with Rabin as a military man; he often referred to the soldiers lost in the battles over these lands and a sense of responsibility to those who had fallen. As in 1974, this was a psychological factor that would appear to have played a part in Rabin's security-related concerns.

However, while all of these concerns may have constituted the factors that could and perhaps did cause the failure in reaching an agreement with Syria, they reflected to a large degree Rabin's deep skepticism and suspicions about Assad's intentions. Israel's academic experts agreed that Assad was interested now in a settlement; intelligence circles knew that at least as early as 1991 Assad had informed his own party that this was a strategic decision for peace; and even political rival Peres (who preferred the Palestinian track) believed this to be the case, worried only about the territorial price that Israel would have to pay.[37] Rabin, however, still viewed the talks as merely exploratory – seeking proof of Assad's intentions. Thus, once again, mistrust lay at the center of Israel's considerations, presumably confirmed by Assad's general refusal either to make a public gesture[38] or to directly spell out what he meant by peace, at least in terms that Rabin judged as sufficient.

These suspicions were apparent a number of times in Rabin's responses to Syrian positions (conveyed publicly or via the Americans) during the years of negotiations. As these talks have been assiduously chronicled by Ross[39] and Rabinovich, we shall deal with only highlights or turning points that may have been critical, illustrating the major factors at play.

From the beginning, the Rabin authorized talks in August 1992, hedging on the territorial issue, together with an effort to gain clear indications of Syria's intentions, had, in fact, already become the major elements of Israel's approach and the mainstay of virtually all subsequent meetings. Syria demanded a commitment to full withdrawal from the Golan; Israel demanded to know just what kind of peace Damascus would provide. In Rabin's terms, as stated in November 1992, "the depth of the withdrawal will reflect the depth of the peace."[40] Syria responded with the demand for "total withdrawal for total peace," altered in April 1993 to "full withdrawal for full peace." Related issues such as timing (phases, overall period), along with security arrangements were to be negotiated; but these too basically depended upon the territory that would be involved, and the nature of the peace. Israel was not willing to make such an explicit withdrawal commitment as a precondition for negotiation; but the issue was not so much a pre-condition but Rabin's need for assurances regarding Syria's intention to make genuine peace – and not just an agreement on non-belligerency, for example, or linked to resolution of the Palestinian issue (implied by "total withdrawal").[41]

Some progress had been made prior to August 1993. At least Syria's demand for "total" withdrawal had become "full"; but Israel was not willing to speak of full withdrawal or provide any indication of the extent of the withdrawal without knowing if Syria's interpretation of full peace meant diplomatic relations, open borders, tourism, trade, and so forth. The context of the talks had changed somewhat in that the Lebanese-based Hizballah had begun violent actions against Israel in the north and Israel had responded with an incursion, Operation Accountability, followed by an American-negotiated cease-fire. While Rabin was concerned that Syria had not restrained Hizballah, he viewed positively Syria's cooperation in the achievement of the cease-fire. In any case, at this time as well as later, Rabin did not allow this theatre of operations to affect the peace talks, or vice versa, even if he believed that the Hizballah attacks were meant to pressure Israel. Another development at the same time was the PLO–Israeli negotiations now underway officially, if still secretly, in Oslo. Both the Americans and Assad believed that Israel was using these talks as leverage on the Syrian track; it is not clear if this was, in fact, the case. Later, Israeli–Jordanian peace talks were also viewed by both Syria and the US as an Israeli pressure tactic, which they may have been, although peace with Jordan was a logical by-product of the progress ultimately made between Israel and the PLO.[42]

Mid-summer 1993 was marked by a stalemate in the Israeli talks with Syria (and also, temporarily, with the PLO), so, therefore, Clinton's Secretary of State Warren Christopher reportedly sought a new approach. This demarche has been described by Ross and Rabinovich, the note takers and only persons present besides Christopher and Rabin. Their versions vary only slightly but critically. According to Rabinovich, Rabin told Christopher:

> ... to explore with Assad, on the assumption that his [Rabin's] demand would be satisfied, first whether Syria would be willing to sign a peace treaty with Israel without linkage to the pace of progress with others; second, whether Syria was ready for a real peace including normalization, diplomatic relations, and the other paraphernalia of real peace; and third whether Syria was ready to offer elements of peace before the completion of withdrawal. Rabin explained to Christopher that he saw the whole process completed in five years and that, given the fact that Israel was

asked to give tangibles in return for intangibles [sic] he wanted tangible proofs of peace before going through a significant withdrawal. What he had in mind was the Israeli–Egyptian precedent of embassies after the first phase of withdrawal.[43]

Rabin raised other issues, particularly regarding security matters, and he insisted that the whole conversation remain secret. Indeed, according to Ross, Rabin said he would deny the proposal should it be leaked.[44] Ross's version of what he termed Rabin's "commitment" was that Rabin "proposed to have us convey the following: He would be prepared to commit to the United States that Israel would withdraw fully from the Golan Heights provided Israel's needs were met and provided Syria's agreement was not contingent on any other agreement." The details, as reported by Ross, were the same as Rabinovich, with the addition of the idea of the US manning warning stations in the Golan.[45]

The discrepancies that were later to become significant issues were, first, how this was to be conveyed to Assad (i.e., as an Israeli commitment or a hypothetical suggestion); and, second, the nature of what Rabinovich called an assumption – namely, just what Syrian territorial demand was being assumed: the international border or the 4 June 1967 lines. With regard to the latter, no line was, in fact, mentioned, though according to Ross, the Americans were authorized to say "full withdrawal." At an earlier Israeli–Syrian bilateral meeting in Washington, the Syrians had told Rabinovich that if the term "full withdrawal" were unsatisfactory, one might use the 4 June 1967 line, in keeping with Resolution 242; but the Israeli side rejected this inasmuch as Rabin continued to avoid any specifics on withdrawal. This was to become important later because there was a difference between the presence of Syrian troops on 4 June 1967 – on the banks of Lake Kinneret (Sea of Galilee) and the former international border (1923), which was some meters back from the shore (a difference of approximately 200 square meters). The difference was the result of the failure of the Israeli–Syrian armistice agreement of 1949 to fully draw a border, leaving a demilitarized area into which both Syria and Israel had advanced over the years. Thus, by 4 June 1967, Syria held land west of the international border in the northeast corner of the lake. The post-1967 war Israeli government decision to return the Golan referred to the international border, and in the early course of the talks with Syria in 1992 it was suggested to Rabin that he use the same reference.[46] This issue may appear unimportant (indeed, the Americans did not see what difference a few meters would make);[47] but this was to become the major point of contention when talks resumed in later years since Israel opposed Syrian access to the waters of the Kinneret.

The Syrians' specific reference to the 4 June line as the meaning of their demand for full withdrawal was stated officially at the end of April 1994 – and caught the Americans by surprise inasmuch as they did not realize the difference. Rabin was said to have responded angrily (to Ross) that "full withdrawal" had always meant to the international border.[48] The Syrians, for their part, were

66 *Failure on the Syrian Track*

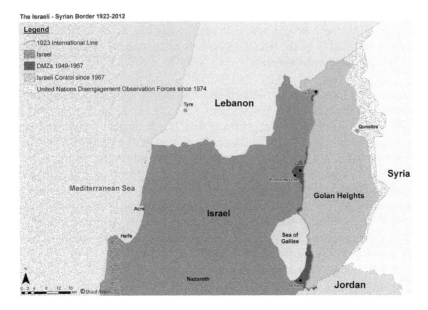

Map 4.1 Israeli–Syrian borders
Source: Shaul Arieli

subsequently to claim that the 4 June line had been their understanding of Rabin's proposal for "full withdrawal."[49] They had good reason to believe this, according to Ross, for when Christopher conveyed Rabin's proposal in August 1993, Assad asked him if Israel had any claim on [Syrian] territory, to which the US Secretary of State answered "No, the Prime Minister spoke only of full withdrawal."[50] And almost a year later, in July 1994, Christopher's conversation with Assad was as follows:

Christopher: I have just come from Israel and I can tell you that at the end of the day and as part of a package in which Israel's needs would have to be met, the United States understands that your needs would be met, and that therefore the meaning of full withdrawal, in these circumstances, would be to June 4, 1967. This only has meaning if you come to an agreement on everything. If you don't come to an agreement on everything, it has no meaning. In any case, this is in our pocket, not yours. It is our understanding, and you will not hear it from them until their needs are met.
Assad: That is clear.[51]

Here, then, is the other variation in the two chief negotiators' accounts. The Americans called Rabin's "hypothetical" a "pocket proposal" and believed Rabin to be committed to it. The bone of contention between Rabin and

Washington was to focus on just what the Americans had been authorized to convey to Assad and how. According to Sagie, Rabin had emphasized to Christopher that his proposal was a deposit to the Americans and was not to be presented to the Syrians without Rabin's explicit consent (neither Rabinovich nor Ross mention such a condition).[52] Rabin did later claim that Christopher had conveyed too much, explaining to his own people that this was one of the perils of going through a third party, for the context of the proposal could get lost – in this case, the condition that Rabin had made repeatedly clear that the withdrawal part could only come if Israel's needs were met regarding the nature of the peace. The package, Rabin claimed, was eroded instead of being kept as a deposit, containing the end-game, until a deal was achieved.[53] Yet still more to the point, Rabin resented both Syrian and American efforts to get him to reaffirm what they called his "commitment" of August 1993. He viewed this as Syrian avoidance of the second part of the matter – namely, the nature of the peace, and an Assad ploy to get Washington to gain Israeli withdrawal without giving anything in return.[54] Indeed, according to Ross, Rabin later made it clear that he believed he had made a mistake in what he had "committed" to them about the Golan in August 1993.[55]

There is no suggestion here of the same kind of mistrust of the Americans that was apparent with Golda Meir or the disdain for them expressed by Menachem Begin. Rabin wanted to work closely with Washington, viewing America as an essential Israeli ally. Yet, according to Uri Sagie, Rabin did feel that Christopher had betrayed his trust by delivering the "deposit" to the Syrians before receiving a similar deposit from Assad. At the least, Rabin was clearly frustrated over what he termed Christopher's mediation (rather than facilitation), negotiating on behalf of Israel instead of overcoming Assad's resistance to a direct channel with Israel.[56]

Contributing to the frustration, on the part of the Americans as well the Israelis, were the distinct and significant differences of interpretations between Jerusalem and Washington not only over the "pocket/hypothetical" deposit, but also over what actually was being accomplished in the negotiations. With regard to the August 1993 proposal, the more immediate divergence in the Israeli and US understanding was over Assad's response. "Very important," is the way Assad characterized the proposal as conveyed to him first by Ross and then by Christopher, commenting to the US Secretary of State that he, Assad, understood that Rabin was referring to full withdrawal.[57] In this connection, he proposed a period of six months rather than Rabin's five years for the withdrawal, and asserted that security arrangements be based on mutual (i.e., Syrian) interests as well. Water, too, would be an issue of mutual interest. As to what Syria would provide (the nature of the peace), Assad preferred the term "normal relations" rather than "normalization," and he said that while he could not mandate trade, he would not block such contacts. More critically, perhaps, he agreed to the Israeli demand that the agreement with Syria not be conditioned on peace agreements with others, though he said that he hoped there would be progress between Israel and the Palestinians.

Believing that Assad had accepted Rabin's basic equation, the Americans viewed this exchange as "an historic breakthrough."[58] Rabin did not. While, according to Ross, the Israeli prime minister did not seem to be troubled by the qualifiers (normal relations rather than normalization, trade), he was disappointed in what he saw as a merely minimal response without a demonstrated readiness to move swiftly to a peace agreement.[59] Rabinovich explains that Rabin had expected *some* bargaining, but he viewed Assad's list of topics – and refusal to offer some public gesture – as the opening of a long drawn-out process that would work against Israel's interests. The Israeli concern was that American endorsement of Assad's demands would lead to pressure that would chip away at Israel's initial positions.[60]

This reaction suggests more mistrust of the Americans than of the Syrians, born perhaps of the concern that since the US had greater leverage over Israel than over any Arab leader, Washington would press where it had a chance of succeeding. Assad might have interpreted the relationships in just the opposite manner, calculating that US–Israeli friendship would work in favor, not against, Israeli positions; but these were indeed matters of perception. What is more certain is that Rabin was disappointed with Assad's response and decided to pursue the Oslo channel. This may have been a tactical decision rather than a conclusion that Assad was not genuinely interested in peace. In August 1993 a breakthrough was imminent on the Oslo-Palestinian track; it provided something concrete with which to go to the Israeli public. Assad's response indicated that the Syrian track was going to be long and drawn out. In fact, there were Israeli observers who believed that Assad was not particularly pressed to gain return of the Golan but was engaging in the talks solely to improve relations with Washington.[61] Rabin may have shared this view; but, in any case, he did not believe that Assad's response had provided sufficiently promising content that could be presented to the public (or the Golan settlers and their supporters in his own party). Rabin told Martin Indyk that "Assad did not give a clear answer but we got a clear answer from Arafat," so, Rabin told Indyk, he went with the cheaper deal in the short run even though the other track would have provided greater strategic benefits over time.[62] Moreover, the Palestinian deal might press the Syrians not to remain odd man out (i.e., work as leverage). But Rabin also said that he could not work on both tracks at the same time and the Palestinian deal would be easier to sell to the Israeli public since it was merely autonomy and in stages, while the only Syrian option Assad might agree to would be nothing less than giving up the whole Golan.[63] Therefore, while talks were to continue secretly with Syria, the beginning of the Oslo Accords prompted an Israeli request in October 1993 for a four month suspension of the Syrian track.

Rabin justified (to Ross) a reluctance to move on Syria (and reaffirm the August commitment) given his even weaker coalition in the Knesset since Shas had bolted after the Oslo signing, leaving Rabin with a minority government of only 56 seats.[64] But the claim that he was too weak politically to move on two tracks at once was somewhat disingenuous inasmuch as he had already begun – and was continuing – peace negotiations with Jordan both before and after the Oslo signing in September 1993, albeit secretly. Rabin could and did maintain to the Americans that the talks with Jordan could serve as pressure on the Syrians.[65] Nonetheless, he was concerned about the public opinion factor regarding still another accord right after Oslo; according to Rabinovich, Rabin preferred to let the Israeli public digest Oslo before moving with Syria.[66]

A similar difference of interpretations between Israel and the United States regarding the possibilities for an agreement occurred when Clinton held a meeting with Assad in Geneva, January 1994. Syria had agreed to Rabin's requested four-month break but reportedly was becoming suspicious of Israel's motives for negotiations with Syria (i.e., were these talks intended simply to bring pressure on the Palestinians?). According to Ross, it was to allay these fears in hopes of resuming negotiations that Clinton decided on the Geneva meeting, while Israel looked upon the summit as an opportunity for the US to secure something public and concrete from Assad regarding peace with Israel.[67] In return, Rabin was prepared to issue statements to the effect that Israel had no claim to the Golan and that the 1981 Golan law did not constitute annexation of the Golan.[68] In Geneva, the Americans once again felt that there had been a breakthrough. Assad came with a full retinue of experts, and, according to the Americans, he provided in a joint written statement with Clinton a commitment to "normal, peaceful relations" as part of a "strategic choice" for peace with Israel.[69] At the closing Clinton–Assad press conference, the US president said that Assad had stated "clearly that it is time to end the conflict with Israel, make peace with Israel, that the peace should lead to normal and peaceful relations."[70] Asked if Assad's agreement to normal relations meant full diplomatic relations, trade and tourism, Clinton responded affirmatively. Assad was then himself asked: "Are you clearly stating unequivocally today that in exchange for full Israeli withdrawal from the Golan Heights, Syria would be prepared to establish normal diplomatic relations with Israel, including open borders, including tourism, the same kind of peace treaty that Israel established with Egypt?"[71] Assad responded with the comment: "Myself and President Clinton completely agreed on these issues, the requirements of peace. We will respond to these requirements."[72]

The Americans were elated by the meeting, both because of a delinking of a Syrian–Israeli agreement from an Israeli–Palestinian agreement and, more importantly because of Assad's written commitment to normal, peaceful relations with Israel.[73] Yet, again, Rabin had quite a different interpretation. He dismissed Assad's comments on normal relations as nothing new[74] and suggested that the delinking of the Palestinian issue was a Syrian attempt to influence the Israeli–Jordanian talks.[75] Rabinovich explained that Assad had been vague – for example, referring to normal, peaceful relations in the context of the region rather than specifically with Israel – while the nature of peace was added only at the end by Clinton or in response to journalists' questions. Rabin's disappointment was particularly keen, perhaps because he had hoped this public appearance by Assad would produce the assurances he needed to convince the Israeli public, and it was his belief that this had not occurred. Israeli media had already responded negatively to what they heard in Geneva (though they may have been predisposed to be negative inasmuch as Israeli journalists were not permitted to pose questions at the press conference). Though Rabin did not see much point in continued talks with Syria – he told the Americans he would give priority to the Jordanians – he did try to temper opponents in Israel by having Ross appear on television with a positive message and also by announcing in the Knesset that should any agreement be reached, he would hold a referendum. The latter, designed to placate domestic opponents, was perceived by both Syria and the Americans as the creation of a new obstacle.

The months following the Clinton–Assad Geneva meeting saw little progress. Israel's skepticism regarding Syrian intentions, along with concern over the way in which the US was conducting the talks, was stronger than ever. Israeli negotiations with Jordan and Oslo-related matters tended to upstage the Syrian track. While Syria, as later reported, viewed the July 1994 clarification brought by Christopher regarding the 4 June 1967 line as a finalization of the withdrawal issue (and therefore opening the way to discussions on the remaining issues),[76] Rabin did not see it that way. Israel continued to demand a phased withdrawal (without specifying lines), each stage of which was to be matched by some element of peace. For Rabin, this was not a technical matter but a need to test the other side in the course of implementation.[77] While some narrowing of differences had been reached regarding the overall time for Israeli withdrawal (Syria was now willing to speak of 16 months), attention in the last months of 1994 was focused on the security issues. However, this was perhaps the one area in which Israeli mistrust was greatest. Various components of a security agreement, such as demilitarization, thinning of troops, and especially early warning stations were critical to the Israeli concept of peace, or, rather, the lack of confidence in peace. For all that Rabin was willing now to speak of peace (to the Knesset) as a component of security, he still defined security in primarily military terms. Positing a continued attitude of enmity on the part of the partner to the peace agreement, one needed to be able to prevent a surprise attack (as explained by then Chief of Staff Ehud Barak to the Americans)[78] or be prepared for a lesser violation of a treaty. In the latter case, an agreement would therefore have to be designed to allow for what one Israeli military expert explained was the Israel Defense Forces' (IDF's) "trip wire doctrine" of immediate military retaliation for any breach of an agreement by the other side.[79] Whether this was an appropriate doctrine or not, it was a clear reflection of the deep-seated mistrust of the intentions of the other side – and even the possibility of sustained peace. Thus, with Syria, as in the case with Jordan in 1967, Egypt in 1973 and 1975, and later with the Palestinians, a critical question (though not the only one) was whether what might be perceived as sensible precautions would be allowed to stand in the way of achieving an agreement altogether.

The security discussions were part of negotiations on what was later called a "non-paper" on Aims and Principles of the Security Arrangements. According to Syrian negotiator Ambassador Walid Mouallem, this was initially produced by the third party, the Americans, but it became the basis for four months of difficult Israeli–Syrian security talks.[80] These negotiations, with American participation, came to an abrupt halt in July 1995 when Assad retreated from a previously agreed procedural matter connected with an impasse over Israel's demand for early-warning stations on the Golan. Eventually there were plans to resume talks in November; but the "non-paper" and disruption of talks were connected not only with Syrian reservations, but also with a domestic Israeli factor that may have been critical.

By the summer of 1995, opposition within the Labor Party had reached the breaking point, with two Labor MKs threatening to leave the party just as the second Oslo agreement (the Interim Agreement) was about to come to a vote in the Knesset – for which these MKs would be sorely needed. Moreover, the "Golan lobby" in the Knesset (which included Labor MKs) renewed an earlier effort to gain legislation that would require a special majority of 70 or 80 members of the Knesset to repeal the 1981 law that had extended Israeli law to the Golan. There was also a proposal in the Knesset that the referendum promised by Rabin require a 65 percent majority for approval of any deal with Syria.[81] Both were intended to tie Rabin's hands in negotiations with Syria. Moreover, the intensified popular campaign against withdrawal from the Golan was assisted by perceived Syrian complicity or at least support for Hizballah attacks against northern Israel communities and the IDF in southern Lebanon.[82] This was accompanied by nasty and violent settler/right-wing demonstrations against the Oslo Accords, often focused specifically on Rabin and fueled by the frequent terrorist attacks by Hamas and the Islamic Jihad.[83] This negative public atmosphere had been further aggravated in June by a leak to the press of an IDF document containing information on the "non-paper," which, opposition leader Netanyahu claimed, attested to Israeli agreement to full withdrawal from the Golan.

The ranks of potential spoilers were broadened by the addition of a campaign in the diaspora. As in 1975, this was conducted by organizations and individuals in the Jewish diaspora in the US who shared the Israeli right-wing opposition to Israeli compromises for peace. Whereas in 1975 it was the Rabin government that urged (or organized) the diaspora campaign in order to reduce US pressure during Washington's "reassessment," this time it was Rabin's Israeli opponents who spearheaded (or, at the very least, assisted) the US diaspora campaign. Focusing on the possibility that American forces might serve as peacekeepers of an eventual agreement on the Golan, an American lobby, press, and letter writing campaign was begun in early 1994 basically opposing the negotiations ostensibly because they would lead to such a deployment (and loss of American lives). Shamir's former aide and negotiator with Syria post-Madrid, Yosef Ben Aharon, along with Yoram Ettinger, who had formerly worked as congressional liaison in Israel's

Washington embassy, traveled to the US to assist the campaign. The effort in the US may have had more of an effect on Assad than it did on Rabin since a major Syrian interest in the talks was to achieve improved relations with Washington, something clearly not assisted by the campaign.

For Rabin, however, the diaspora campaign was but part of the overall difficulties he perceived with regard to winning popular and political support for an agreement, should he ultimately be able to achieve one. There may also have been opponents within the IDF, for the document leaked to the press was actually a somewhat critical internal assessment prepared by the intelligence unit with regard to various proposals raised in the course of the "non-paper" talks. However, there are no indications that there was significant opposition within the Israeli military; Rabin's concern was clearly related to the opposition in the political and also the public sphere. Given the confluence of the various opposition efforts – within the Labor Party, in the Knesset, on the streets – also with regard to the Oslo Accords and the expected Interim Agreement, Rabin was not, as Rabinovich put it, "willing to go out of his way in order to overcome a crisis for which he held Assad solely responsible."[84]

It is impossible to know if or how this crisis would have been overcome if Rabin had not been assassinated just days before talks were to resume. There is no way of knowing if the security factor, specifically the issue of early warning stations, would have prevented agreement. The possibility of US peacekeepers might have become an acceptable substitute for both countries, provided the diaspora lobby of the US Congress could be defeated. The actual extent or line of the Israeli withdrawal – namely, the 4 June 1967 line – was a major but not the only obstacle preventing agreement. Rabin preferred the international line, but he knew that no agreement could be reached without this full withdrawal. He did, however, become increasingly reluctant to concede this as his skepticism over Assad's intentions grew. His skepticism and suspicions undoubtedly influenced his perception of what Assad was or was not conceding, as evidenced by the difference in the Israeli and American analyses at various times, which also resulted in the decline in Rabin's trust of the Americans' role. Whether this skepticism would have been overcome in time is a moot point. Whether it was, in fact, justified is almost impossible to determine. But however much Rabin's estimates of Assad were influenced by his skepticism and lack of trust, or perhaps justified, he did not believe that he had – or perhaps could achieve – enough from Assad with regard to Israel's needs, be they security or political (the nature of the peace) in order to overcome the combination of political spoilers and popular opinion he faced domestically.

Assad was no less a skeptic than Rabin. American accounts clearly indicate that the Syrian leader saw deception and deviousness on the Israel side when Rabin refused to confirm or put in writing the "commitment"/"pocket"/ "hypothetical," when he ignored the Clinton–Assad Geneva summit achievements, and when he suddenly announced that any agreement would be subject to a referendum. Similarly, Assad tended to believe that Israel was merely using the talks as a way of dissipating Syrian opposition to Oslo or as leverage on the Palestinians. His friend Patrick Seale thus went so far as to call the whole period of negotiations with Rabin a "ruse."[85]

It would appear that Rabin's successor, Shimon Peres, encountered similar skepticism from Assad, though he himself appears to have been far less suspicious of Assad than Rabin had been. If Rabin's approach to realization of peace was to begin with mistrust, along with a need to move slowly and reciprocally both to test and to build trust while creating a security arrangements "safety-net,"[86] just in case, so to speak, Peres's approach was quite different. It was not that Peres was less concerned with security; indeed, the military negotiators were to press for various safeguards no less than they had under Rabin. Nevertheless, Peres was particularly interested in the Americans playing an even greater role than previously (by means of an American–Israeli treaty and an American-led regional security arrangement), which might have relieved some of the purely military security concerns. The key to the difference between Peres and Rabin, however, was a different concept of security, specifically Peres's belief in the benefits of economic development and the efficacy of economic ties, creating mutual interests and an interdependency binding the states (and the region) together.[87] For Peres, then, there was no need for a gradual trust-building approach; on the contrary, while there would still be a need for a timeline of mutual steps in the final agreement, the idea would be a swift move to peace and cooperation (including economic cooperation on the Golan), which would neutralize potential spoilers and conquer public opinion. Although Peres did not have Rabin's stature and military credentials in the eyes of the public, he had the benefit of both the shock of the assassination and the mantle of Rabin's legacy to aid him with public opinion. Thus, given the difference between their approaches, the leadership change from Rabin to Peres could have been a factor facilitating a breakthrough. That a breakthrough did not, in fact, result may have been due to a number of counter-veiling factors.

Peres presented his government on 22 November 1995, but he nonetheless faced a key decision regarding the elections scheduled for October 1996. There was a good deal of pressure within the Labor Party to move the elections up, to the spring if not earlier. In considering the options, Peres considered waiting until October if he could obtain a dramatic gesture, such as a summit with Assad, and reach elections with a Syrian accord in hand. His plan also included American security backing (treaty, regional plan, which the Americans repulsed) along with the promise that the Syrian accord would be endorsed regionally, thereby constituting an opening to comprehensive peace. Opposed to the 4 June line, Peres used the formula of borders "on the basis of UNSC resolutions 242 and 338." While Ross claims that Peres did reaffirm Rabin's "pocket" commitment explicitly to the 4 June line, Peres's chief negotiator, Uri Savir, maintained that the exact line was to be decided only after the nature of the peace had been agreed.[88]

Like Rabin before him, Peres sought first to gauge Assad's willingness to make an agreement, and like Rabin before him, he was less impressed than the Americans with Assad's immediate response, particularly since Assad turned down the idea of a summit. A positive sign was the Syrians' agreement to a new framework for negotiations, proposed by the Americans as a series of Camp David-type tripartite meetings, albeit not at the summit level, at the Wye Plantation near Washington. The Israelis brought a significantly broadened negotiating team to what were ultimately two and a half two-week sessions dealing with all of the issues, in plenary and smaller meetings. For Peres, these talks would determine if a deal could be made quickly or, if not, to move up the elections.[89] Although Ross was to claim that more was accomplished in the first week of the Wye meetings than in the preceding four years of talks, it is not clear that the Israelis, or at least Peres, saw it this way. Indeed, the Peres team was deeply divided on this.[90] It was later claimed by Mouallem (and indirectly confirmed by Savir) that he, and Ross, and Savir believed that they would have all the elements of an agreement worked out by June 1996, ready for signing by September 1996.[91] Yet, Peres decided nonetheless to move up the elections. The content of the Wye talks suggests that Peres simply came to the conclusion that an agreement would not, in fact, be achieved that quickly. In the talks, the Syrians indeed balked at the very numerous specific proposals Israel presented in the economic sphere, along with the usual security issues. They were willing to commit only to the earlier general Israeli demand for tourism and trade, arguing that anything more specific would have to wait until there were actually peaceful relations between the two countries. Thus, it would appear that now, under Peres, the Israelis were moving too fast for Assad, and this with regard to the very issues that constituted the critical core of Peres's peace plan. Indeed, Mouallem himself said this when he later explained why Syria could not accept the economic proposals made by the Israelis at Wye.[92]

Peres did make one more effort to continue before publicly announcing his early elections decision. He was willing to wait if Assad would agree to a summit, but Assad once again refused.[93] The last minute bid for a public gesture, sufficient for Peres to wait on elections, suggests another factor at play. No less than Rabin, Peres was faced with continued domestic opposition to the talks with Syria. While the campaign for keeping the Golan (as well as the anti-Oslo hysteria) had quieted down a bit in the wake of the Rabin assassination, public opinion regarding support for compromise with Syria had, nonetheless, dropped. Never high, support for full withdrawal was 31.6 percent in December and fell to 24.2 percent in January, with opposition to any territorial compromise on the Golan up from 30.7 percent in December to 41 percent in January, accompanied by a decline in popular support for Peres as a leader.[94] Moreover, Peres had to face challengers as well as opponents within his own party as pressure for early elections grew. Cognizant of the link between Peres's preference to go to elections with some Syrian achievement to show and the decision on the timing of elections, there were many who believed that the only way Labor could win with Peres at its head would be if the party could take advantage of the upswing of support that had come in reaction to the assassination. This support would not last long. It was presumably in order to push for early elections, if not out of opposition to an accord with Syria, that a number of prominent Labor Party leaders, among them Ehud Barak, who was now Peres's foreign minister, publicly belittled the possibility of reaching any agreement with Syria (implying, therefore, that elections could be held earlier), issuing statements that not only disturbed the Syrians but also contributed to the general opposition to leaving the Golan.[95] Savir has argued that these unhelpful comments may simply have been the customary "hawkishness" adopted with upcoming party primaries in mind.

The decision to move up the elections may well have been critical. Much the way Rabin's announcement of the need for a referendum was viewed by Assad as a sign that Israel was retreating from an accord with Syria, the Peres decision to hold early elections was also viewed by Assad as a sign of reduced importance to Israel of an agreement, especially since the election period would preclude any offer of Israeli concessions or, as Mouallem put it, produce too much uncertainty for any progress to be made.[96] Indeed, as noted above, this may have already been apparent in what were to become increasingly harsh pre-election pronouncements (such as refusal to give up the Golan or return to the 4 June borders) in response to opposition accusations. In any case, circumstances not directly connected with Syrian positions led to a halt in the negotiations. After a series of deadly Palestinian terrorist attacks late February to early March 1996, Peres suspended the talks (it did not help that Syria refrained from condemning the attacks[97]), and then Hizballah (believed by Jerusalem to have been encouraged by Syria[98]) escalated attacks in the north, leading to Peres's ill-fated military action in south Lebanon in April. With these failures and no Syrian agreement to show as a major achievement, Peres lost the election, albeit by only a very narrow margin, to Binyamin Netanyahu, who ran on the slogan that a strong leader was needed to defend Israelis.

Rabinovich's conclusion from the whole period of talks with Syria from 1992 to 1996 was that "at no time were the two countries on the verge of a breakthrough."[99] Ross contradicts this, asserting, rather, that an agreement would have been reached in 1996 if Peres had been elected in May (which he would have been, according to Ross, if not for the terrorist attacks).[100] It was, however, subsequently claimed (reportedly by Uri Savir) that ultimately Peres simply did not believe that he could get the necessary support for a withdrawal from the Golan, given both political opposition and public opinion.[101] In terms of challengers, it may have been the demands of the IDF that could not be overcome.[102] By comparison, Rabin was better prepared than Peres to counter security arguments, from military circles or the public. For Rabin, the security arrangements and signs of "proof" of Syrian intentions – both in the negotiations and in actual implementation of an agreement – were sought in order to waylay or compensate for his own suspicions about the reliability or durability of an agreement, as well as to placate Israeli public opinion. Peres too believed that security arrangements could help in placating opponents to relinquishing the Golan, as would a Syrian gesture such as a summit with

Assad. In addition, given his own past political failures, Peres, according to Savir, did not believe that he could overcome the domestic obstacles, especially public opinion, prior to a mandate as the elected prime minister. However, a significant difference between Rabin and Peres, beyond the security credentials and stature of the former, was the matter of skepticism and therefore testing – in the negotiating process and within the final accord – given the absence of trust. For Peres, trust was not the issue; he appears to have believed that Assad would make peace and, most importantly, that economic interests would ensure its reliability.

An additional factor believed at least by some to have contributed to the failure may have been the reluctance of the United States to play a more forceful or forthcoming role. Savir has argued, much like Rabin himself, that the American mediation role was not the best way in which the Americans could have promoted an agreement. Rather, according to Savir, they should have responded to Israeli security needs in the form of the bilateral treaty and regional security plan that Peres requested. Savir concluded that Clinton was reluctant to do so because of expected Congressional opposition, much the way the stationing of American troops as peacekeepers on the Golan was the subject of (diaspora-encouraged) Congressional opposition.[103] Ross's explanation was more diplomatic: in an election year in America, proposals requiring "massive amounts of foreign aid" would not be welcome.[104] However, Washington also refused to remove Syria from the list of states supporting terrorism; nor was it forthcoming with regard to other Syrian requests. Inasmuch as one of the main, if not the main, motivating factors behind Assad's move toward peace with Israel was his interest in improved relations with the US, American recalcitrance may have played a significant role in the failure, at least up until the Israeli elections brought the process to its final demise.

It is impossible to determine which factor or even combination of factors was responsible for the failure or provided possibly insurmountable obstacles. The list might include the negotiating style of Rabin (too cautious) or of Peres (too fast), Israeli demands themselves (security demands under Rabin, economy-related demands under Peres); domestic political problems (weak coalition and the breakaway Labor ministers for Rabin; the early election issue for Peres); leadership qualities (lack of status, particularly security credentials in the case of Peres); public opinion (public attachment to the Golan; the massive campaign – in the diaspora as well – against withdrawal from the Golan); the absence of trust, actual mistrust, in the case of Rabin, including misperceptions; as well as American missteps: the nature of American mediation (particularly as viewed by Rabin) and unwillingness to meet the demands of either or both sides (particularly with regard to Peres as well as to Assad) that might have greased the wheels of an agreement. Finally, there is also the opponent, Assad, with his own mistrust, reluctance to provide public gestures, and refusal to concede either the security or economy-related demands of Israel. Events unrelated directly to the negotiations brought the talks to a halt – namely, Israeli–Hizballah confrontation and the Palestinian terrorist attacks within

Israel well before the May 1996 elections. Clearly, for Israel, many of these factors were connected or mutually reinforcing; basic mistrust, public opinion, and spoilers were all part of the same picture and led to stiff Israeli bargaining positions in the demands made to Assad, designed to ensure "acceptance" of Israel while preparing for just the opposite.

The change in Israeli leadership with the May 1996 elections significantly altered the political situation in Israel, bringing to power a party that had explicitly ruled out withdrawal from the Golan and a coalition agreement that reiterated this out of ideological opposition to the principle of "land for peace." However, after election, Netanyahu announced that he was willing to resume talks (albeit with no preconditions – i.e., rejecting the Syrian demand to begin where Rabin and Peres had left off). He even obtained a letter from Christopher to the effect that the only agreements reached earlier were, first, the security "non-paper," which was not binding; and, second, oral exchanges, which were even less binding. However, Netanyahu's foreign minister, David Levy, said the basis for talks with Syria would be UNSC Resolution 242, thereby implying some willingness for territorial compromise.[105] And in February 1997 Netanyahu asked the Americans to try to initiate new talks. Without confirmation of what was now termed the "Rabin pocket," however, Assad was unwilling to engage in official talks, although Netanyahu reportedly continued to seek such official negotiations.[106] Secret, indirect talks were, nonetheless, conducted through emissaries such as European Union representative Miguel Moritanos and, more fruitfully, American businessman and former ambassador Ron Lauder. The fact that Netanyahu sought both open and secret channels suggests that he did hope to reach an agreement with Syria, and evidence that emerged only after Netanyahu was out of office – and denied by him – indicates that he was, in fact, contemplating withdrawal from the Golan, ideological reservations notwithstanding.

In the course of five weeks of meetings in the summer of 1998, Lauder and Assad forged two (successive) drafts of a "Treaty of Peace Between Israel and Syria,"[107] one of which was reported to the White House by Lauder only in August 1999 upon Clinton's request, and only later, in November 1999, the second draft (though both drafts were found by incoming Prime Minister Barak's staff in the Israeli Prime Minister's Office in August).[108] The first draft, from 25 August 1998, contained withdrawal to the international border; the second draft, 12 September 1998, was somewhat different and had withdrawal to the 4 June 1967 line.[109] The talks had ended with this, however, since Netanyahu refused to translate the agreement onto maps. His reason was that doing so would prevent deniability – and, indeed, he did later deny that he had made any agreement to withdraw from the Golan and that Lauder had gone beyond his authority. Nonetheless, 14 years later he boasted in a radio interview that he had obtained Syrian agreement for Israel to keep the Hermon.[110] The 12 September 1998 Lauder document mentions only French–American early warning stations on the Hermon; but Netanyahu's reference may have been to a more modest achievement, that of possible

Syrian agreement to limited Israeli personnel participation (a concession that had been discussed in the Rabin talks and later referred to by Barak as having been in the Lauder document).[111] Nonetheless, the comment was an implied admission that Netanyahu had agreed to give up the Golan, and according to the Lauder document and the Syrians, this was to have been to the 4 June 1967 line.

Like the earlier Likud leader Menachem Begin, Netanyahu was apparently willing to forgo ideology, which included settlements, when it came to territory less charged with emotional–religious–ideological meaning than the West Bank. The latter, linked as it was to the identity-threatening Palestinian issue, was Netanyahu's major concern when he took office and sought to shelve the Oslo Accords. Netanyahu may have viewed an agreement with Syria as a major diplomatic achievement, a feather in his cap, that would overshadow whatever minor dissatisfaction there might be in some quarters – domestic or international – to the derailing of the Palestinian track.[112] In fact, it was strong American pressure regarding the Palestinian issue that ultimately – or ostensibly – led to his abandonment of the Syrian track shortly after his refusal to draw maps. According to one account, Netanyahu reportedly felt that he did not have sufficient "political cover" to finalize the agreement once he had made significant promises to the Americans in October to resume some of the Oslo demands (promises that ultimately he did not fully keep).[113] He was, indeed, subject to opposition within his own party and from the right-wing camp over these concessions on the Palestinian issue, and he could not be certain that he would be able to overcome still more opposition. In addition, he still had "spoilers" in his own party, most notably from his defense minister, Itzhak Mordecai, and Ariel Sharon on the Golan issue.[114] While he might have been better able than Rabin or Peres to handle potential spoilers regarding the Golan – since he could garner support from the opposition parties (much the way Begin had overcome opponents within his own party by gaining the votes of the opposition parties), popular sentiment was still against giving up the Golan. A typical poll for the period showed only 9.7 percent "great support" for peace with Syria in exchange for withdrawal from the Golan, 15.9 percent "somewhat support," but a full 40 percent "greatly opposed" and 14.1 percent "somewhat opposed."[115] Thus, it would appear that domestic factors, mainly public and political opinion, were the major factors for the renewed failure to achieve a breakthrough with Syria; but it is not clear if the same matter of mistrust was at play as it was in Rabin's attempts. The scanty information available on the Lauder–Assad talks suggests that Netanyahu was less suspicious and therefore less concerned about the security and peace arrangements. Alternatively, it may have been the case that sufficient progress had already been made by the Rabin and Peres rounds as to leave little left for negotiation; indeed, Lauder was hardly qualified to deal with the fine points of security. In fact, the second draft (12 September 1998) simply called for adoption of the Rabin era Aims and Principles of Security Arrangements. Therefore, if the "treaty" provided by Lauder was, in fact, accepted by both sides, as claimed by Lauder, the factor behind the failure to consummate a breakthrough may well have been Netanyahu's reluctance to deal with both the pressure for concessions on the one (Palestinian) track while making concessions on the other (Syrian) track or, rather, an unwillingness to engage in the necessary political battle at home. According to this analysis, the American factor would have to be taken into account indirectly, for it was American pressure that led to the Oslo-related Wye Agreement that placed Netanyahu in the double bind. Of course, the double bind may simply have been an excuse; Netanyahu may have balked, like Rabin, at presenting a map simply because he was not willing to go through with the deal. For Rabin, this was due to his suspicions that Assad would not, in the end, provide the necessary *quid pro quo* which was deemed necessary in itself as well as for the domestic battle. There is no evidence that Netanyahu had the same reservations. He wanted deniability, not leverage, since apparently he had not yet decided if he would go through with the deal or not, depending upon his estimate of the political cost.

The next change of Israeli leadership promised the elusive breakthrough. Barak was elected with a solid majority and had pledged to take Israel out of Lebanon within a year – a task believed to be dependent upon reaching an agreement with Syria. With this kind of domestic support and viewed quite positively regionally as well as in Washington as someone who could continue where Rabin had left off, Barak signaled his interest in official talks with the Syrians. Secret lower-level talks began outside the region, and although Assad once again rejected a meeting with an Israeli prime minister, he did agree finally to high-level official talks between his foreign minister, Farouk Shara, and Barak. These talks took place briefly in Washington on 15–16 December 1999 and then in Shepherdstown in early January 2000.

As in the previous negotiations, Assad insisted talks begin where they had left off with Rabin; he sought reaffirmation of what was still called the "Rabin pocket." Although initially Barak had told the Americans (July 1999) that while he would not confirm the "pocket," he said that it was more a question of timing (in negotiations) rather than content. According to Ross, Barak did not feel pressed to agree to the 4 June 1967 line since he believed Lauder's (first) claim that Assad had agreed to the 1923 international border.[116] Therefore, Barak was willing only to have the US say that the 4 June 1967 line should "guide" the talks. The lower level talks in the fall (between Sagie, Ross, and Syrian representative Daoudi) adhered to this and much time was spent scouring maps in search of the actual position of the Syrians on that date.[117] When in November Lauder corrected his earlier claim, Barak's reaction was not entirely clear. Ross maintains that Barak still did not accept the "pocket," while others, most notably Dani Yatom, chief of Barak's diplomacy-security staff (and staunch defender), say that Barak now felt he could accept the 4 June position since Netanyahu had gone that far, though Barak was not prepared to have this conveyed to the Syrians yet.[118] Thus, the Syrians were under the impression that Barak, unwilling to reconfirm the "pocket," was actually retreating from past positions, including Netanyahu's.[119]

When the negotiations began in December between Barak and Shara with Clinton, Shara cited a litany of past commitments as conveyed to Assad by Christopher, defining "full withdrawal" as the 4 June 1967 lines. In response, Barak said: "While my government has made no commitment in advance [on territory, in Ross's version], we don't erase history [the past]."[120] This remark was understood by Clinton as well as the Syrians to mean that Barak had agreed; it remained only to delineate this line on a map.[121] Yet, during the break before the January resumption of negotiations, Barak added various demands (among them Syrian agreement for simultaneous discussions between Israel and Lebanon, an upgrade of relations between Israel and Tunisia, announcement of a free-trade zone for the Golan, along with requests for additional US military aid to compensate for leaving the Golan, and other demands[122]), and two weeks later, upon arriving for the January Shepherdstown talks, Barak told Indyk that he "can't do it."[123] Although he authorized the Americans to provide Syria with a statement in writing that it was "the President's understanding that Barak did not intend to withdraw the 'Rabin deposit',"[124] he specifically rejected the 4 June 1967 line. Among other things, he sought a strip of land (for a road) amounting to roughly 500 meters on the northeast shore of the Kinneret and around the source of the Jordan River, as well as a presence in the early warning station on the Hermon. This apparent retreat regarding the 4 June 1967 line (and continued insistence on simultaneous talks with Lebanon) precipitated hostile recriminations from Shara and a scheduled recess that, in fact, became terminal.

Before this occurred, the Americans had presented a "draft treaty" with each side's positions listed, unsettled issues placed in brackets, as a basis for the negotiations. Ultimately, it was this document that led to the end of the direct talks, for it was leaked to the Israeli press, embarrassing the Syrians who, as evidenced in the draft, had made concessions without getting Israeli agreement to full withdrawal.[125] Indeed, according to the Americans, the Syrians had demonstrated much flexibility in the talks even as they continued to demand a commitment and demarcation of the 4 June 1967 line. Feeling betrayed – and humiliated – Assad toughened his position on the Lebanon issue and Syrian media became decidedly hostile.

In view of, or despite, the Shepherdstown failure, the Americans tried to persuade Barak to offer some flexibility so that negotiations might nonetheless resume, but Barak remained firm, particularly on his Lebanon demand. However, Barak needed agreement with Syria in order to fulfill his promise to withdraw Israeli forces from Lebanon – a move that could not be expected to provide security for Israel's northern border in the future without Syria's compliance. For this reason, Barak was willing to provide the Americans with his "bottom" line in Washington's preparation for one final effort: a second Clinton–Assad summit in Geneva on March 2000.[126] This last attempt failed over what Assad interpreted as Israel's continued refusal to commit to full withdrawal. Indeed, Barak was still unwilling to have Clinton convey Israeli agreement to the 4 June 1967 line (he continued to insist on a strip of land on the shore, now to be 400 rather than 500 meters) and a presence on the Hermon; but, according to Ross, he authorized Clinton to say that he, Barak, "'based on a commonly agreed border' was prepared to withdraw to the June 4 line as part of a peace agreement."[127] Assad seized on the ambiguity of the "commonly agreed border" and rejected any further attempt by the Americans to persuade him that this was tantamount to Israeli agreement regarding the 4 June line. It did not help that the next point Clinton presented, according to Ross, was Barak's assertion of Israeli sovereignty over the Kinneret and the Jordan River, explicitly ruling out a border line that touched either of them. Assad proclaimed that Barak was not interested in peace, and after two hours the futile talks came to a close. Two and a half months later, Assad died (shortly after Israel unilaterally withdrew from Lebanon).

There is little agreement as to exactly what went wrong in the Geneva meeting. One version, from a Syrian diplomat of that time, was that Assad – ill as he was – went to the summit in expectation that Barak was going to make the deal (via Clinton) and therefore despaired almost immediately.[128] Indeed, Assad was very ill and appeared to lose all interest in pursuing solutions once he dismissed the very first point that Clinton raised on behalf of Barak, though subsequent points suggested that Assad had not, in fact, misinterpreted Barak's first point. Yet it was also the case that Clinton himself was not in his best form since he was on his way home from a trip to the Far East, sleep deprived, and suffering from stomach upset from something he had eaten along the way.

Whatever happened at Geneva, the overall verdict not only espoused by Clinton himself but also by most of those involved in the four months of talks under Barak, including and especially Barak's chief negotiator Uri Sagie, was that Barak – not Assad – was the main obstacle to a breakthrough in the Israeli–Syrian talks. Assad of the Rabin and Peres period was not the same as the Assad of the Barak period. By 1999, Assad was quite ill, indeed terminally ill, and anxious to conclude a deal for the return of the Golan that would assist in fortifying the future regime of his son and heir, Bashar Assad. Both his willingness to raise the level of the talks and to move quickly attested to this. Further, prospects appeared to be good given the election of a new leader, Barak, in Israel. Indeed, Assad's new approach was met with similar enthusiasm and interest on the part of Barak as he sought a deal with Syria that would allow him to take Israel out of Lebanon within a year. Moreover, Barak was similar to Rabin in his military appreciation of the importance of Syria as an "existential threat" to Israel's security, and also in his preference for dealing with a stable address – namely, a state and a decisive leader – both as distinct from the Palestinians. He also shared Rabin's view that there was a window of opportunity, which, in Barak's eyes had to be exploited while Assad was still alive and before Iraq and/or Iran became nuclear powers.[129]

Yet it was the difference between Rabin and Barak that was a major factor in the failure of Barak's negotiations with Syria. In contrast to Rabin's slow, deliberate approach, Barak moved abruptly and assertively, with a hefty, ostentatious sense of his own abilities. Sagie writes that Barak had once said: "'Give me Assad for a couple of weeks and when I am done with him he will be as Zionist as Herzl.'"[130] This may be apocryphal, but Yatom too refers to Barak's belief that he could hammer out an agreement quickly. According to Sagie, and against Sagie's advice to use subordinates for preparatory steps, Barak accepted Yatom's estimate that by going himself, directly, to the high level talks, he could get an agreement in "two or three weeks."[131] Even after the Shepherdstown failure, Barak sought additional channels to Assad and even told the Americans that he could now win a landslide in a referendum, suggesting that he still thought he could bring Assad to agree to his demands. Certainly Sagie attributes the failure at least in part to Barak's arrogance and cavalier approach to negotiations. He described Barak as cold and volatile.[132] The Americans involved also referred to the problem of Barak's personality, observing that he refused to take advice (theirs) or engage in more subtle tactics where appropriate. This behavior on the part of Barak was not due to mistrust of the Americans – as was the case with Golda Meir, for example, or even Rabin and Peres, who were concerned that the Americans might be prone to give away too much or press Israel too much. Rather, according to Ross, it was Barak's conviction that he knew better how to handle things and preferred that the Americans serve as Israel's "surrogate" at Shepherdstown as well as after.[133] In retrospect, Clinton said of his view of Barak after Shepherdstown: "I was, to put it mildly, disappointed. If Barak had dealt with the Syrians before or if he had given us some advance notice, it might have been manageable ... . As hard as I tried I couldn't change Barak's mind."[134]

Also as distinct from Rabin, it was not a matter of concern that Assad would not be sufficiently forthcoming on security matters of importance to Israel. So long as there was monitoring, Barak claimed his major concern was keeping the Syrians away from the water sources.[135] The rest, he said according to Ross, would work itself out.[136] This would suggest that unlike Rabin, mistrust of the enemy even in circumstances of peace was not a strong factor at least with regard to security measures.[137] Conceivably this was due to the Syrians having scrupulously maintained and regularly renewed the disengagement agreement on the Golan since 1974. While Barak argued that he did not want the Syrians to have control of water sources to the Kinneret, his territorial demand for enough land for a road that would permit Israelis to travel entirely around the Lake, including the northeastern corner, suggests that he was more worried about how he might present the final accord at home. This factor was evident in the fact that he did acknowledge to the Americans that he was willing ultimately to return to the 4 June line because, according to one source, he believed he would be "covered" by the fact that Netanyahu had agreed to this line via Lauder.[138] The suggestion here, and clearly the impression received by the Americans, was that the major factor for Barak was, indeed, domestic public and political opinion. Clinton and Ross both write that Barak's anxiety began to be apparent shortly before the December meeting with Shara, when Barak raised additional demands.[139] The demands themselves were of a nature to render a concession on the Golan more palatable to an Israeli audience – for example, not only withdrawal from Lebanon (which Barak wanted for its own sake) but also elevation of relations with Tunisia, announcements of a planned free-trade zone on the Golan and of additional military acquisitions from the US. In fact, Clinton attributes what he viewed as Barak's retreat to a single factor: the polls.[140] Yatom mentions this factor a number of times as the reason Barak raised the demand for Lebanon talks, or diplomatic relations with Arab states, or increased US military aid, to soften public opinion for the referendum that would be held if agreement were reached. Both Indyk and Yatom speak of Barak's acute concern lest leaks from the talks, particularly regarding an Israeli concession, impede public support; indeed, Yatom notes this as a reason for Barak's refusal to discuss the border before all other issues at Shepherdstown.[141] Uri Sagie, too, saw Barak's concern over domestic opinion and political climate as the major, though not the only, factor causing the failure. Barak as much as said this when he told Indyk, upon arrival for the Shepherdstown talks: "I can't do it because my circumstances have changed. Politically, my hands are tied."[142]

The changed circumstances were the growing strength of the political spoilers and popular campaign against any move from the Golan. These were reflected not only in demonstrations of increasing numbers in Jerusalem and Tel Aviv, but also within the government coalition and the Knesset. Prior to the opening of talks in December, and continuing into January, two of Labor's coalition partners, the National Religious Party (NRP) and the Russian immigrant party Israel b'Aliyah, threatened to bolt the government if a land for peace deal were made with Syria. If they were to do so, Barak's comfortable majority coalition of 68 would be reduced to a minority government of 59 MKs. There was even some question that the 17 member ultra-orthodox religious party Shas, at the time more moderate than the NRP, was wavering in its support of Barak because of economic issues linked to its constituency. Even closer allies, such as the leader of the center party, Shinui, and various well-known Labor supporters expressed reservations. The 13 December 1999 Knesset vote for renewal of the talks with Syria provided little encouragement, for although 47 MKs voted in favor and only 31 against, two of the latter were from coalition parties and some 24 MKs abstained. Moreover, this vote was accompanied by a large demonstration of Golan supporters outside the Knesset. It is no wonder that the Americans were to notice signs of doubt when Barak arrived in Washington the next day. The Third Way group (active during the Rabin period) and leaders of the Golan settlers organized appeals (including a letter to Syrian President Assad), and opinion polls were published frequently for months, some indicating strong opposition, others a close tie. As in the Rabin period, strong elements of the Jewish diaspora in the United States campaigned and lobbied against an agreement. Beginning with Barak's election and continuing all the way into the spring, right-wing American Jewish leaders were once again fortified by visits and messages from Israelis such as Yoram Ettinger. Instead of the earlier argument about American soldiers being dispatched if there were an agreement (a topic that was not prominent in the Barak period), the diaspora campaign focused on Syria as a terror-supporting state not to be trusted, likening Assad to Saddam Hussein.[143]

While the official Israel lobby, AIPAC, supported the government's policy and lobbied strongly for the military package Barak was seeking to sweeten a withdrawal from the Golan, Barak took a number of steps to placate potential spoilers at home. He held meetings with Golan settlers, and Barak supporters organized a counter-campaign highlighting Golan settlers willing to leave in exchange for peace. Barak also acceded to Shas demands, providing most of the party's requests for the 2000 budget, eliminating at least this threat to his coalition.[144] In his December Knesset speech, Barak appealed both to the Lebanon issue – given public interest in Israeli withdrawal from Lebanon – and to Israel's relations with the United States (which was portrayed as most interested in Israeli–Syrian peace), along with Israel's standing in the world, all as incentives. In what was presented as reassurance that he had made no commitments nor agreed to preconditions, he used a phrase he was to repeat in the Washington talks that, nonetheless, "we have not erased the past – neither Madrid nor the substance of the contacts and talks with Rabin, Peres, or even Netanyahu."[145] Thus, while many MKs may not have been privy to the Lauder documents and therefore may not have understood the reference, Barak invoked legitimacy from Netanyahu for withdrawal to the 4 June line. Barak also promised a referendum on any agreement reached with the Syrians, but this brought even greater pressure on him when the Likud introduced a referendum bill (supported by three coalition parties, Shas, NRP, and Israel b'Aliyah) to require a majority of all registered voters, rather than a majority of those voting in the referendum. The proposal, not accepted in the end, was designed to minimize the influence of Israeli Arab voters (in fact, one version of the bill called for a referendum of Jewish citizens only).

The differences of opinion with Barak's own coalition were also reflected in the negotiating team itself. Elyakim Rubinstein, the legal advisor in the Shepherdstown team, discussed with Barak his (Rubinstein's) opposition to withdrawal from the Golan; but he offered and most likely indeed provided unbiased legal assistance. However, Sagie maintains that both Rubinstein and Moshe Kohanovski (a Defense Ministry legal advisor) went over his head and tried to persuade Barak to use the 1923 rather than the 1967 line as a guide for the border. It is possible that such differences – in substance, not tactics – within the negotiating team was a factor in the ultimate failure. Barak himself offered the possibility that someone in the Israeli team was responsible for the 13 January leak of the draft treaty possibly in order to torpedo the talks. But he also theorized, on the contrary, that someone sought to demonstrate that Israel was not compromising, rendering the leak something of a "trial balloon" designed to strengthen public support.[146] Yatom believes it to have been the former; Sagie believes it was the latter.[147] Indeed, Akiva Eldar, the reporter to whom the leak was conveyed, has revealed that the leak came from, and was even confirmed slightly later by, the same source in the Prime Minister's Office while he, Eldar, waited in vain for Barak to call him to tell him not to publish.[148] This explanation of the leak would indeed substantiate the conclusion that domestic opinion – which Barak sought to test in this way, was a major factor.

This could be linked to another factor, as asserted by Sagie, namely a failure of leadership on the part of Barak. Given these domestic obstacles of problematic public opinion and serious political "spoilers," leadership qualities, such as the courage to stand by commitments and take decisive action to overcome obstacles, were lacking. Sagie claims that Barak saw the opinion polls, "got cold feet" and made an about-face.[149] Yet Barak was not known to be indecisive but, rather, calculating if impulsive; he presumably calculated that he could not overcome the domestic obstacles in the face of a referendum. Clinton, however, attributed this to Barak's relatively short time in politics and a lack of understanding of the fickleness of public opinion when it comes to foreign policy.[150] But the personality trait, of refusing to accept advice, played a role in this as well.

Absence of understanding of the other side may have played a role in the failure. For example, as in the past, the Syrians did not appreciate the Israeli concern over public opinion, necessitating confidence-building measures, public diplomacy, or gestures on the part of Syria. The absence of Syrian understanding of this psychological factor among Israelis, crucial in Barak's eyes, was particularly apparent in the refusal of Shara to shake hands with Barak at their December meeting in Washington. On the Israeli side, while Barak (like Rabin) appeared to understand that Assad could not accept anything less than the total withdrawal Israel had accorded the Egyptians, he did not sufficiently appreciate the importance of land – to the last inch – for the Syrians. Barak did not believe that his demand for a strip of land on the shore was asking for much, and he expressed something akin to surprise that such a small demand could make such a difference.[151] Sagie would add that the two leaders had different concepts of peace, with Barak viewing peace as an end in itself, but Assad seeing it merely as a quiet border.[152] Thus, there may well have been misunderstandings in the course of the talks, despite the fact that the Israeli delegation had received expert guidance on cultural as well as political influences on Syrian behavior. There were also personality clashes within the Israeli team, even animosity, particularly between Sagie and Yatom regarding negotiating strategies and tactics. With each claiming that the other did not have Barak's full confidence, these differences may explain what could be viewed (as, indeed, it was by the Americans) as indecisive or erratic negotiating behavior on Barak's part – accepting but then retreating on issues, raising more demands, and the like.

Finally, Indyk maintains that Barak's concerns over public and political opposition notwithstanding, a contributing factor was the absence of stronger intervention by Clinton.[153] He agrees with Clinton, Sagie, and others that

Barak missed a genuine opportunity to reach agreement at the Shepherdstown talks, primarily because of concern over opposition at home.[154] However, Indyk believes that Clinton could have tried to change Barak's mind by means other than his eloquent efforts at persuasion. There were no suggestions or even hints at a reduction of US aid to Israel or a reduction of other types of support. Alternatively, Clinton could have helped with Israeli public opinion by offering the supply of new weapons systems, more intelligence sharing, or even a defense alliance (such as that sought by Peres). Clinton employed neither carrot nor stick. More importantly, according to Indyk, the Americans failed to grasp that Shepherdstown was the moment Assad was willing to make peace; there was unlikely to be another opportunity. In fact, the leak led to a backlash in Syria, and the ailing Assad shifted all that was left to him in time and energy in order to hold the regime together for the transition to his son.

But even when what may have been an opportunity did arise – namely, the Geneva meeting – Clinton did not, in Indyk's view, propose any creative suggestions (e.g., with regard to the issue of the land around the northeast corner of the Kinneret). Yet, as always with the case of hindsight, one may only speculate as to how effective any of these actions by the Americans might have been.

It may be difficult to draw unambiguous conclusions regarding Rabin and Peres's negotiations with the Syrians; many factors, including some from the Syrian side, would seem to account for the failures. In the Barak case, the conclusion of virtually all the participants in the process from the summer of 1999 to the spring of 2000 is that all factors taken into account, the most important would appear to have been Barak's reluctance at the critical moment to try to cope with domestic political and public opposition. While this would attest to the power of public opinion, it may also amount to what Barak's chief negotiator Uri Sagie has called a failure of leadership.[155] For Rabin it was mistrust and skepticism. One might look for entirely different underlying factors for each leader, possibly even economic or simply power-driven interests in holding onto the Golan; yet there is no evidence of these, neither from the negotiations themselves nor from those involved, including the critics.

Notes

1 Yitzhak Rabin, *Pinkas Sherut* [*Service Diary*] (Tel Aviv: *Sifriat Maariv*, 1979): 263 to President Ford during the reassessment and in response to Ford's comment in favor of an "overall Middle East settlement" via the Geneva Conference.
2 Rabin interview to *Davar*, 16 September 1974 (Israel Ministry of Foreign Affairs (MFA), Rabin Speeches, Vol. 3: 1974–1977).
3 Itamar Rabinovich, *The Brink of Peace* (Princeton, NJ: Princeton University Press, 1998); Dennis Ross, *The Missing Peace* (New York, NY: Farrar, Straus and Giroux, 2005); Martin Indyk, *Innocent Abroad* (New York, NY: Simon and Schuster, 2009). A later book mainly on Peres, written by a journalist, not a participant, has some details though possibly not all accurate: Orly Azoulai-Katz,

Ha-ish She-lo Yada' Le-naze'ah: Shimon Peres Be-malkodet Sizyphus [*The Man Who Did Not Know How to Win: Shimon Peres in the Sisyphus Trap*] (Tel Aviv: Yedioth Sfarim, 1996). The only publication from a Syrian participant is an interview by Syrian negotiator Walid Mouallem, "Interview: Fresh Light on the Syrian-Israeli Peace Negotiations," *Journal of Palestine Studies*, 26(2), 1997: 81–94. For non-participant study with particular attention to the Syrian side, see Helena Cobban, *The Israeli–Syrian Peace Talks* (Washington, DC: United States Peace Institute, 1999). Other participant but sparse references may be found in: Uri Sagie, *Orot Ba-'arafel* [*Lights in the Fog*] (Tel Aviv: Yedioth Sfarim, 1998): 153–156, 169, 189, 196–197, 203–204; Bill Clinton, *My Life* (New York, NY: Vintage Books, 2005): 575, 626.

4 Moshe Maoz, *Syria and Israel*, (Oxford: Oxford University Press, 1995), traces Assad's decision to 1988, noting (as does Rabinovich) Assad's rapprochement with Egypt in 1989. Indeed, as early as 1986 it had become clear to Assad that the Soviet Union could no longer be counted on. Galia Golan, *Soviet Policies in the Middle East: From World War II to Gorbachev* (Cambridge, MA: Cambridge University Press, 1990): 278–281.

5 Galia Golan, "Soviet Foreign Policy and the Gulf War: The Role of Domestic Factors," in Patrick Morgan and Keith Nelson (Eds), *Re-Viewing the Cold War: Domestic Factors and Foreign Policy in the East–West Confrontation* (New York, NY: Praeger Publishers, 2000): 179–202.

6 Ross, 2005: 73.

7 The reasons for Syria's participation and also for the decision for peace, as seen by a Syrian member of the Baath Party, at the time a researcher in Britain, may be found in M. Zuhair Diab, "Have Syria and Israeli Opted for Peace?," *Middle East Policy*, 3(2), 1994. The Baath Party was informed of Assad's "strategic decision for peace" in 1991.

8 Ross, 2005: 69.

9 William Quandt, *Peace Process* (Washington, DC: Brookings Institution, 1993): 402, 441–442. Original commitment: "Excerpts of US President Gerald Ford's letter to Prime Minister Yitzhak Rabin on the Issue of the Golan Heights, 1 September 1975," in Benyamin Neuberger, *Mediniyut Hutz Shel Yisrael: Kovetz Mismakhim I* [*Foreign Policy of Israel: Collection of Documents*] (Tel Aviv: Open University, 2004): 335.

10 The Palestinian side will be discussed in Chapter 6 on the Oslo Accords.

11 *Washington Post*, 27 June 1992; Uri Sagie, *Ha-yad She-kaf'ah* [*The Hand that Froze*] (Tel Aviv: Yedioth Sfarim, 2011): 31–32.

12 Rabinovich, 1998: 42.

13 Maoz, 1995: 216–217.

14 Maoz, 1995: 217.

15 Leah Rabin, *Rabin: Our Life, His Legacy* (New York, NY: Vintage, 1997).

16 Knesset speech, 13 July 1992, MFA, Historical Documents, 1992–1994, www.mfa.gov.il/Archive.

17 Protocol, The First Session of the Thirteenth Knesset, Monday, 13 July 1992.

18 Ross, 2005: 89. July 1992 just after Baker's visit.

19 *Haaretz*, 17 August 2012.

20 Eitan Haber in the documentary "Rabin" by Ben Shani on the History Channel, Israel Television, 16 April 2013. See similar comment to Clinton, 2005: 545 and Shlomo Ben-Ami, *Scars of War, Wounds of Peace* (London: Oxford University Press, 2006): 203.

21 Maoz, 1995: 224.

22 *Labor Party Platform 1992*, "Peace Policy" (documents, Israel Democracy Institute).

23 *Haaretz*, 3 July 1992 (elections were 22 June 1992).

24 Maoz, 1995: 127; Rabinovich, 1998: 55; Ross, 2005: 88–89; Indyk, 2009: 18.

25 Rabinovich, 1998: 47 and 55.
26 Specifically, the loan guarantees were needed for the absorption of what was to become nearly 1 million immigrants from the former Soviet Union. The guarantees had been suspended because of Shamir's refusal to halt settlement building; President Bush restored them in August 1992.
27 Ross, 2005: 99.
28 *Yedioth Aharonoth*, 10 September 1992.
29 Asher Arian, *Security Threatened: Surveying Israeli Opinion on Peace and War* (Cambridge, MA: Cambridge University Press, 1995): 103.
30 Arian, 1995: 102.
31 Ross, 2005: 90.
32 Labor MKs Emmanuel Zissman and Avigdor Kahalani were the leaders, along with Yehuda Harel, once quite close to Rabin. Together with a number of MKs, including quite a few Labor members, they had earlier formed a Golan lobby in the Knesset.
33 Yitzhak Rabin, *Rodef Shalom: Neumei Shalom shel Yitzhak Rabin* [*Peace-seeker: Peace Speeches of Yitzhak Rabin*] (Tel Aviv: Zamora-Bitan, 1995): 69–71.
34 Yitzhak Rabin, 1995: 70.
35 Sagie, 1998: 196–197.
36 Rabinovich, 1998: 73. Dani Yatom, *Shutaf Sod: Mi-sayeret Matkal Ve-'Ad Ha-mosad* [*Partner of the Secret: From the Elite Unit to the Mossad*] (Tel Aviv: Yedioth Sfarim, 2009): 135 recounts a similar comment by Rabin.
37 Maoz and Rabinovich being the leading experts, pers. comm.; Rabinovich, 1998: 57.
38 The one public gesture Assad made was to allow exit visas for 800 Syrian Jews, but this was presented as a gesture to the United States, not Israel. He also allowed a visit to Damascus by the US group Americans for Peace Now, including an interview of them on Syrian state television. The group reported that there were also posters on the streets praising the "strategic decision for peace."
39 Less detail also by Indyk.
40 Rabinovich, 1998: 83.
41 It will be remembered that this was how Rabin viewed Sadat's early 1973 offer. See Chapter 3.
42 Indyk, 2009: 141.
43 Rabinovich, 1998: 104–105.
44 Ross, 2005: 111.
45 Ross, 2005: 111.
46 According to Rabinovich, 1998: 57, in the run-up to the beginning of the talks, Peres was concerned about withdrawal to "within 10 meters" of the Sea of Galilee, implying he believed 4 June 1967 was the line being considered. His deputy (Deputy Minister for Foreign Affairs Yossi Beilin) suggested Rabin specify the international border, but Rabin did not want to state any line at that point.
47 Ross, 2005: 146.
48 Ross, 2005: 146. Yet, Uri Sagie claims that in August 1993 Rabin did think that the Syrians would assume full withdrawal to mean 4 June 1967, but did not realize that this line was so unclear a concept as to be subject to varying interpretations (Sagie, 2011: 44).
49 Ambassador Walid Mouallem, then ambassador to Washington and Rabinovich's counterpart in most of the negotiations, later told Helena Cobban that in talks that took place in 1996, Rabinovich actually blurted out: "We even promised you we would withdraw to the 4 June 1967 line" (Cobban, 1999: 74.) Mouallem has also said that according to a Mubarak interview (to *al-Hayat*), Rabin had told Mubarak that he was ready to withdraw to the 4 June 1967 lines (Walid Mouallem, "Light on the Syrian–Israeli Peace Negotiations: An Interview with Ambassador Walid Mouallem," *Journal of Palestine Studies*, 26(2), 1997: 83).

50 Ross, 2005: 113.
51 Ross, 2005: 148. According to Patrick Seale, a British journalist close to Assad, President Clinton telephoned Assad on 25 July 1994, a few days after Christopher had conveyed this "clarification," and both leaders agreed that it was "a major achievement" (Patrick Seale, "The Syria–Israel Negotiations: Who Is Telling the Truth?," *Journal of Palestine Studies*, 29(2), 2000: 70).
52 Sagie, 2011: 44–45.
53 Rabinovich, 1998: 130. Seale later said that Assad had definitely understood Rabin's proposal to be "conditional" provided Israel's needs were met; nonetheless, he viewed it as a commitment (Seale, 2000: 66–67, 77). Seale, however, characterized Rabin's positions as no more than a "ruse" and "a political deception" designed to reduce Syrian opposition to the pending Oslo agreement with the PLO (Seale, 2000: 68).
54 Rabinovich, 1998: 113, 126, 136, 143; Ross, 2005: 94.
55 Ross, 2005: 94, 157–158.
56 Rabinovich, 1998: 130; Indyk, 2009: 108.
57 Ross, 2005: 112.
58 Rabinovich, 1998: 106; Ross, 2005: 114.
59 Ross, 2005: 113; Rabinovich, 1998: 107.
60 Rabinovich, 1998: 107, 136.
61 Aviezer Yaari, "Ha-Golan Beseder Ha'Adifuyot Shel Assad – 1974–94" ["The Golan in Assad's Priorities"], in Moshe Ma'oz, *Ha-golan Ben Milhama Ve-Shalom* [*The Golan Between War and Peace*] (Or Yehuda: Hed Artzi, 1999), maintained that Syrian control of Lebanon was a more important preoccupation for Syria at the time.
62 Indyk, 2009: 89.
63 Indyk, 2009: 89.
64 Rabinovich, 1998: 125–126.
65 Indyk, 2009: 141. Since King Hussein had given up his claim to the West Bank in 1988 in favor of the PLO, negotiations with Israel would not be particularly problematic. Moreover, they would be justifiable, for Jordan, in view of the Oslo Accords with the Palestinians and the talks Syria had conducted with Israel.
66 Rabinovich, 1998: 118.
67 It was in connection with this meeting that Assad allowed the 800 Jews to leave Syria; he also permitted a US congressional delegation to come in search of information regarding Israeli MIAs (Rabinovich, 1998: 127).
68 Rabinovich, 1998: 128.
69 Ross, 2005: 139.
70 William J. Clinton, "The President's News Conference with President Hafez al-Asad of Syria in Geneva, January 16, 1994," The American Presidency Project, www.presidency.ucsb.edu.
71 *Ibid*.
72 *Ibid*. See also Indyk, 2009: 105.
73 Indyk, 2009: 107; Ross, 2005: 140.
74 He called in Sagie to illustrate past Assad statements (in Arabic) of this nature, though Sagie was later to say that he viewed repetition of such statements as signs of Assad's seriousness regarding an agreement, not, like Rabin, the opposite (Indyk, 2009: 108). According to Indyk, both Sagie and Ehud Barak believed that Assad's reference to Israel and normal peaceful relations in the same breath and in the presence of Clinton and the press (as Barak put it) were important.
75 Ross, 2005: 141; Indyk, 2009: 107.
76 Mouallem, 1997: 84.
77 Rabinovich, 1998: 149.

78 Barak briefing to visiting US military delegation, April 1994 (Rabinovich, 1998: 140.) Shortly thereafter the new chief of staff, Amnon Lipkin-Shahak, replaced Barak (who was already preparing his entry to politics).
79 Ron Tira, *Itzuv Mediniyut Yisrael Kelape Suryah* [*Fashioning Israeli Policy Toward Syria*] (Tel Aviv: *Yedioth Sfarim*, 2000), 149–151.
80 Mouallem, 1997: 84.
81 Legislation would have been required for any referendum, and the public debate not only included a call for a 65 percent majority, but also demands to exclude Arab citizens from participating; no bill was actually introduced. The additional bill on the Golan did not pass due to a tie vote (59–59). Rabin was to maintain that the 1981 Golan law had not constituted "annexation" (Rabinovich, 1998: 128). Later, in 2008, a new referendum bill was proposed and passed requiring a referendum for relinquishing any territory under Israeli sovereignty – namely, the Golan and East Jerusalem, both of which had been annexed. In 2013 an effort was begun to pass a stricter law and one that would include the West Bank.
82 Opposition to returning any of the Golan had gone down slightly from 49 percent in 1992 to 44 percent in 1993 and 1994; but in 1995 it went back up, to 50 percent, though those willing to return all of the Golan rose from 6 to 8 percent (Asher Arian, "Israel Security Opinion – February 1996," Memorandum No. 46, JCSS, March 1996). A smaller survey by a different group found in July 1995 that when asked about support for "peace with full withdrawal" or "*status quo*" (remain on the Golan as is without a peace agreement), some 58 percent chose to keep the *status quo*, but a surprising 38.4 percent chose peace with Syria). Tamar Hermann and Ephraim Yaar, Peace Index, Tel Aviv University, 27 July, 1995. Archive of the Peace Index for subsequent years may be found on the Israel Democracy Institute website or the INSS website.
83 Discussed below – for example, demonstrations with posters of Rabin in SS uniform.
84 Rabinovich, 1998: 191.
85 Seale, 2000: 65–77.
86 Yatom, 2009: 183 citing Rabin.
87 See Shimon Peres, *The New Middle East* (New York, NY: Henry Holt, 1993).
88 Ross, 2005: 234; Uri Savir, *The Process* (New York, NY: Vintage Books, 1998): 278.
89 Rabinovich, 1998: 211.
90 Rabinovich, 1998: 210, 215.
91 Mouallem, 1997: 81.
92 Mouallem, 1997: 86–87.
93 Ross, 2005: 243. He told the Americans of his decision even before the beginning of the second round of Wye talks, on 24 January 1996; he told the Syrians via Christopher at the Wye talks, on 29 January 1996.
94 Peace Index, 1995, 1996.
95 Savir, 1998: 281; Ross, 2005: 242; Cobban, 1999: 137–138, has the concerned Syrian reaction.
96 Mouallem, 1997: 82.
97 Syria also refrained from attending the regional anti-terrorism conference initiated by the US in Sharm el-Sheikh in the wake of these attacks.
98 Rabinovich, 1998: 230.
99 Rabinovich, 1998: 235.
100 According to Ross, 2005: 244, if it had not been for the terrorist attacks (and Peres's subsequent narrow loss of the elections) there would have been a peace agreement with Syria.
101 Rabinovich, 1998: 241, claimed that a later article in the Israeli press to this effect was based on Savir as a source ("This is How We Missed the Peace with Syria," 12 December 1997, cited at length in Cobban, 1999, as well.

102 Savir, 1998: 273 on the "powerful voice" of the military in the negotiations. See also, 276, 279.
103 Savir, 1998: 279.
104 Ross, 2005: 234.
105 *Chicago Tribune*, 23 January 1997, http://articles.chicagotribune.com/1997-1-23/news/9701230207_1_israel-syria-netanyahu-gol.
106 Yatom, 2009: 194.
107 Document in appendix of Yatom, 2009: 449.
108 Yatom, 2009: 195.
109 Indyk, 2009: 247 explained that, initially, in August 1999, Lauder presented (to Clinton) the first draft as if it were the final agreement; only upon Syrian denial did Lauder reveal to Clinton in November 199 (letter reproduced in Yatom, 2009: 448) that there was a second draft (the 12 September 1998 document). The Syrians confirmed that this draft superseded the first draft, and Lauder explained to Clinton that while the September draft was agreed to by both sides, the talks could not be completed "until a map of the June 4, 1967 line was provided by Israel" (Yatom, 2009: Appendix, "Letter of Ronald Lauder to the President of the U.S. Bill Clinton from 12 November 1999," 448. See also Ross, 2005: 510–511, 517–519 and Yatom, 2009: 195–196. Yatom, 2009: 198 claims that Lauder's explanations were confirmed by both Mouallem and Moratinos. Yatom also claims that according to Indyk, on the way to his Wye meeting with Arafat, Netanyahu told Lauder to convey to Assad Netanyahu's willingness to present a map personally to Assad in Damascus but the latter refused to meet. This is not mentioned in Indyk's account.
110 *Jerusalem Post*, 11 November 2011.
111 Yatom, 2009: 214, although in the August 1998 draft shown Clinton, this Israeli participation was in brackets, apparently not yet agreed (Ross, 2005: 512) and the 12 September 1998 draft merely adopts the Rabin era "Aims and Principles of Security Arrangements" with no additions.
112 A peace agreement with Syria was not, apparently, Netanyahu's first choice. He preferred a more limited deal whereby Israel would finally withdraw from Lebanon in exchange for an end to Syrian support for Hizballah, but Assad would not discuss Lebanon before the Golan.
113 Wye Accords, signed 23 October 1998, contained a commitment for further withdrawals ("redeployments") of the Israeli military.
114 Ran Edelist and Ron Maiberg, *Ehud Barak: Milhamto Ba-shedim* [*Ehud Barak: His Battle with Ghosts*] (Tel Aviv: Kinneret Zmora-Bitan Dvir, 2003): 128; Yatom, 2009: 198, 220, also mentions Mordecai's opposition.
115 Peace Index, July 1998; Israel Democracy Institute. Asher Arian, "Israeli Public Opinion on National Security, 1998," Memorandum No. 49, JCSS, had 44 percent "absolutely against" returning the Golan.
116 Ross, 2005: 510.
117 Ross, 2005: 526.
118 Ross, 2005: 528; Indyk, 2009: 250; Yatom, 2009: 202, 214.
119 According to Yatom, 2009: 212, the Israelis realized this only later.
120 Ross, 2005: 542–543; Clinton, 2005: 885; Yatom, 2009: 224. Note the same phrase in Barak's 13 December 1999 Knesset speech (www.knesset.gov.il, Protocol, Fifty-ninth Session of the Fifteenth Knesset, Monday, 13 December 1999).
121 The only line appearing on maps was the 1923 international border. Since the waters of the Kinneret had receded since 1967, it was possible – as Israel wished – that the place where Syrian troops had stood in 1967 (touching the water) was now further back from the waterline.
122 Ross, 2005: 544. Barak wanted to negotiate the withdrawal from Lebanon, but the Syrian presence in Lebanon was at least, in part, justified by Damascus as the

92 *Failure on the Syrian Track*

    need to protect Lebanon from Israel, so Syria presumably was not anxious to lose this pretext, nor the leverage provided by its relationship with Hizballah during the Syrian–Israeli talks.

123 Ross, 2005: 545–546; Indyk, 2009: 245.
124 Ross, 2005: 556.
125 *Haaretz*, 13 January 2000.
126 This was preceded by secret but inconclusive talks, including mediation by Saudi Prince Bandar with Assad at Washington's urging.
127 Ross, 2005: 583–584 (see also Yatom, 2009: 268). The wording was taken from the Lauder–Assad document of 12 September 1998.
128 Second-hand confidential account from a Western diplomat.
129 Edelist and Maiberg, 2003: 131.
130 Sagie, 2011 : 119.
131 Sagie, 2011: 118.
132 Sagie, 2011: 116.
133 Ross, 2005: 557; 530–535.
134 Clinton, 2005: 886.
135 Even this, like the security concerns regarding the Jordan Rift Valley, was a bit out of date, at least in the view of the later Sharon government.
136 Ross, 2005: 521.
137 The risk of Syrian interference in the water sources, clearly a threat during the 1950s and 1960s, was not mentioned by Rabin nor by Barak's advisors; later, progress in inexpensive water desalinization made this a less critical matter.
138 Yatom, 2009: 202, 214.
139 Clinton, 2005: 885; Ross, 2005: 543–544.
140 Clinton, 2005: 886.
141 Yatom, 2009: 221 says that Barak was "constantly occupied with problems that he would experience passing the peace treaty in a referendum and continuously thought of points that would help them get the approval he needed in the Knesset and the referendum." See also Yatom, 2009: 230, 235, 241, 250; Indyk, 2009: 260.
142 Indyk, 2009: 251; Gilead Sher, *Be-merhak Negi'ah* [*Within Reach*] (Tel Aviv: Yedioth Sfarim, 2001): 65.
143 See, for example, comments and events presented by Frank Gaffney, head of the Center for Security Policy in Washington, or Morton Klein, president of the Zionist Organization of America, or the Jewish Institute for National Security (*Jewish World Review*, 19 July: 199, www.jewishworldreview.com/0799/golan.html; JTA, 14 January 2000).
144 *Haaretz*, 28 December 1999.
145 "Statement to the Knesset by PM Barak on the Renewal of Israel–Syria Negotiations – Dec-13-1999," MFA (www.mfa.gov.il).
146 Yatom, 2009: 256.
147 Yatom, 2009: 157; Sagie, 2011: 16.
148 Both Akiva Eldar, *Haaretz*, 5 December 2009; *Maariv*, 30 November 2012.
149 Sagie, 2011: 121. Shlomo Ben-Ami used the same expression (Ben-Ami, 2006: 243).
150 Clinton, 2005: 886.
151 Ross, 2005: 547.
152 Sagie, 2011: 66.
153 Indyk, 2009: 285–287.
154 Indyk later said that in December 1999 the Americans concluded that Assad "was apparently ready to do the deal": Shimon Shamir and Bruce Maddy-Weitzman (Eds), *The Camp David Summit: What Went Wrong?* (Brighton, UK: Sussex Academic Press, 2005): 25.

155 Clearly angry over Barak's mismanagement of what Sagie believes was a real possibility of achieving an agreement, he later stated that if an accord had been achieved it would have contained the usual disclaimer of ties with countries not recognizing Israel, Syria would not have drawn close to Iran but rather would have joined the Western-oriented Arab states, and the situation in subsequent years would have been entirely different (*Haaretz*, 17 August 2012).

5 Jordan Again: Failures and Breakthrough

While Israel's positions as put forth in the 1968 Alon Plan seemed to preclude any realistic effort for a peace agreement between Jordan and Israel, contacts and even direct talks continued for many years. Cooperation, particularly with regard to matters connected with the population in the West Bank (e.g., continued use of the dinar, Israel's open bridges policy for movement of people and goods), worked so well that the relationship came to be termed one of "intimate enemies" enjoying *"de facto* peace."[1] This "functional cooperation" (as it was called) was even capped by strategic measures when Israel mobilized forces and flew air sorties in response to King Hussein's request (via the Americans) for assistance against the Syrian invasion of his country during the 1970 civil war with the Palestine Liberation Organization in Jordan. The two states could even be said to have a mutual, or at least similar, interest in weakening the PLO and preventing the creation of a Palestinian state on the West Bank.

"Disengagement" 1974

Though not a party to the 1973 Yom Kippur War (Jordan had sent a symbolic unit to the Syrians[2]), Jordan nevertheless sought participation in the post-war negotiations that focused on disengagement of forces agreements. Both before and after the basically ceremonial Geneva Conference of 1973, the Jordanians proposed a limited agreement in the border area along the Jordan River (Jordan Rift Valley) and Jericho. There were a number of versions of what became known as the "Jericho Plan," the basic idea being to return the town of Jericho to Jordan plus a possible withdrawal of Israeli forces (and settlements) from the Jordan Rift Valley. In secret direct talks in Israel, late January 1974, and again in March, the King proposed an Israeli withdrawal of 10 kilometers but promised that Jordanian forces would not move into the Rift Valley. Prime Minister Golda Meir rejected withdrawal in favor of providing Jordan a corridor from Jericho to the border. For King Hussein, withdrawal from the valley was a step toward an eventual return to the 4 June 1967 lines rather than what he feared was an Israeli bid to implement the Alon Plan.[3]

Meir's position was, indeed, continued adherence to the Alon Plan and rejection of a return to the 4 June 1967 lines. There had been no change in either Israel's position in the intervening years, nor in Meir's conviction that the Arabs were not willing to make peace with Israel. At this time, however, there were also additional factors that made the likelihood of a breakthrough with Jordan most unlikely. Meir was faced with demonstrations of popular protest linked to the Yom Kippur War, and the efforts to form a new coalition after the December 1973 elections were meeting with difficulties. In fact, the effort to include the National Religious Party (NRP) in the new coalition certainly militated against any territorial compromise on the West Bank. Even within the party (the Labor Alignment created between the Labor Party and Mapam in 1968) there had been controversy whether or not to specify the Jordan River in the party platform as Israel's border (sought by Yigal Allon) or only as Israel's "security border" (Dayan) or stating nothing at all about the border (Abba Eban).[4] Therefore, the 1973 platform only declared opposition to the creation of a Palestinian state west of Jordan,[5] and inclusion of a general pronouncement that Israel would not return to the 4 June 1967 lines. The latter, however, was a *sine qua non* for King Hussein.

Shortly after the failure of her talks with King Hussein on the Jericho Plan, Meir resigned her government, and it was some months before Rabin created a new coalition. In presenting his government to the Knesset on 3 June 1974, Rabin spoke of a pursuit of a peace agreement with Jordan "founded on the existence of two independent states: Israel with united Jerusalem as its capital, and an Arab state to the east of Israel. In the neighboring Jordanian–Palestinian state, the independent identity of the Palestinian and Jordanian Arabs can find expression in peace and good-neighborliness with Israel. Israel rejects the establishment of a further separate Arab State west of the Jordan."[6] Inasmuch as Rabin was hoping to get the NRP into the coalition, he adopted Meir's commitment to bring any decision "on concessions involving parts of Judea and Samaria" to the public in the form of new elections.[7] Distinguishing between the new negotiations with Egypt, and also Meir's talks with King Hussein, Rabin's government clarified a month later that the talks with Jordan would not be for a partial agreement (such as a separation of forces) but for a full peace agreement.[8]

Direct talks did, in fact, take place, secretly, including at least three meetings between Rabin and King Hussein, on various proposals similar to those discussed with Meir, and with the same results. Basically, Hussein offered a peace agreement on the 4 June 1967 lines, beginning with partial moves (Jericho Plan); Israel remained firm in its refusal to agree to an ultimate return to those lines. At one point Israel (apparently Peres) suggested that Jordan and Israel share responsibility for the administration of the West Bank and Gaza (civil administration under Jordan; security under Israel) or even joint sovereignty as a permanent arrangement.[9] This set of talks ended with the Arab League decision at its October 1974 meeting in Rabat to recognize the PLO as "the sole legitimate representative of the Palestinian people." There was one more Rabin–Hussein meeting after that on 28 May 1975; but the King, believing that a partial deal with Israel would have forestalled the Rabat decision, told the Israelis (angrily) that they would now have to deal with the PLO.[10] This did not, however, preclude continued contact on other matters and at lower levels. Nor did it mark any change in Jordan's claim to, or involvement in, the West Bank. That was to come much later in 1988.

Although Rabin introduced his government as one that would seek peace agreements with Israel's neighbors, many of the same factors that had prevailed against an agreement with Jordan in 1967 remained operative in 1974 – specifically, and most importantly, the conviction on the part of the government, including Rabin, that the territory (Jordan Rift Valley) was vital to Israel's security as distinct from peace with Jordan. As in the past, the reasoning was that the peace could not be depended upon with regard to future attack, most notably from a third army (Iraqi or Syrian) crossing the Jordan River. This was spelled out in the Labor Party platform, and in presenting his government to the Knesset Rabin said: "Israel will not return – even in the context of a peace treaty – to the 4 June 1967 lines. These lines are not defensible borders, and they constitute a temptation for aggression against us, as has been in the past."[11] Here was the element of mistrust, based on past experience if not of the type ingrained in identity or linked to ideology. Although the general environment was one of somewhat greater trust of Hussein born of cooperation over the intervening years, Rabin explained to an interviewer that while Jordan had refrained from opening a Jordanian front in the 1973 war possibly because of its 1970 war with Syria, those two countries were now moving toward military cooperation which was worrisome for Israel.[12] Thus, while Rabin was willing to consider partial steps in order to "test" the Jordanians, he was nonetheless mistrustful and, therefore, unwilling to budge from his rejection of any return to the 4 June lines.[13]

Other factors that may have impeded a breakthrough in these talks may have been a view of Hussein as too weak domestically, or too vulnerable to pressures from the Syrians and the Palestinians, to risk making peace with Israel. Peres (then foreign minister) had earlier described Hussein "a weak candidate for peace," and Alon (defense minister) apparently shared this estimate, though Alon also believed (as in 1967) that the Jordanian leader would ultimately accept Israel's conditions in order to survive.[14] The varied opinions regarding the King were indicative of another problem Rabin had to face, that of disagreements within his government. Obviously once the NRP joined in September, any suggestion of territorial compromise with Jordan would have been problematic; the coalition might survive without the NRP, but Rabin does not appear to have been interested in the political risk of a coalition with just a one-seat majority. Thus, the potential spoiler factor (the NRP) at least contributed to the failure of the effort, particularly since the NRP was backed up by the newly formed settler organization, Gush Emunim.[15] The group led a vociferous campaign against even a hint that the government might consider territorial concessions in the West Bank.

Additionally, there were disagreements even within the Labor Alignment, with the more left-wing component, Mapam, favoring compromise (though not necessarily with regard to Jordan as distinct from the Palestinians), and people like Alon firmly opposed anything but the limited Jericho Plan, even if the cost were no agreement with Jordan at all.[16] Heated debates had taken place over the 1973 platform, which though accepted by the party, was nonetheless considered too "dovish" by many members. Indeed, the party was now badly divided between "hawks" and "doves," going beyond (and sometimes crossing) the longstanding factional split that predated the 1967 war. Further, the fierce competition between Peres and Rabin was becoming apparent, with Peres taking a hawkish position on the West Bank and challenging Rabin (and Alon) on the possibilities of peace with Jordan. Rabin himself did not yet have a strong political base in the party; he had beaten Peres for the leading position by less than 50 votes when Meir resigned and was challenged by Alon as well.

The admired Six-Day War Chief of Staff Rabin was yet to prove his political abilities, and he was not helped by the political battles and rivalries within his own party. As we have seen, his leadership was an important factor for the progress made on the Egyptian track, but when it came to the more difficult issue of the territories demanded by Jordan, Rabin was said to have failed as a leader. One observer, albeit a clear opponent of Rabin in the Labor Party internal feuds, claimed to quote Kissinger telling his aides (after a visit to the region) that "'This team is incapable of doing anything. We are racking our brains to find some formula, and there sits a prime minister shivering in fear every time I mention the word Jordan. It is a lost cause.'"[17]

Some of this apparent "fear" may have been connected also with Rabin's awareness of the general atmosphere among the Israeli public. The loss of confidence in the Labor government of Golda Meir spilled over onto Rabin, affecting his stature even though he had not been a party to the trauma of the war.[18] Moreover, public opinion was still strongly in favor of the *status quo* in the West Bank.[19] Rabin's attitude toward public opinion, however, was that it was incumbent upon the leadership to persuade the public of the advisability of its policies.[20] Nonetheless, he may not have relished a public debate on the issues involved – not only of the West Bank but also Jerusalem – nor elections, were he to accept Hussein's proposals. Thus, even if he had been inclined to make the concessions demanded by Hussein, domestic political and public opinion might have been impeding factors.

Kissinger apparently did have little regard for Rabin's leadership abilities at the time, even allowing for the problem of Rabin's narrow parliamentary majority. Speaking of the need for Israel to "realistically [face] up to the necessary step-by-step compromises essential for progress to a settlement," Kissinger told the US president in mid-October 1974: "I hope Rabin is the leader to do this, but I must candidly tell you I doubt it ... ."[21] This appraisal did not, however, prevent Kissinger from employing strong pressure on the Israeli leader when Washington deemed it expedient later, in the negotiations with

Egypt. In the Jordanian talks of 1974–1975, it may be the case that beyond the domestic political factors, this outside player, the United States, did play at least an indirect a role in the failure. Although the Americans were perceived by the Israeli media, and possibly even by the government, to be pressing for an agreement with Jordan, Washington's position was, in fact, ambiguous.[22] Kissinger was promoting not only a breakthrough with Jordan but also a second (disengagement) agreement with Egypt, and for most of the summer he expressed no preference between the two. It had been the Americans who had initiated the talks with Hussein when Kissinger traveled to Jordan in January 1974, immediately after the signing of the first Israeli–Egyptian disengagement agreement. It was Kissinger who brought Golda Meir the proposal from Jordan, and the Americans do appear to have been sincere in encouraging an agreement. Yet, it was also the Americans who initiated the second set of talks with Egypt as part of their strategic interest in advancing the budding US relationship with Sadat – at the expense of the Soviets. American ambivalence – or failure, in fact, to press Israel to reach agreement with Jordan – may have contributed to the Rabat decision to favor the PLO over Jordan. Kissinger himself admitted that he did not press for a breakthrough with Jordan and misjudged both his influence with and the attitudes of the Arab states prior to Rabat.[23] Expressing his interpretation, Rabin suggested in a September interview that the US preferred the Egyptian track.[24] And in his 14 October report on his talks in Israel, prior to Rabat, Kissinger implied that it was he who had persuaded Israel (in a three-hour talk with Rabin and his cabinet) to open talks with Egypt, leaving Jordan for later. Yet, Kissinger blamed Israel for the failure of the talks with Jordan. In March 1975, when the Israeli–Jordanian efforts proved fruitless, Kissinger criticized Israel for intransigence (which he somewhat misrepresented by exaggerating the offers made by Jordan), thereby holding Israel indirectly responsible for the Rabat decision favoring the PLO (over Jordan).[25] This reprimand, however, was delivered to a meeting with US Jewish leaders just as Washington had declared its "reassessment" of relations with Israel due to the impasse in the talks with Egypt, suggesting some disingenuousness on the part of Kissinger. Nonetheless, Kissinger had blamed the Israelis in his report to President Ford on the Rabat conference, accusing Israel of offering only "a vague promise [to Jordan and Egypt] to negotiate the surrender of some relatively minor amounts of territory in exchange for a binding long-term agreement on non-belligerency. This was impossible for them to accept and survive politically."[26]

The US position, notwithstanding, the possibility of reaching an agreement with Egypt may have been at least one of the factors in Rabin's decision to downgrade the Jordanian option, even before the Rabat meeting. On 10 September Rabin told the Americans that Israel preferred a deal with Egypt, believing that there was a basis to move forward with Egypt, which did not exist with Jordan.[27] Discussing the rejection of Jordan's proposal for partial Israeli withdrawal, Rabin told the Israeli press that he saw "a chance in the Egyptian direction. I see a possibility and a reason to seek a dialogue with Egypt ... "[28] and, he added in an earlier (26 July) interview, "the Arab world has not so far proved itself capable of taking one step towards a settlement with Israel unless Egypt was leading it."[29] He also implied that withdrawal of some kind could be made with Egypt, as distinct from Jordan (the West Bank) or Syria (the Golan) because of the distance from highly populated Israeli areas.[30]

It is doubtful, however, that the failure to reach a breakthrough with Jordan was due to the availability of the Egyptian alternative, though the alternative did make it possible to respond to the Americans' interest in progress on one front or another, and thus avoid a compromise with the Jordanians. It might be argued that the absence of actual pressure by the Americans played a role in the failure, since Rabin did show signs of sensitivity to American pressure. He was critical of the opposition in Israel for maintaining that one could simply ignore American wishes and expect the continuation of sorely needed American support (and military aid) – especially if Israel were perceived as being too rigid "by taking a stance of 'not one inch'."[31] And, in fact, American pressure, when it was finally applied, did play a major role in the achievement of the Interim Agreement with Egypt in 1975.

It is difficult to conclude that negative public opinion was a factor given Rabin's conviction that leadership should direct (persuade) rather than follow the public; but his coalition's very narrow majority and the divisions within the coalition and even within his party most likely did play a role. Important as these were, the crucial factor was the element of mistrust which defined "security" as "territory" rather than a settlement with Jordan. Rabin, like his predecessors (and most of his successors) was unwilling to pull Israeli forces back from the Jordan Rift Valley (much less withdraw from East Jerusalem, as would have been required for a full peace agreement). This was the essential meaning of Israel's position that it would not return to the 4 June 1967 lines; but Rabin, and most Israeli leaders at the time, could not understand why something short of those lines would not be acceptable to the Jordanians, at least as a first step. To them, King Hussein's insistence on the albeit limited (10 kilometer) withdrawal along the whole line, tied to a commitment to return the entire West Bank, was a sign that Jordan was not serious about making peace with Israel – whether because King Hussein was too weak domestically or within the Arab world, or simply unwilling to accept Israel as a legitimate and independent neighbor. The view that Jordan was not really willing to make peace was fortified by the King's rejection of Israeli offers such as functional cooperation or a condominium between the two states for the West Bank. Thus, Israel had a perception of its adversary that bolstered mistrust and further justified the territorial view of security – and refusal to withdraw even slightly. Was misperception, then, still another factor contributing to the failure? For King Hussein, Israel's refusal to move back gradually (as it had with Egypt and partially with Syria in the troop disengagements) along with the Labor Party's Alon Plan in the background (and even being implemented via settlement building), plus the Israeli government's ambiguous pronouncements on the Palestinians' expressing their identity in a neighboring "Jordanian–Palestinian state," belied any Israeli interest in reaching peace with Jordan. Jordan, of course, had other considerations that served as constraints, particularly the need to appear loyal to Arab and even Palestinian interests while staving off the efforts to bolster the PLO at Jordan's expense. It seems most likely, actually, that both sides did want to reach a peace agreement, but Rabin was correct when he told the Americans that there was no basis to go ahead at this time.

The London Agreement 1987

While there were talks over the years at various levels, there was close to a ten-year hiatus in top-level meetings, with the exception of one Rabin–Hussein meeting before Rabin's resignation in 1977 and the subsequent rise of the Likud to power. In 1984 Labor partially returned to power in a rotation agreement with the Likud. Peres was prime minister for two years with Yitzhak Shamir as foreign minister, reversing the roles after two years; Rabin was defense minister for the whole period. Almost immediately upon taking office, Peres sought to reach a peace agreement with Jordan, meeting King Hussein in London on 19 July 1985. Not only the leadership in Israel had changed; the regional environment was also in a state of flux: the Lebanese civil war remained unfinished, Israel had invaded in 1982 and only now (thanks to the Labor premiership) was withdrawing its troops to a security belt in the south of Lebanon, and the Iraq–Iran war, begun in 1981, continued. The Lebanese civil war and especially the Israeli invasion had had a momentous effect on the PLO, leading to a split in the movement and even, briefly, within the dominant Fatah group, as well as an attempt by Syria to take over the PLO. An early result of these developments was the convening of the 1984 Palestine National Council meeting in Amman, signaling a PLO–Jordan rapprochement – and boycotted by the more radical PLO groups. This was followed by an agreement between Arafat and King Hussein calling for an international conference and noting Arafat's acceptance of UN resolutions (though not explicitly Resolution 242). It was in this atmosphere of PLO moderation that King Hussein tried to maneuver talks between a joint Jordanian–Palestinian delegation and the US, to be followed by negotiations in an international conference. This effort was thwarted, according to Shlaim, not only by Shamir but also by activities of the Jewish diaspora in the US – both due to opposition to American talks with the PLO.[32] By the end of 1985, Hussein's efforts to assist moderate PLO contact with Washington fell apart, both because of Arafat's refusal to provide exactly the assurances Washington demanded and, more directly, because of a Palestinian terror attack that killed an elderly American citizen on a cruise ship, the *Achille Lauro*, in October. The attack led the US congress to enact into law the understanding that Kissinger had given Israel in the 1975 Interim Agreement, whereby the US would not engage in talks with the PLO unless and until it accepted

Israel's right to exist and agreed to Resolution 242. In 1985, Congress added the demand that the PLO also renounce the use of terror.[33]

For Israel, the failure of the attempt to create an American–PLO dialogue and the rift that developed between Hussein and Arafat (whom Hussein called "untrustworthy") seemed to open a way for talks that might meet with Shamir's approval.[34] Peres resumed secret contacts with the King, and in March 1986 Rabin met with Hussein in Europe, followed by talks between Peres, Rabin, and Hussein in Jordan in the summer. They apparently resumed working on the convening of an international conference – perceived as an umbrella under which Jordan could negotiate an agreement with Israel. The idea was finally formulated between Hussein and Peres at a London meeting on 11 April 1987 in a document that came to be called the "London Agreement."

This "historic breakthrough," as Peres's aide, Yossi Beilin, called it, was due to a number of factors, including the resumed animosity between Jordan and the PLO, followed by Hussein's launching of a five-year plan for development of the West Bank, demonstrating his authority where the area was concerned. Moreover, the return of Labor Party figures to the government in Israel provided an opportunity. The modicum of trust that had been created over the years had not been disrupted since the unsuccessful "disengagement" talks; Hussein had, in fact, been a helpful go-between during the Lebanon civil war, and even during the talks in 1985 he responded to a request by Israel to curb PLO personnel living in Jordan by immediately closing the PLO office.[35] That said, Labor was only a partner – to the Likud – in the government, and, moreover, its own platform in 1984 provided little that might produce a peace agreement with Jordan. It specified the areas that must remain under Israeli sovereignty in any future peace agreement: the Jordan Rift Valley,[36] including the northwest shore of the Dead Sea; Gush Etzion; Jerusalem and its surroundings; and also the southern Gaza Strip.

So far as is known, nothing more than the parameters of an international conference were worked out in the London Agreement, but Hussein did clarify that the "goal is peace, not a conference."[37] The conference was to seek a comprehensive peace for the area and security for the states, as well as "respond to the legitimate rights of the Palestinians." Negotiations would be held independently in bilateral committees, with Israel negotiating with a Jordanian–Palestinian delegation with regard to the Palestinian issue. Purely bilateral issues would be discussed between Israel and Jordan. It was, of course, important for Peres that the document stated that there would be no imposed solutions, since the conference was to consist of the five permanent members of the Security Council and the parties to the conflict, invited by the UN secretary general on the basis of Resolutions 242 and 338, and the renunciation of violence and terror.

While the document would require approval by the Jordanian and Israeli governments, the proposal was to have the US present it – and assist each side to gain the needed approval. The problem was that neither Shamir nor the Americans were enthusiastic about the idea. Shamir, who had known about and authorized the secret meetings, including the last one in London, rejected the London Agreement out of hand. He told a meeting of the inner cabinet that it was "a perverse and criminal idea."[38]

It is not difficult to identify the factor at play in Shamir's rejection. He was ideologically dedicated to the idea of "Greater Israel" and fully opposed to territorial compromise on the West Bank. The irony of his swift rejection is that even Labor would not have been willing to meet the conditions necessary for a peace agreement with Jordan at the time. King Hussein had not changed his demand for full return of the West Bank, even if this were to be in stages (as he had indicated ten years earlier as well).

Nonetheless, Shamir was not willing to risk a conference with Soviet involvement, believing that the super powers might try to impose a settlement. He appeared oblivious to the fact that Soviet policy toward Israel and the conflict had already undergone significant changes since Gorbachev's ascension to power in 1985. And he was no more trusting of the Americans than Meir had been and possibly less confident of Israel's importance to Washington than Begin had been. Indeed, American–Israeli relations went through a very difficult period in the early 1980s, over Israel's 1982 invasion of Lebanon, producing the "Reagan Plan" that clearly explicitly ruled out permanent Israeli control of the West Bank. Shamir's mistrust extended also to the UN, which he felt might bring the PLO into the meeting – a more realistic concern, perhaps, given the support for the PLO in the UN. And certainly Shamir did not trust the Jordanians. The Jordanians have described Shamir's behavior and that of his entourage as virtual paranoia at a later meeting that took place at King Hussein's house in London.[39] Shamir's greatest mistrust, however, was reserved for Shimon Peres; he believed Peres had made a secret deal with Hussein, which, according to one source, was how he interpreted the fact that Peres would not give him the document itself (on the grounds that it was to be an American proposal).[40] It was natural enough to assume that a secret deal had been made, inasmuch as the London Agreement was primarily a document of procedural arrangements with no more than the usual general declarations for comprehensive peace. Shamir may have been suspicious by nature, and he may have had reason to mistrust Peres, but the absence of anything specific regarding the parameters of a peace agreement, the "end game," led him to suspect a conspiracy, according to Halevy.[41]

The London Agreement could go nowhere without Shamir's approval, for the government coalition was equally balanced between the Likud and Labor. In the government discussions, the Likud members stood strongly behind Shamir, and Peres did not have the political power to defeat them. Moreover, Peres was not willing to precipitate a coalition crisis by resigning over the issue (as he had reportedly told the Americans he would[42]), presumably because the Labor Party was not prepared to fall from power, though according to Peres it was because his resignation would have required an explanation, thereby violating his promise of secrecy to Hussein.[43]

Beyond the problem of government approval, the other player that was to assist in moving the Agreement along was the United States. However, the Americans were, at best, ambivalent despite the fact that Peres had discussed it with them and, subsequently, claimed that Washington had liked the whole idea.[44] In fact, the US was not particularly interested in an international conference at this time. In response to revived talk of an international conference, in the spring of 1987, Reagan provided hazy, inconclusive responses beyond supporting direct negotiations. Involved in embarrassing Congressional hearings over the Iran–Contra scandal and maneuvering through rapidly changing relations with Moscow, the US administration was neither focused on the Israeli–Arab issue nor willing to bring pressure on either side. In May, Reagan had actually repeated his 1 September 1982 statement that the US would "not support the establishment of an independent Palestinian state in the West Bank and Gaza, nor will we support annexation or permanent control by Israel." US Secretary of State George Schultz, the author of the Reagan Plan, reacted coolly to the London Agreement, though he told Shamir that he was willing to come to the area to discuss it. Shamir suggested that he not come, but he did prevail upon the Americans to help organize a direct meeting with Hussein. Such a meeting did, in fact, take place, in July 1987 in London, with Shamir suggesting Begin's Camp David autonomy plan for Gaza (only). He also agreed to continue talks with Jordan in Washington[45] to deal primarily with practical issues of potential cooperation (in such areas as water, tourism, and so forth), but Hussein, declined, convinced at that point that nothing could come of talks with Shamir. By the end of the year the Palestinian Intifada had broken out, and seven months later Hussein announced Jordan's disengagement from responsibility for the West Bank in favor of the PLO (with the exception of Jordan's administration of the Muslim holy places in Jerusalem). If there had been an opportunity for a breakthrough with the London Agreement, which, in fact, seems totally unlikely, the window for Labor's preferred "Jordanian option" regarding the future of the West Bank was now closed.

The absence of American interest in pushing for a settlement at a time of intense international changes may have been a contributing factor to the failure of the London Agreement. However, the central factors lay within the Israeli leadership: the division of power and the role of ideology. Peres, who negotiated the agreement, had neither the power to pass it nor the will to resign over it. And Shamir and his party, in whose hands the decisive power resided, was dedicated to the ideology of "Greater Israel," diametrically opposed to territorial compromise on the West Bank and inclined to the "Jordan is Palestine" idea. The Labor party was not devoid of similar ideological or at least historic-symbolic considerations to at least part of the West Bank (Jerusalem, Gush Etzion) that may have weakened Peres's struggle to push the London Agreement through the government. Like the Likud, Labor viewed the West Bank as "ours" but supported relinquishing at least some of it. Still, added to these considerations were Labor's unchanged security concerns, part of their ingrained identity-related mistrust of a peace agreement, even with the somewhat more trustworthy (in their eyes) King Hussein. Together these were factors likely to have impeded a genuine breakthrough even if the London Agreement had been seriously considered.

Peace Agreement 1994

By 1994 the regional and global environments had changed drastically, but it took domestic changes within Israel to translate these into factors for a breakthrough. The critical domestic factor was the replacement of the Likud–Shamir government by the election of the Labor Party under the leadership of Rabin. The Intifada, Jordan's disengagement from the West Bank, the 1988 PLO acceptance of the two-state solution, the first Gulf War, the weakening of the PLO, as well as the convening of the Madrid Conference and the beginning of bilateral talks, including Syria, plus the threatened spread of weapons of mass destruction, the emergence of Islamic radicalism, and the collapse of the Soviet Union accompanied by the emergence of the US as the sole super power – all of these could have significantly contributed to a breakthrough for peace, with Jordan as well. They did not do so until the replacement of the Shamir government by Labor in 1992. As we have seen in the discussion of Rabin's motivation for opening talks with the Syrians, all of these factors had led him, and the Labor Party which he now ruled, to seize what he saw as an opportunity and to open talks with all the parties to the conflict.

While the Labor Party platform of 1992 spoke of negotiations with a Jordanian–Palestinian delegation, it also implicitly (not explicitly) provided for the possibility of talks with the PLO. In any case, the platform maintained all the previous specifications of Israeli claims to areas in the West Bank, whatever and with whomever agreement might be reached. In fact, as we have seen, Rabin gave priority to the Syrian track, moving to what he envisaged as a less ambitious track, that of Oslo and the PLO only when the Syrian track seemed less promising. His concept for the West Bank revolved around an interim autonomy agreement rather than a final accord. Insofar as Jordan was in the picture, it would be in connection with the autonomy – despite the fact that Jordan had once again, at the Madrid Conference, declared its readiness to make peace with Israel.[46] Indeed, even after the election of Rabin, the post-Madrid bilateral talks with Jordan[47] did not register much progress, although by the end of October 1992 they had reached agreement on an agenda for eventual peace talks. Israel, however, began to move on the Oslo and Syrian tracks.

Immediately after the 13 September 1993 Oslo Declaration of Principles (DOP) signing on the White House lawn, Israeli and Jordanian representatives signed their agreed agenda and a few weeks later Peres met with Prince Hassan in Washington to discuss economic cooperation. More importantly, on 26 September Rabin met with Hussein in Aqaba, albeit still secretly (though it leaked to Israeli and then foreign media). Rabin reassured the King that the Oslo agreement would not affect Israel's support for the Hashemite regime in Jordan or lead to disregard for Jordan's interests in arrangements that Israel might make with the Palestinians. According to Indyk, Hussein expressed anger over the Oslo agreement with Arafat and the exclusion of Jordan, to which Rabin reportedly answered that it was Jordan that had disengaged from the West Bank, leaving Israel no choice but to deal with the PLO.[48] In any case, at this time, the King was still hesitant about moving quickly to a peace agreement.[49] Most of Rabin's advisors, particularly those involved in the talks with Syria, had gauged that Hussein would not move until and unless there were progress on the Syrian (as well as Palestinian) track.[50] Indyk thought this was, indeed, the problem now.[51] Alternatively, Hussein may simply have been waiting to see what would develop with the two-week-old Oslo agreement. He rejected Rabin's bid to produce a quick agreement and deal with the technical details only later; instead, he proposed working carefully on each aspect of their relations and the issues involved. Discouraged by this hesitancy, Rabin entrusted to deputy Mossad director Ephraim Halevy the task of maintaining contacts with the King (which Halevy had undertaken in the past), characterizing this as merely a "maintenance operation."[52] According to Halevy, Rabin had little patience for Hussein at this point. Moreover, he was reportedly skeptical of Hussein actually going through with an agreement since he had, according to Rabin, gotten cold feet in the past and changed his mind.[53] Yet Shlaim cites Queen Noor to the effect that it was this September 1993 meeting that laid the foundation for the respect and trust that at least Hussein had regarding Rabin.[54]

An incident that almost derailed the potential breakthrough occurred as the result of a secret visit Foreign Minister Peres made to Jordan, at his initiative but accompanied by Halevy at Rabin's request.[55] In a meeting with the King, a four-page document was initialed outlining a peace agreement, including lease of Jordanian lands expropriated by Israel and currently being cultivated by kibbutzim in the area, plus various economic cooperation and other clauses, also calling for normal diplomatic relations and certain Jordanian rights.[56] Upon his return to Israel on 3 November, Peres made mysterious references, on television, to the date as "historic," leading to wide rumors of a secret peace deal between Peres and the King. Hussein was furious because of the breach of promised secrecy at a time when he was not yet sure of the attitudes of Syria and others in the Arab world regarding a Jordanian deal with Israel.[57] The King, therefore, had not been ready to go public just yet. But worse still, Peres had related to the Americans that the talks had produced a breakthrough, precipitating a congratulatory call to Hussein from President Clinton, much to the Jordanian's chagrin.[58] Following this incident Hussein informed Rabin that he wanted to move slowly, and that he preferred that Peres not be included in any future talks.[59]

In a November trip to Damascus, Hussein apparently received a green light from Assad to pursue talks with Israel, but he nonetheless indicated to the Americans that he wanted to work slowly. The absence of urgency on his part may have been due to the fact that the Oslo process had stalled, though Indyk at the time thought there was also a tactical side, to gain greater American support.[60] Rabin, too, was in no hurry in the months that followed, preoccupied perhaps with the problems of beginning implementation of Oslo, and also the resumption in January 1994 of his indirect talks with Syria (following the four-month break he imposed after the signing of Oslo on the grounds that the Israeli public needed time to digest Oslo).

The situation changed entirely in the spring. In his April 1994 visit to Jordan (after his own four-month postponement due to surgery), Halevy reported an entirely different Jordanian attitude: now the King was anxious to reach a speedy agreement.[61] On 11 May Hussein proposed a meeting with Rabin, which took place in London on 19 May. Given the timing, Hussein's change of heart (or tactic) was almost certainly a reaction to the breaking of the logjam in the Oslo process, which was capped by the "Agreement on the Gaza Strip and Jericho" signed in Cairo on 4 May. Both the Syrian and Palestinian tracks now appeared to be moving forward and Jordan might be left out altogether. According to Halevy, Hussein was particularly concerned about Jordanian interests in Jerusalem.[62] There may have been an additional underlying factor (as there had been for Syrian interest in a settlement) – namely, the possibility that progress with Israel would help restore Jordanian relations with the US, lost because of Jordan's support for Saddam in the Gulf War.

Once the King took this decision, matters moved forward quickly. In London, the two leaders agreed to draft a peace treaty, and Rabin agreed for the first time to deal with the issues of Jordanian lands expropriated by Israel, as well as the Israelis' use of water wells on Jordanian territory, and, perhaps most importantly for Hussein, Jordan's rights with regard to the holy sites in East Jerusalem. According to Shlaim, Rabin agreed to give Jordan "special status" in this respect, irrespective of future arrangements with the PLO in the Oslo process.[63] For Rabin, a significant point was Hussein's agreement to public talks in the region – a symbolic gesture of recognition of primarily psychological value. The talks in the region were to be followed by a public "summit" in Washington. Neither of these things had been forthcoming from Syria. For his part, Rabin offered to assist Hussein in his bid to have the Jordanian debt to the US canceled as well as obtain American economic and military aid. As extraordinary as this may sound – Israeli assistance with the US Congress and the White House for an Arab adversary – this had been done before, as early as 1963, when Israel recommended US military sales to Jordan. Israel did, in fact, intervene now on Jordan's behalf. In June, when King Hussein journeyed to Washington, shopping list in hand, Halevy was sent there expressly to fulfill this role. He pressed Ross to consider Jordan's requests with greater flexibility, and at a later stage (in the summer) he organized lobbying efforts on Congress with the help of Israeli Ambassador Rabinovich and members of the Jewish diaspora.[64]

Although the Americans had been somewhat involved, primarily in the form of trips to the region by Secretary of State Christopher and Ross, often with Indyk, their attention had focused on the Syrian track, as we have seen. They were generally well briefed on the Israeli–Jordanian meetings, but they had shown little interest in the Jordanian case up to this point. In fact, Ross and Indyk to some degree viewed the Israeli talks with Jordan as something of a sideshow that would produce very little if there were not the more crucial Syrian deal (in the last they agreed with many of Rabin's advisors), but there was even a tendency to see these moves as a tactic by Rabin to bring pressure on the Palestinians or the Syrians, or both. Nor were the Americans pleased to have their efforts with Syria jeopardized by Rabin's moves toward Jordan, and they communicated or traveled often to Damascus to placate Assad and reassure him of Israel's interests in making peace with Syria. It is possible that the Americans were also less interested because they were not needed; as in the Oslo matter, the protagonists were progressing even without US assistance. Moreover, there was substantial American anger over Jordan's support for "the wrong side" in the war the US had fought against Iraq. While this may not have been the foremost consideration for Clinton, it did affect the US Congress and, therefore, any moves the White House might want to promote on behalf of Jordan. This is why the Israeli and Jewish diaspora assistance would be needed in order to meet Jordan's demands, particularly the request for cancelation of the debt to the US (and help with other country creditors). But more would be needed in order for Washington to concede what Hussein appeared to be presenting as a *quid pro quo*, with Israeli support. As Ross put it: "we would require much greater drama in Jordan's peace-making with Israel" in order to engage Clinton.[65]

The drama Washington sought was a public meeting of Rabin and Hussein, hosted by Clinton, in Washington, and it was in planning this meeting – as well as events surrounding it – that the Americans began to play a major role after Hussein's June visit. Both Rabin and Hussein preferred that their first public meeting take place in the region, prior to Washington, presumably to serve their own domestic purposes. They even set a date for this, much to the Americans' consternation. In response, Indyk exclaimed to Rabin's principal advisor, Eitan Haber, that Israel should treat the White House as something more than the "Kosher caterer."[66] And so it was arranged that there would be a meeting in the region at the ministerial level, followed almost immediately by the Washington show. The "flap" over the location was not the only incident in which the Americans felt they were being made superfluous. When the Americans offered proposals for the Declaration that was to be presented at the White House event now set for 25 July, they found to their surprise that the two parties were already working on it. Only when confronted by the disgruntled Americans, just a few days before the Washington event, Rabin privately showed a draft to Christopher (who was in the region for the ministerial meeting between Shimon Peres and Prime Minister Majali on 20 July). However, Rabin would not give the document to the Americans until almost the last minute, the evening before the White House event, barely in time to have it copied for distribution.

While the Americans were not happy about this treatment, it does not appear that their exclusion was opposition on the part of Rabin to having the Americans involved. Rabin did comment on one occasion that he did not see the purpose of going to the United States for the Declaration since the two leaders lived almost within walking distance of each other.[67] Nonetheless, the reason may simply have been Rabin's desperate fear of a leak, particularly in view of the nearly disastrous effects of the leak after Peres's November meeting with the King. Rabin restricted knowledge of the Declaration to just one or two close associates, excluding Peres up to the last moment – it may be assumed also for personal political reasons.

The price of this strict secrecy was a last minute problem over the wording. Elyakim Rubinstein, the official head of the negotiating team with Jordan, was shown the Declaration in Washington only the day before the signing. Appalled, he pointed out that the phrase stating the "end of belligerency" between the two states was inaccurate; in terms of international law, what was being ended was the "state of war." His legal judgment was upheld by other experts, but it was too late to change the text of the Declaration, for it would have opened the text to demands from those who were now privy to it for the first time. According to Halevy, the solution was proposed by Hussein, who said that he would orally use the term "state of war" in his speech (explaining that the word in Arabic was the same for both belligerency and war).[68] And this is, in fact, what he did, dramatically declaring that the state of war between Jordan and Israel was now terminated.

The whole Washington show was credited to Clinton's "vision and devotion to the cause of peace," as stated in the opening articles of the Declaration. To further assist the White House effort to gain Congressional approval for Jordan's requests, Rabin and Hussein addressed a joint session of Congress together. Halevy stayed on in Washington for a week to work with the Israeli ambassador and diaspora figures in their lobbying effort on behalf of Jordan!

The Declaration itself referred to the previously signed Common Agenda and spelled out future steps, including more immediate confidence-building measures, such as the opening of a border crossing point between the two countries, a direct phone link, and so forth. The only specific commitment, agreed at the London meeting in May, was Israel's respect for the "special role" of Jordan with regard to the Muslim holy places in Jerusalem to be given priority in negotiations on the final status of the city. Such matters as water, borders, and territorial issues were to be negotiated, which they were over the following three months.

Although the confidence-building measures were introduced almost immediately, as promised, the negotiations on the specifics of the final peace treaty were not entirely easy. Teams of experts dealt with the various issues of water, territory, borders, and even refugees, along with security, bilateral relations, cooperation, and so forth. Ross takes credit for the ideas ultimately adopted to overcome an impasse on the territorial issue: namely, what to do with the 340 square kilometers of Jordanian land taken by Israeli kibbutzim over the years – the perennial issue of returning to the 4 June 1967 border albeit in a slightly different form.[69] Meeting with Prince Hassan, he proposed land swaps as well as leasing and other arrangements, and Hassan countered with ideas over water arrangements. Shlaim attributes the solution to the Israeli and Jordanian negotiators, with the two leaders stepping in to resolve problems and details throughout.[70] It was agreed that the border would be adjusted by means of equal-sized land swaps so that the Israelis could continue farming the lands they had taken.[71] In other areas, to be under Jordanian sovereignty, there would be special arrangements or leasing. Further, Israel would provide Jordan with water, based on quantities used by Israel from the Jordanian wells and on future water projects. The various teams produced a draft, and Shlaim recounts that, in the end, it was Rabin and Hussein themselves who worked out the final details in an all-night session at the Royal Palace outside Amman. The Peace Treaty was signed, in the presence of Clinton, in Jordan on 26 October 1994.

There can be little doubt that the major factor enabling, finally, the breakthrough with Jordan was the Oslo Accords. Primarily, of course, the fact that the Palestinians had reached their own accord (to the consternation of King Hussein)[72] freed the Jordanians to move on their own interests without being accused of harming the Palestinian cause or breaking ranks. On the contrary; the Oslo Accords aroused fears in Hussein of being totally ignored in the emerging peace process, shut out of the economic boom that might accompany a change in the status of the West Bank, and possibly even subject to Israel–Palestinian pressure for a Palestinian takeover of Jordan. Thus, Oslo not only freed Hussein to act but actually spurred him into action. However, the critical element in terms of a possible breakthrough was the fact that once the PLO was negotiating for itself, the topic of the West Bank, with its deal-breaking issues (Israel's territorial demands) was no longer a matter for Jordanian–Israeli peace talks. Even the issue of Jerusalem could be treated in a more promising manner since the overall status of East Jerusalem – now to be negotiated between Israel and the PLO – was of less concern to Hussein so long as Jordan maintained its "special role" in regard to the holy places in the city. While negotiations on this and other matters remained necessary, the major barriers impeding agreement since 1967 were now almost totally removed from the agenda. The territories of importance to Israel, for historic or religious or even security reasons, lay within the West Bank rather than what was left of the border between the two countries, along the desert from the Dead Sea to Aqaba. There were no Israeli settlers on the Jordanian side of the border in the south, and there had been little change in the armistice lines of 1949 in the area. What changes or arrangements had intervened were dealt with relatively easily by means of land swaps, leasing, and water sharing.

That fact that the problems were relatively easily overcome (by comparison to negotiations with the Syrians or the Palestinians) attested to a large degree to the factor of trust. Mistrust had played a major role in the past, as we have seen, underlying the demand to hold on to the Jordan Rift Valley – under

110 *Jordan Again: Failures and Breakthrough*

Map 5.1 Israeli–Jordanian Peace Treaty 1994
Source: Laura Zittrain and Neil Caplan, *Negotiating Arab–Israeli Peace*, second ed., 2010, reprinted with permission of Indiana University Press

Israeli sovereignty – with the Jordan River as Israel's eastern (security) border. The presumption was that a peace treaty would not provide Israeli security since a treaty would not prevent an Iraqi or Syrian invasion across that line and into Israeli population centers. The risk factor was, apparently, lower, making it easier to place trust in an accord. Whether it was the difference of risk between the West Bank border and the Arava border, on the one hand, or the relationship of trust between the two leaders, on the other, or both, is difficult to know.

Trust may not have been sufficient to override all the past security concerns with regard to Jordan. For example, several clauses were deemed necessary regarding the non-use of territory for belligerency against the other, including a ban on the stationing of other countries' troops or entering alliances or agreements with hostile third parties. There was also a clause against entering any obligation that conflicted with the Treaty, similar to but less stark than

Begin's insistence in the 1979 treaty with Egypt that the peace with Israel be given priority over any other possibly threatening (for Israel) agreement. Far more illustrative of trust was the reference in the Treaty itself to basing "security relations on mutual trust," joint interests and cooperation, and efforts toward a regional framework for peace. This element of trust, as a factor of security, was borne out by the absence of any mechanism or need for third-party peacekeepers, monitoring, or the stationing of troops, early-warning stations and the like – in short, there was to be nothing beyond the usual border facilities for neighboring states at peace with each other. And the actual measures agreed to (leasing of land for Israeli use, water sharing, and so forth) attest to the degree of trust achieved.

Trust within the final agreement was also the product of the trust built at the leadership level. Both leaders had begun skeptically, with Rabin worried about the possibility that Hussein might retreat. For this reason, Rabin wanted to work swiftly so as not to lose momentum after the Washington Declaration (in stark contrast to his measured attitude toward the Syrian talks). In fact, even a week before the final signing, Rabin reportedly told Halevy to watch over Hussein lest he back down now that agreement had been reached.[73] This was not a case of doubting Hussein's sincerity (as it was with Rabin's concerns about Assad); rather, it was an awareness of the very real problems Hussein would face in making this step and his strength to take them on. The two had, in fact, developed a good deal of trust quite rapidly once they had begun the process of working together. Both Rabin and Hussein spoke of their personal bond and mutual understanding as soldiers as well as statesmen. At the signing ceremony in the Arava, Rabin said:

> Your Majesty, Peace between states is peace between peoples. It is an expression of trust and esteem. I have learned to know and admire the quiet and the smiling power with which you guard your nation and the courage with which you lead your people. It is not only our states that are making peace with each other today, not only our nations that are shaking hands in peace here in the Arava. You and I, your Majesty, are making peace here, our own peace, the peace of soldiers and the peace of friends.[74]

Some of the same element of trust had developed between their aides, particularly between Halevy and the King, over the years of secret contacts as well as in the negotiations.

Leadership may, in fact, have been a critical factor in the Jordan–Israeli peace, not only because of the direct role played by both Rabin and Hussein in the negotiations, but also more basically because of the leaders' decisions to reach peace. As in the case of Egypt, an essential factor was an Arab leader, Hussein, who had the political will to make a separate peace with Israel. Hussein's frequent consultations with Assad and references to the need for comprehensive peace attested to his trepidations. Thus, leadership and courage were part of this political will, though much less so for Rabin than for Hussein;

112 *Jordan Again: Failures and Breakthrough*

nevertheless, flexibility on the part of an Israeli leader was also critical (as was the case with Begin earlier).[75] On the issues that might have made matters difficult for Rabin domestically, such as the refugee issue which Hussein insisted upon noting, the agreed wording in the Treaty was general, referring to the problem as one created by "the conflict in the Middle East." At the same time, Rabin demonstrated flexibility (and sensitivity) with regard to Jordanian concerns by including a clause against the "involuntary movements of persons in such a way as to adversely prejudice the security of either Party" (i.e., the "transfer" of Palestinians to Jordan, occasionally advocated by extreme right-wing politicians in Israel).

For Rabin, however, both the Palestinian and Syrian issues were far more difficult – and demanded far more political courage – in terms of domestic public opinion than the Jordanian issues. While Rabin's popularity had fallen because of the terrorist attacks accompanying the implementation of Oslo, Israelis generally held a positive attitude toward King Hussein.[76] So long as the issue was not the West Bank, agreement with Jordan was, therefore, not a problematic matter for the vast majority of Israelis. Nonetheless, it was still necessary to overcome fears and latent suspicions that the King might not, in fact, go through with his promises – the familiar element lack of public trust in the adversary. A major step in overcoming this was Hussein's agreement to a top-level meeting held in the region itself, just prior to the Washington Declaration. In addition, implementation of the confidence-building measures announced in the Declaration, such as the opening of a crossing point in the south, the installation of direct telephone connections and other measures, was begun almost immediately after Washington, even before the final peace treaty was signed. Perhaps the most effective step, emotionally for Israelis, was Hussein's 3 August flyover of Jerusalem, speaking to Rabin by radio from his royal jet (which he himself piloted). And unlike the case with Assad, the Jordanian leader was willing to meet publicly with the Israeli Prime Minister before the signing of the peace treaty. These steps may have contributed to the overwhelming support for the Israeli–Jordanian Peace Treaty by 86.5 percent of the Israeli public.[77]

The Israeli political scene was also positive. There was party support across the board, with an almost total absence of spoilers. This may have been due to the same risk/trust calculations we have already mentioned regarding the Arava border as distinct from the West Bank. Clinton later wrote: "Unlike the Palestinian agreement, which many Israelis opposed, the Jordan peace pact had the support of nearly everyone in the Knesset, including the leader of the Likud opposition, Benjamin 'Bibi' Netanyahu. The Israelis admired and trusted King Hussein ... ."[78] Even those members of the right wing who had advocated a "Jordan is Palestine" policy found little to oppose in a peace agreement with Jordan exclusive of the West Bank. Ariel Sharon, the main supporter of the Jordan is Palestine idea, merely abstained in a Knesset vote on the Treaty rather than spoil the atmosphere of general approval. The final vote was 105 in favor, 3 opposed, 6 abstained. The only discordant note, though not of a spoiler nature, was the Rabin–Peres feud. The aborted London Agreement (and Peres's failure to resign over it), together with, and especially because of, the leaked November 1993 meeting, led Hussein to demand that Peres be excluded from the negotiations. However, Rabin went much further by preventing Peres from playing almost any role, or, occasionally, even knowing about the talks, much less their content. Peres was, in fact, humiliated and did not hesitate to speak of it. Similarly to the case of his reaction to the 1978 Camp David accords (with regard to the settlements), Peres expressed misgivings about the agreement to grant Jordan a special role in Jerusalem, telling Halevy it was "a very big mistake."

In any case, for Israeli decision-makers, once the West Bank was left for the Oslo process, conditions were ripe for the peace treaty with Jordan: direct channels of communication existed and a degree of mutual trust had developed over the years; both leaderships were interested in making peace and willing to be flexible. In Israel domestic support was assured and regional acquiescence was likely since both Syria and the Palestinians were involved with their own peace processes with Israel as well. The international environment may have contributed, indirectly, since the withdrawal of Soviet involvement in the region affected both Syria and the PLO. The loss of Soviet support was a factor in the decisions of both Damascus and the PLO to pursue agreements with Israel. In turn, insofar as Jordan's position was influenced – either by Syria's acquiescence to Jordanian talks with Israel or by the Oslo breakthrough, or both, the international environment would have been a factor. Moreover, Jordan's interest in repairing its post-Gulf war relationship with Washington and receiving military equipment as well as debt relief may well have been an additional motivating factor for Hussein. In this connection, the Jewish diaspora in America, engaged by Israel in support of Jordan's requests, became a factor as well, assisting Clinton with a possibly recalcitrant Congress.

While the role of the United States was not central throughout, it would appear to have been a necessary factor. This was not always evident by the behavior of the Israelis and Jordanians, ignoring the Americans and even excluding them from information as well as participation. Yet, Washington at the very least provided an incentive for Jordan in the form of improved relations with Washington or concrete benefits, such as debt relief and military equipment. Clinton's public involvement accorded legitimacy to the undertaking, an element suggested, for example, by Rabin's requests for Clinton to address the Knesset (which Clinton did the day after the treaty signing). Once onboard, Clinton provided a leadership role, both in his personal reassurances to Assad and his appearances in the region, but mainly in his efforts to move matters forward to a public conclusion through the cultivation of a relationship of trust with the King.

Rabin was bursting with confidence when he presented the Treaty to the Knesset 25 October 1994, and he addressed a key element of Israeli identity that had often impeded breakthrough in the past: "The peace treaty [with Jordan] is not merely of political significance, but a basic, essential change in our very existence here – no more: 'a people that shall dwell alone.' This is a profound, thorough change, a change that will affect every walk of our lives."

Notes

1 Yehuda Lukacs, *Israel, Jordan and the Peace Process* (New York, NY: Syracuse University Press, 1999): 181–182.
2 Avi Shlaim, *Lion of Jordan* (London: Allen Lane, 2007): 366–369 relates the interesting saga of Jordanian and Israeli efforts to avoid the opening of an Israeli front with Jordan and limiting the direct military exchanges that did occur on the Golan, including one episode that avoided attacking while Hussein was visiting the Jordanian forces in Syria during the war. King Hussein had secretly traveled to Israel in late September 1973 to warn Israel of Syrian plans to launch the war (a meeting thoroughly documented by Israel even on film). See, Uri Bar-Josef, *The Watchman Fell Asleep* (Albany, NY: SUNY University Press, 2005): 89–90; Mordecai Gazit to *Ha'aretz*, 10 January 1998; Yigal Kipnis, *1973: Ha-derekh La-Milhamah* [*1973: The Road to War*] (Tel Aviv: Kinneret, Zamora Bitan and Dvir, 2012): 178–180, though Shlaim, 2007: 364, presents a different interpretation of Hussein's message).
3 Shlaim, 2007: 376–378, has excerpts from the actual text of the 7 March conversation between Golda, Dayan, Rifai, and the King.
4 JTA, 5 August 1969 (http://archive.jta.org/article/1969/08/06/2950433/labor-party-fails-to-act-on-dayan-proposal.).
5 Archive Labor Party, Beit Berl, Platform 1973.
6 Israel Ministry of Foreign Affairs (MFA), Rabin Speeches, 1974–1977. This is virtually word for word the formulation of the party's platform of 1973.
7 *Ibid*. The NRP joined in September 1974.
8 This distinction was repeated over the following months in response to rumors of the Jordanian suggestions for Israeli withdrawal of 10 or 15 kilometers from the Jordan River (i.e., from the Jordan Rift Valley) (see, e.g., Rabin interviews to *Yedioth Aharonoth*, 26 July 1974, and Israel Army Radio, 10 August 1974).
9 Moshe Zak, "Rabin ve Hussein," in Josef Nevo (Ed.), *Shkhenim Be-mavoch: Yahasei Yisrael–Yarden Lifnei Heskem Ha-shalom Ve-aharav* [*Neighbors in a Bind: Israel–Jordan Relations before the Peace Agreement*] (Tel Aviv: Yitzhak Rabin Center, 2004): 111–112; Shlaim, 2007: 382; Shimon Peres, *Battling for Peace* (New York, NY: Random House, 1995).
10 National Archive (US), 1552842, "Memorandum of Conversation," 6 November 1974 (Ford conversation with Israeli Charge d'Affaires, Mordecai Shalev).
11 Speech to the Knesset, 3 June 1974 (MFA, Vol. 3: 1974–1977).
12 Interview with Israel Army Radio, 10 August 1974.
13 Israel television, 20 September 1974 (MFA, Vol. 3: 1974–1977).
14 Shimon Peres, *David's Sling* (London: Weidenfeld and Nicholson, 1970): 259. By the 1990s, Peres apparently changed his estimate to a more positive one of Hussein (Peres, 1995: 260–261).
15 Created in April 1974 as an ideological wing of the NRP.
16 An interviewer tried to draw Rabin out over this disagreement; *Yedioth Aharonoth*, 26 July 1974.
17 Matti Golan, *The Secret Conversations of Henry Kissinger* (New York, NY: Quadrangle/*New York Times* Books, 1976): 226.
18 Rabin had returned from duty as ambassador to Washington only months before the war, and he joined Meir's government, as minister of labor, only after the 31 December 1973 elections.

19 A poll mid-1974 showed 65 percent of Israelis favoring the return of none or only a small part of the West Bank (Asher Arian, *Security Threatened* (Cambridge, MA: Cambridge University Press, 1995): 102.
20 Interview to *Davar*, 16 September 1974 (MFA).
21 FRUS, Arab–Israeli Dispute 1969–1976, XXVI, Doc. 110, "Draft Telegram from Secretary of State Kissinger to the President's Deputy Assistant for National Security Affairs (Scowcroft), undated (to be passed to the President)". Nigel Ashton, *King Hussein of Jordan* (New Haven, NY: Yale University Press, 2008): 180, too quotes similar sentiments delivered by Kissinger to the British Foreign and Commonwealth Secretary earlier in January 1974.
22 In response to interviewers' questions about US pressure to deal with Jordan, Rabin on one occasion challenged the term "pressure" and on another occasion said: "I don't think that the USA is presently trying to influence us as to which state to choose" (*Yedioth Aharonoth*, 26 July 1974; Israel Army Radio, 10 August 1974 (MFA). He repeated this in September but suggested that the US preferred Egypt in order to keep the Soviets out (interview to Israel Television, 16 September 1974, MFA).
23 Henry Kissinger, *The White House Years* (Boston, MA: Little, Brown, 1979): 1141.
24 Interview to Israel Television, 16 September 1974 (MFA).
25 FRUS, Arab–Israeli Dispute, 1969–1976, XXVI, Doc. 168, "Memorandum of Conversation," 31 March 1975. Some months after Rabat, on 28 March 1975, Senator George McGovern held a secret meeting with Arafat in Beirut in which they discussed the possibility of a Palestinian state limited to the West Bank and Gaza. Arafat's responses were actually positive but also contradictory (FRUS, XXVI 1969–1976, Doc.167, "Telegram from the Embassy in Lebanon to the Department of State," 29 March 1975).
26 FRUS XXVI, Doc. 112, "Memorandum from the President's Deputy Assistant for National Security Affairs (Scowcroft) to President Ford," 30 October 1974.
27 FRUS, XXVI, Doc. 99, "Memorandum of Conversation," 10 September 1974. The Israeli government decided formally, before Rabat (FRUS, XXVI, Doc. 107, "Memorandum from the President's Deputy Assistant for National Security (Scowcroft) to President Ford," 14 October 1974.
28 IDF radio, 10 August 1974 (MFA).
29 Interview, *Yedioth Aharonoth*, 26 July 1972.
30 IDF Radio, 10 August 1974.
31 Interview to *Davar*, 16 September 1974, following a trip to Washington.
32 Shlaim, 2007: 429.
33 "Codification of Policy Prohibiting Negotiations with the Palestine Liberation Organization," in US Senate and US House of Representatives, Committee on Foreign Relations and Committee on Foreign Affairs, Legislation on Foreign Relations through 1987, Vol. 1 (Washington, DC: US Government Printing Office, March 1988): 529–530.
34 There are a number of explanations – some contradictory – for the collapse of the Hussein–Arafat agreement. See, for example, Ashton, 2008: 245.
35 Peres, 1995: 267; Shlaim, 2007: 434. Yeshayahu Ben-Porat, *Sihot 'im Yossi Beilin* [*Conversations with Yossi Beilin*] (Tel Aviv: Hakibbutz Hameuchad, 1996): 89–94.
36 The Jordan River was now called Israel's "security border," wording that had crept in over the years; but since Israeli sovereignty was to be maintained as well as a presence, the change was not particularly meaningful (*Platform of the Alignment for the Eleventh Knesset*, July 1984, Labor Party Archive, Beit Berl).
37 Shlaim, 2007: 443. The London Agreement may be found in Laura Zittrain Eisenberg and Neil Caplan, *Negotiating Israeli–Arab Peace* (Bloomington, IN: Indiana University Press, 2010): 195.

38 Shlaim, 2007: 446, citing a *New York Times* report, 13 May 1987.
39 Shlaim, 2007: 449.
40 Ephraim Halevy, *Man in the Shadows* (New York, NY: St. Martin's Press, 2008): 12. (Halevy, of the Mossad, had accompanied Peres to the London meeting.)
41 *Ibid*. See also Yitzhak Shamir's autobiography, *Summing Up* (Boston, MA: Little, Brown and Company, 1994): 169.
42 Shlaim, 2007: 445.
43 Peres, 1995: 270.
44 Peres, 1995: 267, 270, said he had coordinated with Washington and had both prior and post London enthusiastic support from Schultz, Thomas Pickering (ambassador to Tel Aviv), and Richard Murphy (special representative to the Middle East).
45 Washington had suggested tacking on a meeting to the tail end of a super power summit (Shlaim, 2007: 450).
46 Lukacs, 1999: 186.
47 Despite Shamir's insistence that Palestinians participate only as part of the Jordanian delegation to Madrid, during the bilateral talks the delegation divided into bilaterals of each with Israel.
48 Martin Indyk, *Innocent Abroad: An Intimate Account of American Peace Diplomacy in the Middle East* (New York, NY: Simon and Schuster, 2009): 95. See, also, Zak, in in Nevo, 2004: 94–97.
49 Shlaim, 2007: 525–526.
50 Uri Sagie, *Orot Ba-'arafel* [*Lights in the Fog*] (Tel Aviv: Yedioth Sfarim, 1998): 189, 203–204. (Sagie claims this to have been the consensus at a meeting in Washington on 26 August 1993, which included Ehud Barak, Danny Rothchild, Elyakim Rubinstein, and Deputy Defense Minister Mota Gur.)
51 Indyk, 2009: 95.
52 Halevy, 2008: 3.
53 Shlaim, 2007: 529.
54 Shlaim, 2007: 526, citing Queen Noor, *Leap of Faith* (London: Weidenfeld and Nicholson, 2003): 364.
55 Indyk, 2009: 100; Halevy, 2008, though all of these sources and others describe the incident, the same way.
56 Shlaim, 2007: 528–529.
57 Shlaim, 2007: 529; Indyk, 2009: 103.
58 Ashton, 2008: 302–303 said an angry letter had been sent to Hussein by Arafat as well.
59 Indyk, 2009: 103.
60 Indyk, 2009: 104.
61 Halevy, 2008: 83. See also, Marwan Muasher, *The Arab Center* (New Haven, CT: Yale University Press, 2008): 29.
62 Halevy, 2008: 82. Jordan also wanted to be party to discussions of refugee issues (Muasher, 2008: 29).
63 Shlaim, 2007: 534.
64 Shlaim, 2007: 538–539. See also Halevy, 2008: 93.
65 Dennis Ross, *The Missing Peace: The Inside Story of the Fight for Middle East Peace* (New York, NY: Farrar, Straus and Giroux, 2005): 172.
66 Ross, 2005: 179.
67 Halevy, 2008: 91–92.
68 Halevy, 2008: 94–96. Ross, 2005: 184, has a different version, claiming that Rabin wanted more than an "end of belligerency"; but the King was not yet ready to go further. In fact, neither Hussein nor Rabin had noticed the matter; Rabin, as in the 1974–1975 talks with Egypt, had unsuccessfully sought agreement to the end of belligerency – something short of "end of war."

69 Ross, 2005: 186. This was not land necessarily taken in war (like the Golan or the West Bank), but rather desert areas gradually cultivated, in a sort of creeping annexation, by Israel.
70 Shlaim, 2007: 541–542.
71 The text of the treaty may be found in Zittrain Eisenberg and Neil Caplan, 2010: 217–228. Quotations below are from the official Israeli version, MFA.
72 He was angered by the surprise – Arafat told him of the Oslo talks only on 23 August 1993 – and also because, according to Shlaim, he had sought to work together with the PLO in the post-Madrid talks in order to preserve Palestinian interests (Shlaim, 2007: 516–524).
73 Halevy, 2008: 214.
74 Rabin speech, "Signing Ceremony of Israel-Jordan Peace Treaty," 26 October 1994 (MFA, Press Room, 1994).
75 Hussein would have a more difficult task of explaining peace with Israel to his predominantly Palestinian population. "Address to the Nation," 15 November 1994 (www.kinghussein.gov.jo/speeches_letters.html).
76 A September 1994 poll asked about the credibility of Arab leaders: 75 percent thought Jordan's King Hussein was credible, while 7.5 percent ascribed that quality to Arafat (42 percent said they were frightened by him). Some 48.5 percent saw Hussein as honest, 0.9 percent Arafat. (Dan Leon, "Israeli Public Opinion Polls on the Peace Process," *Palestine–Israel Journal*, 2(1), 1995: 57, citing Modi'in Ezrahi poll).
77 Tamar Hermann and Ephraim Yaar, *Peace Index*, October 1994 (Israel Democracy Institute).
78 Bill Clinton, *My Life: The Presidential Years* (New York, NY: Vintage Books, 2005): 626.

6 Oslo I
Breakthrough and Failure

The breakthrough

The Oslo Accords between Israel and the Palestine Liberation Organization constituted the most significant breakthrough since the 1979 Israeli–Egyptian peace agreement. Moreover, they were perhaps the most important breakthrough altogether for Israel inasmuch as these Accords opened the way to resolution of the issue at the heart of the Arab–Israeli conflict, the conflict with the Palestinians over Palestine/*Eretz Israel*. The Oslo Accords became possible, first of all, because of the November 1988 PLO decision to declare a state (with East Jerusalem as its capital) based on United Nations General Assembly (UNGA) Resolution 181 that had called for the creation of "a Jewish state and an Arab state" in Palestine, to accept United Nations Security Council (UNSC) Resolution 242 that carries with it the right of all states in the region "to live in peace within recognized and secure borders," and to reject the use of violence or terror. This decision was followed by more explicit renunciations of terror, virtually dictated by the Americans, in a speech by Arafat to a 13 December 1988 UN meeting in Geneva, as well as in a press conference three days later, which included the explicit recognition of Israel's right to exist.[1]

These moves by the PLO were the culmination of nearly 15 years of often bloody internal debates over the ultimate objective: a Palestinian state in all of Palestine with the destruction of Israel (as stated in the PLO charter of 1965), or a two-state solution with the creation of a Palestinian state in 22 percent of mandated Palestine, next to the state of Israel.[2] The Intifada in the occupied territories, initiated by local Palestinians in December 1987, was probably the most important factor leading to the 1988 decision, not only attesting to the insufferable situation of the Palestinians under occupation but also challenging the PLO leadership in Tunis to break the impasse that maintained the occupation. A number of other factors contributed as well, such as the expulsion of the PLO leadership from Lebanon to relatively distant Tunisia as a result of the Lebanon War of 1982; the repeated failure of the Arab states to defeat Israel or intervene to save the PLO (as evidenced in the Lebanon War); and a longstanding interest in reaching the Americans, intensified by the weakening of Soviet support as Gorbachev changed Moscow's attitude toward the PLO, calling for a "balance of interests" between Israel and the Palestinians in his meeting with Arafat in Moscow in 1986.[3]

In one sense, the 1988 PLO decisions were analogous to Sadat's 1977 decision to go to Jerusalem. They represented the change on the adversary's side that was essential for a breakthrough. However, there were a number of other factors, for Israel, that would, in fact, turn these decisions into the breakthrough they enabled, transforming the conflict.

The Shamir government had already rejected not only the Peres–Hussein London Plan in 1987, but also proposals by US Secretary of State Schultz in 1988. The PLO statement and Arafat's speech did nothing to change Shamir's deep-seated belief that the Jewish state would never be accepted by the Arabs, US-induced Palestinian statements notwithstanding. Indeed, prior to Arafat's press conference the Israeli PM termed the UN speech a "monumental act of deception,"[4] and he subsequently criticized the opening of the US–PLO dialogue that followed the speech. Nonetheless, the Americans expected some kind of official reaction, and it did come, in the form of an Israeli "peace initiative" announced in May 1989. This plan explicitly ruled out both negotiations with the PLO and the creation of a Palestinian state. Although it was presented as a plan of Prime Minister Shamir and Labor Party Defense Minister Rabin, Rabin explained in subsequent interviews that it was, in fact, his plan.[5] It was a replica of the 1978 autonomy plan with its call for elections in the territories for a delegation to discuss an interim period of autonomy. The only new element was a call for negotiations with all of Israel's adversaries in the region for a comprehensive peace agreement. For Rabin, this may have been a genuine initiative to try to end the Arab–Israeli conflict due to his concerns over developments in the region, in particular, Iranian nuclear plans, as well as the Intifada that had broken out.[6] Despite the explicit rejection of the PLO, there were, at this time, factions of Rabin's own party less opposed to speaking with the PLO, and members of Labor were, in fact, meeting privately not only with West Bank Palestinian leaders known to be associated with the PLO, but also with PLO officials in track two meetings abroad.[7] Similarly, in response to the PLO's November 1988 decision, the more or less mainstream peace movement Peace Now had already held a massive rally in Tel Aviv in December under the slogan "Speak Peace with the PLO Now." Thus, there were changes taking place outside and inside Israel at the time, ultimately producing the breakthrough of Oslo in 1993.

Chronologically, we have the following. The Iraqi invasion of Kuwait in August 1990 brought about an American commitment to seek resolution of the Arab–Israeli conflict once the Gulf crisis was resolved. This "sequential linkage," as distinct from Saddam's demand for direct linkage (withdrawal from Kuwait/Israeli withdrawal from the occupied territories) was a promise the US gave both to Syria and Gorbachev for their agreement to the creation of the anti-Iraq coalition. In compliance, the US (with the Soviets), convened the Madrid Conference in 1991, with Syrian participation (unlike the 1973

120   Oslo I: Breakthrough and Failure

Geneva Conference) and local Palestinians as members of the Jordanian delegation. US pressure ensured Shamir's agreement to the conference, with a promise that the PLO would not participate and the US would not support the creation of a Palestinian state. After the formal opening, the parties divided into prolonged bilateral and multilateral talks with regional and international participation. On leaving office Shamir had this to say of the Madrid process: "In my public activity I know how to display the tactics of moderation, but without conceding anything on the goal – the integrity of the Land of Israel ... I would have carried on autonomy talks for ten years and meanwhile we would have reached half a million [Jewish] people in Judea and Samaria."[8] Although the 22 June 1992 elections had brought Labor to power, with Rabin as prime minister, the bilateral Israeli–Palestinian–Jordanian talks faltered and, in January 1993, Israel began secret back-channel talks with the PLO in Oslo. Born of informal Israeli–PLO contacts, these talks were authorized by deputy Foreign Minister Yossi Beilin and Foreign Minister Shimon Peres and initially conducted in a track two Norwegian conference with Norwegian Foreign Ministry involvement. When this Oslo channel showed significant progress, Rabin made it official, though still secret, by sending Uri Savir, director general of the Foreign Ministry, to lead the talks in May 1993.[9] The PLO delegation was already being led by Arafat's close associate, PLO executive member Abu Ala.

The success of the Oslo talks, which produced the Declaration of Principles (DOP) and Letters of Mutual Recognition that opened the Oslo Accords, was due to a number of specific factors linked to the negotiations themselves (described in penetrating if contradictory detail by both Uri Savir and Abu Ala).[10] The track two (unofficial), informal, and secret nature of the talks were all critical, for the negotiators were able freely to suggest and weigh alternatives, change positions, and consult others, even after the arrival of Savir and the legal advisor to the Israeli Foreign Ministry, Yoel Singer. The degree of personal trust that developed facilitated compromises, assisted by informal interventions on the part of the Norwegian hosts and even intermediation between the Norwegians and Arafat.[11] It helped that the Israeli negotiators, the two academics who initiated the process, Ron Pundak and Yair Hirshfeld, were determined peace advocates long engaged in efforts to find a solution to the conflict, as was Uri Savir. A similar determination was evident among their Palestinian interlocutors – a determination that led the PLO negotiators to accept compromises on important issues, such as acquiescence to the Israeli demand (specified by Rabin) that Jerusalem not be included in the autonomy arrangements, or that settlement construction not be mentioned (since the Labor Party had already declared its commitment to such a freeze).[12] As in the case of the 1978 Camp David agreement with the Egyptians, side letters were used on points the sides could not agree upon for the DOP – namely, a commitment by the Palestinians to end the Intifada and a commitment by Israel not to close PLO institutions in East Jerusalem, conveyed to Norwegian Foreign Minister Holst. While the Palestinians did win some concessions, significantly the inclusion of a West Bank town, Jericho, in addition to Gaza for the initial agreement,[13] asymmetry of power favored Israel and was perceivable in the outcome. But it was not simply a matter of weakness; a further factor for success was the fact that Arafat wanted the Oslo talks to succeed. The Israelis (and Americans) attributed this to Arafat's interest in gaining a physical foothold in the territories so as to assert his leadership over the increasingly active local Palestinians and also to meet the emerging challenge from the relatively new Hamas.[14] Indeed, both the Israelis and the Americans believed that Arafat purposely stalled and complicated the bilateral talks in Washington (between only local Palestinians as per Israel's Madrid related demands[15]) in order to demonstrate both his leadership and control, along with the priority of the Oslo channel, where the PLO was directly involved. On the Israeli side, Rabin was not keen to deal with the PLO; he had given the green light to the Oslo track with, apparently, little expectation that it would lead to anything.[16] He became somewhat more interested following receipt of a letter from Arafat and Holst's account of a meeting with Arafat, both during a critical period in the talks in mid-July, tending to indicate that the PLO leader was serious about reaching agreement.[17] Peres described the letter as reflecting "qualities of moderation and responsible statesmanship" not always apparent in public or diplomatic encounters with Arafat.[18] Nonetheless, still skeptical of Arafat's intentions, Rabin continued to prefer the talks taking place with Syria via the Americans, as we have seen. It was only when that track fell behind the successful Oslo channel that Rabin opted for agreement with the PLO in August 1993.[19]

Beyond the specific factors that made for the successful talks in Oslo, a number of underlying factors accounted for the historic breakthrough in the conflict represented by what became known as the Oslo Accords (ultimately, some seven agreements, including the DOP and the Interim Agreement known as Oslo II, plus additional protocols and the Letters of Mutual Recognition). An important domestic factor was the significant change that had occurred within the Israeli public over the years. For example, the aforementioned peace demonstration urging talks with the PLO could not have been expected to take place ten years earlier. During the ensuing period, the Lebanon war had occurred, dividing the Israeli public (as well as its powerful diaspora abroad) for the first time during actual wartime. The Israeli role in the Sabra and Chatila massacres, condemned by an unprecedented 400,000 strong demonstration in Tel Aviv, further divided the public regarding the conflict.[20] While not immediately reflected in election results – due to a number of generally unrelated factors within the Israeli electorate, opinion polls over the 1980s were showing a gradual increase in Israelis' willingness to compromise over the occupied territories. This gradual change showed an upward swing toward willingness to compromise during the Intifada.[21] Indeed, the Intifada, which to a large degree precipitated the 1988 PLO decisions, played a very large – perhaps even the central – role in the "ripeness" of the Israeli public for the Oslo Accords.

The Intifada, while a basically unarmed uprising, nonetheless threatened Israelis' personal security within the country as well as within the occupied territories, due to knifings, Molotov cocktails, and the like. Perhaps more importantly, the uprising demonstrated that the *status quo*, which had been favored by most Israelis, could not be sustained. The Palestinians would no longer quietly acquiesce to the occupation, and the now apparent dynamic did not seem to be working in Israel's favor. In other terms, it was becoming clear that, perhaps, these territories were not enhancing Israel's security but possibly actually harming it. Even security-related self-interest appeared to dictate a change and a willingness to compromise. This did not reflect altered convictions about the Palestinians or the Palestinians' cause, however.[22] Polls indicated that hatred and fear of the Palestinians, rather than understanding or sympathy, increased among Israelis during the Intifada.[23] A certain war-weariness (more like "fed-up"; "had enough of this conflict") may also have been at play among the public, as people speaking to the media or simply in casual comment often expressed the wish to just get on with their lives, without all the turmoil of the conflict.[24] This attitude may even have been connected with globalization, which was bringing significant changes to Israel's economy, and society. The dismantling of much of the welfare state, privatization, competition, consumerism, and individualism were all developments that affected solidarity, willingness to make sacrifices or tolerate risks. For many, they prompted a more calculating cost/benefit analysis of the relative value of holding onto or abandoning the territories.[25]

These were the sentiments that led to the election of Rabin in 1992. By the time the Oslo Accords were made public, there had been significant changes in Israeli attitudes from those before the Intifada, both with regard to the occupied territories and Israel's future prospects. Polls indicated a 20 percent decline between 1987 and 1993 in Israelis' confidence that the country could win another war against the Arab states (a decline probably related later to the 1991 Gulf War SCUD attacks on Israel); but this sentiment had also been accompanied by a sharp rise in the belief that peace was possible, prompted most likely by the convening of the 1991 Madrid Conference, but sustained in the polls of 1993 as well.[26] And support for returning part or all of the territories had risen to an astonishing high of 71 percent by the beginning of September 1993 (a week before the Oslo Accords).[27] It was not surprising, therefore, that the Oslo Declaration of Principles, signed on 13 September 1993, received 65 percent support in Israeli public opinion.

Many of the factors that led to the changes in Israeli public opinion were instrumental in bringing about the shift in Israeli policy that came with the new leadership of the Labor Party and Rabin. As we saw with regard to Syria, Rabin came to power with the purpose of reaching peace agreements. His evaluation of changes and developments in the domestic, regional, and international environments had led him to believe in the possibility and, indeed, necessity of doing so. The collapse of the Soviet Union, which weakened previously anti-Western Arab states, and the emergence of Israel's closest supporter, the United States, as the world's dominant power, including in the Middle East in the wake of the American show of force in the Iraq War, begat increased interest by the Arab states in positive relations with Washington. This interest was also augmented by the perceived threat to their regimes from Islamic extremism. All of these developments were understood by Rabin as creating an opportunity for Israel, as we have noted. Some of these same factors had played a role in the PLO's 1988 decisions; but the final dissolution of the Soviet Union and, particularly, the PLO's support for Saddam Hussein in the Iraq War had virtually crippled the organization by causing it to lose its main financial backers, Saudi Arabia, in addition to the loss of political backing from Moscow. An isolated and weakened PLO, interested in finding a way to repair (resume) contact with the US, as well as challenged by local Palestinian Islamist elements and possibly others, had rendered the Palestinians an easier adversary with which to negotiate.

If these factors constituted something of a "pull" toward a peace initiative, a beckoning opportunity, other factors represented something of a "push" or necessity. Rabin's widow, Leah Rabin, was later to say that the Intifada brought about a change in Rabin, leading him as early as 1989 to the conclusion that the occupation must end.[28] Indeed, this would appear to have been the major factor at play for Rabin with regard to the Palestinian track. Uri Sagie saw this not only connected to the Intifada but also linked to Rabin's concern over the Iranian nuclear preparations and the need, therefore, to remove the Arab–Israeli conflict and the Palestinian issue from the Middle East equation.[29] Rabin himself made this connection in his first speech to the Knesset as prime minister and on subsequent occasions, saying: "If we succeed within five to seven years to conclude peace, or almost peace, with the Palestinians, Jordan and afterwards Syria, we will have largely limited the motivation for an arms race."[30] The decline in the resilience of the Israeli public – apparent not only during the Iraq SCUD attacks but also in the Intifada – was also a matter of concern, "pushing" in the direction of ending the conflict.[31] This was joined by the growing realization that there was no military solution to the Intifada.[32] Furthermore, the demographic ramifications of holding onto the occupied territories were a longstanding issue for the Labor Party – namely, how to remain a Jewish and democratic state if Israel continued to hold onto the West Bank and Gaza (i.e., how could Israel maintain its Jewish character – a Jewish majority – if it upheld democratic rights for all those under its control, including those within the occupied territories).[33]

Rabin spoke of a "window of opportunity" estimated (on different occasions) at five, or seven, or ten years' possible duration, in which it was imperative upon Israel to make peace. In both the Labor Party election campaign and in his inaugural speech to the Knesset, Rabin appeared to give priority to the Palestinian issue. Yet, he still was not willing to deal with the PLO. He had often said in the past that speaking with the PLO could only be about a Palestinian state, which he opposed.[34] Moreover, for Rabin, the PLO remained a "terrorist organization" even as he presented to the Knesset his decision to work with it. This decision came, as he explained, only after it became clear that local Palestinians were no substitute (they answered to the PLO).[35] Nor was Jordan, since the King had renounced his claim to the West Bank, dispelling Rabin's earlier conviction (e.g., contained in the Labor Party 1992 platform) that the Palestinian issue would be resolved within the context of Jordan. If the Intifada were to be stopped – the immediate matter on the agenda – and any kind of settlement were to be sought, there remained only one address, formalized in Rabin's Letter of Mutual Recognition of the PLO "as the representative of the Palestinian people" for the commencement of negotiations "within the Middle East peace process."

In the past it had been almost a mantra in the Labor Party that speaking with the PLO was out of the question, for the only topic for such a dialogue would have to be Palestinian statehood – something Rabin and the Labor Party expressly rejected.[36] In this sense the content of the DOP itself was a factor facilitating the breakthrough, for it provided only for an interim agreement on Palestinian autonomy, leaving the final status of the West Bank (i.e., independence and related issues) to a later date, as much as five years down the road. Thus, like Begin, who devised the original autonomy plan – a plan adopted virtually in its entirety by Rabin in 1989 and presented in his first speech to the Knesset after his 1992 election, and also ensconced in the DOP – Rabin could live with open-endedness. However, like Begin, Rabin was also quite clear that Israel would not return to the 4 June 1967 lines, and he stated a number of times that he would not agree to a Palestinian state; at most, what might emerge would be a Palestinian "entity less than a state."[37] Thus, the Oslo Accords, officially adopted in the form of the 1995 Interim Agreement known as Oslo II, constituted a limited agreement with no commitment regarding the future and creating no immediate danger for Israel. Withdrawal from Gaza was not considered a security risk; indeed, both the public and the military had come to regard Gaza as a liability. Moreover, Israel was to retain responsibility for external security as well as the security of the settlers, including the roads they traveled on, while determining, alone, the areas from which the Israel Defense Forces might "redeploy." Insofar as there was a degree of risk, Rabin reassured the Knesset (while presenting the DOP) that "we believe that these are calculated risks and that they are not capable of damaging the security or threatening the existence of the state of Israel any more than existing dangers. In any case, the might of the IDF, the best army in the world, is at our disposal if and when we are, God forbid, put to the test."[38] Further, in this same speech on 21 September 1993, he explained that given the PLO's terrorist history, specific steps had been demanded in the form of commitments, made by Arafat in the Letters of Mutual Recognition, which Rabin enumerated: "recognition of Israel's right to exist in peace and security, the resolution of any differences peacefully and through negotiation, the promise to renounce and cease terrorism and violence in Israel, the occupied territories and everywhere else. ... , to regard as null and void the articles in the Palestinian Charter that are incompatible with

Israel's right to exist and the peace process, and to bring about their repeal."[39] The Letters of Mutual Recognition, perhaps the most important, least reversible of the Oslo documents, were actually suggested by Israel's legal advisor at Oslo. The purpose was to obtain just this *quid pro quo*, a change in the PLO doctrine, thereby ensuring that recognition of the organization in no way implied legitimation of the PLO's ideology denying Israel's right to exist.[40] As Uri Savir put it, the DOP was a "practical guideline," but "now we were dealing with the ideological roots of the conflict."[41]

From this it is clear that trust was not a factor; Rabin even asserted that while he believed the Palestinians (and the Arab states) "want peace," "we place our trust in no one – but ourselves. In any agreement, in any situation, and under any condition, the security of Israelis will be in the hands of Israelis."[42] Thus, because of the absence of trust, Israel pressed for maximum control and, as we shall see below, security measures that themselves impeded the development of trust. Actually, the absence of trust was built into the Accords themselves. The gradual, interim nature of Oslo was designed to test the Palestinians by moving incrementally through limited steps over a three- to five-year period. This was consistent with Rabin's conviction that while the Arabs would never make peace with Israel, this might change, and also his comment to the Knesset in July 1992 that he did believe that peace was possible.[43] Presumably it was hoped that a degree of trust might be created during this time; indeed, the negotiators both in Oslo and subsequently spoke of the need for attitude changes and grassroots activities to develop trust. Recommendations for such activities, known as people-to-people endeavors, were included in the Oslo II agreement.[44] Rabin, for his part, said that a leader "must go before the pack, but not too far ahead" lest he find that no one is behind him any longer.[45] This said, his approach to leadership, as noted earlier, was to lead, and persuade, rather than follow the public: "It [the government] must do everything to prove that the line it believes to be right is the correct one, and must try to influence public opinion [to that effect]."[46]

Indeed, from the day he came to office, Rabin strove to do whatever persuading might be necessary for the skeptics and potential spoilers in Israel, particularly within the political establishment. In his very first speech to the Knesset (before Oslo) and almost every subsequent speech and interview, he referred to the changed environment, directly challenging the deep-seated "victim" mentality of Israelis.[47] "No longer are we necessarily 'a people that dwells alone,' and no longer is it true that 'the whole world is against us.' We must overcome the sense of isolation that has held us in its thrall for almost half a century. We must join the international movement toward peace, reconciliation and cooperation that is spreading over the entire globe these days – lest we be the last to remain, all alone, in the station."[48] Seeking to change those elements of Israeli identity that stood in the way of a breakthrough, he repeated these sentiments to the graduating class of the National Security College in August 1993. Rabin referred again to the "siege mentality" developed over the years, and he told the highest ranks of the Israeli army and security establishment: "In the face of the new reality of the changing world, we must forge a new dimension to the image of the Israeli. This is the hour for making changes, for opening up, for looking around us, for engaging in dialogue ... for making peace. We must view this changing world through eyes informed by wisdom; note that it is no longer against us."[49]

Implicitly deriving his legitimacy from his security credentials, at no time did Rabin let the public forget that he was first a military man and, therefore, personally keenly aware of Israelis' losses and sacrifices in the past. Beyond legitimacy, these references indicated a realism and empathy difficult for spoilers to challenge. Nor did he ignore or minimize terrorism, but rather expressed the need to work for peace despite terror (promising to "pursue peace as if there were no terrorism, and fight terrorism as if there were no peace process," a paraphrase of Ben Gurion in World War II regarding the British White Paper).[50] In time, he also took pains to distinguish between the PLO and those committing the terrorism: Hamas and the Islamic Jihad.[51] He occasionally referred to Arafat's efforts to combat terrorism, and in the summer of 1995 he was frustrated to the point of anger over Arafat's failure to rein in these elements; yet, some observers believe that Rabin did develop a degree of trust in Arafat by the time of his presentation of the Oslo II agreement to the Knesset on 5 October 1995.[52] Nonetheless, even as he noted the abandonment of terror by those under Arafat's authority, he also drew attention to the fact that the PLO had not yet implemented its commitment to change the Palestinian Covenant, which, Rabin said, he viewed "as a supreme test of the Palestinian Authority's [sic] willingness and ability ... ."[53]

While Rabin's leadership qualities – namely, his willingness to adapt his views to changing circumstances, his stature, security credentials, and his rhetoric – were critical factors, his was not the only leadership that contributed to the breakthrough. The Oslo process was, in fact, the brain child of Shimon Peres, the "dove," who authorized and persevered despite Rabin's reservations. It was Peres who ironed out many of the differences with the PLO that arose in the negotiations for the various Oslo agreements, particularly at critical points for the original DOP and the Oslo II Interim Agreement of 1995. Peres also played a significant role in promoting public support; Rabin's biographer Yoram Perry maintains that Peres "was able to lift the public on the wings of his vision."[54] Perhaps somewhat of an exaggeration, this view does point to Peres's contribution in the diplomatic arena, his bold regional initiatives, and his enthusiastic dynamism in contrast to Rabin's more hesitant, plodding, and cautious approach. Savir characterized the two leaders as "visionary" and "pragmatist," respectively.[55] Politically, the rivalry between the two remained; but their public display of cooperation was important in the "selling" of the Accords to the public.

With the Peres and Rabin camps working together there were few problems within the party over the Oslo Accords, although Barak, as interior minister, abstained in the Knesset vote on the Oslo II Interim Accord out of disagreement over the redeployment arrangements. During the talks for Oslo II in the summer of 1995, there were apparently differences between the political and the military echelons over security arrangements and redeployment plans, Rabin's preoccupation with security notwithstanding. However, as we saw in connection with the Syrian track, Rabin could count on the loyalty of the military, particularly of IDF Chief of Staff Amnon Lipkin-Shahat, who played a central role in the negotiations for Oslo II (as chief negotiator), along with Major-General Uzi Dayan (in charge of the security sub-committee) and Major-General Danny Rothchild (in charge of transferring the civil administration).[56] The domestic political problems, as well as potential spoilers, derived from the fact that the ruling coalition held only a very small majority. Initially, it was composed of parties with a total of 62 members of the Knesset (Labor, Meretz, and Shas) and the support of the two Arab and three Hadash MKs outside the government coalition. The small ultra-orthodox party Shas, with its six members, had threatened to bolt the coalition several times over various issues unrelated to the peace talks, and it finally did so in the summer of 1993. Thus, Rabin was left with a minority government of 56, expanded to 59 in December 1994 (with the addition of a small splinter party previously in the opposition), dependent upon the support of the two Arabs and former Communist parties (total five MKs) outside the coalition. In Israeli politics, this was a very weak government, indeed, and the opposition of right-wing and religious parties led a vociferous, even violent popular protest, as we shall see below. Rabin's government had weathered the 23 September 1993 vote of no-confidence on the DOP by a 61 in favor, 50 opposed, 8 abstentions Knesset vote;[57] the historic Oslo breakthrough as officially enshrined in the Interim Agreement known as Oslo II passed the Knesset by just one member's vote (61 to 59). In each of these votes, not all the coalition MKs voted in favor – a further sign of the political weakness of Rabin's government. Thus, while the domestic political picture had changed, providing a government interested in peace – without which the breakthrough could not have occurred – its durability was far from certain.

One last factor to be considered is that of the American role. It might be claimed that the major breakthroughs in the Israeli–Arab conflict were achieved, at least initially, without American involvement, *viz*. Sadat's trip to Jerusalem, peace with Jordan, and the Oslo Accords. This would, indeed, seem to be the case with regard to Oslo, inasmuch as the major agreements of the Oslo Accords were negotiated by the parties themselves. US claims to the contrary, the US role does not appear to have been a major factor even in the achievement of the Interim Agreement (Oslo II). The Americans, in the person of Dan Kurtzer (then deputy assistant secretary of state for the Near East), were, in fact, regularly and directly briefed by the Israelis throughout the talks in Oslo, well before the official – and personal – notification to Warren Christopher of the achievement of the DOP. Clinton, who writes that he was informed of the channel at the beginning as well as at the end, believed that Christopher had "done a good job of keeping them on track" by stepping in to resolve difficult issues and matters of implementation.[58] Ross describes numerous personal interventions, most notably with regard to the Letters of Mutual Recognition and at critical junctures of the negotiations for Oslo II. He speaks of daily telephone calls with both sides and of the exertion of pressure, by himself or Christopher, on many occasions in order to keep the process moving, offering his assistance after every meeting (related to Oslo II). He also says that the parties used him to persuade the other side and their respective leaders.[59] Ross attributes a far greater, even occasionally critical role to himself and the Americans than do any of the participants or the later authoritative team-analysis by American experts.[60] In fact, the later Kurtzer *et al.* account notes that the chief negotiators excluded the American representative, Ross, from substantive discussions, even hiding a draft agreement from him at an August 1995 meeting on Oslo II. Yet, Ross himself admits that the United States was skeptical of the Palestinian track and preferred to concentrate on the Syrians.[61] The later American analysis provides further explanations for American neglect, at least with regard to the DOP and Mutual Recognition:

- The PLO was unpopular in the US because of its support for Saddam Hussein in the Iraq War; and the US had broken off its earlier dialogue with the PLO over a 1990 resumption of terrorism.
- Clinton believed that his predecessor, Bush, had been too hard on Israel with regard to loan guarantees sought by Shamir and the issue of settlements.
- Clinton perceived the Oslo track as the project of Peres, who was not, in his opinion, a popular leader.
- Connected with this, Rabin, whom Clinton liked and even admired, had not himself briefed the Americans on Oslo nor indicated his preference for the Palestinian track.[62]

Additionally, according to this team, there may have been little interest because the US had neither initiated nor played a central role in Oslo, and, possibly, Washington simply stayed with the Madrid process inherited from the previous administration. Indyk adds the US conviction that Rabin was merely using the Palestinian track as leverage on the Syrians, or vice versa.[63]

An additional factor is noted by Ross, at least with regard to the post-DOP negotiations. According to Ross, it was clear that the Israelis and Palestinians wanted – and needed – to make their agreements themselves. He said that Abu Ala preferred working with Savir, with whom he had developed a bond of trust, and did not want third-party suggestions; the Israelis believed that the Palestinians' commitment lay in their willingness to persevere in the face of difficulty, without resorting to a third party.[64] He adds that Rabin did not want the US in the negotiations, except "to keep the Palestinians from changing the ground rules," while the Palestinians were interested in the Americans only if they were "to lean on Israel" to show greater generosity.[65] Aaron David Miller maintains that "Rabin was worried that if the Americans got involved, we'd level the playing field at a time when he [Rabin] wanted to keep the pressure on Arafat."[66]

Ross is correct that the Israelis, at least, did not seek US involvement. Amnon Lipkin-Shahak later said that at the time (negotiations for Oslo II) there was no real need for a bigger US role, but, also, there was concern that the US might have added issues that Israel did not want – namely, political matters – while Israel wanted to focus on security.[67] Savir explains that the negotiators preferred that the parties reach agreement on their own, and, therefore, strongly opposed mediation or third-party intervention on substantive matters, although they were open to assistance "in persuading the sides to be flexible" when problems arose.[68] Ben Ami cites a positive American role in this respect, and Savir confirms Ross's involvement in some of the more difficult negotiations for Oslo II, especially during an impasse in August, when, according to Savir, Israel decided to use the Americans as a lever to gain Arafat's acquiescence on various points. Ross sent the US Consul in Jerusalem, Ed Abington, to speak with Arafat, although at the same time he sent Indyk to both Rabin and Peres.[69] Savir attributes great importance to what he called the Americans' network of ties in the final efforts on Oslo II. These included also the Egyptians and even King Hussein, whom the Americans called in at critical times. Clinton saw US involvement as providing, among other things, broad connections and a degree of legitimacy by virtue of Washington's backing. He later wrote of the importance of having the DOP signed on the White House lawn in order to show the countries of the region that Rabin and Arafat were truly committed and, also, in the belief that "a billion people around the globe" as witnesses would "make them more committed."[70]

Oslo failure

Much has been written about the reasons for the failure of the Oslo Accords, by participants and analysts alike, often providing convincing evidence as to why one factor or another played *the* central role.[71] As in the case of a breakthrough, so too with failure (as we have seen in the previous cases), it is most likely that a number of factors were responsible, often interacting with each other without necessarily having been the single most significant factor. One often heard explanation was the absence of the "ripeness" factor in Israel due to the top-down set of agreements, simply presented to the public without preparation. While it was, indeed, the case that the Oslo talks were held in total secrecy and little if any preparation of the public was attempted, the changes that had occurred in public opinion, particularly in response to the Intifada, would suggest that the public was "ready" for compromise with the Palestinians. In fact, the public may have been ahead of the leadership in its growing support even for the creation of an independent Palestinian state, as indicated by the polls as early as 1992–1993. One set of polls had public willingness to accept the creation of a Palestinian state increasing from 20 percent in the late 1980s to 36 percent by 1993 or 40 percent in another poll of the same year.[72] Further, once the Accords were signed, an (often since forgotten) groundswell of grassroots contacts, joint ventures, and popular exchanges occurred as Israelis (and Palestinians) began a process of dismantling the dehumanization of the enemy generally internalized over the long years of conflict. Meetings were held between Israelis and freshly released prisoners (who spoke the Hebrew learned in Israeli prisons); Palestinian and Israeli families sought to create a joint kindergarten and family outings, to name just two such efforts. Not only did the term "Palestinian" connoting a people or nation, come into use, but Israeli media, for example, presented Arafat satirically in a sympathetic and benevolent way, breaking down the stereotype to some degree. Yet, the Accords were gradually to lose this broad public support as other factors led to the ultimate failure of Oslo.

A basic misperception, or rather difference in conception of Oslo by the two protagonists, would appear to have been an important factor in this failure. The Israeli leadership, certainly Rabin, viewed the Oslo Accords as a path to end the occupation and provide self-rule for the Palestinians. This in his view would bring peace with the Palestinians even though he clearly stated that he envisaged no more than "an entity which is not a state" for the Palestinians. The Palestinians, however, had quite a different perception of Oslo, viewing it as a first step on the path to statehood, as stated very clearly, for example, in a paper presented by the Palestinian negotiators in 1994: "Our aim is the establishment of a Palestinian state in accordance with the 1967 border."[73]

This difference in the basic perception of Oslo led to endless negotiations and arguments with regard to the jurisdiction, composition, and power of the organs of self-rule to be exercised by the Palestinian Authority (PA) provided by the Accords. While the DOP and Oslo II stipulated that the West Bank and Gaza Strip would be viewed "as a single territorial unit,"[74] Israel did not see this as according full PA control (that might be perceived as akin to sovereignty) over the whole area. Palestinians pressed, for example, for a parliament (Israel envisaged a "self-governing Council" as distinct from the legislative council actually created by the PA), or the title "president" for the head of the PA, Palestinian police on the borders, and so forth. Indeed, it was this and other types of disputes that led to delays in implementation, delays which themselves became a factor contributing to the failure, along with the lack of implementation or perceived violations of the stipulations of the Accords – for example, the presence of many more light weapons among the Palestinian police than allotted by the agreements, the low number of Palestinian prisoners released, Israel's failure to create a safe passage from Gaza to the West Bank, the failure of the Palestine National Council (PNC) to draw up a new covenant (after it had, finally, voted to abrogate the articles demanded by the agreements), along with delayed "redeployments" of the IDF, and similar matters.

Oslo II (like the DOP) also clearly stated that "agreements reached for the interim period "should not prejudice or preempt the final status negotiations" (Article V, 4); yet, Israel continued to expropriate land and expand settlement construction. Technically this did not violate the Accords, for Israel had refused to include anything in the agreements regarding settlement construction. Although Rabin was no friend of the settler movement, he apparently chose to avoid confrontation with the settlers (even rejecting the removal of settlers from Hebron after the fatal attack by a settler on Moslem worshippers there) until it might be absolutely necessary in connection with the determination of the final status and borders of the territories. For the Palestinians, however, settlement construction was interpreted as a violation of the Oslo ban on permanent changes and, more importantly, suggested that Israel had no intention of leaving the territories since it was, in fact, expanding its non-military presence on the land.

This, however, points to another factor: lacunae and ambiguities in the Accords themselves, despite the negotiators' efforts to include as much detail as possible. One such lacuna was the absence of a serious monitoring mechanism to ensure implementation. The agreements did provide for a small observer group and possible arbitration, but neither was accorded clear authority, duties, or significant personnel. The only observer group eventually organized, for example, consisted of a relatively small number of Norwegians posted in Hebron (TIPH). Without monitoring to ensure implementation or to deal with the perceived violations, these became a source of frustration and mistrust for many on both sides. Ambiguity over security became an equally if not more important factor. The Accords called clearly for Israeli responsibility not only for the security of the settlers and the roads used by them but also for "external security." We know from the negotiators that what was intended by "external security" was Israeli responsibility for the borders, with Jordan (the Jordan River) and with Egypt (from Gaza).[75] Yet, in practice, as Israel redeployed its forces in accord with Oslo II, an indeterminate network of checkpoints was created throughout the territories both to protect the settlers and to place the IDF in control of entry and exit to towns or areas handed over to the Palestinians in what could be construed as "external security." This may not have been the intention, but the result was that Palestinians found their movements more rather than less restricted inside the territories themselves. Moreover, the express exclusion of Jerusalem from the jurisdiction of the PA and the Oslo II arrangements was, apparently, interpreted by Israel as the basis for closure of the city to Palestinians from the West Bank and Gaza. Palestinians now had to seek permits for entry to East Jerusalem or travel through it in order to get from one place in the West Bank to another (such as Ramallah to Bethlehem).

Increased restrictions, closures of the territories, and a drastic reduction of the number of Palestinians permitted to work in Israel were indirectly related to the very nature of the Oslo Accords (i.e., the "interim" nature of the agreements, designed to stretch over a five-year period, unclear targets or delineations, and no clear goal or end-game in sight). In such circumstances, opponents to compromise could and did do everything possible to delay and ultimately torpedo the agreements, putting up a last, desperate stand, as it were. On both sides there were significant numbers or at least politically powerful elements whose positions – nationalist, religious, or ideological – were not accommodated by the Accords or opposed them. On the Israeli side these spoilers were led by religious West Bank settlers, in particular, but also joined by nationalist Likud supporters for whom territory held implacable ideological (historic–national) significance. One may only speculate if these cloaked or were joined by economically motivated stakeholders with vested interests in holding onto the West Bank.[76] As leader of the parliamentary opposition, Netanyahu had called Rabin "worse than Chamberlain" in the Knesset session on the DOP, and greeting Oslo II he accused Rabin of "causing national humiliation by accepting the dictates of the terrorist Arafat."[77] The latter was expressed from the speaker's balcony at a demonstration in Jerusalem in which posters and an effigy showed Rabin in a Nazi SS uniform. These public protests became still more vociferous and even violent as Palestinian spoilers intensified their actions through terrorism. Violent Palestinian opposition came from the religious, Islamist elements outside the PLO (more radical groups within the PLO objected to the Accords but did not instigate violence). Almost from the first days of Oslo, Hamas and Islamic Jihad engaged in terrorist attacks inside Israel itself, with an ever-increasing death toll among the civilian Israeli population. In the first year alone, after the signing of the DOP, 149 Israeli civilians were killed in terror attacks.[78] Although Arafat eventually presented a security plan to end these attacks, following innumerable Israeli demands, his ability to do so was not certain. Spoiler actions tended to feed each other, as terrorism led to Israeli countermeasures – namely, closures and further restrictions, viewed by Palestinians as collective punishment – which, in turn, made it difficult for Arafat to appear to be doing Israel's (anti-terrorist) work for it against his own people. No real crackdown was apparent until the spring of 1996. But, coming as it did in the wake of four of the most serious terrorist attacks (in which over 60 Israelis were killed), Arafat's compliance was too late to stem the tide of Israeli disillusionment with Oslo. By the beginning of 1995, 49 percent were "disappointed" or "very disappointed" with the peace process (around the time that Rabin, Peres, and Arafat were receiving the Nobel Peace Prize).[79] Indeed, a graph plotting public opinion among Jewish Israelis in this period clearly shows the link between terror attacks and declining support (as well as belief) in Oslo (as distinct from fluctuations in negotiations).[80]

Taken together, the delays, disputes over, and lack of implementation, violations, settlement expansion, increased restrictions by Israel, and acts of terrorism by Palestinians all served to whittle away at whatever modicum of trust had been generated by the signing of the Accords. The initial enthusiasm for Oslo did not eliminate skepticism; as expected, deeply engrained psychological factors, the sense of victimhood, and fear were still present even as support for the process was apparent. The idea of an interim period was to a large degree designed for the purpose of building trust where little or none existed, as Israel was to gradually withdraw and Palestinians were gradually to assume self-rule. Theoretically, at least, as this process moved along, Israeli control over security would diminish; but when these developments did not occur as planned, trust not only failed to emerge – instead, mistrust and suspicion led to greater, not less, Israeli control, while Palestinians had expected greater freedom. Indeed, the period intended by the Israeli leadership to test the other side and potentially build trust had just the opposite effect. Asked if they agreed or disagreed with the statement "most Palestinians have not accepted the existence of Israel and would try to destroy it if possible, even if the PLO leadership is negotiating with it," as many as 49 percent of Oslo supporters expressed agreement, (64 percent of Oslo opponents expressed agreement) in a December 1994 poll.[81] A poll in October 1994 showed just 48 percent popular support for Oslo, falling to its lowest point in the Rabin period to 45.5 percent in April 1995.[82] The outcome might have been different had there been an end-game in sight, for belief that the process would, in fact, ultimately lead to an independent state might have placated Palestinian opponents or at least provided greater tolerance on the part of the Palestinian population and greater willingness, or ability, on the part of the PLO to crack down on Hamas and the Jihad in time.[83] That, in turn, might have neutralized some of the Israeli opposition. Actually, the open-endedness of the Accords created expectations that themselves became self-defeating, as Israelis and Palestinians were to wonder, respectively, how settlement building and terrorism could be reconciled with the other side's intention to make peace. Additionally, Israelis – indeed, even the Labor Party, as we have seen – considered the occupied territories "ours," a view that had been strengthened by the erasure of the green line (1949–1967 *de facto* border) from official (and school) maps, weather reports and the like.[84] Therefore, the Accords were perceived as an Israeli concession, "giving" something (some of the land) to the Palestinians, which presumably should be appreciated. Moreover, the initial enthusiasm had not only raised expectations but had also created the incorrect sense that peace had already been achieved. Many to this day referred to Oslo as a "peace agreement." As the process broke down, its flaws became evident, and the spoilers' actions – in particular, terrorism – dominated, the response tended to be that "peace" was failing. Israeli author Amos Oz characterized this situation in a radio interview with the analogy that it was as if you were to wake up a patient in the middle of an operation and asked him how he felt. But the public did not see it this way – "peace" was not working very well, it was not bringing security.[85] Thus, the spoilers' actions, particularly the murderous terrorist acts of Hamas and Islamic Jihad, but also the threatening and ultimately fatal opposition of nationalist–religious Israeli spoilers, succeeded in dealing the final blows to Oslo. The assassination of Rabin (by a religious Jewish student – ironically at the close of a massive rally in support of the government's peace policy under the slogan of "Peace yes, Violence no"), followed some months later by the four devastating terrorist attacks, led ultimately to the election of the Likud once again, in May 1996. American pressure brought some movement forward, but under Netanyahu the Oslo Accords were more or less moribund. Disillusionment with the process, on both sides, laid the foundation for an even greater mistrust than had preceded Oslo. Public support for peace, even explicitly a two-state solution, remained despite this, but the

134   Oslo I: Breakthrough and Failure

mistrust began to outweigh any belief that an ultimate agreement could, in fact, emerge.

Some might add still one more factor contributing to the failure: mistakes or inaction on the part of the Americans. One Palestinian has maintained that the US was "shy" and "should have intervened." Indeed, Kurtzer *et al.* share this view, noting assurances made to the Palestinians prior to Madrid that the US would be a "driving force" in the peace process.[86] Palestinian expectations, based on these assurances, may have been themselves problematic, for the US never took pains to disabuse the Palestinians of the belief that Washington could "deliver" Israel in response to PLO demands. The more common criticism of the Americans, however, is that they should have pressed Israel on the settlement issue and the Palestinians on the terrorism issue, providing some form of monitoring, and even proffered at least a suggestion of an end-game.[87] Aside from the fact that the US actually continued to give priority to the Syrian track throughout the Oslo period, there was also a problem of differences of opinion within the US team, too little communication and coordination between the special envoy (Ross) and the State Department, and misunderstandings of Israeli intentions. It is possible that still another element made it difficult for the US to act more forcefully: the activities of the Jewish–American diaspora. It must have been at least perplexing if not harmful that the American Israel Public Affairs Committee (AIPAC), the leading Israel lobby in Washington, was at odds with Rabin regarding Oslo, even to the point of working at cross purposes over the matter of Congressional backing for aid to the PLO – a measure supported by the Israeli government.[88] One can only speculate as to how much, if at all, American intervention or a stronger role might have succeeded in reducing the effects of the many factors that bore more directly on the failure of Oslo.

Finally, one must ask if there were not an underlying factor, actually a basic flaw in Israel's conception of the Oslo Accords – namely, Israeli's view of peace as compatible (or achievable) with the priority given to security. It was not an accident that Oslo lacked an end-game. Although Rabin and the Oslo Accords themselves left the final status for later negotiations, Rabin made the government's view of the final arrangement quite clear in a number of speeches, including his last speech to the Knesset, 5 October 1995, presenting Oslo II. There he spoke not only of "an entity which is less than a state," but spelled out various parameters that would be demanded by Israel. Among these, "united Jerusalem," including specifically the settlements of Givat Zeev and Maale Adumim (not located even within the municipal borders expanded after the 1967 war), under Israeli sovereignty, and also "the security border of the State of Israel [to] be located in the Jordan Valley, in the broadest meaning of the term." In theory, this could be accommodated by just a military presence (Rabin was rumored to have spoken even of limiting such a presence to 30 years); but his speech indeed left open the question of sovereignty in the Jordan Rift Valley. His use of the term "broadest meaning" suggested more than a presence on the line of the Jordan River, and, in fact, the Labor Party platform had clearly stated that Israel would demand the Rift Valley (and northwest Dead Sea) as Israel's security border "under Israeli sovereignty").[89] Rabin mentioned further demands, such as demilitarization, retention of Gush Etzion, Beitar [Ilit], Efrat, and other "communities" and the establishment of "blocs of settlements in Judea and Samaria, like the one in Gush Katif [Gaza Strip]." The intention of this explicit presentation of the final agreement as he saw it (and, he reminded the Knesset, as expressed in the Labor Party platform) was most likely intended to assuage concerns over the size of withdrawals that might result from Oslo II. To this end, Rabin used Labor Party terms rarely heard in those years, defending his willingness to give up (some) territory as the only alternative to the eventual existence of a "bi-national state with millions of Palestinian Arabs" in Israel – the old Labor demographic concern to keep the state democratic but also Jewish.

Thus, ending the occupation would solve Israel's problem, according to Rabin. He believed this would bring peace, but only with certain conditions, including territorial, just as his party had believed in 1967 and later, that such conditions would bring peace with Jordan. The territorial demands are even somewhat surprising given Rabin's own admission, to Clinton, that changes in modern warfare rendered territory far less important, or as Clinton reports Rabin's comments: "in the Gulf War, when Iraq fired Scud missiles into Israel, he realized that the land did not provide a security buffer against attacks with modern weapons ... ."[90] Yet, the conditions delineated by Rabin a month before his death were no different, indeed a bit harsher, than those of his predecessors: the same security concerns (fears), the need to hold onto the Jordan Rift Valley, as well as the attachment to East as well as West Jerusalem, remained unaltered. Would Rabin have ultimately given these up in favor of a peace agreement with the Palestinians, as he gave up his opposition to dealing with the PLO and his aversion to Arafat? We will never know, but there is nothing in his or his government's statements at the time that suggest such a change was about to occur.[91]

To sum up the factors that led to both the breakthrough and the failure of Oslo, from the Israeli point of view, we can point to many changes. First, and crucial, was the change in Israeli leadership: the replacement of the Likud (Shamir) by Labor (Rabin, and also Peres) and with this a new interpretation of developments in the international, regional, and bilateral (Israeli/Palestinian) environments. At the same time, there were also domestic changes in the socio-economic situation (globalization, individualism, war weariness), in personal security (the Intifada), and public opinion (willingness to compromise, support for a Palestinian state). These factors apparently served to reduce the identity threat in that they contributed to the view that the territories did not constitute a vital or essential part of our existence, and that, rather, a compromise on the territories might even provide greater security. Once the leadership change occurred and the Oslo period began, the previously strong emotional or psychological factors such as hatred, fear, and victimhood gave way to hope and a degree of confidence. Albeit somewhat surprising, given the depth of such feelings, this development may have been at least aided by two additional elements: first, the fact of an actual agreement (which included explicit recognition of Israel's right to exist and concrete benefits for Israel); and, second, trust, not in the enemy but in a leader who possessed solid security credentials and known to have shared much of the public's skepticism (some would have said realism) in the past.

The element of trust in the leadership was lost with the assassination of Rabin. Peres did not have sufficient security credentials to weather the difficult challenges of the Hamas terror attacks in early 1996, and he had a reputation for dovishness and over-optimism (apparent in his often mocked vision of a "new Middle East"). The work of the spoilers played a major role in the failure, along with flaws in the agreements themselves – and their implementation or lack thereof, which both strengthened the spoilers and contributed to a loss of what little trust had begun to develop between the two publics. It is not easy to undo or eliminate ingrained fears and an inherent sense of victimhood, or to overcome years of hatred and dehumanization of the enemy. Thus, it is not surprising that these sentiments began to re-emerge with the disappointment over Oslo. Yet, they were not to dominate entirely or to fully eradicate the progress that had been made at least with regard to the public's attitude toward the importance (or lack thereof) of the territories and its willingness to compromise even if it dampened the belief that compromise was, in fact, possible. It was on this basis that an effort to revive and complete the Oslo process could and would be initiated when Labor returned to power in May 1999. Subsequent leaders were to admit the importance of the transformation that had, in fact, occurred in the conflict itself with the mutual recognition of Israel and the Palestinians and their respective rights that was the essence of the Oslo breakthrough. The rise of Hamas and the return of Netanyahu challenged these achievements through the use of past methods of violence, intimidation, and manipulation of fears.

Notes

1 See Chapter 3: US commitment to Israel not to speak with the PLO until certain demands were met by the organization. Arafat made his 1988 speech in Geneva because the US would not grant him a visa until these demands were met, finally, in the 16 December 1988 press conference: acceptance of UNSC Resolution 242, recognition of Israel's right to exist, renunciation (not just condemnation) of the use of terror.
2 One of the more authoritative Palestinian elucidations of the 1988 decision is presented by the late Abu Iyyad, who together with Abu Jihad and Arafat founded Fatah. Salah Khalaf (Abu Iyad), "Lowering the Sword," *Foreign Policy*, Spring 1990: 78, 91–112. At the time he was the head of security and intelligence for the PLO, later killed apparently by the renegade organization of Abu Nidal.
3 Abu Ala cited the link between the Oslo talks and the PLO interest in the US, particularly in view of the changes in the international environment. Ahmed Qurie (Abu Ala), *From Oslo to Jerusalem* (London: Tauris, 2006): 36–37.

Oslo I: Breakthrough and Failure   137

An additional factor was Jordan's renunciation of its claim to the West Bank at the end of the summer 1988.
4 Foreign Ministry of Israel (MFA), www.mfa.gov.il/, Reaction by Prime Minister Shamir to Arafat's speech, 13 December 1988.
5 Interview as Defense Minister to *Haaretz*, 21 April 1989 (MFA, Vol. 11–12: 1988–1992). The 1988 elections had once again produced a virtual tie between Likud and Labor, but the new national unity government did not include rotation this time.
6 Additional factors will be discussed below.
7 Secret contacts had been going on for some time, even by persons linked to the Likud; the government under Peres in 1984 authorized talks with the PLO ostensibly on the matter of MIAs. Shimon Peres, *Battling for Peace* (New York, NY: Random House, 1995): 263–264.
8 *Maariv*, 26 June 1992; *New York Times*, 27 June 1992.
9 This would not have been possible before the rescinding (19 January 1993) of Israel's law banning contracts with the PLO. Nonetheless, Rabin did not want any news of the Oslo channel to leak, preferring to maintain the official bilateral channel in Washington as if it were the only channel.
10 Uri Savir, *The Process* (New York, NY: Vintage Books, 1998); Qurei, 2006; see also Ron Pundak, "*From Oslo to Taba*: What Went Wrong?," Survival, 43/3: 31–45, and by non-participants, David Makovsky, *Making Peace with the PLO* (Boulder, CO: Westview, 1996); Mahmoud Abbas (Abu Mazen), *Through Secret Channels* (Reading, UK: Garnet Publishing, 1995); Jane Corbin, *Gaza First: The Secret Norway Channel to Peace Between Israel and the PLO* (London: Bloomsbury, 1994).
11 The Norwegians did not take part in the negotiations but assisted when crises arose, most notably by means of 12 July 1993 trips to Arafat in Tunis and Rabin and Peres in Jerusalem by Foreign Minister Holst (Savir, 42). Savir (83) also said that it helped that Egypt, Morocco, and Tunisia were frequently consulted and supported the talks.
12 Savir, 1998: 72, 75; Qurie, 2006: 171, 177.
13 See Abu Ala's demands for inclusion of the West Bank, beginning with Jericho, in the DOP (Qurie, 2006: 130–134, 171–172). A discussion of this issue between Mubarak and Rabin in Cairo, in April 1993, may have had something to do with Rabin's agreement to add Jericho (Peres, 1995: 286).
14 Savir, 1998: 42. Shlomo Ben-Ami, *Scars of War, Wounds of Peace* (New York, NY: Oxford University Press, 2006): 190; Martin Indyk, *Innocent Abroad* (New York, NY: Simon and Schuster, 2009): 88.
15 Shamir had ruled out not only PLO people but also East Jerusalemites and diaspora Palestinians. Rabin relinquished regarding the last two, still hoping to avoid the PLO directly, but it was an open secret that the negotiators at the bilateral talks received orders from Tunis.
16 Beilin, the official who initially authorized the Oslo track, claimed that Rabin agreed to it simply to give his rival Peres something to do; Rabin considered the really important track to be the talks that he controlled –namely, the Syrian track. Beilin notes this as one of the paradoxes of Oslo since the track that Rabin was "on the point of scrapping in June" turned out to be the one that got him a Nobel Peace Prize (Yossi Beilin, *Touching Peace* (London: Weidenfeld and Nicholson, 1999): 135.
17 Savir, 1998: 38, 42; Peres, 1995: 294–295; Dennis Ross, *The Missing Peace: The Inside Story of the Fight for Middle East Peace* (New York, NY: Farrar, Straus and Giroux, 2005): 108 (Rabin showed the letter to Ross).
18 Peres, 1995: 295.
19 Itamar Rabinovich, *The Brink of Peace* (Princeton, NJ: Princeton University Press, 1998): 114–115.

20 The demonstration, organized by Peace Now and a number of political parties, including Labor, demanded – and achieved – an official Commission of Inquiry into Israel's role in the Lebanese Christian forces' massacre of civilians in the two Beirut refugee camps.
21 Jacob Shamir and Michal Shamir, *The Anatomy of Public Opinion* (Ann Arbor, MI: University of Michigan Press, 2000): 171.
22 Examining polling results over a 30+ year period, Shamir and Shamir found that Israeli public opinion tended to rise in favor of willingness to compromise in reaction to breakthroughs or hope (such as the 1975 interim agreement on Sinai, and the peace agreement with Egypt), but also in periods of greater violence – e.g., 1973 war, the 1983 attack on Israeli military HQ in Lebanon, the first Intifada.
23 Unpublished polling data from Dahaf survey conducted for Galia Golan and Naomi Chazan's project on Attitudes and Behavior of Israeli Women on War and Peace, unpublished.
24 Hanna Levinsohn and Elihu Katz, "The Intifada is not a War: Jewish Public Opinion on the Israel–Arab Conflict," in Akiva Cohen and Gadi Wolfsfeld (Eds), *Framing the Intifada: People and Media* (Norwood, NJ: Ablex Publishing Corporation, 1993): 53–61. An early perception of this is Mark Tessler, "The Intifada and Political Discourse in Israel," *Journal of Palestine Studies*, 19(2), 1990: 43–61.
25 The Israeli stock exchange "soared" 10 percent in the week following the signing of the DOP and leading businessmen published an ad congratulating Rabin and Peres: Uri Ben-Eliezer, *Old Conflict, New War* (New York, NY: Palgrave Macmillan, 2012): 37. See, also, Guy Ben-Porat, "'Dollar Diplomacy,' Globalization, Identity Change and Peace in Israel," *Nationalism and Ethnic Politics*, 12, 2006: 455–479, and Ben-Eliezer, 2012: 34–35.
26 Optimism regarding the possibility of peace was reflected in the 1992 party platform even of the Likud, as well as Labor. For this and other positive changes, see Neta Oren, "Israeli Identity Formation and the Arab–Israeli Conflict in Election Platforms, 1969–2006," *Journal of Peace Research*, 47(2), 2010: 193–204.
27 Poll taken 7–8 September 1993 commissioned by the American Jewish Committee, published in part in the *Jerusalem Post*, 13 September 1993. My thanks to Dr. Hanna Levinsohn of the Guttman Institute for providing me with details of the complete poll.
28 Lea Rabin, *Rabin: Our Life, His Legacy* (New York, NY: Vintage, 1997).
29 *Haaretz*, 17 August 2012. See Rabin's presentation of his government to the Knesset, 13 July 1992, (MFA), Rabin Speeches, Vol. 13–14: 1992–1994.
30 Yitzhak Rabin, "Nitzul Pesek Ha-zman," ["Exploiting the Time Out,"] *Politika*, 44 (March), 1992: 28.
31 Yitzhak Rabin, *The Rabin Memoirs* (Berkeley, CA: University of California Press, 1996): 366–367; *Haaretz*, 20 July 1993; Eitan Haber interview, History Channel, Israel Television, 16 April 2013; Ben-Ami, 2006: 203, 208.
32 Perry, "Afterword," in Rabin, *The Rabin Memoirs*, 1996: 351–355, Ben-Ami, 2006: 190, 209.
33 Bill Clinton, *My Life: The Presidential Years* (New York, NY: Vintage Books, 2005): 545, cites Rabin's comments to him on this; this position appears in the Labor Party platform from at least as early as 1981.
34 For example, Rabin interview to *Davar*, 16 September 1974, or to *Maariv*, 10 February 1989.
35 Rabin speech to the Knesset (Protocol, The One Hundred and Twenty-ninth Session of the Thirteenth Knesset, Tuesday, 21 September 1993).
36 See Rabin interview, Israel Television, 20 September 1974 (MFA, Vol. 3: 1974–1977).
37 For example, Knesset speech, 5 October 1995 (MFA, "PM Rabin in Knesset – Ratification of the Interim Agreement"); speech at Tel Aviv University," 18 November 1992 (MFA, Vol. 13–14: 1992–1994; see also Labor Party platform of 1992.

Oslo I: Breakthrough and Failure 139

38 Translation, Perry, "Afterword," in Rabin, 1996: 406–407 (slightly more complete than the MFA excerpted version of the speech).
39 The speech is a paraphrase of the letter, which in fact does not mention "repeal" of Charter clauses but rather a commitment "to submit to the Palestine National Council for formal approval the necessary changes in regard to the Palestinian Covenant" (MFA, Vol. 13–14: 1992–1994, 107; Israel–PLO Mutual Recognition, Letters and Speeches, 10 September 1993).
40 Savir, 1998: 35.
41 Savir, 1998: 69.
42 Speech December 1993 (no exact date or occasion listed; Perry, Appendix G, in Rabin, 1996: 413).
43 Knesset, 13 July 1992: "We believe wholeheartedly that peace is possible, that it is imperative, and that it will ensue" (MFA, Vol. 13–14: 1992–1994 and references in 1974 to testing "in practical terms" Arab intentions, Interview, Israel Television, 20 September 1974, MFA, Vol. 3: 1974–1977).
44 The Israeli Foreign Ministry set up a unit to deal with people-to-people activities and funds were provided by the US and other countries.
45 Rabin, 1996: 378.
46 Interview with *Davar*, 16 September 1974 (MFA, Vol. 3: 1974–1977).
47 An interesting study of the presentation of Oslo by the leadership, see Nimrod Rosler, *Political Context, Social Challenges, and Leadership: Rhetorical Expressions of Psycho-social Roles of Leaders in Intractable Conflict and its Resolution Process – The Israeli-Palestinian Case*, PhD thesis, Hebrew University of Jerusalem, 2012.
48 Speech to Knesset, (MFA), Rabin Speeches, Vol. 13–14: 1992–1994, 13 July 1992.
49 Speech, Perry, Appendix D, in Rabin, 1996: 397–398. Delivering a eulogy at the 1994 funeral of General (retired) Yehoshafat Harkabi, Rabin praised Harkabi for being able to change his opinions in view of changes in the world and new circumstances. Upon leaving the funeral, I commented to General (retired) Shlomo Gazit that I thought Rabin was speaking of himself. Rabin's speeches continued to demonstrate this view.
50 This is one of those comments that have entered Israeli memory, but I have not been able to find the original source.
51 Speech to the Knesset, 5 October 1995 (MFA, PM Rabin in Knesset-Ratification of Interim Agreement).
52 Clinton, 2005: 545; Ross, 2005: 208; Rabin, 1996: 364–365; Savir, 1998: 243.
53 Speech to the Knesset, 5 October 1995 (MFA).
54 Rabin, 1996: 374. Virtually all of the participant accounts of the Oslo period attest to the degree of cooperation the two were able to muster, both in the political sphere and publicly.
55 Savir, 1998: 78.
56 Savir, 1998: 117, said the appointment of these military people created some friction between Peres and Rabin, and Makovsky claims these three actually replaced the political negotiators. Nonetheless, Peres did, in fact, continue to play a central role, along with Savir and others (Makovsky, 1996: 144).
57 One MK absent. Most of the abstentions were from Shas, which, unlike the other religious parties at that time, was willing to give priority to human life over the possession of territory.
58 Clinton, 2005: 542.
59 Ross, 2005: 196.
60 Daniel Kurtzer, Scott Lasensky, William Quandt, Steven Spiegel, and Shibley Telhami *The Peace Puzzle* (Washington, DC: USIP, 2013).
61 Ross, 2005: 104. See, also, Indyk, 2009: 84.
62 Kurtzer et al., 2013: 42.

63 Indyk, 2009: 84.
64 Ross, 2005: 196–197, 200, 207.
65 Ross, 2005: 123.
66 Aaron David Miller, *The Much Too Promised Land* (New York, NY: Bantam Books, 2008): 250–251.
67 Interview to Kurtzer group, 2009, Kurtzer et al., 2013: 47.
68 Savir, 1998: 129.
69 Savir, 1998: 205.
70 Clinton, 2004: 542.
71 Savir, 1998; Ben-Ami, 2006; Ross, 2005; Clinton, 2005; Miller, 2008; Peres, 1995; Beilin, 1999; Kurtzer et al., 2013; Abbas (Abu Mazen), 1995; Qurie (Abu Ala), 2006; Rabin, 1996; Gilead Sher, *Within Reach* (London: Routledge, 2006); Yoram Meital, *Peace in Tatters* (Boulder, CO: Lynne Rienner Publishers, 2006); *Daniel* Lieberfeld, *Talking* with the Enemy, (Westport, CT: Praeger,1999); Eisenberg and Caplan, *Negotiating Arab–Israeli Peace* (Bloomington, IN: Indiana University Press, 2010); Galia Golan, *Israel and Palestine: Peace Plans and Proposals from Oslo to Disengagement,* (Princeton, NJ: Marcus Weiner Publishers, 2007); Moshe Ma'oz, Robert Rothstein, and Khalil Shikaki (Eds) *The Israeli–Palestinian Peace Process* (Brighton, UK: Sussex Academic Press, 2002); Dean Pruitt, "Ripeness Theory and the Oslo Talks," *International Negotiations*, 2, 1997: 237–250; Edward Newman and Oliver Richmond (Eds), *Challenges to Peacebuilding* (Tokyo: UN University Press, 2006); Avi Shalim, "The Rise and Fall of the Oslo Peace Process," in Louise Fawcett (Ed.), *International Relations of the Middle East* (New York, NY: Oxford University Press, 2009); Edward Said (Ed.), *Peace and Its Discontents* (New York, NY: Vintage Books, 1996).
72 Asher Arian, "Israel and the Peace Process: Security and Political Attitudes in 1993," Memorandum 39, JCSS, Tel Aviv University, 1993" 10; Jacob Shamir and Michal Shamir, "The Dynamics of Public Opinion on Peace and the Territories," Final Research Report, September 1993, cited in Galia Golan, "Israel and Palestinian Statehood," in Winston Horne (Ed.), *Global Convulsions: Race, Ethnicity, and Nationalism at the End of the Twentieth Century* (New York, NY: New York University Press, 1997): 176.
73 Savir, 1998: 99.
74 Arafat told an interviewer a few days after the DOP signing: "The most important component of the agreement is not the provision stating the Israelis will withdraw from Gaza and Jericho but rather the acknowledgment that the jurisdiction for the Palestinian Authority covers all occupied Palestinian territory"(*al-Duster*, 19 September 1993, cited in Kurtzer et al., 2013: 49).
75 Savir, 1998: 105.
76 Some analysts argue that the occupation, from the beginning, was and is designed by Israeli governments as a colonialist enterprise exploiting Palestinian land, labor, and resources (see, e.g., Neve Gordon, *Israel's Occupation* (Berkley, CA: University of California Press, 2008).
77 Kol Israel, 21 September 1993, cited by Avi Shlaim, "The Rise and Fall of the All-Palestine Government in Gaza", *Journal of Palestine Studies*, 20(1), 1990: 37–53.
78 Eisenberg and Caplan, 2010: 186.
79 *Ibid*.
80 Tamar Hermann and David Newman, "A Path Strewn with Thorns: Along the Difficult Road of Israeli–Palestinian Peacemaking," in John Darby and Roger MacGinty (Eds), *The Management of Peace Processes* (Basingstoke, UK: Palgrave Macmillan, 2000): 119.
81 December 1994 poll cited in Dan Leon, "Israeli Public Opinion Polls on the Peace Process," *Palestine–Israel Journal*, 2(1), 1995: 57.

82 Following a series of terror attacks. Peace Index, April 1995 (Israel Democracy Institute).
83 It did so but only after the assassination and four devastating terrorist attacks that played a large role in the defeat of Peres, and the Oslo process, in the elections of May 1996.
84 See note 79 in Chapter 3: the difference between Labor and Likud being not over the right to the land but the willingness to give up part of it.
85 The once self-declared leftist journalist Ari Shavit wrote an article on what he called the old peace – that didn't work: "After Israel gave the Palestinians most of Gaza, the first bus blew up at Dizengoff Square. After Israel gave the Palestinians Nablus and Ramallah, buses started to blow up in downtown Jerusalem and Tel Aviv." He suggested giving up the dream of peace and coming up with something new, something more modest to manage the conflict (*Haaretz*, 9 February 2012). Like so many others, he incorrectly identified the Oslo Accords with a "peace" accord, while in fact they were no more than an interim agreement, and he viewed Israel as "giving" something of its own to some other side.
86 Riad Malki, "No Peace Agreement: Israel–Palestine," in Edwin Corr, Joseph Ginat, and Shaul Gabbay (Eds), *The Search for Israeli–Arab Peace* (Brighton, UK: Sussex Academic Press, 2007): 181; Kurtzer et al., 2013: 56.
87 Kurtzer et al., 2013 : 55–56, Miller, 2008: 252; Riad Malki, 2007: 181.
88 Ross, 2005: 132.
89 Former chief of staff (and, in 2013, later defense minister), Moshe Ya'alon quoted this speech as proof that Rabin adhered to Israeli sovereignty over the Jordan Rift Valley. Ya'alon said this when he was deputy prime minister in an interview to *Haaretz* on 14 June 2012.
90 Clinton, 2005: 545.
91 At the end of October 1995, Beilin and Abu Mazen had secretly completed a set of understandings – including the two-state solution – which they hoped would be the basis for the final status negotiations. Beilin planned to show it to Peres for the first time at a meeting scheduled for 11 November and subsequently to Rabin. The assassination occurred on 4 November (Beilin, 1999: 178.)

7 Oslo II
Barak and Camp David

While Netanyahu, who won the May 1996 elections by a very narrow majority, announced the Likud-led government's willingness to continue the Oslo agreements, he did almost nothing in the way of implementation. In fact, he was later unwittingly filmed boasting to settlers that by interpreting the Accords as he wished – for example, defining designated military zones in a way that suited him – he "stopped the Oslo Accord" unconcerned about the US reaction because "America is a thing you can move very easily, move it in the right direction ... they won't get in our way."[1] Although Palestinian violence had greatly diminished due to Arafat's crackdown on Hamas elements in the spring of 1996, three days of violence broke out in the fall of 1996 in response to the government's opening of a controversial tunnel under the Temple Mount (Haram al-Sharif). This prompted the Americans, with the help of King Hussein, to press Netanyahu to implement the long delayed withdrawal from most of Hebron in January 1997.[2] When other obligations and further redeployments failed to materialize, the Americans organized another meeting between Netanyahu and Arafat which produced the Wye River Memorandum, signed on 23 October 1998. This provided specific percentages and times for the remaining redeployments, along with other previously promised Israeli obligations (release of prisoners, opening of a safe passage between Gaza and the West Bank, etc.), while the Palestinians were committed to various security measures, anti-incitement, and a second abrogation of the PLO Covenant (demanded by the Likud since the first abrogation had failed to produce a new *written* version of the document). Most significantly, for the first time, the Americans were made part of the agreement; they were to provide monitoring and actual participation in an Israeli–Palestinian–US security coordination committee and to facilitate the final status talks. President Clinton himself was to address a Palestine National Council (PNC) meeting once again abrogating the Covenant, which he did in Gaza in December 1998. The promised airport in Gaza was opened; but almost no other part of the Wye Memorandum was implemented on the Israeli side. Netanyahu suspended it before the end of the year on the grounds that the Palestinians were not abiding by their security obligations.[3] His period in office ended in May 1999 with almost all the Oslo II requirements – in particular, the last redeployment, prisoner releases, safe passage between Gaza and the West Bank, still pending and final status talks frozen since 1996.

Camp David

The virtual abandonment of Oslo became, actually, a factor favorable to a positive change and revival of the initial Oslo breakthrough. While there was widespread dissatisfaction with the Netanyahu government on domestic issues, the loss of any forward momentum, accompanied by clear signs of American frustration with Israel, was at least one factor in the decisive electoral victory of Ehud Barak and his party in the May 1999 elections.[4] Despite the flaws of the Oslo Accords – indeed, the failure of the process – and the disappointment that had led to Netanyahu's 1996 victory, the majority of Israelis still supported Oslo and, even more so, negotiations with the Palestinians (though not with Syria).

A further factor that might provide for renewed breakthrough was the fact that Barak won a decisive victory over Netanyahu (in Israel's first and only direct election of the prime minister), and he created a broad coalition of his Labor party (renamed One Israel), Meretz, Israeli b'Aliyah (the Russian immigrant party), Shas, the Center Party, and Yahdut HaTorah, adding slightly later the National Religious Party (NRP). The coalition guidelines were clearly in favor of resumed efforts for peace, and domestic expectations were high. Moreover, Barak himself had a good deal of legitimacy not only by his personal election but also due to his stature as Israel's most decorated soldier, a former chief of staff of the Israel Defense Forces (IDF), and, as promoted in Labor's electoral campaign and asserted by Barak himself, Rabin's protégé destined to continue Rabin's legacy.[5] International expectations were also high, especially among the American administration, which was both relieved and more than anxious to assist in an invigoration of the peace process. So, too, the regional actors – namely, Egypt and Jordan – were hopeful Barak would bring a welcome change. Most importantly, perhaps,

Table 7.1

Month	Negotiations Index	Oslo Index	Syria Index
January	64.5	52.3	42.1
February	65.7	52.8	43.9
March	64.5	55.2	43.6
April	66.8	56.8	42.9
May	67.1	54.5	42.9
June	65	52.1	42.8
July	64.7	55.7	47

Support for Negotiations – 1999, adapted from Tamar Hermann and Ephraim Yaar, *Peace Index – 1999* (Israel Democracy Institute, Peace Index Archive, www.idi.org.il). See also, Asher Arian, *Israeli Public Opinion on National Security 1999*, (Tel Aviv: JCSS-Tel-Aviv University, 1999).

the Palestinians were pleased with Barak's victory. They were encouraged by the view of Barak as Rabin's successor (and the coalition guidelines that promised to halt the construction of new settlements that had characterized the Netanyahu government). Moreover, Barak's initial pronouncements contained many references to his wish to rebuild trust and partnership toward peace.

Yet, the promising beginning notwithstanding, the first weeks of Barak's term bore the seeds of the ultimate failure of Oslo. Preferring the Syrian track, primarily because of his promise to withdraw all Israeli forces, finally, from Lebanon within a year, Barak postponed the remaining Wye obligations, most notably further redeployments. To allay Palestinian concerns and US pressure over this abandonment of an official agreement, Barak agreed to make a formal commitment to his new plan in the form of the Sharm el-Sheikh Memorandum of 4 September 1999. This specified a new timeline for the final redeployments and called for the drafting within five months (by January 2000) of a framework agreement for a final accord (primarily agreement on the core issues) – that is, still another accord which itself was to be concluded within a year, by 13 September 2000. Barak delayed the opening even of these "framework" talks, and, after many difficulties and unfulfilled promises, he carried out only a fraction of even the Sharm commitments. In January he announced indefinite delay of further redeployments on the grounds that final status talks were now underway.

In fact, the real reason for this critical decision was different: Barak had abstained from the 1995 vote on Oslo II because of his opposition to further redeployments, and in connection with Wye, he told the Knesset just four days after the Sharm memorandum that: "implementation of the redeployments as stipulated in the Wye Memorandum schedule was potentially harmful to the political and security interests of the state of Israel," since Israel would be leaving territory – that is, giving up "assets," without obtaining anything in return – a *quid pro quo* that could come only in final status negotiations.[6]

Talks of various kinds and at different levels took place between January 2000 and the July 2000 summit at Camp David: Clinton's team, often joined by Secretary of State Madeleine Albright, met with both Barak and Arafat and their respective negotiators; two sets of final status talks – both secret but one considered a particularly secret "back channel," and more individual contacts via emissaries of a totally unofficial nature.[7] Aside from issues connected with the Wye and Sharm commitments, and gestures requested (e.g., Arafat's request that Israel withdraw from three villages around Jerusalem to offset the delay of the last redeployment), differences arose not only over the issues of Jerusalem and security but even the very need to discuss these issues and at what level. With the Syrian talks now collapsed, Barak authorized a round of secret high-level talks (in Stockholm) on permanent status issues, conducted by Shlomo Ben-Ami and Gilead Sher with Abu Ala and Hassan Asfour. Some progress was made in these talks, though Barak himself was not amenable to all the compromises suggested by the negotiators. A stalemate appeared to have been reached, and Barak decided the time had come for real decisions, which he maintained could only be made at the leadership level. Moreover, there was renewed pressure of a possible PLO unilateral declaration of a state at the September deadline, and on the ground there had been renewed, albeit brief, Palestinian violence on Nakba Day (Arabic for catastrophe, the anniversary of the founding of the state of Israel). Barak now pushed for the Americans to organize a summit. Generally the Israelis (at least as expressed by two central negotiators, Shlomo Ben-Ami and Gilead Sher, along with Barak himself) believed Arafat was avoiding any final decisions; the Palestinians thought they were being pushed into a trap; and the Americans thought the two sides were far too apart on the issues to warrant a summit. Nonetheless, with US elections in November (and the party conventions in the late summer), the Americans conceded to Barak's pressure to move ahead. According to Ross, who was present, in gaining Arafat's agreement Clinton promised the Palestinian leader that he "would not blame Arafat if a summit failed."[8]

One might argue that there were still, nevertheless, some favorable factors that might provide a breakthrough. For example, there was Barak's promise, determination, and interest in reaching an agreement, particularly after his failure with the Syrians and his weakening political position. For Arafat, there was the opportunity – perhaps for the first time – to achieve statehood, for although Barak spoke publicly only of "separation" between Israelis and Palestinians, preliminary talks had clearly referred to an agreement that would include a Palestinian state.[9] And public opinion on both sides still favored an agreement – in the case of Israeli Jews, even with the prospect that a Palestinian state would result.[10] In addition, there was a US president seeking to complete what had begun on his White House lawn in 1993, and to do this in the little time left of his term in office.

Yet, the Camp David summit was convened in an atmosphere of extreme mistrust on the part of Israeli and Palestinian protagonists. Arafat felt deceived by Barak's earlier preference for Syrian talks and his reneging not only on the Wye agreements but even on his, Barak's, own subsequent commitments, including withdrawal from one or two of the Jerusalem villages as promised.[11] As he told Ross on one occasion, if Barak could not deliver even on the matter of the villages, how could he be expected to deliver on the big issues?[12] Barak, for his part, believed Arafat to have been devious, purposely non-committal, and not really interested in making peace with Israel. Only if Arafat were pressed to the wall – that is, forced to make a decision – would this view be proven true or false in what was understood by Sher, and the Americans, to be Barak's process of "unmasking" Arafat.[13]

Domestic political factors also contributed to the inauspicious convening of the Camp David summit. Barak's coalition had been steadily losing no-confidence votes in the Knesset; coalition partners were voting against government-supported bills; Ahdut Hatorah had resigned in 1999 (over a religious matter); and other parties, particularly Shas, threatened repeatedly to resign. As Camp David drew nearer, right wing non-governmental organizations

(NGOs) took to the streets in noisy disturbances and large demonstrations, which were only meekly met by counter-demonstration from the peace camp. Finally, on the eve of Camp David, Shas, the NPR, and Israel b'Aliyah all left the government because of the summit, and Foreign Minister David Levy announced that he would not attend. Thus Barak went to Camp David as the leader of a minority government, facing demands for new elections. Amnon Lipkin-Shahat said later that Barak wanted to move swiftly to a summit because "opponents of the peace process were ready and eager to take action and unless the move was swift, the cabinet would have to face protracted demonstrations and campaigns."[14] It might be argued that Barak's precarious political position was, in fact, one of the reasons for his haste to hold a decisive summit. Success might redeem him while failure would be presented as his "unmasking" of Arafat and proof of his, Barak's, steadfast adherence to Israel's interests. Whether this was Barak's motivation or not, his domestic political problems did not bode well for the flexibility and courage that would be needed to achieve a breakthrough at Camp David – a factor that was already evident with regard to Barak's "cold feet" (as Uri Sagie put it) at the Shepherdstown talks with Syria.[15] It did not help matters that Arafat, too, had to face internal political differences. These were broadly related to the failure of Oslo but also to tension between local leaders and returning PLO officials, dissatisfaction with corruption and dictatorial methods of the Palestinian Authority (PA), juggling for power within Fatah and the PLO, all aggravated now by the fact that Arafat was virtually coerced by the Americans to agree to a precipitous summit for which neither he nor his colleagues believed the ground sufficiently prepared.[16]

Given this background, it is not surprising that Barak and Arafat did not directly negotiate at Camp David; their teams met – collectively, individually, and in committees, while Clinton (and Secretary of State Madeleine Albright plus aides) met directly with the two leaders individually as well as with members of the teams. The purpose was to formulate a Framework Agreement – that is, principles regarding the core issues of the final status for the West Bank (including Jerusalem); but in essence the negotiations sought to delineate just how a final agreement, with a Palestinian state, would look. Thus, the major issues – and disagreements – revolved around borders, which was directly connected with the issue of the settlements – namely, the number of settlers who would have to be moved or might be accommodated, perhaps with the introduction of land swaps; security, primarily the issue of an Israeli presence in the Jordan Rift Valley and control of the border with Jordan, early warning stations, use of air space and the like; refugees – namely, the right of return, Israeli acknowledgment of responsibility, return only to the Palestinian state; and the issue of Jerusalem, focusing on sovereignty over East Jerusalem, the Old City, the holy places – specifically the Temple Mount/ Haram al-Sharif area. Formal agreement was not reached on any issue and positions of each side changed sometimes numerous times, with differences between proposals – even apparent agreement – in committee sessions, on the one hand, and the views of the respective leaders, on the other. Moreover, due primarily to Barak's fear of leaks (that might hurt his already weak political position at home), there was no formal record kept beyond individual note taking, and no formal written proposals. Thus, it is not easy to determine the exact or necessarily final positions of either side.[17]

Barak's proposals, presented to Clinton after a week of the talks, were as follows: Israel was to maintain 9 percent of the West Bank with the possibility of a 1 percent swap of an area south of the Gaza Strip; this would include annexation of a strip of land along the Jordan River. In addition, there would be an Israeli military presence (i.e., military control) in another 10 percent (possibly 6 percent) within the Jordan Rift Valley for no more than 12 years (down from an original plan for 20 years).[18] In the course of the talks, Barak raised the percentage Israel would hold permanently to 13 percent, finally settling on 10–12 percent depending, for example, on inclusion of the safe passage from Gaza to the West Bank or other small areas.[19] Security arrangements were not specified in the first offer, but Barak apparently agreed to an international presence at some point on the Jordan River border; he sought five warning stations (subsequently reduced to three) and access roads in case of an emergency. His position by the end of the talks included demilitarization of the Palestinian state.

While he spoke only of a satisfactory solution to the refugee problem, his position in the talks rejected any reference to UN Resolution 194 (of 1949)

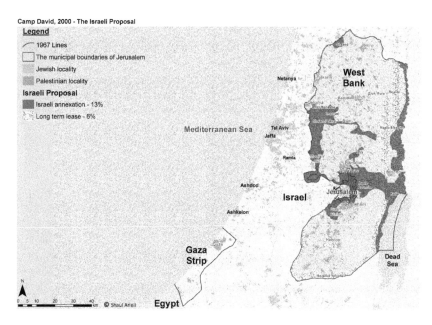

Map 7.1 1 Israeli Proposal Camp David 2000
Source: Shaul Arieli

since it was viewed by the Palestinians as according the *right of return* for all refugees (the relevant clause: "Resolves that the refugees wishing to return to their homes and live in peace with their neighbors should be permitted to do so at the earliest practicable date").[20] Barak did allow for unlimited "return" to the Palestinian state (as if this were a concession) but not to Israel, with the exception of limited numbers (at one point suggesting 7,000–10,000 over ten years),[21] through family reunification arrangements, as was the practice already, in any case. Nor would Israel accept responsibility for creation of the refugee problem although it would participate in international efforts of compensation and resettlement.[22] Thus, Barak held to Israel's traditional position on the refugees, which derived from the fear of an influx of even a small percentage of the 3 to 4 million Palestinian refugees that might eventually put the Jewish population in the minority within the state of Israel.[23] With regard to Jerusalem, Barak offered Palestinian sovereignty in the Muslim and Christian quarters of the Old City and in seven or eight of the nine outlying East Jerusalem neighborhoods (within the municipal borders expanded by Israel in 1967) and "custodianship" over the Temple Mount/Haram al-Sharif area, but under Israeli sovereignty. There was also the idea of functional autonomy (zoning, planning, security, law enforcement) for the "inner ring" of East Jerusalem. At various stages in the talks, Barak retreated on some of these ideas, but he also eventually added to them – for example, he was willing to include a few neighborhoods in the inner ring for the Palestinians (though would concede only "symbolic sovereignty" to them). He also added the idea of a Presidential Compound in the Old City and the often mentioned idea of expanding the border to include the village of Abu Dis, which could be the seat of the Palestinian capital.[24] And he also seemed amenable to various ideas of "functional sovereignty" for the Palestinians or Israeli "residual sovereignty" or Palestinian "custodianship" over the mosques on the Temple Mount/Haram al-Sharif, but added the demand that Jews be permitted to pray on the Temple Mount/Haram al-Sharif. Barak took his Jerusalem offers off the table altogether in the last days of the talks in angry response to Arafat's rejection of American proposals (an incident we will discuss below). With whatever terms Barak offered on Jerusalem, he demanded that the agreement declare the conflict ended.

The Palestinians considered any Israeli presence in the West Bank or control (including roads and air space) to be a violation of their sovereignty, though at one point Arafat was apparently willing to allow early warning stations (though no permanent Israeli military presence[25]). The only map the Palestinians would show gave Israel 2.5 percent of the West Bank for settlements (and access roads to them from Israel).[26] In the course of the talks, and in response to heavy pressure from Clinton, Arafat reportedly accepted some of the Americans' and Barak's ideas, including even unequal swaps, compromise wording on the refugee issue (i.e., no specific demand for "right of return," but nonetheless reference to Resolution 194), and agreement to an "end of conflict" stipulation in the final accord (provided all the issues were resolved).[27] The major sticking point was East Jerusalem. Arafat would not compromise on the issue of sovereignty, particularly (though not only) over the Temple Mount/Haram al-Sharif. His basic position was simply for each to keep its own areas – namely, East Jerusalem Palestinian, West Jerusalem Israeli, though he gradually agreed to speak of dividing the Old City quarters and Israeli sovereignty over the Western Wall (the bottom of the Temple Mount/Haram al-Sharif as distinct from the top, where the mosques stood). However, the critical issue, around which the final discussions revolved, was sovereignty over the Temple Mount/Haram al-Sharif itself. His main argument was his responsibility to the entire Muslim world ("a billion Muslims will never forgive me") if he relinquished Haram al-Sharif, Islam's third holiest site, and that he would rather kill himself.[28] Thus, at least in the eyes of the Americans, Jerusalem became the key; if the Jerusalem issue were resolved agreement might be reached on the other issues.[29] Clinton personally sought assistance from various Arab leaders, but none was willing to weaken Arafat on this issue.

When no Framework Agreement had been reached by the time Clinton had to leave for a G-8 meeting in Asia, it was decided that instead of disbanding as planned, the delegations would stay at Camp David and work with Albright until Clinton's return. Before departing, the Americans had presented a bridging proposal on the issue of Jerusalem: Palestinian custodianship over the mosques and churches, sovereignty in the Muslim and Christian quarters of the Old City, Israeli sovereignty in the Armenian and Jewish quarters and in the inner circle neighborhoods of East Jerusalem, plus functional autonomy for the inner circle. Arafat rejected the proposal (Barak was not entirely happy with it either and Clinton criticized him for retreating on previous positions[30]). To persuade the Israelis to remain while he was away, Clinton apparently told Barak that Arafat had agreed to the bridging proposal, or according to a different version, that Arafat agreement would be secured and so negotiations could then take place (in Clinton's absence) on the basis of that proposal.[31] To Arafat, he merely said that Barak agreed to stay, at the very least leaving the impression that they would negotiate the Jerusalem issue.[32] It was left to Albright to explain to Barak that, in fact, Arafat had not agreed to the American proposal, to which Barak responded by saying that there would be no formal discussions at all and secluded himself in his cabin more or less for the duration. In the two days of talks after Clinton's return, Barak took his own Jerusalem offer off the table, and the Palestinians, for their part, retreated on some of their positions regarding refugees and security. Finally, hoping that a solution on Jerusalem might provide the sorely needed breakthrough, the Americans concentrated on the issue of the Temple Mount/Haram al-Sharif – to no avail. Neither Barak nor Arafat would compromise on sovereignty over the Temple Mount/Haram al-Sharif. And so Camp David ended, with the US president complementing Barak for his efforts, by implication blaming Arafat for the failure.

The inauspicious circumstances of the convening of Camp David certainly were important factors contributing to the failure, but other factors also played a role. The public Israeli version spoke to innate fears and emotions of Israelis, attributing the failure to a Palestinian insistence on the right of return of the refugees – something that resonates with the Israeli public as a Palestinian wish to flood Israel with Arabs and thus eliminate the Jewish state, along with a demand to dividing Jerusalem, thereby denying and depriving Israel of a symbol of its historical legitimacy. The Palestinian version was that Israel sought to create a truncated entity divided into cantons, each surrounded and thereby controlled externally by Israel (in terms of movement of goods, people, and so forth), bereft of sovereignty due to continued Israeli military presence in the Jordan Rift Valley and elsewhere, along with continued occupation of East Jerusalem.[33] Actually, each side blamed the other, claiming in mirror-like accounts that the other side refused to budge from its positions. Behind this was the claim that an underlying factor was the negative motivation of the other side: that Arafat (or Barak) did not come to the summit intending to reach an agreement. Whether true or not, this claim points to the important factor of trust, or rather mistrust, as each leader viewed the other as harboring "devious objectives."[34] It is impossible, perhaps, to know if Barak (like Rabin) believed that Arafat would ultimately accept Israel's conditions for an agreement, but he was clearly skeptical and even contemptuous of Arafat's intentions, as evidenced by his idea of "unmasking" the Palestinian leader. Arafat seems to have had few if any illusions that Barak would make an offer that the Palestinians could accept, which may be why he did not put any counter proposals on the table. At most, the Palestinians surmised, Israel would try to force an accord on them, on Israeli terms (and with American assistance), seeking agreement to an "end of conflict" without resolving all the issues, in particular Jerusalem.[35] Some members of his delegation even admitted that Arafat did not expect or try to reach an agreement ("we just did not engage" Mahmud Rashid told Aaron David Miller).[36] Moreover, Arafat was similarly mistrustful of the Americans, viewing them as tied to the Israelis rather than an "honest broker."

Mistrust related not only to the motivation or intentions of the parties but also led to misunderstandings and prevented progress. There was a tendency to disbelieve each other's arguments or explanations – for example, their references to problems of domestic public opinion. Arafat thought Barak was simply making up his alleged domestic political problems, while Barak never seemed to believe that Arafat really did have to prove his steadfastness to his own public. Albright reports that Barak "dismissed the idea that Arafat needed help controlling Palestinian extremists."[37] Of particular importance was Israel's refusal to take seriously Arafat's claims of responsibility to the Palestinians and to the Muslim world for the matter of Jerusalem. Exaggerated declarations that concessions on Jerusalem would "kill him" did nothing to weaken Israeli skepticism.[38] Actually, Indyk also was skeptical and believed that Arafat simply used the Jerusalem issue as a way of ending the talks "honorably" in the eyes of his public.[39] Of no less importance, however, was Arafat's failure to understand Israel's attachment to Jerusalem, specifically the Temple Mount, and Barak's unbending attitude on the matter. Seizing on what he claimed was Barak's "surprising" demand for the right of Jews to pray on the Temple Mount (something actually banned by Israel throughout the occupation, for religious as well as security reasons), Arafat dismissed the purported Israeli interests (and thus, by implication, legitimacy) in Jerusalem as a simple fabrication, claiming the Jews' ancient temple had actually been in Nablus.[40]

If mistrust and mutual suspicions were the main factors in the failure is difficult to determine, for other factors also played a negative role – whatever element of trust or mistrust was at play. A number of participants point to the process itself – namely, the absence of structure, organization, strict agenda, or timeline. Because work was in committees and people usually dealt with a specific topic, the overall picture and possibility of trade-offs got lost. Positions raised informally or even in a committee were often changed or ignored or somehow lost in the shuffle (sometimes the result of differing positions, possibly power struggles, within the delegations). The role of the Americans is blamed for much of the procedural anarchy, according to most of the American participants themselves. As Miller put it, "we did not run the summit, the summit ran us."[41] Clinton did not maintain a structure or provide firm guidelines, and he did not play a strong enough direct role (despite his angry outbursts against Barak and also against Abu Ala). The Americans often failed to follow up on proposals or suggestions, and they announced – and then abandoned – procedures (usually after Israeli objections or Palestinian recalcitrance). Clinton lost the earlier trust he had enjoyed from Arafat by actually behaving as the Palestinians feared he might – namely, consulting first with the Israelis, and only then presenting (and often adjusting) American proposals to the Palestinians. This was in keeping with Clinton's promise to Barak that there would be no surprises, but it greatly reduced, if not destroyed, his efficacy as a mediator. In fact, by the end, and despite frustrations over zigzagging in Israeli positions and an effort to maintain impartiality, Clinton (and the whole US team) believed that Barak was taking unprecedented steps to reach an agreement, particularly in his unexpected willingness to discuss any arrangements at all regarding Jerusalem. This positive attitude to Barak, however, was reflected in US pressure on Arafat, contributing to the Palestinians' sense of US–Israeli collusion. In addition, the Americans' role was weakened by the fact that they had failed to appreciate the central role that was to be played by the Jerusalem issue and, therefore, they had not prepared any of their Arab allies to weigh in on the issue of the Temple Mount/Haram al-Sharif. The result was a last minute – unsuccessful – American scramble to garner Arab support for a compromise (while the Palestinians and even the Israelis had kept various Arab leaders informed on a regular basis).

More basic to the procedural issues and US conduct of the summit, an important factor was the asymmetry of the talks. Israel was, indeed, the powerful side, and it held all the cards for the most part. The impression the Israelis gave, implicitly and sometimes even explicitly, was that Israel was "giving" the Palestinians something, often referring to Barak's "generosity" (which, it was said, should not be expected from subsequent Israeli leaders). Unlike negotiations over the Sinai or the Golan Heights, Israeli leaders did not view this as a negotiation over territory belonging to the other side but, rather, as "disputed" land (the official version) or even "ours." The Israelis of Camp David may not have felt the same emotional "rights of ancient ownership" that the previous Labor leaders (including Rabin) felt for the West Bank; but their attitude and proposals clearly ignored the fact that the Palestinians viewed Palestine as their historic homeland – and not something the Israelis could "give them" or not.[42] Actually, the Palestinian point of view was that they were the ones who were "giving" inasmuch as they had agreed in 1988 (and in Oslo) to settle for just 22 percent of mandated Palestine, abandoning 78 percent to Israel, in favor of a state in just the West Bank (including East Jerusalem) and the Gaza Strip. This had been their "historic compromise," but now Israel was asking them to make further compromises. Here, too, the Israeli negotiating style played a role, for despite the asymmetry of power (evident in their attitude), Israelis conducted negotiations as if they were on a level playing field, expecting bargaining of a tit-for-tat nature, a give and take, that the Palestinians – as the party under occupation – felt they could not and need not match. Indeed, in their eyes they were the wronged party, the victim of past (and present injustices), and as typically the case in asymmetrical negotiations, the less powerful party, the Palestinians, appealed to justice, and international law, while the stronger party, Israel, countered with the future benefits that the Palestinians stood to gain.[43]

A further factor that did not help this situation was Barak's personality. As already evident in the Syrian talks, Barak's style could only be described as arrogant and cold. Clinton and even Barak's own negotiators tried to warn him of the problem and soften his approach. In the pre-Camp David talks, Sher warned him against speaking as if delivering "an edict from the conqueror to the conquered," and at Camp David Yossi Ginossar, who had long been in back channel, personal contact with Arafat, criticized Barak for "always dictating to them." Ben-Ami added that Arafat perceived Barak's "high-handed manner" as "disrespectful."[44] Albright spoke of Barak's "people skills leaving much to be desired. He let people know that he thought he was smarter than them ... not a smart tactic."[45] Clinton referred to this as "cultural differences," which he listed as one of the reasons for the failure of the talks.[46] But in addition to personality, Barak's tactics were also problematic. He did not want to reveal his bottom line or even principles lest Arafat use them as a basis or mere starting point for further concessions. He preferred to leave his final positions to the very last. In a way similarly to Rabin, Barak did not even trust the Americans not to give away his, Barak's cards. Thus, his approach was all or nothing, which in the analysis of Malley and Agha, left Arafat fixated on potential traps, "fretting about a potential ploy," rather than searching for alternative proposals. Barak's approach derived also from his fear of leaks (which is why he did not want proposals in writing) lest Israeli positions get out before there was a Palestinian *quid pro quo*. As in the talks with the Syrians, Barak had his eye on domestic politics and potential spoilers at home. Part of his tactic in this connection was to take tough positions and make harsh statements in public, which did little to persuade the Palestinians that there was much to negotiate.

News that the issue of Jerusalem had been put on the table did leak out, and even as the negotiators were contending with numerous obstacles, opponents in Israel launched vociferous campaigns against Barak's ostensible sell-out. Given the absence of a majority government on the eve of Camp David and the decline in his personal support, Barak was particularly sensitive to the news from home. Even before the summit, he had continued settlement building and allowed the wild cat outpost construction in order to avoid alienating or provoking the settlers and the National Religious Party.[47] He had also sought to placate opponents – from the Center Party as well as the right-wing – by using language similar to that of Rabin – namely, referring often to his military past, his recognition of the "cost" of peace but also the "new life" that peace would bring for Israelis, albeit without Rabin's effort to tackle Israelis' victimhood complex. He even used Rabin's comment of a "window of opportunity" of five to seven years, despite the fact that seven years had passed since Rabin made that calculation. Generally, Barak not only employed rhetoric similar to that of Rabin, he also invoked Rabin as his mentor (and, like Rabin, he also referred to Menachem Begin's compromise for peace as a form of legitimacy in the eyes of the right-wing).[48] Further, he promised a referendum, to placate his opponents, though public opinion polls were quite favorable regarding a peace accord prior to Camp David. Nonetheless, Barak may have been justified in his concern over the power of the spoilers. There were members of his own team – non-party experts or, for example, the Center Party MK Dan Meridor, who reflected some of the spoilers' or at least more conservative views. Meridor, originally (and later once again) a member of the Likud, told Ross at the end of the summit: "I personally feel we were lucky Arafat did not agree because we were giving up too much."[49] He was not alone at Camp David in thinking this, and it was just this reaction that Barak had repeatedly warned of and, indeed, anticipated throughout the talks. Thus, potential rejection within Israel operated, as it had with Syria, as an important factor in the failure of the summit, weighing as it did on each issue discussed (as it did for the Palestinians as well).[50] However, it also reflected a related factor, evident also in the Syrian talks: a failure of leadership on the part of Barak.

With regard to the issues themselves, the potential domestic political battle at home also operated as a factor. Similarly to the negotiations with Syria, "security" – while invoked and sought (in the form of early warning stations and a presence in the Jordan Rift Valley) – was viewed by Barak equally if not more as a matter of domestic public opinion than pure security. The demands on security are often attributed to the influence of military people in the negotiations, and Ben-Ami was to explain that "peace, just like war, has always been a military or militarized affair in Israel" because of the strong involvement of the security establishment. As a matter of fact, some of the issues of early warning stations and access were brought up by the military experts at Camp David.[51] But other factors were also at play. As we have seen, even Rabin, despite his explanations to Clinton that changes in the nature of warfare reduced the importance of some of these measures, still sought an Israeli presence, even apparently sovereignty over the Jordan Rift Valley, mainly out of mistrust that a peace agreement would last. At Camp David Abu Ala was to remark (as had both King Hussein and Hafez al-Asad before him) that "Instead of making peace, you [Israelis] always look more as if you are getting ready for the next war."[52] However, in preparatory talks with the Israeli delegation (including Sher), Major-General Shlomo Yanai had noted that expanding the narrow waist of the country was far more important for Israel's security than the Jordan Rift Valley. From a hard security point of view, there was no need for full Israeli control or sovereignty over the Jordan Rift Valley, even if these were desirable. Noting this IDF estimate (which was ultimately accepted, in part, by Barak at Camp David[53]), Sher explained that, in fact, the issue of the IDF presence in that area was more of a psychological one than security. Its function was to relieve the anxieties of the Israeli public.[54] Presumably, it was also a matter of responding to the political spoilers on the right. Barak opened almost every public exposition of his peace policy with the imperative of maintaining Israel's security, and like his predecessors, he did not believe that a peace agreement would bring "the peace of Europe" in the short run.[55] Yet, this did not appear to be an overriding factor, as it had been for Rabin and others before, perhaps because of the changed circumstances as explained by Yanai. It fact, while Barak appeared to remain steadfast on the security demands, this issue may have been on its way out, so to speak, as a "deal breaker." Rather, in the negotiations, Barak seemed more concerned to demonstrate to the home-front that he had not in any way sacrificed or neglected Israel's security needs.

The new deal-breaker was contained in the various border proposals – namely, the number of settlers who could be accommodated determining the amount of land to be annexed by Israel and the amount left for the Palestinian state. This issue, along with the matter of land swaps, was not determined primarily by security considerations. The problem of Israel's narrow waist (and therefore the future Palestinian border with Israel) that carried the danger of Israel being split into two by an attack was to be dealt with primarily by the demand for demilitarization of the Palestinian state and the ban on entry of any foreign army west of the Jordan River. Yet, the main consideration regarding this border and the amount of land to be annexed by Israel was, in fact, determined by the matter of the settlers. Barak's criterion was accommodation of at least 80 percent of the settlers (in settlement blocs adjacent to and absorbed by Israel). Given the number of settlers at this time, even this "concession" on the border would have meant moving tens of thousands of settlers – a practical if not ideological issue, on the domestic front, rather than a security problem. In fact, the talks at Camp David may have marked the point at which the deal-breaking security issues were beginning to take second place (due to changes in the nature of warfare) to a new deal-breaker: the settlements as the determining factor for the Palestinian border. This had been the very intention of the right-wing advocates of the settlement enterprise, but it was little different from Labor's objective when it began building settlements in 1967 in order to create "facts on the ground" to stake a claim to the territory. The major difference was in numbers, for in the interim the number of settlers, under later Labor and Likud governments, including those of Rabin, Peres, and Barak, had grown from some 1,500 West Bank settlers in 1972 (the first year for which official statistics are available) to 198,300 by the end of 2000.[56] Thus, the "1967 border" would now become a domestic issue of the first order not because of security considerations and not only because of ideological opposition, but because of the very practical issue of evacuating tens of thousands of settlers.

Solutions for the city of Jerusalem were also weighed largely along the lines of what could be sold to the public, given the already proven divisive nature of the issue.[57] Thus, the Israeli delegation held intense discussions not only regarding what the Palestinians might accept but what the public at home could take regarding "dividing Jerusalem." Dani Yatom urged de-mystifying the issue for the negotiations, recalling how Israel had changed (and manipulated) the borders of the city according to various interests. Joined by the two military men Lipkin-Shahat and Yanai, as well as the diplomat Oded Eran, they broke down the matter to just what were the important aspects of the Jerusalem issue. ("What is this Jerusalem of ours that we do not want to divide?" asked Yanai.)[58] And so the discussion focused on mundane considerations of demography and daily life in the city – as distinct from what they viewed as the historic–symbolic importance of the city for Arafat. Reacting to this, Elyakim Rubenstein, the religious member of the delegation, expressed his discomfort with this way of treating the issue on the grounds that maintaining the "internal cohesion of Israeli society [presumably dependent upon a united Jerusalem] is more important."[59] Yet, most agreed that it was primarily, if not only, the Temple Mount that constituted Israelis' emotional and historic attachment to East Jerusalem and therefore this was the issue upon which they should concentrate. Yatom called this site of the two ancient temples "the cradle of Jewish culture"; Barak called it the "the anchor of the Zionist endeavor, even though this effort was largely secular." He may have simply been carried away by the rhetoric (indeed, Ben Gurion might have taken issue with Barak's characterization); but this is what had Barak worried. He saw the issue of the Temple Mount within the context of the weighty nature of the decision he would have to take inasmuch as this was the aspect of the issue that would have repercussions, as he said, "for millions of people."[60] Compromise could be made on practical, territorial matters, such as the various neighborhoods of the city or the quarters in the Old City, but it would be virtually impossible to take on the prospect of giving sovereignty of the Temple Mount to the Palestinians. Just prior to Camp David, a poll indicated some 89 percent of Israelis were opposed even to a Palestinian capital in East Jerusalem.[61] Jerusalem was an issue of public opinion, but it also touched on an additional factor linked to identity, history, and religion. Nonetheless, Barak himself fully understood that there would be no agreement on "end of conflict" without a solution to the Jerusalem issue. Similarly to his dilemma (and his failure) in the case of Syria, he apparently was not certain that the first – "end of conflict" – would outweigh the domestic opposition (or the support that would be lost) by "dividing Jerusalem," since that was the compromise necessary, though perhaps not sufficient, for reaching a peace agreement with Arafat.

If Barak shied away from the political, maybe even public challenge of "dividing Jerusalem," his position on the refugee issue was not entirely dictated by such a factor. The "right of return" of the refugees was a genuine concern of every Israeli government (and the public) because of the demographic effect of a massive return envisaged by accepting this principle. Yet, there was a possible compromise on the refugee issue that Barak avoided. Sher believed the Palestinians' "core" position was more a demand for recognition of responsibility than actual return.[62] And this was, indeed, reflected in the formulations of the Palestinians' avoidance in the talks of the phrase "right of return" (until the final collapse of the talks). They sought Israeli acknowledgment of responsibility for the creation of the problem, according greater attention to the practical side of the issue – namely, numbers. Barak had demonstrated awareness of this possible compromise, having publicly expressed "regret" over the suffering of the Palestinians; nonetheless, he maintained the traditional Israeli position explicitly ruling out acknowledgement of any Israeli responsibility for creation of the problem.[63] Barak spoke mainly of a satisfactory solution, and the issue was not the major focus of the negotiations. Ben-Ami maintained that this was the main topic and obstacle in the talks, but he was alone of all the participants (at least whose accounts are available); all the rest agreed without hesitation that Jerusalem (primarily the Temple Mount/Haram Sharif) was the major issue and deal breaker. *Post-factum*, however, it was politically more expedient for both Israelis and Palestinians to highlight disagreement over the "right of return."[64] For the Israeli public this was an effective and acceptable explanation for the failure; for the Palestinians it was important for the delegates to indicate that they did not abandon the masses in refugee camps and the diaspora (as they had been accused of doing in the Oslo Accords).

This is not to say that agreement was reached on all the issues besides Jerusalem; far from it. Arafat was probably genuine in believing that he could not go back to his public (and the hardliners in and outside the PLO, much less some in his own delegation) with a state that would consist of less than the entire West Bank (22 percent of Palestine, with or without swaps) and fractured into separate areas by Israeli access routes along with continued Israeli military presence in the West Bank and sovereignty over the Muslim holy places (with only Palestinian "custodianship"). Thus, assuming that these were, in fact, Israel's final positions (what came to be termed Barak's "generous offer,[65]), one might well conclude that the major factor for the failure of Camp David was that Israel's maximum offer could not meet the Palestinians' minimum needs, even though Barak did go further than any previous Israeli leader, including Rabin. The fact that the two sides were simply too far apart on the issues was true at Camp David, but if all the other factors or perhaps even some of them had not been present, or different, it is possible that greater agreement could have been reached. Indeed, later negotiations – under different leaders – would attest to this, as we shall see below.

Arafat expected further negotiations; having insisted that the summit was premature, he may even have set out to prove this, proposing and expecting continued talks – which, in fact, did ensue. Yet, neither Barak nor Clinton saw it this way, and Clinton, reneging on his earlier promise not to place blame for failure on Arafat, praised Barak's efforts, leaving little doubt as to who the guilty party was in his eyes. While Clinton's intention was to politically bolster Barak in Israel, most of the American and Israeli participants agreed with Clinton's analysis, even as they acknowledged many other negative factors on their own part. In any case, Clinton (and Barak's) assignment of responsibility to Arafat would become a major factor in subsequent failures to achieve a breakthrough.[66]

Talks actually did continue after Camp David, with two formal attempts once again at resolution: the Clinton Parameters for an agreement presented by Clinton on 23 December 2000 and Israeli–Palestinian talks at Taba in January 2001. The Clinton Parameters were one last attempt by Clinton, just weeks before leaving office, to overcome the differences between the two sides on virtually all the core issues in order to reach an "end of conflict." Building on the various proposals that had been raised, and ignoring the phrase "right of return," he came up with options regarding resettlement of the refugees in other states, or in the Palestinian State, or in Israel but granting Israel control over the number it would allow. These steps would then constitute fulfillment of Resolution 194. On the territorial issue, the new state would be in Gaza and 94–96 percent of the West Bank (the exact figure varied but was summarized by Clinton as 97 percent), compensated by 1–3 percent in land swaps. There would be an international presence in the Jordan Rift Valley, gradually replacing the Israelis over a three-year period, with a limited Israeli presence for an additional three years under international authority and with the right to re-enter in case of emergency; three Israeli early warning stations with Palestinian personnel as well for a period of ten years, to be renewed only by mutual consent; Palestinian sovereignty over airspace (with agreements for Israeli use); and non-militarization (rather than demilitarization) of the Palestinian state. On Jerusalem, the Clinton Parameters provided the simple formula of Arab neighborhoods to be under Palestinian sovereignty, Jewish neighborhoods under Israeli sovereignty (a far cry from the preferences of either Israel or the Palestinians[67]) with a sharing of the Temple Mount/ Haram al-Sharif: Palestinians on top, the Israelis below (i.e., the Western Wall) and some agreement regarding excavations underground. In sum, as

158 *Oslo II: Barak and Camp David*

Clinton put it, the Palestinians would get their capital in Jerusalem and the Israelis would finally get recognition of their capital in a large part of Jerusalem. On all of these issues, some of the Israeli demands were accommodated, some of the Palestinian demands, but compromises and deviation from previous bottom lines would be necessary from both parties.

Clinton did not present the Parameters as a bridging proposal or starting point, but rather as a plan to be accepted or rejected, leaving only details of implementation for negotiation. He gave a four-day deadline, and clarified that if no agreement were concluded within two weeks (when he would no

Map 7.2 Clinton Parameters (approximation)
Source: Copyright Washington Institute for Near East Policy, reprinted with permission

longer be in office), these ideas would "be off the table."[68] Israel met the deadline and agreed that the Parameters could be a "basis" for discussion on condition that Arafat also agreed, adding a number of reservations regarding virtually all the security measures, borders, refugees, the Old City and the Temple Mount.[69] Clinton viewed these as within the Parameters. One might speculate that Barak conditioned Israel's acceptance of the Parameters to that of Arafat's acceptance in the expectation that Arafat would not, in fact, agree. There is no evidence one way or another on this, but given Barak's aversion to bucking public opinion, and the overwhelming opposition of the public to the clauses of the Parameters, when published, Barak's conditional acceptance may have been purely tactical.[70] Actually, Arafat neither agreed nor rejected the Parameters, but rather presented reservations, suggestions, and questions, even in a meeting with Clinton well after the deadline. Clinton records that while younger members of Arafat's entourage apparently pressed for acceptance, Arafat did not give a yes or a no until an affirmative reply only 18 months later – long after Clinton was out of office.[71]

Despite the hiatus of the Clinton Parameters, Barak – now facing an election he was slated to lose – made one more attempt. He sent what peace supporters termed a "dream team," consisting of dovish Labor and Meretz leaders, to meet with the Palestinians in Taba on the Israeli–Egyptian border. Unofficial reports of the 18–27 January 2001 meeting attest to progress on most issues, particularly on the refugee issue and also a retreat (approved by Barak) from the demand for annexation of the strip along the Jordan River (though the demand for a military presence in the Jordan Rift Valley for a period of time remained).[72] However, Abu Ala, in the closing statement on the meeting, not only ignored these advances but even referred to the Palestinian demand for the "right of return" – code words (in the eyes of the Israeli public) for a Palestinian plan to flood Israel with refugees and thereby end the state of Israel. Thus, although the final statement was upbeat regarding some of the progress made and future possibilities, Taba could only be understood as still another failure, this time with Israel's most moderate negotiators.

There were factors that could have occasioned breakthroughs with Clinton's Parameters and the Taba meeting. Following a provocative visit by opposition leader Ariel Sharon (which Arafat had urged Barak to prevent), violence had broken out on 28 September leading to a full-scale, armed Intifada matched by broad use of the Israeli military. A desire to end the bloodshed, at least in theory, could have operated as incentive to reach a breakthrough. There was also the pressure of Clinton's imminent departure from the presidency and therefore the wish to have an agreement in place, possibly binding upon the incoming president. Finally, there was the fact that the Israeli negotiators were, indeed, men who genuinely sought an agreement. Moreover, they were sent by Barak in the hopes that their success would bring him victory in the elections two weeks later.

Yet, negative factors were also at play. The violence of the al-Aksa Intifada served as "proof" in the eyes of the Israeli public that Barak had been correct when he said after Camp David that the Palestinians were not a partner for peace. Opinion polls showed a decline in support for a Palestinian state, a shift to the right among the electorate, and an increase in the perception of the Palestinians as a threat to Israel's security – even existence – shortly after the beginning of the Intifada.[73] Linking the violence to the "right of return" demand was viewed as the continuation of the Palestinians' longstanding determination to "throw the Jews into the sea." Government, military, and media figures claimed (untruthfully as later was ascertained) that Arafat had planned the uprising in advance with the goal of destroying Israel.[74] Just as the violence could and did work in the negative rather than a positive direction, Clinton's imminent departure weighed heavily against making any concessions since he would not be around to back them up or pursue them. Nor was it likely that the incoming US president (from the opposite party) would seek completion of his predecessor's endeavors. Conversely, there were some who maintained that Arafat held out because he thought he might get a better deal from George W. Bush, whose family had oil interests tied to the Middle East and whose father had, in fact, been willing to take a strong position against Israeli intransigence when president.[75] Finally, there really was little reason to believe that Barak could or would win the upcoming election in the atmosphere of violence and opposition that had forced the dissolution of his unpopular government. His successor, Ariel Sharon, was not only the leader of the right wing but in the eyes of many he was a symbol for hardline Israeli positions and preferences for use of force. There was certainly no reason to think that Sharon would adhere to or implement any agreement that might have been made by Barak. Therefore, as with Clinton's disappearance, so too with that of Barak, one may conclude that there was little incentive for Palestinian concessions at this time. The Camp David summit may have come too early for some, particularly the Palestinians, but its timing, in any case, did not portend much success; the post-Camp David efforts clearly came too late.

The Camp David and post-Camp David peace efforts were not a total failure, however, for, just as Oslo produced mutual recognition, these talks produced Israeli agreement, for the first time, to the two-state solution, even though this was not proclaimed officially. Yet, mistrust, lack of leadership, spoilers and public opinion, cultural clashes and personality issues, procedural flaws, third party deficiencies, along with identity-related symbolism, and poor timing all played a role. It is impossible to accord relative weight to these factors, but all or most contributed. The failures of Camp David and the post-Camp David meetings were the product not only of circumstances and developments particular to each of them, but also of the failure of Oslo and all the factors that had brought that failure about.

Notes

1 Video of Netanyahu 2001 visit to the settlement of Ofra, leaked and aired on Israel Television Channel 10 in 2010 (IMEUdotnet, available on YouTube).

2 The Hebron Agreement was negotiated in a meeting between Netanyahu and Arafat in Washington for withdrawal from 80 percent of Hebron. This marked the first time a Likud prime minister agreed to give up an area in the West Bank.
3 For details, Galia Golan, *Israel and Palestine: Peace Plans and Proposals from Oslo to Disengagement* (Princeton, NJ: Markus Weiner Publishers, 2007): 29–34.
4 He changed the name of the Labor Party to One Israel, incorporating the new, miniscule dovish religious party Meimad. This was Israel's only election in which there was separate balloting for the prime minister (individually) and for the Knesset (by party).
5 Victory Speech by Prime Minister elect Ehud Barak, 18 May 1999 (www.MFA.gov.il).
6 Protocol, The Twenty-sixth Session of the Fifteenth Knesset, Wednesday, 8 September 1999. See also, Gilead Sher, *Within Reach: The Israeli–Palestinian Peace Negotiations* (London: Routledge, 2006): 2.
7 Many of the negotiators on both sides later provided written accounts: Bill Clinton, *My Life* (New York, NY: Vintage Books, 2005); Dennis Ross, *The Missing Peace* (New York, NY: Farrar, Straus and Giroux, 2005); Shlomo Ben-Ami, *Scars of War, Wounds of Peace* (New York, NY: Oxford University Press, 2006): 190; Martin Indyk, *Innocent Abroad* (New York, NY: Simon and Schuster, 2009); Aaron David Miller, *The Much Too Promised Land* (New York, NY: Bantam Books, 2008); Madeleine Albright, *Madame Secretary* (New York, NY: Harper Collins, 2003); Mahmoud Abbas (Abu Mazen), *Through Secret Channels* (Reading: Garnet Publishing, 1995); Ahmed Qurie (Abu Ala), *From Oslo to Jerusalem* (London: Tauris, 2006); and Sher, 2006.
8 Ross, 2005: 633; Indyk, 2009: 293.
9 In its 1997 party convention, the Labor Party had accepted the idea of a Palestinian State and it was in the platform for the 1999 elections, though both had clauses that would limit sovereignty (Labor Party Archives, Beit Berl, 2-021-1997-190, 13 May 1997, 28–37). See also, Neta Oren, "Israel Identity Formation and the Arab–Israeli Conflict: Election Platforms, 1969–2006," *Journal of Peace Research*, 47(2): 193–204.
10 The *Peace Index* at the end of June 2000, in anticipation of Camp David, found a clear majority (61 percent) of the Jewish–Israeli public (and even more in the Israeli Arab public) "presently supports the Israeli-Palestinian negotiating process, despite the widespread opinion that this will lead to the establishment of an independent Palestinian state" (*Peace Index*, June 2000, Israel Democracy Institute).
11 One of these was Abu Dis, on the outskirts of Jerusalem, slated in some back channel talks to become the capital of the Palestinian state. When Barak announced the idea to the Knesset he received a political onslaught and retreated from the promise.
12 Ross, 2005: 632.
13 Sher, 2006: 23; Ross, 2005: 628–629; Albright, 2003: 484.
14 In Shimon Shamir and Bruce Maddy-Weitzman (Eds.) *The Camp David Summit: What Went Wrong?* (Brighton, UK: Sussex Academic Press, 2005): 44.
15 Uri Sagie, *Ha-yad She-kaf'ah* (Tel Aviv: Yedioth Sfarim, 2011): 121; also Ben-Ami, 2006: 243 (see Chapter 3).
16 Akram Hanieh, "The Camp David Papers," *Journal of Palestine Studies*, 30(2), 2001: 75–78; Robert Malley and Hussein Agha, "Camp David: The Tragedy of Errors," *New York Review of Books*, 9 August 2001; Ron Pundak, "From Oslo to Taba: What Went Wrong?," *Survival*, 43(3), 2001: 31–45; Khalil Shikaki, "Ending the Conflict: Can the Parties Afford It?," in M. Ma'oz, R. Rothstein, and K. Shikaki (Eds.) *The Israeli–Palestinian Peace Process: Oslo and the Lessons of Failure: Perspectives, Predicaments and Prospects* (Brighton, UK: Sussex Academic Press, 2002): 37–46.

17 Unofficial roughly day-by-day accounts by participants may be found in Shlomo Ben-Ami, 2006; Gilead Sher, 2006; Dennis Ross, 2005; Martin Indyk, 2009; and Akram Hanieh, 2001, as well as more briefly in Clinton, 2005; Albright, 2003; Robert Malley and Hussein Agha, 2001. Sher, in particular, provides a great deal of detail regarding informal as well as formal discussions, including numerous proposals and changes that may or may not have actually been agreed upon at some point.
18 Sher, 2006: 53, and interviews.
19 An Israeli map prepared by the IDF prior to Camp David (May 2000) had 66 percent of the West Bank for the Palestinians, 17 percent for Israel, and 17 percent under "special status" (i.e., mostly Jordan Rift Valley areas to be under Israel for a period of time). In the Stockholm talks the same time, the map prepared had Palestinian territory of 76 percent, Israel 13.3 percent, and 10.1 percent special status. At Camp David, Barak positions were believed (by the Americans) to vary between 88.5 percent and special status 11.5 percent to 92 percent, 8 percent Israel with land swaps of 9:1 (Michael Herzog, "Minding the Gaps: Territorial Issues in Israeli–Palestinian Peacemaking," The Washington Institute, Policy Focus 116, December 2011, Appendix).
20 The official Israeli position was that Resolution 194 did not grant the right of return but, nonetheless, Israel opposed any reference to it.
21 Though he told his negotiators that Israel would go up to 20,000 (Sher, 2006: 99).
22 In his "inaugural speech" to the Knesset on 6 July 1999, Barak expressed "recognition of the suffering of the Palestinian people." Later he went further than any prime minister in the past when he expressed "regret" over the suffering, but on both occasions he asserted that Israel was not responsible (i.e., the regret was "not, under any circumstances, based on a feeling of guilt or responsibility for the emergence of the conflict and its results") (Protocol, The Eleventh Session of the Fifteenth Knesset, Tuesday, 6 July 1999; *Haaretz*, 12 October 1999).
23 The number of Palestinian refugees as a result of the 1948 war was 600,000–700,000.
24 The addition of Abu Dis and other villages, presumably together with East Jerusalem, would be called al-Quds (the Arabic name for Jerusalem).
25 Albright, 2003: 486.
26 The Palestinian map had 97–98 percent with 2–3 percent for Israel and equal land swaps (Herzog, 2011: Appendix).
27 Indyk, 2009: 324.
28 Ross, 2005: 84; Indyk, 2009: 325. He also told Clinton that if he accepted the Barak ideas, "there'll be a revolution. I will be killed" (Indyk, 2009: 314).
29 Indyk, 2009: 316; Albright, 2003: 487, said borders and refugees were easy compared to Jerusalem.
30 Sher, 2006: 84.
31 First version, Indyk, 2009: 329 and Albright, 2003: 490–491; second version, Sher, 2006: 94.
32 Albright, 2003: 490.
33 This can be found in an *Haaretz*, 24 July 2001 report on a pamphlet published by the Palestinian negotiations unit sometime after the summit (PLO Negotiation Affairs Department, "Camp David Peace Proposal of July 2000," www.nad-plo. org.) See also, Mustafa Barghouti, "Generous to Whom," *al Ahram* weekly on-line, 10–16 May 2001, no. 533 (www.weekly.ahram.org), as well as Robert Malley and Hussein Agha's second account, "Camp David and After: An Exchange," *New York Review of Books*, 13 June 2002.
34 Term introduced by Oliver Richmond for someone negotiating not in good faith but rather to use the process to gain time, legitimacy, allies, face saving or to avoid concessions. (Oliver Richmond, "The Linkage Between Devious Objectives

and Spoiling Behavior in Peace Processes," in Edward Newmann and Oliver Richmond, *Challenges to Peacebuilding – Managing Spoilers During Conflict Resolution* (Tokyo: UN University Press, 2006): 244. A Palestinian participant, Samih al Abed echoed Israeli sentiments, saying the Palestinians "felt that the Israelis were not seriously seeking to finalize an agreement at that time" (Shamir and Maddy-Weitzman, 2005: 76).
35 Hanieh, 2001: 85, 86, 92, 93; Malley and Agha, 9 August 2001.
36 Miller, 2008: 298.
37 Albright, 2003: 486.
38 Indyk, 2009: 314.
39 Indyk, 2009: 314, 316.
40 Indyk, 2009: 313, 325. He had often used this to bolster the Arab's unique claim to Jerusalem: Daniel Kurtzer, Scott Lasensky, William Quandt, Steven Spiegel, and Shibley Telhami, *The Peace Puzzle* (Washington: USIP, 2013): 145.
41 Miller, 2008: 298.
42 Al Abed later said of this attitude: "If Israel had come and said, 'perhaps for strategic and future concerns, we need to modify the green line, but in the way that will cause minimal damage and will allow both of us to live with' that would have been an acceptable opening argument. We could have sat down and looked at these areas, examining Israel's interests there. If we could have accommodated the Israelis and if there were no harm to the Palestinians in terms of territorial contiguity, population, natural resources or other issues, then I cannot see any reason why we could not have reached an agreement" (Shamir and Maddy-Weitzman, 2005: 76).
43 See, Karen Aggestam, "Mediating Asymmetrical Conflict," *Mediterranean Politics*, 7(1), 2002: 69–91; Louis Kriesberg, "Changing Conflict Asymmetries Constructively," *Dynamics of Asymmetric Conflict*, 2(1), 2009: 4–22; W. McCarthy, "The Role of Power in Getting to Yes," in W. Breslin and J. Rubin (Eds), *Negotiation Theory and Practice* (Cambridge, MA: Harvard Program on Negotiation, 1991); William Zartman and Jeffrey Rubin, "Symmetry and Asymmetry in Negotiation," in William Zartman and Jeffrey Rubin (Eds), *Power and Negotiation* (Ann Arbor, MI: University of Michigan, 2000); and Galia Golan, "Asymmetry in Cross-Conflict Collaboration: Is There a Gender Factor?," *Peace and Conflict Studies*, 18(2), 2011: 164–191.
44 Sher, 2006: 4; 86, 87. See also Ben-Ami, 2006: 253.
45 Albright, 2003: 458.
46 Clinton, 2005: 911.
47 The opposition of the NRP was the reason Barak reneged on his promise to Clinton to withdraw from the three villages around Jerusalem (Sher, 2006: 48). Shortly thereafter he admitted in an interview that he had handled the matter mistakenly by treating it separately, arousing a political row, rather than simply including the villages in a regular redeployment (*Haaretz*, 19 May 2000).
48 For example, speech presenting his government to the Knesset on 6 July 1999; *Haaretz*, interview 19 May 2000; *Jerusalem Post* interview, 19 May 2000, eve of Camp David statement, 10 July 2000 (all available on MFA website).
49 Ross, 2005: 709.
50 There were differences of opinion within the Palestinian delegation, too, reflecting, upon occasion, some linked to power struggles or broader differences within the PLO (Ross, 2005: 208; Ben-Ami, 2006: 282–283).
51 Ben-Ami, 2006: 247, said the military were "sometimes overwhelmingly involved" in negotiations under Barak; see also Sher, 2006: 34–35, 53.
52 Ben-Ami, 2006: 247.
53 He relented regarding sovereignty but wanted a military presence for 10–12 years, if not more.

54 Sher, 2006: 34–35. Yanai said leasing or sharing protection of the Palestinian–Jordanian border between Israel, Palestine, and even a third party would be acceptable in terms of security. He also said that a small Israeli contingent temporarily would do.
55 *Haaretz* interview, 19 May 2000.
56 Central Bureau of Statistics. If East Jerusalem were added, the 1972 total number of settlers was 10,149 and in 2000 the total was 370,548.
57 A familiar campaign slogan of the Likud was that Labor would "divide" Jerusalem, and when news broke that discussions of Jerusalem were taking place at Camp David, there were demonstrations using this line.
58 Sher, 2006: 78.
59 Sher, 2006: 78.
60 Sher, 2006: 79.
61 Asher Arian, *Israel Public Opinion on National Security*, Memorandum 56, JCSS, July 2000.
62 Sher, 2006: 62, also 53.
63 Knesset speech, Protocol, Twenty-eighth Session of the Fifteenth Knesset, Monday, 4 October 1999; speech to cabinet on guidelines for Camp David summit, 9 July 2000 (MFA, Vol. 18: 1999–2001). His fifth point was: "No Israeli recognition of legal or moral responsibility for creating the refugee problem."
64 This deceptive post-conference campaign by Israel was noted also by Indyk and Ginossar in Shamir and Maddy-Weitzman, 2005: 55–56, 103, respectively.
65 The *Peace Index* at the end of July 2000 asked: "Do you feel that the positions presented by Barak at Camp David for the final stage of the peace process were too tough, too conciliatory, or appropriate, meaning not too harsh and not too yielding?" The majority – 44 percent – replied that they were too conciliatory; only 9 percent deemed Barak's positions too harsh, and 35 percent felt they were appropriate. Fewer women (40 percent) than men (48 percent) believed Barak was too conciliatory.
66 The *Peace Index* found, at the end of July 2000, that 67 percent of Jewish Israelis believed the Palestinian side to be entirely or in large part responsible for the failure of Camp David.
67 For the Palestinians this would mean agreeing to the Jewish settlements in East Jerusalem.
68 Ross, 2005: 809, has the text of the Parameters.
69 For example, Barak did not believe 80 percent of the settlers could be accommodated in 4–6 percent of the West Bank (INSS, *The Israeli Palestinian Negotiation File*, "Response of the Government of Israel to the Ideas Raised by President Clinton Regarding the Outline of a Framework Agreement on Permanent Status, 5 June 2001," 2013: 172).
70 *Peace Index*, July 2000: 63 percent of Israeli Jews objected to the clause, stating that sovereignty over Jerusalem would be divided between Israel and the Palestinians in accordance with the composition of its residents. On the Temple Mount proposal, 66 percent were opposed. The strongest opposition – 77 percent – came on the proposal according refugees the right to return to the Palestinian State, with Israel to absorb (maybe) tens of thousands of refugees for family unification and humanitarian reasons. Some 60 percent opposed transferring 95 percent of West Bank territory to the Palestinians, leaving Israel with only 5 percent of the land on which 80 percent of the settlers would be concentrated (32 percent were in favor and 7 percent didn't know).
71 Clinton, 2005: 936–938, 943–945. There are other versions, including one by Yossi Beilin to the effect that Arafat did give a response in January (albeit after the deadline) that Clinton took as a "yes," but that is not what Clinton himself recounts (Yossi Beilin, *The Path to Geneva: The Quest for a Permanent*

Agreement, 1996–2004 (New York, NY: RDV Books, 2004): 224. On the acceptance: *The Guardian*, 22 June 2002.

72 Miguel Moratinos, there as an observer for the EU, produced an account of the talks that can be found at www.ariga.com/treaties/taba/html. According to Herzog, Beilin, and private sources, Israeli offers at Taba varied between 92–94 percent for the Palestinian state, though there is little clarity regarding the extent of swaps and inclusion or not of the Latrun salient, areas of Jerusalem, and more. Herzog, 2011: Appendix; Beilin, 2004: 246. The principle was to provide the Palestinians with the equivalent to 100 percent of the land occupied in the West Bank in June 1967 (some 5,860 square kilometers) plus Gaza, though not necessarily the exact border.

73 Asher Arian, *Israel Public Opinion on National Security*, Memorandum No. 60, JCSS, August 2001. The "Focus Section: Public Opinion" of the *Palestine–Israel Journal*, 11(3&4), 2004/2005, has a number of public opinion studies and analyses; see also The Peace Index for 2000.

74 For example, Barak interview, *Haaretz* magazine, 6 September 2002; or in order to internationalize the conflict or improve leverage. Chief of Staff Moshe Ya'alon, *Haaretz* magazine, 8 August 2002 in order to improve leverage or internationalize the conflict. For the evidence regarding Arafat's effort to prevent the outbreak (though not to stop it subsequently), see Colonel Ephraim Lavie, interview, *Haaretz*, 13 June 2004; Reuven Pedatzur in *Haaretz*, 21 October 2011, and even Albright, 2003: 494, plus Israel's escalation rather than agreement to Arafat-requested cease-fire, Ephraim Lavi and Matti Steinberg, *Haaretz*, 27 February 2013 and the 2007 Israeli documentary film *A Million Bullets in October* by Moishe Goldberg containing interviews of past senior Israeli officials and advisors.

75 Usually suggested in popular commentaries, such as the blog by "Clive" posted on 29 June 2002 on the Free Republic site (www.freerepublic.com/fouc/news/708295/posts). A long article on Prince Bandar indicated that Arafat was warned that this would not be so (Ella Walsh, "The Prince," *The New Yorker*, 24 March 2003). Some believed the Intifada was intended to internationalize the conflict or at least pressure for a "better deal."

8 Olmert's Near Breakthroughs
Annapolis Process and Syrian Talks

The failures of Oslo and Camp David spawned one of the most difficult and violent periods in the Israeli–Palestinian conflict: the second Intifada (termed the al-Aksa Intifada by the Palestinians) and Israeli military retaliation accompanied by reoccupation of areas in the West Bank. In addition, there was periodic, heavy shelling on Israel from Hamas and Islamist groups in Gaza and two major Israeli attacks on Gaza, along with a second war on Lebanon. A good part of the period between Sharon's replacement of Barak in the February 2001 elections and the opening of the Annapolis Conference in November 2007 was spent in trying to end the violence and forge a path to resumption of a peace process. But it was also a period of complex developments inside both Israel and the Palestinian Authority, and within an entirely changed global and regional context that included the 9/11 attacks on the US, the 2003 Iraq War, and the growing power of Iran as well Islamic radicalism in the region.

For the Israeli leadership, the major challenge was the violence of the Intifada and the domestic pressure that it created for some kind of government action, beyond the use of military force. Arafat's death in 2004 had done nothing to alter the stalemate, though it did bring an end to most of the Intifada related violence. But the total absence of negotiations between Israel and the Palestinians did give rise to important voices from military and former security leaders in Israel urging conciliatory measures to strengthen the new, apparently moderate leader of the Palestinian Authority (PA) and the PLO, Abu Mazen.[1] This pressure, combined with a widely publicized, detailed "peace agreement" – the Geneva Initiative – modeled by a track-two effort of Israeli and Palestinian public and security figures, prompted Sharon to undertake an extraordinary unilateral step: full Israeli disengagement from the Gaza Strip. Announced at the end of 2003, and implemented in August 2005, the disengagement entailed the evacuation of some 8,500 settlers and all Israel Defense Forces (IDF) from the Gaza Strip, along with the evacuation of four sparsely populated settlements in the West Bank. Sharon's motivation was not entirely clear – beyond his own stated need to pre-empt the imposition of unfavorable plans upon Israel, meaning presumably the Geneva Initiative.[2] One possible motive was that he simply sought to divide and thereby weaken the PA, cutting off

Gaza from the West Bank; another possibility was that it was a first step in a plan for further, even large-scale withdrawals from the West Bank. Indeed, the latter idea is what the Americans were told in Washington by Sharon's Deputy Prime Minister Ehud Olmert shortly after the disengagement.[3] Still another explanation was the growing realization in right-wing circles of the demographic issue (whereby Jews would soon be outnumbered by Arabs in the total area held by Israel). Disengagement from the Gaza Strip would "remove" some 1.3 million Palestinians from Israeli control. The evacuation of the settlers in August 2005 was a politically tumultuous event – earlier Sharon had actually had to leave his party (which rejected his plan) and create a center party, Kadima;[4] but it was also one that proved that relatively large-scale evacuation of settlements could be carried out.

As a purely unilateral measure, however, the disengagement was to have a serious negative effect. In abjuring the strategy of negotiation of Abu Mazen's Fatah, the move appeared to prove the value of Hamas's strategy of violence for achieving Israeli withdrawal, thereby strengthening the Islamist Hamas at the expense of nationalist Fatah and the PLO. Combined with Palestinians' disenchantment with Fatah corruption and ineffectiveness, along with other factors such as the electoral system, Hamas's enhanced reputation led to a solid victory in the January 2006 elections and the creation of a Hamas-led government of the PA. Israel refused to have anything to do with a PA run by Hamas, inasmuch as the organization rejected the existence of Israel. Both the US (which had Hamas listed as a terrorist organization) and the Quartet[5] adopted Israel's ban on Hamas, also accepting its conditions that Hamas cease terrorism and disarm terrorist groups, recognize the right of Israel to exist, and accept all previous agreements signed with Israel. This meant not only boycott of the PA but also the withholding of funds and suspension of contacts and agreements, although Israel could and did meet with Abu Mazen in his capacity of chairman of the PLO and even as president of the PA.

Just a few weeks before these Palestinian elections, dramatic events had occurred in Israel as well: in early January 2006 Sharon suffered a stroke and went into an irreversible coma.[6] He was replaced temporarily by his deputy Prime Minister Ehud Olmert, who then went on to win the March 2006 elections at the head of Kadima. Actually, Olmert, former mayor of Jerusalem and long-time Likud politician, was not a popular figure; he had placed relatively low in the Likud Knesset primaries of 2003, but his choice by Sharon as deputy prime minister now projected him unexpectedly to power. Presenting himself as the past partner to Sharon, Olmert ran in the March 2006 elections on the promise to undertake unilateral disengagement from the West Bank. He preferred to call this "convergence," which in its Hebrew meaning was closer to the idea of "pulling inward;" it came to be called "realignment." Without providing specifics, Olmert advocated evacuation of the settlements from most of the West Bank (later approximated at 92 percent of the West Bank) – namely, those settlements east of the fence/wall (or a changed demarcation of this barrier) that the Sharon government had begun to build.

This "security barrier" as it was to be called officially had actually been a Labor Party proposal at the height of the Intifada, the idea being to prevent terrorist incursions into Israel proper. The line of the barrier approved by the Sharon government would veer into the West Bank, east of the "green line," encompassing roughly 10 percent of the West Bank. A proposed line for a fence in the Jordan Valley was not approved by the government; it would have provided *de facto* annexation of still more land. With the withdrawal proposed by Olmert, roughly 60,000 settlers (according to some estimates) were to be moved to settlement blocs west of the fence (i.e., near the "green line") that would be annexed to Israel.[7] The withdrawal remained unilateral, presumably as a continuation of Sharon's ideas, but now, also, because of the ascent of Hamas in the January elections.[8]

Nothing was said of withdrawing the IDF along with the settlers – in fact, Olmert said that the "operational range" of Israeli security forces would "not be limited," and he saw the Jordan River as Israel's "security border." He gave few details regarding the future border, though he spoke of keeping Ariel, Gush Etzion, and other settlements around Jerusalem as well as a united Jerusalem.[9] He presented his plan as an alternative should negotiations not be possible – that is, should the PA remain under a government led by Hamas. However, by this time, the parameters for negotiations had undergone significant changes since their September 2000 disruption. Although Olmert only gradually began to say so directly, it was now public knowledge that future negotiations – if they occurred – would have the explicit goal of creating a Palestinian state next to the state of Israel.

Public and official acknowledgement of agreement to a Palestinian state was conspicuously absent from previous Israeli government positions, including, as we have seen, that of Yitzhak Rabin. In fact, Rabin had said explicitly that the result of final status talks would be "an entity less than a state."[10] The negotiations at Camp David in July 2000 were based implicitly, but only implicitly, on the idea that a Palestinian state would emerge. The Clinton Parameters used the term Palestinian state, but neither the Israelis nor the Americans had officially or publicly embraced the goal of creating a Palestinian state. Surprisingly, it was military hawk Ariel, as head of the then Likud-led government, who did so on 23 September 2001 in a little noticed speech in Israel ("The state of Israel wants to give the Palestinians what nobody had given them before: the possibility to establish a state").[11] Subsequently Sharon repeated the position, saying, for example: "In the end we [Israel and the Palestinians] will reach a solution in which there will be a Palestinian state but it has to be a Palestinian state by agreement and it has to be a demilitarized state."[12] Presumably on the basis of this change in Israel, and in the interests of forging a broad coalition that would include the Arab states for his post-9/11 onslaught on terrorism, President George W. Bush too spoke of the vision of two states. He did this almost casually, in a press conference after a meeting with Congressional leaders on 2 October 2001, possibly as a "trial balloon" purposely launched by the White House (with Israeli approval).[13] This then was formally and officially pronounced by Bush in his 10 November 2001 speech to the United Nations General Assembly. Bush's UN comments were subsequently incorporated almost word for word into a UN Security Council (UNSC) resolution affirming a "vision of a region where two states, Israel and Palestine, live side by side within secure and recognized borders" and in his 24 June 2002 Rose Garden speech.[14] This last outlined Bush's idea of a Palestinian state, in provisional borders, to be achieved once the Palestinians rid themselves of Arafat, destroyed the infrastructure of terrorism, and adopted the accoutrements of democracy. These demands were later spelled out in greater detail in the April 2003 Road Map, presented by the Americans in the name of the Quartet. The Road Map was designed to guide the parties through various stages, including the declaration of a state in provisional borders, before reaching final status talks. But the preamble of the Road Map set the goal of a Palestinian state, and the document was adopted by the Israeli cabinet (albeit with 14 reservations). In presenting it to the Knesset for approval, Sharon told the Likud faction that it was necessary to "end the occupation," adding: "You may not like the word, but what is happening is an occupation – to hold 3.5 million Palestinians under occupation. I believe that is a terrible thing for Israel and for the Palestinians."[15] A page had been turned even if qualified by preconditions (to be met by the Palestinians), and accompanied by continued violence on the ground and Israeli settlement construction, without any negotiation process in place.

Still another, also little noticed, page had been turned in the region at the same time as the adoption of the two-state solution by Israel's right-wing government. Meeting in Beirut in February 2002, the Arab League unanimously adopted a slightly revised version of a Saudi peace plan in what became known as the Arab Peace Initiative (API). The brain child of the Jordanians and the Saudis, the Initiative was probably the most significant step with regard to Israel in that country's brief history, for the API not only proclaimed the rejection of military means for solution of the conflict, but also outlined steps for accepting Israel in the region. It stated the usual formula calling for Israeli withdraw to the 4 June 1967 lines (the idea of land swaps was already commonly accepted – and officially added to the API some years later, in 2013), the creation of a Palestinian state with its capital in East Jerusalem, and a "just, agreed upon" solution to the refugee issue. These two last clauses, and especially the latter one, had been carefully and purposely formulated in deference to Israeli concerns. Thus the word "East" was specified rather than the customary more general – and emotionally charged – reference simply to Jerusalem. But more significantly, the phrase regarding the refugees for the first time added the words "agreed upon," meaning that a solution could not be forced upon Israel. Resolution of the refugee issue would have to be agreed between Israel and the Palestinians. The refugee clause had not been in the original Saudi proposal; it was added upon Syrian demand, but not only did it have this more conciliatory wording, it also omitted a specific mention of a "right of return," making do with a reference only to United Nations General

Assembly (UNGA) Resolution 194. As already noted, Israel maintains that Resolution 194 did not actually grant the "right of return," but Jerusalem has always objected to any mention of the resolution because it does allow for refugees ("willing to live in peace with their neighbors") to choose to return. The API reference could thus be interpreted in various ways, but the point, as noted by the person who actually formulated the clause – the Jordanian Foreign Minister Marwan Muasher – was to find wording (the new phrase "agreed upon") that would calm Israeli fears of an inundation of refugees that could challenge the nature of the state.[16] Aside from the more conciliatory wording of the refugee clause, the most significant part of the API was the pledge that if these steps were taken, along with Israeli withdrawal from the other areas taken since 4 June 1967 – namely, from Syria and Lebanon – all 22 Arab states (including Palestine) pledged to "Consider the Arab–Israel conflict ended, and enter into a peace agreement with Israel, and provide security for all the states of the region" and "Establish normal relations with Israel in the context of this comprehensive peace."[17] The API was subsequently endorsed by the 57-member Islamic Conference, which included Iran.[18] It is possible that the Saudi initiative, first suggested by Crown Prince (later King) Abdullah in an interview with Tom Friedman in the *New York Times*, was a means of improving the country's image given the involvement of Saudi citizens in 9/11.[19] However, its adoption (and repeated subsequent reconfirmations) by the entire Arab League was more likely due to the common interest of the Arab states to end the conflict that had come to serve as a rallying point for radical forces in the region considered anathema to their regimes and a threat to their continued power. But coming as it did, in the midst of some of the worst terror attacks that, in fact, prompted an Israeli military assault on the West Bank and reoccupation of various areas in the spring of 2002, the Arab Peace Initiative was virtually ignored by Israel, though it was included in the later Road Map.

In general, it was the ongoing violence that precluded Israeli interest in or progress toward negotiations, including implementation of the Road Map.[20] According to the Israeli interpretation (often supported by the Americans), the steps within the stages of the Road Map were to be taken sequentially, rather than in tandem. This meant that first the Palestinians should implement *all* the anti-terrorism and democratization measures (the focus of Bush's post-9/11 policy), before Israel would undertake its obligations and move onto subsequent stages. The result was what amounted to a continuation of the diplomatic void, and it was into this void that Sharon introduced his disengagement plan in December 2003. The Americans were impressed that Sharon was willing to give up Gaza, and in response to his request that the president provide assurances regarding Israeli interests in the West Bank, Bush altered America's traditional policy on the settlements. In a 14 April 2004 speech and letter, Bush noted that future borders were to take into consideration "new realities on the ground, including already existing major Israeli population centers ... it is unrealistic to expect that the outcome of final status negotiations will be a full and complete return to the armistice lines of 1949."[21] At the same time, Sharon provided Bush with assurances that he was not ignoring the Road Map despite pursing unilateral disengagement.

Notwithstanding the Road Map, Sharon's disengagement in fact introduced an entirely new direction – and method – that may have impeded rather than facilitated resumption of a peace process, whatever Sharon's ultimate intentions. Yet, unilateralism was the path that Sharon's successor, Olmert, chose to follow when he came to power in 2006. Between the continued violence (that now included rocket attacks from Gaza), and the strength of Hamas now ruling the PA and boycotted by Israel, the US, and the other Quartet members, there appeared little hope for any other path. Circumstances were to change, however, and with them a chance for a breakthrough was to emerge in less than a year, leading ultimately to the Annapolis Conference.

The factor most basic to a breakthrough was the change that occurred in Olmert himself. Active in Likud politics from his youth, Olmert was one of the Likud "princes" – that is, the son of pre-state right-wing underground activists. He had voted against the accords with Egypt and against Oslo, criticized Barak's reported concessions at Camp David, and, as an enthusiastic advocate of "greater Israel," he had actively supported settlement construction in East Jerusalem during his tenure as mayor, as well as in the West Bank. Although he himself specified the late 1990s as the time of his transformation to supporting the two-state solution, his public pronouncements gave little evidence of this position until 2003, and even then only slightly. Judging from his speeches, interviews, and his own accounts, it was primarily the demographic factor that brought about the change. For Olmert, it was imperative that there be a Jewish majority in the area ruled by Israel, which obviously would not be the case if Israel continued to hold onto the occupied territories. Like the Labor Party before him, Olmert understood that if Israel were to remain democratic it would have to give the vote to all the inhabitants – leading then to a bi-national state, in which Jews would soon no longer be a majority. In addition to the demographic issue, the second Intifada also weighed heavily upon Olmert. He spoke often and graphically of the terrorist attacks, particularly the suicide bombings in Jerusalem, where as mayor he had visited victims' families, often eulogizing at funerals. He referred to this later as "the most arduous time of my life."[22] Thus, as early as 2003, he spoke of the need to evacuate much of the West Bank.[23] While demography and the Intifada apparently persuaded him that time was not working to Israel's benefit, the views of his family also played a role in his thinking, as he himself suggested. His wife Aliza was known to be left wing in her political views, and their children, as young adults, were identified with the radical left. In retrospect, he said: "I am proud that I was able to admit, first of all to myself, then to my family, and eventually to the public at large, that in 2005 I didn't think what I had thought 20 years earlier."[24] Actually, Olmert did begin publicly to reveal much of this change in a surprising speech he gave (in place of an ailing Sharon) at a Ben Gurion memorial in 2003. This was followed by an extensive interview in which he spoke of all of these matters, later repeated for the most part in his election campaign in 2006.[25] His conclusions were withdrawal, and in his pragmatic approach the method was to be unilateral, despite his talk of a preference for negotiations.

The major factor that led Olmert subsequently to abandon unilateralism was the Second Lebanon War in the summer of 2006. The war was precipitated by the Hamas capture of an Israeli soldier near the Gaza Strip, followed by a similar incursion by Hizballah in the north and the capture of two Israel soldiers. The Israeli response was a full-scale military attack on Lebanon and then a smaller onslaught against Gaza. Since Israel had ended its occupation of southern Lebanon unilaterally in May 2000, the Hizballah action defied the wisdom of unilateral withdrawals (i.e., withdrawing without agreements, particularly agreements on security measures). But it was not only the demise of the unilateral idea that led Olmert to seek an alternative policy. A second reason was Olmert's weakened position as a result of the war. There was serious post-war criticism of his government's handling of the crisis. Some of the protests related to the unpreparedness of the IDF, some to what was perceived as a restraining of the army in order to avoid Israeli casualties, some were related to the continuation of the war days after a cease-fire had been achieved diplomatically, and some (far fewer) were related to the doubtful need for the attack altogether. In response, a state commission was appointed to examine the conduct of the war. While the commission eventually supported Olmert's decisions, his earlier interest in a breakthrough on the Palestinian issue may now have been augmented by a wish to redeem his political standing and improve his reputation. These had been further tarnished by press accusations of corruption that had been appearing since early 2006.[26] Such charges were to multiply and hound Olmert, eventually forcing him to resign in 2008.

An American factor was also at play. Secretary of State Condoleezza Rice had been pressing for greater priority to the Arab-Israeli issue since the beginning of Bush's second administration. The US itself was in a weakened position in the region following the Iraq War and the unraveling of both the political and security scene in Iraq. The longstanding pressure from America's Arab allies, especially Saudi Arabia, for moves to promote a breakthrough on the Palestinian front had only been strengthened by Israel's harsh response to the Intifada and now the war in Lebanon. Moreover, and perhaps even more importantly for the Saudis, the absence of progress on the Palestinian front, coupled with Israel's actions, strengthened the Saudi's enemy Hamas. The Iraq Study Group, an independent bi-partisan commission set up by Congress under the auspices of the US Institute of Peace, and headed by James Baker and Lee Hamilton, had also linked progress on the Israeli–Palestinian track with America's overall interests in the region.[27] And Rice saw this as a crucial element for the building of an alliance against Iran.[28] All of these factors may explain Rice's proposal in September 2006 to Olmert's advisors Shalom Tourgeman and Yoram Turbowitz regarding the need to initiate permanent status talks, possibly in an international meeting to jumpstart an Israeli–Palestinian peace process. Although Olmert is reported to have rejected the idea of moving to final status talks (according to US Assistant National Security Advisor Elliot Abrams, who opposed Rice and her policies, particularly this one), Israeli efforts were made in October to commence bilateral talks in Jerusalem.[29]

Olmert invited Abu Mazen to his official residence, and, after a number of postponements by Abu Mazen, the first meeting took place on 23 December 2006 amidst an unusual Israeli display of formal recognition, including Palestinian flags. According to an Olmert interview, he went out of his way to be forthcoming, even offering Abu Mazen such things as the transfer of Palestinian funds held by Israel, beyond the sum requested by Abu Mazen. Indeed, on leaving the meeting, the Palestinian leader is quoted as saying: "A new era has begun."[30] There followed regular talks, usually bi-weekly, on one or two occasions joined by Rice. Olmert remained opposed to an international conference, preferring bilateral talks, though the idea that was emerging was to hold negotiations on a final agreement that would be held in reserve (a shelf agreement) until the Road Map was implemented. Olmert even told the American Jewish Conference of Presidents in early February 2007 that "there will not be an international conference."[31] Elliot Abrams had actually been telling the president that American Jews were not sympathetic to the conference idea, although it does not seem to be the case that the diaspora played a role in Bush's continued skepticism about a conference at this time.[32] Be that as it may, in March 2007 the Palestinians formed a national unity government composed of Fatah and Hamas, thereby precluding any official US contact with the Palestinian Authority. In fact, because of this, Rice had to meet separately with Olmert and Abu Mazen on her March 2007 trip to the region.

Annapolis was an American – actually, a Rice – initiative, and a number of factors may account for Bush's agreement finally to hold an international conference. Rice's persistent argument that the Palestinians needed a "political horizon" apparently convinced the US president that a framework or shelf agreement envisaging a state might provide the incentive needed for the realization of the democratization measures he advocated. Bush has written: "If wavering Palestinians could see that a state was a realistic possibility, they would have an incentive to reject violence and support reform."[33] The timing of the decision to hold a conference was apparently connected with the violent coup staged by Hamas in June 2007 that led to a formal split – with Hamas ruling Gaza and Abu Mazen the West Bank. Israel and the United States could now deal with Abu Mazen, who still held the title of president of the PA (Hamas's Haniyeh, now leading in Gaza, had been prime minister of the National Unity Government). In fact, there was now a US interest in strengthening Abu Mazen lest Hamas spread its gains to the West Bank. A helpful move was the appointment of a new PA government under Prime Minister Selim Fayyad, a politically unaffiliated economist well known and respected by the US. In addition, the Americans calculated that Abu Mazen needed an agreement now more than ever in order to halt Hamas's progress, and, therefore, he would be ready for a conference.[34] Thus, just one month after the Hamas coup, Bush announced that there would be an international conference.

Olmert agreed primarily because of the Americans, though he still preferred bilateral talks, and eschewed both American and international involvement, believing that more progress could be made – namely, greater flexibility and pragmatism could be achieved from the other-side if third parties or more were not present. Similarly, grandstanding, efforts to exploit the third party, and also leaks might be avoided. Nonetheless, Olmert did see international support as an important factor; he considered the "everyone is against us" attitude nurtured by many Israeli right-wing politicians merely a self-fulfilling and dangerous tendency. More specifically, if a deal were made with the Palestinians, he would need both diplomatic and economic backing from the Americans for his domestic political battle. Thus, it was characteristic of Olmert to take care to keep Washington informed of his decisions, even revealing to the administration his plan for unilateral withdrawal before revealing it to the Israeli public in 2006.[35] Nonetheless, Olmert sought to avoid any opening or broadening of his negotiations with the Palestinians, acquiescing to the Americans' Annapolis idea (preferring to call it a meeting rather than a conference) only if it were to constitute no more than a launch of the bilateral path. Probably more than simply a matter of avoiding outside pressure, this was evidence of Olmert's over-riding preference to negotiate quietly. The potential opposition within his own party and government was an important factor; any indication that he might actually be considering concessions, in discussion of final status issues, could "bring down my government," he told the Americans.[36] This was to be a key factor in Olmert's handling of the conflict and negotiations altogether. Yet, at the time, there was also something to be gained by a show of international support, given the steep decline in Olmert's popularity and the accumulation of corruption charges against him. A meeting in the presence not only of the American president, but foreign ministers from over a dozen Arab countries, including Saudi Arabia, plus Muslim Pakistan, Malaysia, Turkey, and Indonesia, and the Arab League secretary-general, some 20 additional countries and representatives of the European Union, UN and others could provide a needed boost to his sagging prestige. Many may have believed this to be his only motivation, but subsequent developments suggest that Olmert thought that the American-sought meeting might at least provide backing, especially for Abu Mazen, helpful for reaching an agreement in the later, quiet bilateral talks. In any case, due both to the leadership in Israel and the US, along with the changed circumstances, Annapolis was presented – and perhaps was – the launching pad for a potential breakthrough at the bilateral level.

The willingness of Arab states, in particular Saudi Arabia, to send high-level officials to the Annapolis meeting was the result of the changed regional environment that had itself produced the Arab Peace Initiative. Syria, now ruled by Bashar al Assad, appeared to be less interested inasmuch as it sent only a deputy foreign minister, but, in fact, at the time Damascus was engaged in secret unofficial talks and track two meetings to reach an agreement with Israel as well. Syrian initiatives in this direction had begun in 2004, with approval of Foreign Minister Walid Mouallem, leading to a series of unofficial meetings despite an official rebuff by Israel. The negative Israeli position was most likely due to America's opposition to dealing with Syria at the time, though Sharon himself was not particularly interested. During this period, while Sharon was still prime minister, Olmert was aware of the Syrian overtures, some of which were made in contacts with Israelis at Pugwash meetings – a channel used in the past, for example, for semi-official contacts between the US and the Soviet Union. The main channel that developed, however, was one initially facilitated by Turkey, in 2004, and subsequently continued by Switzerland under the auspices of Swiss Foreign Ministry Middle East Chief Nicholas Lang. Alon Liel, former director-general of the Israeli Foreign Ministry (and formerly ambassador to Turkey), met several times in Europe with Ibrahim Suleiman, a Syrian businessman permanently located in Washington. For a period of time, there was also a channel with a more direct representative from Damascus, also authorized by Muallem and in touch with Liel, as well as other Israelis, including this author. Senior Israeli officials were kept aware of all of these contacts. The Swiss-facilitated Suleiman-Liel channel was used for meetings throughout 2005–2006, including eight meetings of the Swiss mediator with Syrian Vice-President Farouk Shara and Foreign Minister Walid Mouallem. During the 2006 Lebanon War, the group claims to have met with Olmert's top advisor Turbowitz.[37] According to a later interview by Suleiman to the Israeli press, Turbowitz was given a proposal for steps toward official talks, but Olmert turned it down.[38] The proposal reportedly was the draft of a peace agreement prepared by the Suleiman-Liel team. Later, in January 2007, the plan was purposely leaked to the Israeli press, presumably in order to provoke the opening of official talks. At that time, Olmert, who was now acting prime minister, claimed to have had no knowledge of the talks (which was not, in fact, true), and he publicly rejected any dialogue with Syria unless Damascus ended its support for terrorist groups and its destabilizing activities in Lebanon and Iraq.[39] Press reports claimed that the US was the obstacle;[40] Washington still held Syria responsible for the 2005 murder of Lebanon's former Prime Minister Rafic Hariri and also for harming US efforts in Iraq. Yet, conservative Republican Dov Zakeim, who had served in the administrations of both Bush Sr. and George W. Bush, was involved at the early stages of the talks via Pugwash meetings in Washington. He even went to Damascus for talks with Muallem during late 2004 to early 2005, not long after he resigned as Comptroller of the Department of Defense. In addition, Vice-President Cheney (a good friend of Olmert's[41]) had been "kept in the picture" regarding the talks all along, according to "senior officials" and also Suleiman.[42] The leaders of the Iraq Study Group, James Baker (a close confidante of the administration) and Lee Hamilton (a good friend of Suleiman, maybe even the initial go-between), along with some of the members of the Iraq Study Group were also aware of the talks possibly from the very beginning. The knowledge, even participation by some of these figures, may have been indications of at least tacit US approval – at the least there was no active US interference. By the spring of 2007 there were more open signs of a change in the US attitude. Although the Bush administration rebuked Democratic Speaker of the House Nancy Pelosi for traveling to Damascus for a meeting with Assad in April 2007, the very next month Secretary Rice held a half hour discussion (which she publicly described as "cordial"[43]) with Muallem on the sidelines of a conference in Sharm el-Sheikh. And by November 2007 Washington was willing, even if reluctantly, to invite Syria to Annapolis.[44]

The factors that may have prompted Washington to change its attitude, at least toward Israel's talking with the Syrians, were attributed to pressure from the Arab states; but there was also domestic pressure in the US to engage Syria in order to move it away from Iran and bring it closer to the moderate Arab center in the region. This was the recommendation of the Iraq Study Group, which saw a potential for Syria to operate as a stabilizing factor with regard to Iraq and possibly the region as a whole. For Syria, the initiative once again to open talks with Israel was primarily motivated by an interest in improving relations with the US, particularly to obtain an end of US sanctions and removal of Syria from the list of governments supporting terrorism. The road to Washington might pass through Jerusalem, which, under Olmert, appeared to be open (though not officially) to exploring any avenue. This was not the generally held opinion; most observers believed that Israel could never work on two tracks (Palestinian and Syrian) at the same time – indeed, in response to a query about talks with Syria, Olmert even spoke of reluctance to deal with two "heartrending" sacrifices at one time.[45] Moreover, public opinion was far from supportive of an opening toward Syria. Some 52 percent of Israelis polled opposed responding positively to a Syrian initiative.[46] Nonetheless, there were factors in favor of pursing a dialogue with Damascus. At a minimum, talks with Syria could act as leverage on the Palestinian track (something the Americans had once thought Rabin was trying to engineer); alternatively, the Syrian track might serve as a substitute if the Palestinian track failed once again. The security establishment may also have played a role, for there were signs that the military were interested in an opening to Syria after the 2006 war, though the Mossad was skeptical about the likelihood of success.[47] It would appear that the major factor, despite US hesitations, was Olmert's perception that Syria was seriously interested. The draft peace agreement, as published in *Haaretz* on 15 and 16 January 2007, suggested that Syria was somewhat more forthcoming than in earlier negotiations with regard to Israel's demands for:

1   staggered withdrawals (though they still disagreed on the length of the implementation period);
2   early initiation of diplomatic steps;
3   mutual but unequal force reductions (in favor of Israel 1:4); and
4   Israeli control over the headwaters of the Jordan River and the Kinneret.

There were also reports of a possible American agreement with Syria that Damascus would end support of Hizballah and Hamas, and there were reportedly Syrian assurances that Damascus would distance itself from Iran.[48] Israel, for its part, would grant Syria use of the headwaters and agree to US (rather than Israeli)-led early warning posts on the Hermon. The border would be the 4 June 1967 line, the location of which was to be determined jointly. An innovation in this draft agreement was the provision for the creation of a "peace park" on the Golan Heights, to be under Syrian sovereignty and administration but open to all.[49] Although Olmert not only denied any knowledge of this draft accord and made no mention of Syria in the lead-up to Annapolis (for him Annapolis was all about the two-state solution with the Palestinians), he did agree to the Syrian demand that Syria be on the agenda of Annapolis. This was accommodated by the broadening of the event with a "discussion group on regional peace."[50] Moreover, as early as February 2007, Olmert had sent out informal feelers and then engaged in direct talks with Syria, via the Turks. Olmert's reasons for pursuing a Syrian track were linked – both positively and negatively – to the 2006 Lebanon War. The war had highlighted the unpreparedness of the Israeli home front and the complexity of the defense of Israel's north in case of future conflict with Syria. Thus, there appeared to be a vital security interest in peace with Syria. On the more positive side, Assad's restraint during the war and, later, his total silence in response to an Israeli attack on a Syrian nuclear facility 6 September 2007 suggested that Bashar Assad was a mature, responsible leader who might be a serious interlocutor, possibly even one willing to act independently of his ties to Iran.[51] In fact, Israel's estimate, as in past times, was that Syria was interested in joining the Western-oriented Arab "center" and moving towards the US rather than maintaining its present orientation. And, as in the past, the road to Washington could only pass (if at all) through Jerusalem, certainly in the eyes of the Americans at this time.

An additional factor for the convening of Annapolis and possible breakthrough at least on the Palestinian track was favorable Israeli public opinion about the desirability (even need) for Israeli–Palestinian negotiations. The November 2007 Peace Index a few weeks before the Annapolis opening showed 70 percent support, although only 38.9 percent of Israelis thought talks would lead to peace in the near future.[52] Signs that this was a realistic appraisal could be found in the still different Israeli and Palestinian expectations and problems regarding the meeting. These, in fact, suggested that there would be serious obstacles on the path toward a breakthrough. The very invitation issued by the Americans was the subject of dispute, with Israel objecting to any reference to an end product – namely, a "peace agreement," or discussion of the core issues, as preferred by the Palestinians and Arab invitees. Nor did Olmert want mention of the Arab Peace Initiative as a "basis" for the meeting (despite the fact that he himself had referred to "positive parts" of "the Saudi initiative" as early as 27 November 2006).[53] Olmert preferred a bland invitation, including little more than the bare essentials of time and place of the meeting, and he reportedly was angry when the invitation did mention the API.[54]

More promisingly, he agreed to the invitation's stated objective: "the launch of bilateral negotiations toward the establishment of a Palestinian state and the realization of Israeli-Palestinian peace ... ."[55] But that was as far as he was willing to go publicly. Thus, there were even more differences over the joint statement that was to have laid out the basis or principles for the conference. After months of effort, with American involvement, the parties were unable to reach agreement in time for a frame of reference joint statement. Here, too, the sides made do with a last minute, relatively bland statement read out by Bush at the opening.

The major factor for these differences, as we shall see below, would appear to have been Olmert's preferred method for dealing with peace talks. Cognizant of potential spoilers even within his own government, he chose to keep his intentions known only to a small number of associates and advisors while avoiding public discussion of issues that might stir up opposition and impede the talks. Thus, he constructed the ensuing negotiations to proceed on three parallel tracks: the first, most important track was between himself and Abu Mazen, sometimes just one-on-one; the second track was between his foreign minister (and rival) Tzipy Livny and her Palestinian counterpart Abu Ala, with American participants. Occasionally Rice joined both tracks as well as meeting with each of the leaders during their visits to the US or Bush's visits to the region. The third track was composed of committees dealing with the infrastructure necessary for whatever was agreed on the various issues – that is, the more technical matters in order to prepare the ground for implementation once agreement was reached at the top level.

The turning point in the negotiations occurred, apparently, in May 2008. At a private dinner at the prime minister's residence, Olmert told Rice that the negotiations under Livny would not finish before Bush's term ended and, therefore, he wanted more direct talks, via a "trusted agent" from each side. He said that he knew what Abu Mazen needed and these could be briefly written in a few pages, the critical issues being Jerusalem and the refugees. He proposed the following, according to Rice's account: "enough land," roughly 94 percent of the West Bank plus swaps; Jerusalem as the capital of the two states with an Israeli mayor and a Palestinian deputy mayor for a joint city council selected by both populations according to their percentages in the city's total population; Israeli security for the holy sites; a committee composed of "wise people" from Saudi Arabia, Jordan, Palestine, Israel, and the US to administer – that is, "to oversee but not politically rule" – the Old City; and the entry to Israel of approximately 5,000 refugees under the rubric of family reunification.[56] He said that eight security demands prepared by then Defense Minister Barak would most likely not be accepted by Abu Mazen and therefore suggested that the Americans work with Barak and the IDF on a proposal. When Rice conveyed these ideas to Abu Mazen the next day, the Palestinian leader reportedly said that the refugee proposal was a problem but suggested he and Olmert deal with everything themselves rather than through "agents," to which Olmert agreed.

Actually a few weeks earlier, on 4 May, the Palestinians had presented maps in the Livny-Abu Ala channel, outlining the areas intended for the Palestinian state and swaps (1.9 percent allowed for Israeli annexation), along with ideas regarding Jerusalem.[57] While Rice participated in a 15 June 2008 meeting with this group, and much of the information appears to be the same as the ideas presented in the Olmert-Abu Mazen channel, it is far from clear how much the two channels were, in fact, synchronized on the Israeli side. Indeed, the absence of close synchronization, noted by Rice, seemed to be implied in Olmert's decision to handle the negotiations himself, disdaining to a large degree Livny's track.

The two leaders met over the next months on all the final status issues, one of the main bones of contention being the Israeli demand to annex the settlement of Ariel which juts into the West Bank roughly 16 kilometers beyond the "green line." In the summer there were numerous – not always accurate – leaks, particularly with regard to the Jerusalem issue, but all the parties involved refrained from publicly responding. The final, apparently decisive meeting between Olmert and Abu Mazen took place on 16 September 2008, well after Olmert's July announcement that he would resign and one day before the new head of Kadima was to be selected.

There are many accounts of the proposal made by Olmert on 16 September, including revelations by both leaders, as well as a myriad of leaked protocols of the Livny-Abu Ala talks.[58] According to Olmert's own accounts and interviews accorded over time, the Israeli proposal followed the lines of the ideas conveyed to Rice in May.[59] Regarding the territorial aspects, the border would be based on the 1967 lines, with Israel annexing 6.3 percent of the West Bank (some of Olmert's accounts said 6.5 percent, presumably depending upon what was included; the 40 kilometer tunnel for passage from Gaza to the West Bank was not included since it was to be under Israeli sovereignty but Palestinian control); previously demilitarized areas would be equally divided, and land from within Israel amounting to 5.8 percent of the total area of the West Bank would be accorded to Palestine in a swap (in exchange for the 6.3 percent annexed by Israel for the settlement blocs, areas around Jerusalem, and the areas added to Jerusalem by Israel in 1967).[60]

Abu Mazen, in his accounts,[61] proposed just 1.9 percent for Israeli annexation. Rejecting inclusion of Ariel, he based his figures on his calculation of the amount of land actually taken up by the settlements. In fact, at that time the settlements took up 2 percent, and five years later Israel's right-wing deputy foreign minister, claiming that settlements were not an impediment to peace, inadvertently strengthened the Palestinians' bargaining position when he said that the settlements actually took up only 3 percent of the West Bank. An Israeli advocacy group, "Stand With Us," went even further by claiming that the settlements took up only 1.2 percent of the West Bank.[62] Of course, the Israeli negotiating position was based on the fact that the settlements were in scattered locations and therefore needed to be encompassed in "blocs" to provide safe access once attached to Israel. Under Olmert's plan to annex

180 Olmert's Near Breakthroughs

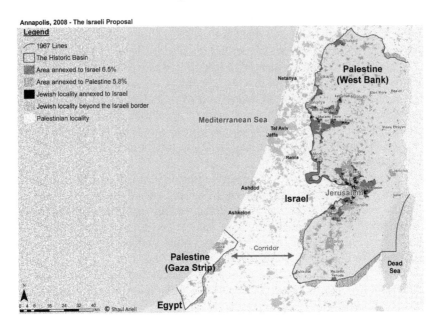

Map 8.1 Olmert Proposal 2008 (approximation)
Source: Shaul Arieli

6.3 percent, some 85 percent of the settlers (as of 2008) could be accommodated in the settlement blocs, necessitating the evacuation of roughly 45,000 settlers (some estimated as high as 70,000 and even 120,000 depending upon the map used – under Abu Mazen's proposal, some 74,000 settlers, according to other estimates as many as 160,000, would have to be moved, accommodating only 75 percent of the settlers).[63] These figures depended upon various delineations of the blocs (and possibly of East Jerusalem); but according to the State Census taken in 2008 there were 296,700 settlers in the West Bank (and 193,700 in East Jerusalem).[64] The criterion for the Palestinians was territorial contiguity for their state, and Abu Mazen's most consistent objection was to the Israeli inclusion of Ariel. For Israel, the major concern was the number of settlers who would have to be moved.

Regarding Jerusalem, Olmert adopted Clinton's proposal that the Jewish neighborhoods/settlements built in expanded East Jerusalem after the 1967 war would be under Israeli sovereignty, while the Arab neighborhoods would be under Palestinian sovereignty. These areas could be considered the capital of Palestine if the Palestinians so wished. The "holy basin" would be open to worshippers of all faiths but under a trusteeship of Saudi Arabia, Jordan, Palestine, Israel, and the US, which would be responsible for setting the procedures and regulations for this area and visitors to it. In this way, the previously critical matter of sovereignty over the Temple Mount/Haram al Sherif within the "holy basin" was not addressed, placing the whole matter on

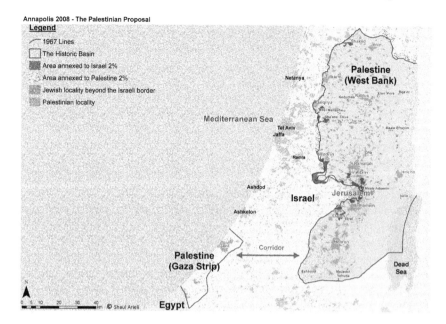

Map 8.2 Abu Mazen Proposal 2008 (approximation)
Source: Shaul Arieli

a more practical level. It was assumed by both leaders that the *status quo* regarding the administration of the Islamic sites would continue, under the Wakf.[65] Abu Mazen is said to have agreed to Olmert's formula, though inclusion of some areas, such as the formerly divided Abu Tor and parts of Silwan, were still undecided but not considered (at least by Olmert) to be problematic.[66] Abu Mazen did resist Israeli's annexation of the settlement of Har Homa, alone of the 13 or more Jewish neighborhoods/settlements built by Israel after 1967 in the expanded borders of the city. Clearly sensitive on these matters (subsequent to the *al Jazeera* leaks), Abu Mazen's later accounts in the Arab world said that final agreement had not been reached regarding Jerusalem.

On the refugee issue, there are several versions of what was proposed. Olmert reports that he would agree ("in the spirit of the Arab Peace Initiative") to the absorption of 5,000 refugees at the rate of 1,000 a year – a figure based amazingly on an estimate of the number of people who could fit into the Muqata (presidential compound of the PA, but also upon the fact that the absorption at that time of some 5,000 Sudanese refugees in Israel had not affected the nature of the state).[67] This would constitute an end of all claims and would be accompanied by a written declaration of Israel's sensitivity to the suffering caused the Palestinians uprooted from their homes as a result of the conflict, as well as something about the suffering of Israelis and the Jewish people as a result of the wars.[68] Israel would assist in the creation of an international fund to compensate refugees for their losses. Olmert said later that the final number of refugees could, in fact, be negotiated later and might even reach the figure of 15,000, but no more than that.[69] Olmert insisted, however, that Abu Mazen never set a specific figure to which the Palestinians might agree, although various figures were mentioned in Palestinian conversations with the Americans, such as 20,000 or 40,000. One senior administration source reportedly said that Abu Mazen told the Americans that he would agree to 40,000 to 60,000.[70] Olmert specifically clarified later that as early as their December 2006 conversation Abu Mazen had assured him: "'I know how sensitive you are to the refugees. I can tell you one thing: We are not aspiring to change the nature of your country.'"[71] Indeed, Abu Mazen was often to repeat such sentiments, saying that he would be guided by the API reference to a "just and agreed" solution. Contrary to Olmert's accounts, however, a long paper published by Saeb Erekat claimed that Abu Mazen had, in fact, spoken of 15,000 refugees per year over a ten-year period.[72] According to Akiva Eldar in *Haaretz* on 26 February 2010, the Arabic version of this paper contained no numbers, and Olmert dismissed Erekat's account with the comment that the only talks that mattered were those that he had held with Abu Mazen.[73]

The security measures were based on the eight points provided by Barak and proposals from American envoy James Jones. Olmert and Abu Mazen accepted the use of Clinton's term "non-militarized" state for the Palestinian state, the agreement being that the Palestinians would have only a strong security force for law enforcement. According to Olmert's proposals, no foreign army would be permitted to enter Palestine, and, as in the case of the Israeli–Egyptian peace agreement, the Palestinian state would not enter any military agreement with a state that did not have diplomatic relations with Israel. The eastern border – the strip of the Jordan Rift Valley along the Jordan River – would be patrolled by an international force; on some occasions Olmert specified that this would be the North Atlantic Treaty Organization (NATO).[74] Israel would have the right to defend itself beyond that border if foreign troops were amassed there. Similarly, Israel would maintain the right to pursue terrorists across the border with Israel, would have two early warning stations, and access to and military use of both the airspace over Palestine and the electromagnetic communications spectrum. Abu Mazen agreed with what he called Israel's right to negotiate the use of Palestinian airspace. More importantly, he maintained that there was agreement for an international force on the eastern border, commenting that he had received Washington's agreement to NATO (under the Americans, according to some accounts).[75] Rice comments that she, in fact, consulted the NATO chief about this.[76] Jordan was also consulted about an international force to be on the Jordanian, not Palestinian, side of this borer. Elliot Abrams, however, denies that the use of NATO was even suggested, citing Turbowitz to the effect that Israel consistently rejected the use of NATO or any other outside force except as observers.[77] This was, indeed, the position of the Israeli negotiators in the Livny-Abu Ala channel;

guided by the old identity-related mistrust, they adhered to all of Barak's eight points, demanding an Israeli military presence, as revealed in an *al Jazeera* document.[78] However, comments by both Olmert and Abu Mazen clearly indicate that this traditional deal-breaking demand – now basically outdated by changes in warfare – was not included in Olmert's proposals. Olmert himself said most explicitly in a 2013 interview: "I completely gave up on having an Israel presence in the Jordan Valley," though he said that Israelis could be in warning stations along the mountain range (Ba'al Hazor and Har Eval, which are roughly in the center of the West Bank).[79] Summing up the security arrangements, Abu Mazen told the *New York Times*: "We do not claim it was an agreement, but the file was finalized."[80] He explained that he could not call it an agreement because the principle of the negotiations was that "nothing was agreed until everything was agreed." But he was later to tell various audiences that security was, in fact, the only area that had been finalized.[81] Olmert confirmed "more or less" Abu Mazen's description of the security measures, but Abrams quotes Turbowitz to the effect that security was barely discussed and that nothing was agreed.[82] This may have been due to ignorance since the advisors, Turbowitz and Tourgeman, were not always included in Olmert's talks with Abu Mazen.

Most of Israel's positions had been conveyed to Abu Mazen in his meetings with Olmert, and on 16 September Olmert presented them together with a map. He and Abu Mazen have recounted many times that the map was shown to Abu Mazen with Olmert's request that he sign it on the spot. Abu Mazen requested a copy of the map and when Olmert refused, they agreed to have their aides and a Palestinian map expert meet the following day.[83] The Palestinians canceled that meeting and there were no further meetings while Olmert was in office; neither side has offered an explanation for that. However, canceling the meeting, the Palestinians expressed interest in Olmert's proposals and said they were leaving for Jordan and Egypt to get their reactions (a response initially viewed by Israel as encouraging). Israel too dispatched people who sought, and received, Jordanian and Egyptian support for the proposals.

Saeb Erekat has said that during an Abu Mazen visit to Washington on 18 December 2008, it was agreed with the Americans that the negotiators would come to Washington on 3 January 2009 to review everything achieved in preparation for handing over all the information to the incoming US administration.[84] Abu Mazen maintains that the two leaders (or Tourgeman and Erekat) were to go to Washington on 3 January to try to work out their differences over the territorial issue: 6.3 percent versus 1.9 percent since, according to some of his accounts, everything else had been more or less resolved. The Israeli attack on Gaza broke out on 27 December, but Abu Mazen has said that he was still willing to go through with the January meeting, although Olmert was not.[85] Olmert claims that he never knew of any such meeting but that he would have accepted the invitation if one had been issued.[86] A brief comment in Bush's memoires sheds some light on this apparent misunderstanding – or contradiction. According to Bush, Olmert was to deposit his proposals with him (presumably in Olmert's November trip to Washington); Abu Mazen, in his planned December visit, would express his agreement, and then the two leaders would be invited to Washington to finalize the deal. However, according to Bush, Abu Mazen in his December visit did not agree to Olmert's terms. This would explain the invitation that Olmert says he never received, for it may never have been issued, while it would also explain Abu Mazen's expectations of a meeting to take place in January. Rice too refers to Abu Mazen's refusal to provide agreement in December, suggesting not only that the problem was Olmert's soon to be ended term in office but an additional factor: that the new head of Kadima (and likely next prime minister), Tzippy Livny, "had urged me, (and, I believe, Abbas) not to enshrine the Olmert proposal."[87] She added that Abu Mazen had been told "by numerous Israelis, including some of Olmert's closest advisors, that the lame-duck prime minister did not have the legitimacy to deliver the deal."[88] Elliot Abrams also asserted that Livny had sent a similar message to Abu Mazen, to "wait for her," and that Abu Mazen told Bush that he received such messages from people in Olmert's government.[89]

Olmert's plan, however, had been to have the agreement signed on 16 September and then, "before presenting it to our own peoples," delivered immediately by both leaders to the UN Security Council followed by the General Assembly (UNGA), then a joint session of Congress, then the European Parliament, then a ceremony at the White House, to be followed by a massive international meeting at the seam line between East and West Jerusalem, and then Israeli elections "with the accumulated impact of this process at our backs."[90] While this may sound like more of a fantasy than a plan, the idea was, indeed, to present the agreement to the Security Council possibly as early as the opening UN session at the end of September. Erekat had said a few weeks before the September meeting that Olmert was pressing for a deal because the Americans wanted to present a joint document to the UNGA annual opening in the presence of heads of state later in the month.[91] Elliot Abrams claims that when Rice came to the region in August, it was clear that there would not be sufficient time for a final status agreement and, therefore, she suggested a framework agreement. Abu Mazen, according to Abrams, was insistent that there be a final agreement and proposed simply continuing the talks.[92] Abrams, who even before the opening of the Annapolis process believed that the circumstances were not ripe for an agreement, did not view the timing factor (created primarily by the corruption charges responsible for cutting short Olmert's tenure) as an impediment to an agreement. Rather, he maintains, the more Olmert was harassed and his resignation demanded, the weaker he became and therefore the more concessions he was willing to make.[93] Yet, Olmert himself did not consider the timing – his imminent departure from office – to be an obstacle to reaching agreement, for he maintained that the agreement would be confirmed by others, specifically the US, which would take it to the Security Council, and as he would convey to the Syrians as well (see below), it would be confirmed in the Knesset and presented as part of Kadima's platform in the upcoming elections. Thus, the elections would become something of a referendum on the agreement itself.

In presenting his proposal to Abu Mazen, Olmert had said "even in fifty years there will be no Israeli government that will offer you what I have offered."[94] Both leaders later said that there was no actual Palestinian rejection and that they could have completed a final status agreement within "two months."[95] In 2010, Olmert told the Israeli press "we were a hair's breadth away from a peace agreement. ... the negotiations had not ended," and he believed the remaining issues could have been resolved by "half a percent here, half a percent there."[96] However, his earlier comments had not been so positive; in July 2009, for example, he said: "To this day I cannot understand why the Palestinian leadership did not accept the far-reaching, unprecedented proposal I offered them."[97] Political considerations may account for the different Olmert comments, for in the immediate aftermath Olmert had an interest in trying to prove that any failure was the fault of the other side, while later he sought to prove that he and Abu Mazen had been very near to success (and could be again in the future), whereas his successors were not. His later version may well have been accurate, nonetheless, not only because it was confirmed by Abu Mazen but because it was also confirmed in 2011 by Sharon's former (conservative) political advisor Dov Weisglass, who would have had little reason to praise the "seriousness and determination" of the Palestinians under Abu Mazen as he did to the Israeli paper *Yedioth Aharonoth* on 25 January 2011.

Like every Israeli leader before him, Olmert expected the other side to agree with Israel's terms. As in the case of Barak, Olmert's terms indeed went further than any offer in the past, but unlike Barak, Olmert's terms were far more realistic and came quite close to the needs of the Palestinians. In part, they were in response to Palestinian compromises, for example, regarding Jerusalem, but they also constituted Israeli compromises on such things as traditional Israel demands for sovereignty in all of Jerusalem and a security presence in the Jordan Rift Valley, or at least along the Jordan River. The two red lines of Eshkol, Golda, Rabin, and, to some degree, Barak were gone (the red lines of right-wing leaders Begin, Shamir, and Netanyahu began much further away from minimum Palestinian needs). Olmert was to explain these two cardinal "concessions" in some detail. Regarding Jerusalem, Olmert took what he called a realistic position. Israeli sovereignty over the whole city would have meant "270,000 Palestinians inside Israel's security barrier," he said in his last New Year's interview as prime minister on 29 September 2008.[98] In addition, even as former mayor of Jerusalem, he said, he came to realize that the city had never really been united, nor had the government ever sought to truly unite it, for it was beyond Israel's capacity to make the two parts equal in standard of living, infrastructure, quality of life, and the like. United Jerusalem was "merely a slogan."[99] Moreover, he said, Israelis certainly had no attachment to Jabel Mukaber, for example, or Abu

Dis; they – and, by implication, many other places – were not part of historical Jerusalem, while the "special magic" of Jerusalem for Jews was "not dependent on whether Jerusalem's sovereignty includes Abu Dis or Jabal Mukaber"; even the Temple Mount, sensitive an issue as it was, required "understanding and even a sense of restraint."[100] With regard to the Jordan Rift Valley, Olmert spoke more generally of the need to withdraw from most if not all of the territories, explaining that with military strategists the considerations were "all about tanks, land, and controlling territories and this hilltop and that hilltop. All these things are worthless."[101] And, he added, in another interview, if a "rocket has a range of 60 kilometers, so what do you need a border 60 kilometers from where it [the border] was in order to make more defensible? Because we are not afraid that in the east there will be a ground attack that will cut Israel in two, like we were forty years ago … . It's a different reality. The main things [sic] are rockets, which can cross borders anyway."[102] This would suggest a rational, purely military line of thinking with no connection to the issue of trust. Olmert acknowledged the changed nature of warfare and military doctrine previously acknowledged by Rabin. Yet, unlike Rabin or his predecessors, in so doing he was willing to overcome the element of mistrust that had dictated a continued demand for an Israeli military presence, even control. Realizing the changed security demands, Olmert was willing to rely on others – namely, an international force under the Americans, to prevent a ground attack by an enemy across Palestine's border into the Jordan Rift Valley – insofar as that might still be a threat. In this era of rocket warfare, he explained, he gave up on a military presence in the Jordan Valley "because I could protect the line of the Jordan River through an international military force on the other side of the Jordan River."[103] That he still did not fully trust the Palestinians, or perhaps their ability to control all Palestinian groups, was evident in his maintenance of the remaining security demands – namely, demilitarization of the Palestinian state, two Israeli early warning stations on the mountain range roughly in the center of the West Bank,[104] the various clauses about enemy armies, the right of pursuit (of terrorists), and so forth. However, despite the changed circumstances (the nature of warfare), these safeguards had been considered insufficient by past Israeli leaders at least up to and possibly including Barak for Israel to overcome its ingrained mistrust and therefore abandon the deal-breaking demand for a "security border" along the Jordan River (i.e., a military presence, if not sovereignty, in the Jordan Rift Valley). So it is not clear if it was the element of trust/mistrust that underwent a change or rather a change in the concept of what constituted a threat and therefore just what security measures remained essential. If these remaining demands would have constituted deal-breakers depended upon the adversary – and in the case of Abu Mazen, they did not.

It is possible that similar considerations were at play in Olmert's negotiations with the Syrians that had been begun in February 2008 and were taking place at the same time. Israel finally acknowledged, on 22 May 2008, that peace talks were being indirectly conducted with Syria through the mediation of the

Turkish government. The decision to make this public was the initiative of the Syrians, who wanted to test the seriousness of the Israeli side. But Israel itself had become increasingly persuaded that Assad was serious about reaching an agreement and perhaps willing to meet Israel's conditions. The press and public response in Israel, however, was skeptical to say the least, viewing Olmert's announcement as a "spin" designed to divert attention from the latest corruption charges against him.[105] According to one poll, 49 percent of Israelis said they believed Olmert was merely trying to draw attention away from new police charges, while only 38 percent said they thought the talks were really meant to promote peace.[106] While there is little information on the content of the talks themselves, the draft agreement negotiated by the unofficial group and reportedly rejected by Israel in 2006 could have served as basis for the talks. Olmert would reveal very little publicly, explaining that he knew what the Syrians wanted – the Golan – and they knew what Israel required. He refrained from providing the Syrians an explicit commitment for full withdrawal – something the Syrians sought, as they had in the past but now also especially because they felt that they had been left out to dry by Barak's retreat at Shepherdstown. The most Olmert would say publicly (and possibly even privately) was his statement in late September 2008: "We must be prepared to give up the Golan, but Damascus knows it must change the nature of its relationship with Iran and its support for Hizballah."[107] Once out of office he said that his requirement had been that Syria break off military cooperation, though not necessarily diplomatic relations, with Iran.[108] By December 2008, the Turkish mediated talks had served their purpose. They had been viewed by Olmert primarily as a vehicle to determine the seriousness of Bashar Assad's interest in reaching an agreement, in particular the Syrian leader's willingness to accommodate Israel's interests regarding Iran and Hizballah. Satisfied by the responses received via the Turks, Olmert went to Ankara in December 2008 to propose the next step. Israel had determined that the time had come for more concrete talks on specific issues such as security arrangements (to be updated from those of the Rabin and Barak periods, drawing upon the lessons of the Second Lebanon War) and the delineation of the elusive 4 June line, matters that required direct talks between experts. In Ankara, Olmert was present as Prime Minister Recep Tayyip Erdogan relayed this message between the Israeli leader and Assad by telephone. As a result, according to Olmert, they were "hours" away from opening direct negotiations by means of a meeting to be held with the Syrian foreign minister.[109] The long phone mediation dealt with a joint statement on the opening of direct negotiations. While Olmert had to leave before the statement was finished, a Turkish official subsequently said that the statement was expected to include adherence to the "understanding reached by Rabin" (apparently the "pocket" agreement) on full Israeli withdrawal from the Golan in exchange for peace and security arrangements, plus the elucidation of what would constitute the normalization of their relations.[110] In December 2009 a Syrian Foreign Ministry statement said that every Israeli prime minister since the Madrid Conference had agreed to withdraw to the 4 June 1967 line.[111] Assad himself claimed that all that had remained was to finalize the exact delineation of the 4 June 1967 line, but that Olmert wanted first to consult with his cabinet.[112] Israeli press accounts claimed that the direct talks were never opened due to the Israeli attack on Gaza just a few days after the Ankara phone exchange. Erdogan was said to have been angry and felt deceived by Olmert, and therefore broke off contact and the mediation. In fact, however, contacts continued even during and after the Gaza attack, so the fact that the direct talks never materialized may have been due at least in part to some other consideration. As with the Palestinians, Israel had conveyed to the Syrians the idea that if agreement were reached, it would be enshrined in Kadima's platform for the upcoming elections (as well as the UN Security Council) and thus very likely to be implemented, since Kadima was expected to win. Such assurances notwithstanding, the Syrians, apparently, were not willing to take that chance. They may have concluded (like the Palestinians, perhaps) that Olmert could not make a deal, or a deal that would hold, given his limited time left in office.

The negotiations with the Syrians were far less advanced as well as far less complicated than those with the Palestinians, but the final break in both would appear to have been Olmert's limited time left in office, though the impact of the attack on Gaza cannot be entirely ruled out (since the Syrians knew of his resignation, long since announced, well before December). If the underlying factor was, in fact, Olmert's limited time in office, this factor itself was the product of the corruption charges against him that led to his resignation. One might speculate that had Olmert responded earlier to the Syrian overtures (or the US had changed its position on Syria earlier), there might have been time to reach an agreement. A similar argument regarding earlier moves on the part of Israel, connected also to the approaching end of Bush's term in office, might be applied to the Palestinian case as well. One interviewer even pointed that out to Olmert, who replied that the issues with the Palestinians were complicated matters that took some 36 meetings to develop (evolve), especially on the Palestinian side. Moreover, until the corruption issue appeared, there had been no reason to believe that he, Olmert, would not have sufficient time to reach an agreement. In addition, he said, if progress had been made earlier, the corruption issue would simply have been brought up earlier (a claim somewhat tenuous inasmuch as the press accusations had begun as early as February 2008). In any case, Olmert argued, he had met the one-year deadline set at Annapolis, though he ignored the fact that he had already announced his resignation in July 2008, possibly leaving the Palestinians doubtful about chances for completion even at that earlier stage. The timing may, in fact, have been the critical factor for Abu Mazen, as Bush was to conclude himself. Calling the timing the major cause of the failure, Bush said that Abu Mazen "did not want to make an agreement with a Prime Minister on his way out of office."[113] Similarly to the dilemma the Palestinians had faced with the Clinton Parameters, the concern remained that whatever was agreed, including concessions, with the incumbent in Israel (as well as

Washington) would have little value with the successor, leaving the Palestinian leader exposed to domestic criticism with nothing concrete to show in return. The claim that Abu Mazen may have refrained from going forward in expectation that the next prime minister, presumably Tzippy Livny, would make a better offer, as implied in the messages reportedly conveyed to "wait for her," does not hold much water. Livny had been far less forthcoming than Olmert in her negotiations with Abu Ala, and any alternative to Livny – namely, Netanyahu –would surely be less accommodating. Actually, Abu Mazen urged the Americans to continue the talks, and he claims that he clung to the possibility that there might still be time, despite the Gaza invasion, for the Americans to help them bridge the remaining differences on the territorial percentages.

Other factors may have contributed to the failure on the Israeli side – for example, domestic political opposition that threatened to be a serious obstacle to a breakthrough. Much of this was driven by ideological (nationalist and/or religious) attachment to the territories, coupled with identity-related mistrust of the enemy, characteristic of the right wing and most religious parties. Olmert's comfortable majority (71 MKs) coalition began to fall apart as early as 17 January 2008 when Avigdor Lieberman pulled his Israel Beiteinu party (11 MKs) out of the coalition. Lieberman was protesting the Annapolis process, which he said was based on the concept of land for peace (Labor's old declared policy) rather than what, in his opinion, should have been the principle of the talks: "exchange of territory and population."[114] He had long been championing the idea of transferring to the Palestinians various areas of Israel heavily populated by Arabs in exchange for parts of the West Bank. The departure of this party left Olmert with a coalition strength of 60 plus 15 non-coalition supporters (the MKs from Meretz, Hadash, and the Arab parties). But, also in January, Shas, with its 12 MKs, began threatening to resign as well if the issue of Jerusalem were put on the negotiation agenda. Both leaks from the talks, and Likud accusations that "Kadima is selling Jerusalem to our enemies," prompted almost continuous threats from Shas throughout Olmert's tenure.[115] Labor, also a member of the coalition, was not much help to Olmert, for that party joined several no-confidence votes in the summer of 2008, occasionally supporting the call for early elections. Thus, Olmert had to deal not only with mounting corruption charges and impending indictment (as well as rockets fired from Gaza), but also with increased political opposition from his own coalition partners in addition to that of the Likud and the parties further to the right.

Olmert was not particularly successful in dealing with these spoilers; he lost many of the no-confidence votes and managed to avoid a decision on early elections only because he resigned from the Kadima leadership in July, prompting the party's early primaries for his replacement. Back in early 2006, when he was still pressing for unilateral "realignment," Olmert had countered critics with promises to keep Ariel (he even campaigned there for the March 2006 elections) along with other settlements, as well as an eternally united Jerusalem.[116] During the Annapolis process in 2008, he emphasized the importance of fixing permanent borders for Israel. However, when elements of his proposals to Abu Mazen were leaked, he offered no compensating comments to his political opponents, but rather boldly and simply said to the Likud from the Knesset podium: "whatever negotiations we hold, you will call it 'surrender' because you do not want peace."[117] His only political concessions were to Shas in an effort to sustain the coalition. He promised Shas that the Jerusalem issue would not be decided in these negotiations, and he made various offers (possibly deals), such as restoring government child subsidies that had previously been reduced. In addition, he did try to placate – or at least not provoke – the settlers; he continued to build settlements (4,056 new houses in the West Bank, 40 percent of them east of the fence/wall or the expected settlement blocs) and refrained from removing unauthorized outposts called for in the Road Map.[118] Olmert later said that he had explained to the Americans that in implementing outpost evacuations there might be "bloody confrontations between the security forces and the settlers [in which case] nobody would talk about peace, but only the fact that we were heading toward a civil war."[119] Similarly, he went on to explain regarding settlement construction that he did not want to go through "daily battles," particularly over Jerusalem neighborhoods, although he did promise not to proceed with the especially controversial construction plan outside Jerusalem known as E-1. At the same time, he enlisted the Americans to help him prop up his coalition, during Bush's visit to the country in January, by having the American president speak with the entire Israeli cabinet at a dinner at the prime minister's residence, and again in a speech to the Knesset on Israel's 60th anniversary in May.[120] But Olmert also had to reassure the Americans, as well as Abu Mazen, over the following months that his government would be strong enough to make a deal.

Olmert also enlisted American assistance on the security issues under negotiation, saying that he wanted the US to "work this out to the satisfaction" of the Israeli military. He told Rice that he could "sell this deal but not if the IDF says it will undermine Israel's security. That's one thing no prime minister can survive."[121] Whether the military establishment could, in fact, be considered a potential spoiler is not entirely clear. As a result of the second Intifada, the IDF was determined to maintain responsibility for Israel's security, specifically to prevent intrusions and the right of pursuit of terrorists. For them trust of Palestinian, or even shared, responsibility was unacceptable. Specifically, Defense Minister Barak objected to Olmert's abandonment of one of his eight recommended security measures – namely, the Israeli military presence in the Jordan Rift Valley, at least as a trip wire along the Jordan River border.[122] And there were, indeed, rumors that the two were not getting along, to which Olmert responded that "we don't always agree on everything but we respect each other. Well at least I respect him ... I can't speak for him."[123] Later, Olmert accused Barak, along with Livny, of having sent people to Abu Mazen to tell him not to sign, though it is not clear that this was due to differences over security issues or simply politically motivated antagonism.[124] Moreover, Olmert's concern over the opinion of the IDF was not necessarily a sign of total opposition from the military, but rather his effort to ensure that there would not be objections that, as he implied to the Americans, might frighten the public with regard to the security provided by his peace proposal.

Another spoiler impediment may have come from a different direction and, according to Olmert, may well have had a critical impact. This factor was the diaspora, or diaspora circles in the US allegedly engaged by right-wing opponents in Israel. On at least one occasion much later, Olmert accused Americans "from the extreme right wing" who transferred "millions and millions of dollars" and "aimed to topple me ... who spent millions of dollars in order to stop me."[125] If this was, in fact, true, and there were many rumors to this effect at the time, these spoilers together with their allies in Israel may well have achieved their objective, having perhaps ferreted out or possibly even fabricated some of the scandals that were the undoing of Olmert, and his peace efforts, in the end.

The Kurtzer *et al.* study of US policy suggests that the American handling of the process was also a contributing factor to the failure. While Abrams would argue that there was too much involvement by Rice (and the State Department), the Kurtzer group maintained that there was not enough. According to their conclusions, the US did not step in when there were problems, nor did it offer bridging proposals or follow up matters that had been suggested.[126] The Americans, in fact, sent mixed messages, particularly those sent by Rice as distinct from those by Vice-President Cheney who visited Israel in March 2008, and the US team was, in fact, divided and in dispute amongst themselves. For his part, while Bush insisted on a consistent position of American support for Israel, he had no intention of mediating or taking the kind of active role assumed by his predecessor; this was even more decidedly the case with regard to the Syrian track. Nor did either Israel or the Palestinians want the US to play that kind of role. For Olmert it was not a question of not trusting the Americans; he actually had an excellent relationship with Bush and trusted him implicitly. He apparently believed that direct talks with Abu Mazen would be more productive than if a third party were present – something that was proven in a way by the failure to reach a common statement in the American led pre-Annapolis meetings. All that Olmert sought from the Americans with regard to the involvement of the US was that he not be "blindsided"; he asked Washington to inform him before making any proposals.[127] Abrams might claim this was because Olmert and Rice did not get along, and that Olmert rejected or mistrusted many of her positions.[128] This may have been the case, but there are no indications that this was a factor in the failure. Indeed, Rice's pressure to attain an agreement and her direct role even in some of the negotiations may have operated as positive factors, certainly to get things moving and possibly also to achieve progress, however limited the American role was meant to be.

Similarly, the nature of the negotiating process itself – namely, the Livny track alongside the Olmert track – has been noted as a negative factor, particularly because the two Israeli leaders were political rivals, and the two tracks were often out of sync with each other. Not only did Olmert tend to dismiss the importance of Livny's role, actually ignoring that track, but he also often dealt privately with Abu Mazen, even excluding his aides whom he would brief after the fact.[129] On the whole, the separation of the two tracks was the result of Olmert's negotiating and leadership styles, both of which may actually have been positive factors behind what ultimately was a "near breakthrough." Peace-making is a very controversial undertaking in Israel, with political spoilers coming even from the ranks of the peacemakers' own party or advisors, as was indeed the case with Olmert, as well as from other elements of the political establishment. For this reason, it was important for Olmert to keep the whole process "under the radar" as far as possible, seeking to avoid conflicts and arguments that might torpedo the whole process. Rice was even to complain that in the midst of general skepticism (in Washington, as well as in Israel), it was not permitted to speak of the progress that was being made.[130] Avoiding the pitfalls of political spoilers, Olmert was later to explain this as part of his concept of leadership. He told an interviewer in 2010 that "the leadership must direct the public to take the path that the State of Israel must take – not in the direction dictated by several irresponsible, populist, overexcited and inflamed members of the [Likud] central committee."[131] His leadership concept extended also to the way in which he conducted negotiations, dealing, like Sadat in the past, mainly with principles while leaving the details for "finalization" to others, who would merely provide the necessary specifics for implementing what was decided by the very top level. He was also a leader who was willing to take risks and sought to demonstrate his ability to make decisions and carry them through. According to a number of his associates, he not only was willing, but actually enjoyed "thinking out of the box" and shattering accepted myths (such as the myth that Israel cannot negotiate on two fronts at the same time). In addition, unlike Barak, Olmert both sought and listened to advice, even beyond his inner circle – providing a basis, it appears, for his comments regarding both the Palestinians and the Syrians that he knew what they needed.

Unlike Barak, Olmert does not appear to have been driven by or concerned with how the public would respond to a peace agreement (provided the military did not reject it, as noted above in his conversation with Rice on security matters). His concept of leadership resembled that of Rabin; he stated that a leader was to lead, not follow the public: "the test of a leader is the ability to make decisions, even those that are not popular in the eyes of part of the public."[132] In the case of the Syrian talks, public opinion could have played a spoiler role if secrecy had not been maintained, but in the case of the negotiations with the Palestinians, public opinion (as distinct from the political echelon) was actually a positive factor. It is true that skepticism among the public regarding a possible breakthrough only increased as Olmert's position became weaker; by May 2008 virtually half the public (49.6 percent) thought the government under Olmert did not have a mandate to be negotiating and

61.4 percent thought Olmert should resign. However, support for negotiations was still 70.9 percent at this time, just before Olmert presented his peace proposal to the Americans in May. Support fell to 63 percent in the following months, but remained steady at that figure until new elections were called at the end of October 2008.

It was not just his concept of leadership that played a role, but also Olmert's personal development. At least as he has explained, he had undergone significant change not in his ideological devotion to the concept of Greater Israel, but in his understanding of Israel's interests. The factors that brought about the change, as we have seen, were a new grasp of the demographics – with the possibility of an Arab majority leading to a bi-national state if Israel held onto the occupied territories, the impact of the second Intifada with its implications for future violence, and even the left-wing views of his family. This was reflected in his willingness to adopt what he saw as a more realistic position regarding sovereignty over Jerusalem (and possibly over the Temple Mount), as well as his understanding of what was or was not needed to protect Israel from future threat.[133] He does not appear to have been guided by trust in the Palestinians, but he also was not guided by mistrust, accepting, as he did, third-party safeguards rather than holding to a concept of security that in the past had rendered a peace agreement impossible. In this sense, Olmert was a pragmatic leader, possibly with regard to Syria as well. A motivating factor in the talks with Syria may have been Olmert's wish to offset the decline in his popularity amidst the accumulating charges against him, although only some 25 percent expressed support for giving up the Golan in exchange for peace with Syria (mainly because the majority of Israelis thought the *status quo* would continue with Syria even without peace).[134] Nonetheless, Olmert had, in fact, sanctioned the earlier unofficial talks, presumably out of the same pragmatism apparent in his efforts with the Palestinians. He may have seen the positive effect an Israeli–Syrian (as well as Israeli–Palestinian) peace would have within the region, and most importantly for Israel, the possibility of moving Syria into the pro-Western Arab center, separating Syria from Iran and limiting aid to Hizballah. Such an outcome may have particularly resonated with Olmert because of his unpopularity over the Second Lebanon War, which was perceived in Israel as having fallen short of dealing a serious blow to Hizballah. The talks with Syria ended before there was any clear indication of how the final accord, if there were one, would look; but Olmert had already publicly admitted that the Golan would be returned. If he wanted an agreement, it was clear that the 4 June 1967 line, however it might be determined, would have to be respected. There was also the possibility of deriving legitimacy from the progress – or at least promises – made by some of his predecessors on the substantive issues of a peace agreement with Syria.

Leadership changes in both of Israel's adversaries may have been a factor in Olmert's thinking and possibly in the near achievement of a breakthrough. Abu Mazen was a leader who had clearly identified himself with moderate positions, and one who needed an agreement in order to counter the growing strength of Hamas and prove the justice of the path chosen by Fatah. Abu Mazen was a weak leader, and he had to be cautious in the face of domestic pressure to forge reconciliation with Hamas; but like Olmert, he was a realist who understood that compromises might have to be made regarding Jerusalem and the refugees if a deal were to be achieved. Additionally, both he and Bashar al-Assad appeared to be more trustworthy in Israeli eyes than their predecessors, Arafat and Hafez al Assad. When Bashar Assad assumed his father's position, he was touted by many as a Western-educated man, a professional rather than a politician, far more modern and, perhaps, more moderate than his father. It was Assad who initiated the opening of talks with Israel, most likely out of an interest in repairing relations with Washington, but also, perhaps, to garner the prestige and political strength as a leader in his own right that regaining the Golan would accord him in Damascus. And, as noted, he demonstrated both maturity and responsibility in his restrained responses to Israeli actions in Lebanon and the attack on the Syrian nuclear facility.

It is difficult to know just how determined Assad was to reach an accord with Israel, but with regard to Abu Mazen and also Olmert, an additional factor that gave reason to believe that a breakthrough might be forthcoming was their political will to reach an agreement. A critical element for any settlement, such a political will was apparent in the exchanges between the two leaders, as evidenced in the compromises both were willing to make despite the cost each knew he might have to bear, in popularity or support, for each of the compromises. Abu Mazen maintains that he believed there was the basis for a deal and that he fully expected a continuation of the talks with Olmert, aided by the Americans, in order to bridge the final gap in January while both Bush and Olmert were still in office. Olmert, for his part, may have calculated that the gamble was worth it, initially because he believed this was the path Israel must take, later perhaps because it was also a path that might save him politically. He was also convinced that settler–right-wing opposition notwithstanding, a package deal that carried with it an end of conflict and peace would be accepted by the majority of the Israeli public. This was evident in opinion polls, particularly the studies conducted quarterly by Yaacov Shamir. Abu Mazen was aware of similar findings among the Palestinian public in the polls conducted in parallel to Shamir, by Khalil Shikaki. Both these experts, interviewing Israelis and Palestinians, respectively, consistently found opposition to specific compromises (on Jerusalem, on the refugees); but when they presented a final deal (with these compromises) as a package, majority support was assured. For an Israeli policy-maker this was an important factor, for it was an indication of just how much the situation had evolved since the Oslo Declaration of 1993. The two-state solution was now the assumed objective, the creation of a Palestinian state accepted; the 1967 borders were clearly the basis for the future border, with territorial compensation in the form of swaps also understood; arrangements for sharing and even dividing parts of Jerusalem had been put on the table and long under discussion; a prime minister had openly and repeatedly stated that the Golan would be returned and plans developed for future arrangements; settlements had been evacuated even from the West Bank in the disengagement, and in that same arrangement Israel had even set a precedent by agreeing to third-party responsibility for a security border (an EU rather than Israeli presence on the Gaza border with Egypt). Arab countries – namely, Egypt and Jordan – had been accorded deep involvement in Israel's relations with the Palestinian Authority on such critical issues as security. And a positive contribution of the Americans in the Annapolis process was to cultivate a factor previously missing: broad Arab support for the talks, secured through regular consultations conducted by Secretary Rice. The factor of a changed regional environment made this possible. What had only been understood by Rabin in theory during the Oslo period had by now been enshrined in the Arab Peace Initiative. The Arab regimes saw that their interests lay in the achievement of resolution to the conflict, and for this they were willing to accept Israel's right to exist, open normal relations, and ensure security for all.

All of the above factors were favorable for a breakthrough. Yet Olmert's efforts produced only a near breakthrough due to some, if not all, of the negative factors also at play. The critical factor would appear to have been the corruption charges and resignation of Olmert, which prevented any continuation that might have produced a breakthrough. But contributing to this were the political weakness of Olmert, the spoilers who corroded his political base and decimated his coalition, to a large degree due to ideological objections, alongside Abu Mazen's own weakness due to the split among the Palestinians and the spreading strength of Hamas, both leading to a cautious approach by Abu Mazen. We may never know if Abu Mazen's hesitancy after the 16 September meeting was due to that factor – that is, his concern that he could not get the deal past his own spoilers, or if, as the Americans believed (as some Israelis suggested to Abu Mazen), the Palestinian leader decided that it was simply not wise to make a deal with an Israeli prime minister on his way out of office. If the Palestinian partner would have ultimately consummated a deal, we can never know. Similarly, we may never know if the talks with the Syrians that were about to take a more direct and apparently decisive turn would have succeeded. Here, too, it was a matter of timing or, more to the point, perhaps, the Israeli attack on Gaza that ended the talks. In the Syrian case, virtually all of the parameters of an agreement had been discussed and even worked out unofficially in the past, and conditions (the positive factors) seemed ripe for an agreement. In the case of the Israeli–Palestinian conflict, the near breakthrough was due to a large degree to Olmert's willingness to forego the past ideological, nationalist, and mistrust-producing identity-related factors that had impeded a breakthrough on the part of his predecessors, going all the way back to the days following the 1967 war. New impediments might be created (e.g., the demand from Netanyahu after he came to power in 2009 that the Palestinians recognize Israel as a Jewish state), while other favorable factors may disappear in Israel, in the adversary, in the region, internationally or otherwise; nonetheless, under Olmert, the Annapolis process – and possibly even the process with Syria – did constitute a near breakthrough at the time.

Notes

1. See Sharon's former bureau chief Dov Weisglass (*Haaretz*, 7 January 2013) on the effects this had on Sharon.
2. Sharon speech to the IDC Herzliya Conference, 18 December 2003 (www.idc.ac.il).
3. Condoleezza Rice, *No Higher Honor* (New York, NY: Crown, 2011): 382–383. Olmert later told an interviewer that Sharon had originally planned to remove 17 settlements from the West Bank (Ben Birnbaum, "It's Just a Matter of Time," *The New Republic*, 19 March 2013). In fact, he had asked the Israel National Security Council to look into various options, including evacuation of all the West Bank settlements. Dov Weisglas, *Arik Sharon - Rosh Hamemshala*, (Tel Aviv: Yedioth Aharonoth-Sifriat Hemed, 2012), 212-217; MFA, *Knesset Speech by Prime Minister Sharon on the Disengagement Plan*, 15 March 2004.
4. Together with leading figures from Labor, among them Shimon Peres.
5. Created in 2003 to deal with the Israeli–Palestinian issue; it consisted of the US, UN, Russia, and the EU.
6. He was pronounced brain dead by an outside expert neurologist in April 2006 and was kept on machines, by request of the family, until his death in 2014.
7. Olmert tended to refrain from specifics, saying only that Israel would keep "as much as is needed" in large blocs, including the settlement of Ariel (Israel Television, Channel 9, 30 March 2006).
8. Olmert may actually have been the source of Sharon's disengagement plan in response to demographic concerns.
9. Olmert speech presenting his government to the Knesset, 4 May 2006 (MFA); David Makovsky, *Olmert's Unilateral Option: An Early Assessment*, Washington Institute for Near East Policy, Policy Focus No. 55, May 2006.
10. His last speech to the Knesset (MFA, "PM Rabin in Knesset – Ratification of the Interim Agreement," 5 October 1995).
11. Kadima party website, www.yallakadima.co.il/fullArticleDetails.aspx?id=4148; www.pmo.gov.il/PMO/Archive/Speeches/2001/09/Speeches8394.htm.
12. Reuters, 11 November 2001. Sharon also reconfirmed this in press conferences with Bush, 7 February 2002 and 7 May 2002.
13. BBC News, 2 October 2001 (bbc.co.uk/2/hi/middle_east/1570599.stm).
14. UNSC Resolution 1397 (2002), adopted 12 March 2002.
15. AP, 26 May 2003; Kadima website: www.yallakadima.co.il/fullArticleDetails. aspx?id=4148. Can be viewed on YouTube: http://youtu.be/shgGvpkUMp4 (YouTube has the incorrect date – this was not Sharon's "last speech").
16. Marwan Muasher, *The Arab Center* (New Haven, CT: Yale University Press, 2008): 120–122, 127–128. Muasher had been Jordan's first ambassador to Israel.
17. Beirut, 28 March 2002 (AFP) – the official translation as published on the Arab League internet site. In a booklet in Arabic and English publicizing the API in 2012, the East Jerusalem Palestinian Center for Democracy and Community Development spelled out quite explicitly that the right of return was purposely omitted and not meant. See also, Muasher, 2008: 127–128.
18. It was even reconfirmed at the twelfth Islamic Summit Conference in Cairo, 6–7 February 2013 (with the participation of Ahmadinejad), including a final communique that also explicitly accepted the two-state solution (Cairo Final

Communique, ww.mnlfnet.com/OIC/12th%20Islamic%20Summit_Cairo%20Final%20Communique.pdf).
19 *New York Times*, 17 February 2002.
20 As had previous plans (proposals of the Mitchel Committee, Tenet, Zinni) for returning to talks. Galia Golan, *Israel and Palestine: Peace Plans and Proposals from Oslo to Disengagement* (Princeton, NJ: Marcus Weiner Publishers, 2007, 2nd edition): 63–68.
21 Rice, 2011: 280; "Remarks," The White House – George W. Bush and letter from Bush to Sharon, 14 April 2004.
22 *Yedioth Aharonoth*, 8 September 2010, published four chapters of Olmert's forthcoming book. Excerpts in English can be found in Jennifer Hanin, "Exclusive: Olmert's Own Words," 7 February 2011 on actforisrael blog.
23 *Yedioth Aharonoth*, 2 December 2003.
24 *Ibid.* He reportedly said in 2005, on the eve of the disengagement, that he was sorry that Begin was not alive so that he could publicly recognize to him that "he was right and I was wrong" about pulling out of Sinai (cited without a source in Makovsky, 2006: 10).
25 *Yedioth Aharonoth*, 2 December 2003; "Olmert's Bombshell," *Middle East Mirror*, 5 December 2005; speeches 24 January 2006, IDC Herzliya Conference; *Haaretz*, 8 February and 8 March 2006.
26 Beginning in February 2006 (e.g., in *Haaretz*, 8 February 2008, in connection with the purchase of a private home some years earlier).
27 The final report was published only in December 2006 but its recommendations were already common knowledge by the fall of 2006. James Baker and Lee Hamilton *et al.*, *The Iraq Study Group Report* (New York, NY: Vintage, 2006).
28 Rice, 2011: 550–551.
29 Elliot Abrams, *Tested by Zion* (New York, NY: Cambridge University Press, 2013): 200–202. Avi Issacharoff, "Exclusive: 'I am still waiting for Abbas to call,'" 24 May 2013 (www.thetower.org).
30 Issacharoff, 2013.
31 PM Olmert addresses the Conference of Presidents of Major American Jewish Organization, 8 February 2007 (MFA, press releases)
32 Abrams, 2013: 202. Bush himself refers to this skepticism: George Bush, *Decision Points* (New York, NY: Crown Publishers, 2010): 408.
33 *Ibid.*
34 Rice, 2011: 600.
35 *Haaretz*, 14 March 2006.
36 Rice, 2011: 204.
37 Most of this information can be found in *Haaretz*, 16 January 2007.
38 Interview to Y-Net (*Yedioth Aharonoth*) reported by *Haaretz*, 21, 2007, to prove that Olmert was aware of the contacts.
39 *Haaretz*, 17 January 2007; Jason Brookhyser, "The Syrian Turn," *American Diplomat*, August 2007; Olmert to *Der Spiegel*, 11 December 2006.
40 For example, *The Economist*, 20 January 2007.
41 *Yedioth Aharonoth*, 8 September 2010.
42 *Haaretz*, 17 January 2007.
43 *New York Times*, 30 November 2007.
44 AP, 4 April 2007.
45 *New York Times*, 29 November 2007 (at the close of Annapolis).
46 Tamar Hermann and Ephraim Yaar, *Peace Index: February 2007* (Israel Democracy Institute).
47 Alon Liel, "Syria Comes to Annapolis," *Palestine–Israel Journal*, 14(4), 2007: 17. Former security heads such as Yaacov Perry, David Kimche, and Amnon

Lipkin-Shahak joined Liel in creating an NGO promoting peace negotiations with Syria (*Haaretz*, 28 January 2007).
48 *Haaretz*, 16 January 2007.
49 For details of this, with maps, see Frederic Hof, "Special Report: Mapping Peace between Syria and Israel," USIP, March 2009. Most of these parameters of a treaty, including the peace park idea, were based on a proposal of the International Crisis Group in 2002 in which Hof participated, and Hof's original proposal in 1999 for an Environmental Preserve under Syrian sovereignty on the Golan.
50 Liel, 2007: 17.
51 There had been a break in the indirect contacts following the September attack, but talks resumed in November.
52 *Peace Index, February 2007*.
53 Speech at Ben Gurion memorial, *Haaretz*, 27 November 2006. Rice, 2011: 604. In the spring of 2007, Olmert had passed up an Arab-supported proposal (initiated by an Israeli peace group) to address the Arab League in Cairo in support of the Arab Peace Initiative, preferring to proceed with the conference that Rice was pressing for (*Haaretz*, 9 August 2012).
54 Rice, 2011: 604.
55 MFA, "Announcement of the Annapolis Conference," US Department of State, 20 November 2007.
56 Rice, 2011: 651–652.
57 Clayton Swisher and Ghada Karmi, *The Palestine Papers: The End of the Road?* (London: Hesperus Press, 2011): 30–31; 139–150.
58 Leaked from the negotiation unit of the PLO and published online by *al Jazeera*. Many of the documents may be found in Swisher and Karmi, 2011.
59 *Yedioth Aharonoth*, 8 September 2010; Bernard Avishai, *New York Times*, 7 February 2011.
60 *Haaretz*, 17 December 2009, published what it claimed to be Olmert's proposed map, though this was largely inaccurate, based as it was on Abu Mazen's memory of what Olmert had shown him. A later calculation interpreted this to account for 85 percent of the settlers to be accommodated in the settlement blocs, taking up 6 percent of the West Bank slated for annexation to Israel, with the 5.8 percent returned in swaps from land inside Israel and the remainder left for the passage between Gaza and the West Bank. Shaul Arieli, *Zekhut Ha-chashivah* (Tel Aviv: Touch Print Press, 2010): 21.
61 Avishai interview, repeated innumerable times in conversations in Israel, Ramallah, and abroad.
62 Zeev Elkin to a Brazilian newspaper, *O estado de S. Paulo*, carried by *Haaretz*, 21 August 2013: "West Bank: Settlements, Communities, and Facts on the Ground," www.standwithus.com.
63 *Haaretz*, 17 December 2009; Ben Birnbaum, "The End of the Two-State Solution," *The New Republic*, 11 March 2013; Arieli, 2010: 22.
64 Central Bureau of Statistics, http://cbs.gov.il/ishuvim/ishuvim_main.htm.
65 Bernard Avishai, *New York Times*, 7 February 2011.
66 *Ibid*.
67 Olmert attributes the Muqata comment to the Americans regarding the basis for the number of refugees to return (Olmert interview, Birnbaum, 19 March 2013).
68 *Yedioth Aharonoth*, 8 September 2010.
69 Birnbaum, 11 March 2013. He made a similar comment to Elliot Abrams (Abrams, 2013: 289).
70 *Ibid*.
71 Birnbaum, 19 March 2013. Abu Mazen made similar comments in internal discussions and even on Israel television, channel 2, 1 November 2012 speaking of "returning" to his birthplace Safed only as a visitor, for which he was criticized by many Palestinians.

72 Saeb Erakat, "The Political Situation in Light of Developments with the US Administration and Israeli Government and Hamas' Continued Coup d'etat: Recommendations and Options" can be found on www.prrn.mcgill.ca.
73 Birnbaum, 19 March 2013.
74 Bernard Avishai, *New York Times*, 7 February 2011.
75 Abu Mazen has said this repeatedly to Arab, Israeli, American, and European audiences – for example, Mahmoud Abbas, "I Reached Understandings with Olmert on Borders, Security," MEMRI, 16 November 2010 (speech in the UAR); see also "Meetings of Mahmoud Abbas with Jewish Leaders," no date or publisher; and meeting with Israeli MKs on 22 August 2013 (*Haaretz*, 23 August 2013). See also, Daniel Kurtzer, Scott Lasensky, William Quandt, Steven Spiegel, and Shibley Telhami *The Peace Puzzle* (Ithaca, NY: Cornell University Press, 2013): 228–229; *New York Times*, 27 January 2011.
76 Rice, 2011: 654.
77 Abrams, 2013: 290.
78 2 July 2008 security talks, Jerusalem (Swisher and Karmi, 2011: 189; *al Jazeera*, 25 January 2011).
79 Tower.org, 24 May 2013; Arieli, 2010: 22.
80 Bernard Avishai, *New York Times*, 7 February 2011.
81 Abbas, MEMRI.
82 Olmert to Birnbaum, 19 March 2013; Abrams, 2013: 290.
83 According to one account (Avi Issacharoff, Tower.org, 24 May 2013), Abu Mazen met late that night with PLO leadership and advisors, sketching his memory of the map on PLO stationary, but there is nothing in this report of their reaction to his description of Olmert's offer.
84 Saeb Erakat, "The Political Situation in Light of Developments with the U.S. Administration and the Government and Hamas's Continued Coup d'État," *Journal of Palestine Studies*, 49(3), 2010: 197–201.
85 PLO, "Meetings of President Mahmud Abbas with Jewish Leaders," undated: 53 and conversations with Israelis.
86 Birnbaum, 19 March 2013.
87 Rice, 2011: 713. Olmert said the same thing regarding Livny at a *Jerusalem Post* conference in New York (*Jerusalem Post*, 2 August 2013). See also *Jerusalem Post, Sof Ha-shevua* and *UPI*, all on 24 May 2013, in which Olmert said Barak as well as Livny had sent such messages to Abu Mazen.
88 Rice, 2011: 724.
89 Abrams, 2013: 285, 291 and also quoted in Birnbaum, 11 March 2013.
90 Birnbaum, 19 March 2013.
91 *Haaretz*, 31 August 2008. In his memoirs (Bush, 2010: 409–410), Bush briefly mentions a plan to publicize the agreement; Abrams, 2013: 291, has still another version of the idea. Neither as grandiose as Olmert's suggestion nor mention of the UN.
92 Abrams, 2013: 279–280.
93 Abrams, 2013: 233 (in reference to willingness to negotiate).
94 *Yedioth Aharonoth*, 8 September 2010. Also in Birnbaum, 19 March 2013.
95 Tower.org quotes Abu Mazen later in reference to Olmert's proposal: "This is the best offer we've ever gotten from Israel and the best we will ever get" (17 May 2013); Erakat told Mideast Web that Olmert's offer had been the most advanced ever and that the two sides were quite close (Mideast Web, 21 July 2010). Both Abu Mazen and Olmert were to insist that the Palestinians never said no Avishai; Birnbaum, 19 March 2013; Abu Mazen, Reuters, 4 October 2012.
96 Birnbaum, 19 March 2010; *Maariv*, 15 April 2010.
97 *Washington Post*, 17 July 2009; *Haaretz*, 17 December 2009.
98 *Yedioth Aharonoth*, 29 September 2008.

99 *Maariv*, 15 April 2010; Birnbaum, 19 March 2013.
100 *Maariv*, 15 April 2010.
101 *Yedioth Aharonoth*, 29 September 2008.
102 Birnbaum, 19 March 2013.
103 Tower.org, 24 May 2013.
104 Arieli, 2010: 22.
105 *Yedioth Aharonoth, Maariv*, and *Haaretz*, 22 May 2008.
106 *Yedioth Aharonoth*, 22 May 2008.
107 *Yedioth Aharonoth*, 29 September 2008 (see also, *New York Times*, 29 September 2008).
108 Interview to *The Australian*, 28 November 2009; *Yediot Aharonot*, 20 April 2008.
109 Olmert speech to INSS conference, Tel Aviv, 14 February 2010.
110 *Haaretz*, 13 February 2009.
111 *Haaretz*, 11 December 2009.
112 Reuters and *Haaretz*, 19 March 2009 (Assad interview to the Italian *La Republica*).
113 Bush, 2010: 410.
114 *Haaretz*, 17 January 2008.
115 See Likud statement, *Haaretz*, 3 August 2008.
116 For example, *Haaretz*, 8 February, 14 March 2006.
117 See www.knesset.gov.il, Protocol, Two Hundred Twenty-fifth Session of the Eighteenth Knesset, Wednesday, 25 June 2008.
118 *Peace Now Settlement Watch* (*Haaretz*, 7 October 2008). Olmert abandoned the dismantling of outposts after the forced evacuation of Amona in early February 2006.
119 *Yedioth Aharonoth*, 8 September 2010.
120 Abrams, 2013: 263–264; *Haaretz*, 10 January 2008; 6 June 2008; Protocol, Special Session, Two Hundred Thirty-second Session of the Seventeenth Knesset, Thursday 15 May 2008.
121 Rice, 2011: 652.
122 Noted on Israel television, Channel 10, 29 July 2013. As noted in Chapter 7, at the Taba talks, Barak had allowed negotiators to forego Israeli sovereignty over a strip of land along the Jordan River (demanded at Camp David) but still sought an Israeli military presence for an unspecified period of time in the Jordan Rift Valley.
123 *Yedioth Aharonoth*, 20 April 2008.
124 *Sof Ha-shevuah, Jerusalem Post* and UPI, 24 May 2013.
125 Interview to CNN, 5 May 2012.
126 Kurtzer *et al.*, 2013: 220.
127 This was in particular reference to security proposals (Rice, 2011: 652).
128 Abrams, 2013, describes in detail one serious argument in front of the president, but refers to many differences of opinion throughout his account.
129 For example, Kurtzer, et al., 2013: 226.
130 Rice, 2011: 656, in reference to the May 2008 proposals.
131 Interview to *Maariv*, 15 April 2010.
132 *Ibid*.
133 Additional considerations brought others from the right wing to similar conclusions (most notably, Tzippy Livny) regarding Israel's increasing isolation in the world and the challenge even to its very legitimacy.
134 24.8 percent, *Peace Index*, May 2008.

9 Conclusions

It is difficult to accord causal value to factors. For example, even if, statistically, breakthroughs have occurred following changes in leadership, it is not certain that the new leader was the decisive (sufficient) factor even if important (necessary). Even if it were possible to find statistical indications in such a limited number of cases, it would be difficult to quantify the impact or relative weight of the various factors, such as public opinion, negative as well as positive, and it is equally difficult to quantify intangibles such as leadership status or legitimacy, trust/mistrust, personality traits, or political will, to name but a few of the factors found in the cases of breakthroughs in Israeli peacemaking. These, at least, are identifiable factors, but one is hard put to even identify, much less quantify, something like "thirst for power." There was no direct evidence of the "thirst for power" factor in the available material, including participant accounts and psychological analyses of Israeli peacemaking. Therefore, one can only guess when or if such a factor played a role; at most it would be cloaked in the guise of other factors.

Addressing first the failures, of which there are more cases than breakthroughs, the over-riding factor would indeed appear to have been intangible ideological (nationalist and/or religious) identity-related factors on the part of the Israeli leadership, to which domestic (and diaspora) spoilers contributed. Mistrust, born of the deeply engrained belief that the Arabs would never accept Israel's legitimacy, nurtured by an historical (as well as government-manipulated) sense of persecution and victimhood, had become part of Israelis' identity. Mistrust was particularly strong among the Labor leaders immediately after the 1967 war and later in the cases of Golda Meir and Rabin with regard to all of Israel's adversaries. The rejection of Egyptian offers before the Yom Kippur War, and Rabin's hesitations in talks with both Egypt and the Syrians, were signs of this attitude; it was even apparent in Rabin's failed talks with Jordan over a partial agreement. His mistrust of the Palestinians, specifically the PLO, long ruled out talks with the organization, based as it was on Rabin's conviction that the Palestinians sought a state in all of Palestine and the right of return of all the refugees, both of which would eliminate the state the Jews had created: Israel. The later changes in PLO policy (the 1988 acceptance of Israel's right to exist and the two-state solution) lessened some of these concerns though they did not fully eliminate Rabin's mistrust. For Barak, mistrust appeared quite strong with regard to the Palestinians, almost surprisingly less so with regard to the Syrians, at least as an over-riding factor. In almost all these cases, mistrust led to deal-breaking demands on the part of Israeli leaders when it came to the West Bank, Egypt, or Syria, as precautions against future attack. Thus, there was a preference for what was seen as "security" over peace. The exceptions to this were Begin and Olmert (and possibly Barak). Probably only moderately less mistrustful, Begin and Olmert, each for his own reasons, was determined to reach an agreement and therefore willing to stop short of deal-breaking demands, making do with those safeguards that were obtainable. Barak seemed to be moving toward a somewhat more flexible position, at least for the distant future (due to the changes that occurred in the nature of the security threats). Still, security demands prompted by lingering mistrust contributed to the failures of both Barak's negotiations at Camp David and Shepherdstown, as they had for Rabin before then. Clearly, the perception of the threat influenced the degree or nature of the mistrust in all the cases; but only Olmert found a way to deal with the threat as he perceived it, and the underlying mistrust, so as to prevent failure.

There were those who attributed the preference for "security over peace" to the influence of the military on the political echelon or in the negotiations themselves. This claim is based on the premise that it is the duty of the military to be mistrustful – that is, to prepare for the worst case scenario. The influence of the military (or former military) may have been a factor in the early years (under the Eshkol, Meir, and even the first Rabin governments), but it does not appear to have been a significant factor in the later failures. In fact, in some cases, the military played a positive role in support of breakthroughs (1978 Camp David, Oslo), and even in the case of the Barak Camp David failure, the military experts were occasionally more flexible than the political. This was due to their concentration on the nature of the military threat, rather than a matter of trust as such, and the nature of the military threat had undergone a change. Only later did this change directly affect the thinking of the political echelon.

Mistrust also contributed to failure by precipitating misinterpretation of the adversary's intentions. Deep mistrust led the post-1967 war government to focus only on the "three no's" of the Khartoum conference, thereby misinterpreting the relative moderation of the final resolution that both Jordan and Egypt had engineered in order to open the way for some kind of agreement with Israel. In the wake of this misinterpretation, Israel also missed the significance of the acceptance of Resolution 242 by Egypt and Jordan a few months later. Similarly, Sadat's proposals of 1971 and 1973 were met with more than skepticism due to the government's misinterpretation of Egypt's ultimate intentions (though some in the government apparently did believe the peace offer of 1973). Suspicion and apparently misinterpretation of Syria's willingness to make peace marked Rabin's negotiations via the Americans, and possibly

Barak's efforts as well. At the very least, Israel's negative interpretations of the adversary's intentions (Jordan, Egypt, Syria) may not always have been justified, and they were often contested by more positive interpretations on the part of third parties. Actually, for Rabin mistrust was perhaps at the core of his peacemaking approach. It was apparent not only in his occasional misinterpretation of Syria's positions and his insistence upon proofs of Assad's peaceful intentions, but it was also built into the Oslo Accords (viz. their interim nature), along with Rabin's avoidance of any commitment to the creation of a Palestinian state and insistence upon the Jordan River as Israel's security border.

In the end, mistrust also affected Israel leaders' political will or determination to pursue an agreement. Not only did it generate deal-breaking security demands but, also, the belief that a genuine peace agreement was unattainable. This belief was characterized by the post-1967 Eshkol and Meir government approaches and Rabin's attitude toward the Palestinians for many years (though he was will to test). It was also apparent in Rabin's negotiations with Syria that dragged on and on, eroding whatever political will may have existed on either side.

Ideology – that is, nationalist ideology in the case of Labor governments – contributed significantly to policy with regard to the West Bank. All of the Labor leaders, including the "younger" generations of Rabin, Peres, and Barak, adhered to the attitude, indeed the conviction, that the territory of the West Bank is "ours," to keep or give up, to control, to divide, as they saw fit – perhaps depending upon other factors. For the right-wing and religious parties, ideology (whether nationalist or religious or both) obviously stopped at the "it is ours," with nothing of *Eretz Israel* to be relinquished. Insofar as Labor was willing to keep or "give up" part of the land, the party claimed to be guided purely by security-related considerations. Yet its ideological stance was apparent in the settlement project it undertook and supported from 1967 onwards. Settlements such as those in Gush Etzion or the Gaza Strip belied the purely security argument, with settlements ultimately becoming a deal breaker themselves, due to pragmatic if not ideological considerations, in the territorial discussions under the later governments of Barak and of Olmert (as the security relevance of the Jordan River border diminished). But even earlier, for Begin the ideological attachment to the settlement enterprise almost prevented the breakthrough of the Camp David accords with Sadat.

The other "deal-breaker" behind the failures was the Israeli position on East Jerusalem. Historically, before 1967, the difference we saw above between Labor and the right wing with regard to the West Bank was generally the same regarding Jerusalem. Given other considerations, some compromise on Jerusalem was viewed as possible (viz. Ben Gurion's acceptance of the 1947 Partition Plan despite the absence of Jewish sovereignty over Jerusalem). But after 1967, until 2008, this difference virtually disappeared, as both political camps defined Jerusalem as the historic as well religious focus of Jewish legitimacy in this land. Even the secular Barak, who was willing to consider relinquishing control of at least some parts of East Jerusalem, would not forgo Israeli sovereignty over the Temple Mount even when it constituted a deal-breaker.

Religious and nationalist ideology, along with mistrust, was the main factor among the spoilers from the political echelon (though economic interests may also have motivated some). One may assume that there were economic interests among those who sought to hold onto the occupied territories; but aside from pointing to actual business deals and investment, it is hard to find evidence of direct influence on the political echelon (unless one adopts a single factor analysis that explains the occupation as a colonialist enterprise of Israeli governments since 1967). In the failures (and in the breakthroughs) the political spoilers did not make life easy for the leaders who sought peace agreements, but the degree to which they negatively influenced the process varied. The political spoilers, with their threats to the government's majority and encouragement of public opposition, weakened Rabin and Barak, despite the legitimacy both of them had in the eyes of the public. For Barak this was to be a critical factor, at least on the Syrian track, as he questioned his ability to get an agreement past the government and the Knesset. Right-wing governments, such as that of Begin, did not have this problem to the same degree inasmuch as they could count on the support of the opposition, Labor and the left, in case of an agreement. The spoilers within Begin's own camp did have some impact upon the content of the agreement actually reached with Egypt, but not to the point of preventing the breakthrough. Insofar as spoilers from the political establishment allied with or encouraged public action against the government in the Oslo period, they could certainly be counted among the various factors responsible for the failure. The assassination of Rabin, largely due to incitement created by the political and public opponents to Oslo, brought a halt to the process that Peres was unable and Netanyahu was unwilling to revive. Precipitous decisions by Peres to advance elections brought a halt to the talks with Syria as well, though Netanyahu did authorize resumption of at least indirect talks (via Ron Lauder) in 1998.[1] Some might argue that timing was a critical factor for the 2000 Camp David and later Annapolis failures, namely, in both cases, the impending departure from office of both the Israeli leaders and the American presidents. Olmert, however, would argue (indeed, he has argued) that the timing was, in fact, the result of political spoilers who harassed him incessantly with corruption allegations even of their own creation, to the point of cutting short his period in office. If his accusations were true, they could be held responsible for the shortened time period left for reaching a final agreement (though the Gaza war may also have been a factor, further cutting short the time remaining). Blaming his opponents, Olmert (but also Abu Mazen) considered timing to have been the critical factor that rendered the Annapolis process only a "near breakthrough." Somewhat connected to this, Olmert's political rivals (with their advice to Abu Mazen that he wait for a new leader) may have been a factor in the Palestinians' hesitation to conclude a deal with Olmert as he was leaving office, though that could only be considered one of many factors in the failure.

The role of political spoilers was closely linked to popular action and public opinion, though it is always difficult to determine to what degree public opinion, as such, contributed to policy decisions. In the aftermath of the 1967 war, public opinion does not appear to have been a factor in the government decisions that prevented a breakthrough with Jordan. Similarly, public opinion does not appear to have affected Golda Meir's decisions regarding Egypt. Nor was public opinion in opposition to the positions of the government in either case. While public opinion during Rabin's second period opposed compromise on the Golan, this was not a critical factor in Rabin's decisions or hesitations. This same negative public sentiment, and public opinion as a factor at all, would seem to have come into play for Peres – who moved quickly, perhaps too quickly, in order to amass popularity prior to elections. Public opinion played a far larger role in the Barak period, possibly even a critical role, as suggested by President Clinton and chief negotiator Uri Sagie, among others, in connection with Barak's retreat and the failure on the Syrian track. Yet, for all that Israelis had been negatively affected by the failure of Oslo and then the violence of the second Intifada, public opinion did not work against a breakthrough in the Annapolis process. The Israeli public, as reflected by opinion polls and surveys, continued to support negotiations, even after Olmert's legitimacy to make an agreement had been compromised.

The role or impact of public opinion depended to a good deal on the leader's concept of leadership. Rabin, like the generation of leaders before him, and the pragmatic Olmert after him, adhered to a concept that one should lead, not follow, the public, though he was perhaps more cautious than Olmert. Rabin believed that one should not get too far ahead of the public, and he therefore sought what he would need to bring to the public in order to gain its support for an agreement (particularly with the Syrians). However, at most this was but one factor for Rabin. Basically, his confidence that he could bring about a shift in public thinking contributed to his undertaking talks for peace on both the Syrian and the Palestinian tracks when he came to power. As such, it was a significant factor contributing to the Oslo breakthrough. In the case of Olmert, the role of the concept of leadership is clearer. At most, Olmert was concerned only that the military establishment be sufficiently satisfied as to be able to reassure the public with regard to the security arrangements. The decline in his popularity may even have motivated him further to work for a breakthrough, but there is no evidence that it worked as a negative factor except insofar as it affected the adversary's belief in Olmert's ability to deliver, or not, in the end. This effect, however, is related more to status and legitimacy of the leader than to public opinion regarding an agreement or the modalities of an agreement. The lack of security credentials and status worked against Peres and may actually have been a decisive factor in his failure to sustain the Oslo process after the terrorist attacks of February and March 2006, leading then to the election of Netanyahu.

Leadership style may also have been a contributing factor to the failures. Rabin's slow, deliberate, and mistrustful manner may have discouraged his adversary Assad; it may have led to missed opportunities to achieve a breakthrough. Yet, the opposite approach, Peres's hasty moves and abrupt shift to a different set of Israeli demands, may have aroused Assad's suspicions no less than Rabin's hesitation had. And Barak's arrogance, with regard not only to his adversaries but even to his own colleagues, therefore leading him to forego advice, contributed greatly to the problematic nature of the negotiations themselves and the resulting failures.

Indeed, the nature of the "process" was also an important factor. In the case of the Oslo Accords, for example, the interim nature of the agreement and inherent flaws, such as the absence of monitoring or guarantees for implementation, played a large role in their failure. During the later part (post-Rabin) of the Oslo period, and particularly under Barak, the Israeli method of negotiating was a decidedly negative factor, especially at Camp David. Israeli negotiators approached the talks as a bargaining session of give-and-take: each side gives a little, takes a little, a tit for tat of mutual compromises. But this implied equality or symmetry that the Palestinians saw as misplaced. Not only did they see themselves as the side that had been deprived (by Israel) of what was rightfully theirs, they also had already made their critical "historic compromise," the abandonment of their goal of a state in all of Palestine and a willingness to make do with just the territory occupied by Israel in 1967. Moreover, inasmuch as all Israeli leaders (and their negotiators), from the Eshkol government to Olmert's, adhered to the attitude that all of the land was "ours," they approached each issue as if Israel were making a concession by "giving" the Palestinians a certain amount of the West Bank, for example, or a neighborhood or two in East Jerusalem, and so forth. Even Olmert told Abu Mazen that his was a "generous offer," fully expecting Abu Mazen to appreciate what Israel was willing to "concede" in the way of territory in the West Bank or in East Jerusalem. This offensive and condescending, as well as unjustifiable, approach may well have contributed at least somewhat to the failure of Oslo, more perhaps to that of Camp David. Israelis believed that they were, in fact, granting concessions to the Palestinians, not just because the West Bank or East Jerusalem was currently in Israel's possession but because these areas "rightfully" belonged to Israel. As a result, Israeli negotiators faulted the Palestinians for trying to gain such "concessions." Even in dealing with the Egyptians and Syrians, in which cases Israel did not relate to the territories involved as "disputed" (with the exception of the exact 1967 line), it nonetheless employed a "bargaining," give-and-take approach that may have contributed to the failures that occurred. In the case of Begin with Sadat, this approach marred the pre-Camp David negotiations to the point of nearly preventing a breakthrough.

Another aspect of the process considered by some to have contributed to failure in the Annapolis negotiations and probably also both the talks with the Syrians and the Barak–Arafat Camp David talks was the guiding principle that nothing was agreed until everything was agreed. Both American and Israeli participants were later to view this as a flaw, though the Palestinian participants may not agree; in fact, this principle did leave the way open to trade-offs, particularly on the more problematic issues. Still another process-related factor was the use of a third party, which may have been a contributing factor to the failures insofar as it replaced the potentially trust-building effect of direct, person-to-person talks. Yet, while direct talks with King Hussein over the years contributed to trust, they did not manage to overcome the differences over substantive issues (until those issues had undergone change). Moreover, in the case of Begin and Sadat, frequent personal contact actually led to animosity, necessitating third-party involvement. Similarly, personal contact did not help in any of Barak's negotiating attempts. Yet, the involvement of a third party, specifically the Americans, could be problematic. The older generation, for example, the Eshkol and Meir governments, and also to some extent Rabin, did not fully trust the United States to act on their behalf, particularly during the Nixon period but also even in the earlier Johnson period. Israel did not grant much weight to American advice in the post-1967 period nor was it always candid with the Americans (e.g., about the fact that Israel was holding meetings with King Hussein shortly after the war). In this sense, the suspicious view of the third party may have limited the possibility of using US assistance to achieve a breakthrough. Indeed, Israeli suspicions of the Americans may have led them to reject steps or proposals that might have led to a breakthrough – for example, with Jordan, possibly even Egypt. Rabin, however, went further; he believed that the Americans had actually hurt the chances for a breakthrough by means of faulty mediation between himself and Hafez Assad. Barak, too, thought the Americans played a problematic role with the Syrians (e.g., in the Geneva summit) and especially at Camp David. Many on the US team faulted themselves and/or Clinton for not conducting the Camp David talks more actively, productively, or authoritatively. High-ranking US observers also attributed the failure of the Annapolis process at least in part to the absence of US involvement as well as inconsistencies or policy differences on the American side. The Jewish American diaspora played a minor role, often a negative one with regard to the achievement of a breakthrough, particularly during the Oslo process. Yet, there is no evidence that this was an important much less critical role in the final analysis, despite the diaspora's generally right-wing lobbying of the US Congress on both the Syrian and Palestinian issues. The only exception would be if Olmert were correct in his accusations that the diaspora was linked politically and financially to the political opposition in Israel, providing the material and funds for the campaign against him that ultimately brought him down, and with him his peace efforts. If there were truth to these accusations (which are not as farfetched as they may appear), then one could conclude that the diaspora did, indeed, play a critical role in the failure of the Annapolis process, causing both a crisis of timing and an erosion of confidence in Olmert's ability to make a deal.

An additional outside factor may have been the regional environment. In the post-1967 war period there were signs of change in the thinking of the regional actors, but Israel misread these signs, as noted above. Thus, Israel's failure to comprehend the positive change in attitudes within the region was a contributing factor to the failure with Jordan, if not Egypt as well. Although it was basically mistrust that led not only to the failure to perceive the change but also motivated Israeli's deal-breaking positions, the failure to engage the region may have contributed to the failure of Barak at Camp David. The future of Jerusalem was of importance to the Arab states as well as the Palestinians, but Israel (and America's) failure to engage and cultivate Egypt and Jordan before the issue was raised at Camp David did negatively affect the outcome of those talks. Later comprehension of this mistake was to play a role in the near-breakthrough of the Annapolis process.

Notwithstanding the positive role the region might but did not play, this was not necessarily critical, as evidenced by the success of the Begin–Sadat Camp David summit despite strong regional opposition to such a breakthrough. Other factors outweighed this problem, particularly determination of the adversary, as we shall see below. The role of the adversary was a key factor in the failures; certainly, Israeli leaders attributed failure, indeed all the failures, to the recalcitrance of the adversary, whether King Hussein, Hafiz Assad, Arafat or even, to some degree, Abu Mazen. Their failures to accept Israel's "offers" were attributed to various motives and factors difficult to prove or disprove.

Although it was under Arafat that the PLO changed its policy in 1988 and accepted the two-state solution, doubts remained about Arafat's intentions. Was he really interested in peace with Israel or did his failure to curb Islamic spoilers – Hamas and Jihad terrorists – during the Oslo period indicate the opposite? Did his hesitation to consider various compromises at Camp David – for example, over Jerusalem – indicate disinterest in reaching an agreement or a genuine belief that he had to contend with naysayers in his own camp or even the Islamic world (with regard to the Haram al Sherif)? Or did Arafat genuinely believe that Camp David was intended by Barak as a trap or, at the least, that it had been convened before the complicated issues had been sufficiently deliberated to lead to agreement? Did he believe that he could get a "better deal" by holding out (as in a bargaining situation) or at a later time, possibly even with a new president – one of the explanations for his ambiguous response to the Clinton Parameters? All or even some of the doubtful or negative intentions attributed to Arafat could account for the failures of Oslo and Camp David. Arafat was not an accommodating or even trustworthy negotiating partner – certainly not in Israeli or even American eyes – and he demonstrated only minimal acknowledgement of Israeli legitimacy. Similarly, Hafiz Assad was not an easy partner. He was a suspicious, cold, and distant adversary who refused even to provide confidence-building measures, rejecting direct talks at the summit level that might have produced greater trust and flexibility on the Israeli side. As was the case with Arafat, Assad's apparent inflexibility was interpreted ultimately by Israel as an absence of a genuine interest in peace with Israel – and therefore the cause of the failures.

On the background of the underlying mistrust, failure was therefore attributed to the intentions and positions of the adversary, despite the fact that Israel's positions or proposals may have been genuine problems for the other side. Obviously, if the adversaries had accepted the Israeli positions, failure would have been averted both with the Palestinians and the Syrians, but that is to ignore the nature of the proposals themselves. The deal-breakers with the Palestinians – namely, Israel's claims to almost all of East Jerusalem and the Temple Mount, the security demands regarding the Jordan Rift Valley or at least the Jordan River border, and the later territorial demands in order to accommodate the majority of the settlers – were all major factors for the failures. The apparent inability to resolve the last of these (the territorial issue) may therefore have been a critical – perhaps even the critical – factor in the failure of the Annapolis process insofar as there was a failure. Yet, deal-breaker proposals came not only from the Israeli side. Palestinian demands on the refugee issue might have been a deal breaker for Israel if all other matters had been resolved. The Palestinians did not view this issue any less a justifiable grievance than their claims to the areas occupied in 1967. But for Israel the introduction of claims from 1948 was perceived as challenging Israel's legitimacy altogether, or at the least an effort to take over the state, demographically, and therefore clearly constituting a deal-breaker. Since final discussion of the refugee issue was never reached, neither at Camp David nor in the Annapolis process, it is impossible to know if compromises that had been suggested (e.g., those of the Clinton Parameters) would have produced a breakthrough or if this issue would have led ultimately to failure. On the Syrian track, Israeli demands regarding the albeit miniscule territorial issue of the northeast corner of the Kinneret was the apparent cause of the failure, but subsequent progress on this issue suggests that other, already noted factors, including mutual mistrust, played a more important role.

Finally, among the negative factors – namely, those contributing to failures – there is the matter of leadership changes. Aside from the Rabin to Peres succession, which did play a negative role, the other changes generally occurred after the failures had already taken place: Netanyahu's succession to Peres, and later to Olmert; or Sharon's succession to Barak. Of course, one might argue that had these leadership changes not taken place, along with those that occurred in Washington as well, negotiations might have been resumed and led to breakthroughs. In fact, contacts of various kinds were resumed both with the Syrians and the Palestinians even under the new, conservative Israeli leaders; but these contacts did little if anything to reverse the earlier failures, and, particularly in the case of Netanyahu, the leadership change was a decidedly negative factor with regard to a possible, future breakthrough.

Turning to factors for success, leadership changes were, however, major factors in the breakthroughs and near-breakthrough that occurred. On the domestic scene, the shift from Labor-dominated governments to the Begin government of 1977 surprisingly led to the first breakthrough: the peace with Egypt. A personal meeting with Sadat and the achievement of a full peace agreement with Egypt were objectives set by Begin. Unlike his predecessors, Begin was willing to pay the price that a peace agreement would clearly entail, and it was this willingness that would play a critical role, together with other factors, in the ultimate breakthrough. Similarly, the later leadership shift from the intransigent Likud leader Shamir to Rabin in 1992 (indeed, from the conservative Likud to the more liberal Labor Party) was one of the keys to the Oslo breakthrough. In each of these cases the leadership change was a necessary if insufficient factor. In the case of Olmert, it is not certain if the shift from Sharon to Olmert was a key factor inasmuch as Sharon's own apparently changing objectives remain unclear. But it was the new leader, Olmert, who initiated the policy that led to the near-breakthrough of the Annapolis process.

Begin and Rabin both enjoyed status and legitimacy as leaders insofar as they were respected for their integrity and judgment. Despite his small parliamentary majority, Rabin had the added virtue of his military standing. While in the cases of Begin and Rabin their status contributed to their successes, it is not clear that the absence of such status would have negatively affected Olmert's efforts in the long run. In any case, other factors played equal if not more important roles in the breakthroughs, including and especially those factors that guided each of these leaders himself. In an indirect way, ideology was the motivating factor for Begin as he sought to avoid pressure to relinquish the West Bank (*Eretz Israel*). By withdrawing from Sinai he could claim fulfillment of Israel's obligations, as he chose to interpret them, under Resolution 242. For Rabin, and especially for Olmert, it was actually a matter of putting ideology aside as they engaged in a reappraisal of the importance or role of the occupied territories for Israel's future. As we have seen, it was not that trust replaced mistrust as a major factor for any of the three leaders, but rather the changed estimate on the part of each of them regarding the nature of the threat to Israel's interests. This revised view of the threat operated as a "push" for a new policy, not necessarily in Zartman's meaning that a stalemate had been reached but, rather, something close to a "breaking point" – namely, the conclusion that the old path was not working (a form of stalemate, perhaps) but, in fact, was leading to harm and must not be allowed to continue. For Begin, the reassessment was the many lives lost in the Yom Kippur War; for Rabin and Olmert, it was the instability inherent in the continued occupation as demonstrated by the first and second Intifadas, respectively. In addition, Rabin and Olmert both had concerns related to the home front; for Rabin these had been highlighted by the Scud attacks of the first Gulf War, and for Olmert by the rocket attacks of the second Lebanon War. The demographic issue, long a consideration in Labor Party thinking, now plagued both these two leaders. Thus, all three underwent shifts in their estimates of the dangers facing Israel, particularly Rabin and even more so Olmert (mainly, but not only, in response to various types of violence). And these shifts acted as something of a "push" toward peace efforts. For Begin, there was something of a "pull" towards peace in the form of the changed leadership in Cairo and, also, the estimate that without Egypt the Arab states (i.e., Syria) would not risk a war against Israel. For Rabin, the changed international and regional political environment (collapse of the Soviet Union, the new American-led world order, the Arab states' turn to the US and their concern over the rise of radical Islam, the weakening of the PLO because of the loss of Soviet backing and also the loss of Saudi financing after the Iraq War) created a "window of opportunity." This was accompanied by a negative time factor – namely, anticipation of the spread of weapons of mass destruction in the region. For Olmert the regional factors were not cardinal though they were positive: a mutuality of interests *vis à vis* Iran, along with an Arab interest in ending the Palestinian conflict, as reflected in the Arab Peace Initiative and declared Arab willingness to normalize relations with Israel in return. But for Rabin and, especially, for Olmert, the threat to Israeli interests posed by continuation of the occupation was cardinal, promising as it did renewed bloodshed, a threat to Israeli democracy or, even worse in their eyes, a bi-national state. All of these factors contributed to the Israeli decisions to pursue agreements, but many of them, such as the changed regional factors, also played a role in the achievement of the breakthroughs themselves, as we shall discuss below.

Domestic political factors, despite the strength of spoilers and shaky coalitions, played a positive role insofar as the leaders could point to public support. In reaction to Sadat's dramatic visit, public mistrust and fears were greatly reduced, as were concerns by many politicians regarding Egyptian interest in peace (i.e., acceptance of Israel). In addition to the public support for a peace accord with Egypt, there were now also broad expectations that agreement would ensue. Even Begin acknowledged these expectations as a factor that weighed in favor of returning from Camp David with an agreement. Given his own leadership strength and abilities, he did not appear in need of bowing to the spoilers beyond certain accommodations to their sensitivities, but he also benefitted from the support of the Knesset opposition and therefore was able easily to withstand the skeptics in his own camp. Rabin too benefitted from public opinion, as did Olmert, despite the fact that Olmert did not enjoy the same status and legitimacy of either Begin or Rabin. The effects of both Intifadas on the public's desire to see an end to the conflict with the Palestinians were important factors (possibly in addition to the underlying changes of Israeli society from one guided by a collective ethos to one based more on competitive individualism). The failure of the Oslo process and Camp David, followed by the trauma of the second Intifada, created deep skepticism as to the possibility of a breakthrough, but this did not hamper the public support for the effort to reach an accord. While less strong, support for an agreement even with Syria was apparent, at least in the Olmert period. Like Begin (and unlike Barak), however, both Rabin and Olmert believed that leadership would outweigh opposition. All three believed that the leader's duty was to determine the nation's goals and to pursue them, whether these were popular or not, confident that in the end the public would be led.

In the cases in point, a critical factor was the political will of each of these leaders – namely, the determination to find a way to achieve the goal or engineer a breakthrough. Thus, process had something to do with success.

Begin employed diplomatic tricks, ambiguous formulations, separate assurances or disclaimers, many of which bordered on deceit. These were, in part, due to his own beliefs, but also in response to the sensitivities of his own camp. He also sought the advice and interventions of advisors and colleagues. Together, all of this attested to his determination to find a way to achieve an agreement with Egypt. Rabin, ever skeptical, employed different tactics, both for the achievement of the initial breakthrough and in the Oslo process itself. Albeit without much enthusiasm, he allowed skilled, peace-oriented (in Israeli terms "dovish") individuals chosen by his political rival, Peres, to conduct back channel negotiations to create a basis for movement. While the end product varied little from ideas Rabin himself had proposed many years earlier, the key was the change in Rabin's thinking (noted above) that allowed a peace process to be conducted with the previously rejected partner, the PLO. Rabin then agreed to proceed on a step-by-step basis, in a form of a testing but basically patient approach that consisted also of direct bilateral talks with Arafat as well as the use of private intermediaries. All of this attested to Rabin's determination to reach an agreement with the Palestinians. We do not know how far this determination would have extended or what he would have been willing, ultimately, to do in the final status talks, but the continued breakthrough in the form of Oslo II, despite the actions of the spoilers on both sides, suggested a strong political will on Rabin's part to achieve an agreement.

While neither Rabin nor Olmert later made more than a minor (rhetorical) effort to calm opponents, they both, however, did seek to placate the settlers. Each of them permitted the continuation of potentially deal-breaking settlement construction; but in the cases of both leaders, this was designed to ease the process until a final reckoning would have to be made with the settlers. Olmert's negotiating tactic was particularly constructive, relying on quiet and direct, person-to-person talks of a nearly secret nature. He tended to disregard the more detailed discussions undertaken by his supposed representative, Livny, leaving the decision-making to himself and relying on the lower-level expert groups to prepare the infrastructure for implementation of the eventual agreement. This was a top-down, bottom-up approach (that ignored the middle track) and avoided publicity. Moreover, Olmert sought advice and agreed to compromises out of a pragmatic (and realistic) approach to find devices – for example, with respect to Jerusalem, specifically the holy places – in order to come as close as possible to minimum Palestinian demands. This attested to his political will and determination to achieve a breakthrough, and while there was no final accord on the two potential deal-breakers, for the territorial percentages needed to accommodate maximum number of settlers, and the number of refugees Israel would accept to accommodate the Palestinians, nonetheless, Olmert – and Abu Mazen – later claimed that these issues too would have been solved, and failure prevented. A similarly pragmatic and realistic approach was to be applied by Olmert to the Syrian track, and initially the negotiating technique was similar – virtually secret top-level talks, albeit through a mediator. How and by whom the planned direct talks would have taken place was not revealed. Although such talks reportedly were to be held between foreign ministers, here too Olmert planned only for bilateral expert meetings (on specific issues) to implement the decisions reached in principle between the leaders themselves, in whatever manner that took place.

The successful use of a third party – namely, the Americans in the breakthrough with Egypt, the Norwegians in connection with Oslo, and the Turks with regard to the Syria – certainly suggests a critical factor. To a lesser degree, Morocco and Rumania also played positive roles. Yet, this factor, specifically the role of the Americans, did not significantly change the cases that ended in failure. While the difference from the failures lay in the many other factors at play – or missing – even in the successful cases, the role of the third parties varied. The American role was already evident, if indirect, in Begin's decision to move on the Egyptian track due to the Israeli leader's concern over the changes that the new US president (Carter) had introduced in American policy. The new policy was one far more sensitive to the Palestinian issue and geared to obtaining a comprehensive peace agreement (as distinct from his predecessor's step-by-step method), which would mean pressure on Israel regarding withdrawal from the West Bank. More directly, the role of President Carter, personally, in the Camp David talks was an important, even critical factor. It was not just Carter's presence and authority but also his thorough preparation, his assistance (virtual micro-management), and his persuasion in devising the formulations and compromises achieved that enabled the peace agreement that was finally signed in March 1979. Similar efforts by Clinton at the second Camp David fell short, not just because of other factors (which, indeed, were at play), but also because of the shortcomings in the Americans' approach, an absence of more forceful direct intervention. Yet, while earlier the Americans had not been involved in the initial breakthrough in Oslo, their public backing by means of the White House ceremony did help in its promotion. They may also be said to have significantly assisted later in the achievement of Oslo II. But it was Norwegian facilitation that had brought the two sides together at a time when the formal Madrid negotiations in Washington were at an impasse. And the quiet mediation by the Norwegians, including talks with Arafat in Tunis, for example, should not be ignored as a contributing factor. There was minimal American involvement in the Israeli peace agreement with Jordan; nor was there any need for much involvement once the Oslo Accords had been negotiated (eliminating the major issues between Israel and Jordan and providing legitimation for Jordanian moves). Moreover, Washington was not entirely happy with Jordan (after the Iraq War) or with digression from the Syrian track at the time. Yet, it had an indirect role since the prospect of repairing relations with the US was part of Hussein's objectives. In this, the diaspora played a (rare) positive role for the breakthrough. Mobilized by Israel, diaspora leaders pressed Congress to cancel the Jordanian debt, as requested by Hussein in the peace talks. On the whole, Washington limited itself to minor procedural proposals, along with public backing for formal talks (which the Americans claimed to have initiated) at a White House ceremony, and then at the final signing ceremony, belying the fact that the US had played only a marginal role.

This was not the case with Syria. A third party had always been necessary between Israel and the Syrians, even after the ascent to power of Assad's son Bashar. At least some third-party involvement was required presumably due to Syrian hostility to Israel, and the preferred candidate was the US given Syria's interest in using an accord with Israel as a means to improved relations with Washington. When the Americans were unwilling, other third parties previously informally involved – primarily, the Swiss and the Turks – became options. Once Israel, under Olmert, decided to pursue the Syrian track, Turkey was the preferred choice given both the desirable improvement that had occurred in Israeli–Turkish relations and Turkey's position as a regional player as well as a member of the North Atlantic Treaty Organization (NATO). We know very little of the Turkish role itself except that in addition to Ankara having been supremely discreet, its role was both direct and at the highest level. It was also, apparently, successful.

On the Palestinian track, Olmert did not believe that the Americans were needed or that any third party would necessarily render the talks easier. He viewed personal, bilateral talks as the most conducive method for reaching compromises. There were Americans who did not share this view, and also those who maintained that the absence of effective American involvement contributed to the failure, insofar as there was a failure. Nonetheless, the Americans *can* be credited with having provided backing for the initiation of the process already undertaken by Olmert. More importantly, they can be credited with harnessing official regional support for the Annapolis process along with possibly critical Arab support for the compromises reached on Jerusalem and other issues. As noted above, such support was not solicited or nurtured in time for the Barak–Arafat talks at Camp David; both the Americans and the Israelis avoided that mistake in 2008, suggesting a learning curve. In those earlier talks, the regional atmosphere had also been generally positive, despite Barak's zigzagging on the Oslo track and failure with Syria; but by 2008 the region's leaders were far more united around a coherent position, as demonstrated by the Arab Peace Initiative that continued to be reconfirmed. Nevertheless, the American effort to keep the Arab states engaged (prompted by Saudi pressure on Washington), alongside continuous Israeli contact with Egypt and Jordan, was a major factor.

Finally, there is the role of the adversary and, more specifically, leadership changes on the side of the adversary. Israeli leadership, Israeli proposals, the nature of the processes, as well as the contributions of domestic political and public opinion factors, along with regional and third-party factors, would all ultimately affect or be affected by the critical factor of the adversary. Sadat, Abu Mazen, and possibly even Bashar Assad, each in his own time and in his own way, appeared more trustworthy and promising than their predecessors. King Hussein had long enjoyed Israeli trust, rebuilt in direct contacts over the years after the 1967 war. Thus, Jordan and Israel were able relatively easily to resolve the issues around the small amount of Jordanian land taken by Israel over the years and the water sources involved. Other issues that had previously tried Israeli trust, and violated it – namely, the security issues related to the West Bank or the more recent deal-breaker of the settlements – were no longer relevant to Israeli peace with Jordan since King Hussein had returned his claim to the West Bank to the Palestinians in 1988. And whatever remaining claim or interest Jordan had with regard to the holy sites in Jerusalem had been accommodated in the Israeli–Jordanian peace treaty, to be finally ensconced later in Palestinian–Israel agreements. Indeed, King Hussein was to become an important mediator between Israel and the Palestinians during the Oslo period, and under his son and heir, King Abdullah, Jordan assisted Israel in security arrangements with the Palestinians. Moreover, Jordan also played a major role with regard to the Arab Peace Initiative.

The advent of Sadat to power in Egypt brought a new vision for his country that included a shift in international orientation, to the US, and an end to conflict with Israel. Sadat understood the psychological nature of the conflict for Israelis, and it was this aspect that he confronted directly in his visit, particularly in his speech to the Knesset. Thus, although it was initially Begin who had sought a personal meeting, it was Sadat, with his dramatic visit to Jerusalem, who penetrated the barriers of Israeli mistrust. Other factors played a role, even a critical role perhaps; but Sadat's extraordinary act, opposed not only by most of the Arab countries but also by many of Sadat's own officials and colleagues, was the key that opened the door to the peace treaty. And his ultimate cooperation at Camp David – in agreeing to the ambiguities and devices of Begin – made the peace possible.

Nothing as dramatic as the Sadat visit occurred or could have been expected from the new leadership in Syria. Bashar Assad basically revived his father's efforts to shift the country's orientation westward as well as to regain the land lost to Israel in 1967. Like his father, he agreed to Syrian participation in a conference that opened a peace process with Israel, and, albeit with reservations, he endorsed the Arab Peace Initiative. Whether he would prove a less difficult, less suspicious negotiating partner was not brought to a test inasmuch as Olmert's time ran out and subsequent tentatives on both his and Israel's parts dissipated with the stirrings of the "Arab Spring" and subsequent civil war in Syria.

Abu Mazen, however, was a distinctly different leader from Arafat and while far less an authoritative figure, he nonetheless inspired far more trust as an individual. His longstanding rejection of violence had made him a preferred candidate for power in the eyes of the Israelis and the Americans, even before Arafat's death. As a leader, he was willing to provide confidence-building measures, most notably security assurances – and actions – that provided an opening for Israel to resume serious final status discussions with him. Unquestionably, Abu Mazen was a far more flexible and creative negotiating partner than Arafat regarding the formerly deal-breaking issues of Jerusalem and Israeli security interests. Whether he ultimately would have been as forthcoming on the remaining territorial issue or, as he claimed, on the refugee issue is still not known. Abu Mazen was to insist that the deal could have been made had time not run out. He appeared to have the necessary political will; he may not have had the necessary political power. But his leadership played a critical role in the near-breakthrough produced by the Annapolis process.

The willingness of Israel's adversaries, Sadat, King Hussein, Abu Mazen, and possibly Bashar Assad, to make peace with Israel was the result of the more pragmatic – and realistic – approach that had begun to characterize the region's leaders over the years. Indeed, some of the pragmatism had been apparent even among their predecessors. But the additional, perhaps new, characteristic common to Sadat, Hussein, and Abu Mazen was a greater understanding of Israelis – their history, their fears (despite the might of the Israel Defense Forces), and even their need to have their legitimacy in the region acknowledged. These leaders, in particular the Palestinian, may not have fully accepted this legitimacy – namely, acceptance of the Jews as a people with a right to self-determination and on this piece of land. Nonetheless, they understood and, more importantly, were willing to agree officially to the "*right* of Israel to exist within secure and recognized borders" in the region – without necessarily spelling out the basis of this right. For Israel, this phrase was the heart of Resolution 242; it was the core of the conflict with the Palestinians in particular. Eventually even Arafat had been willing to acknowledge this right in the PLO's historic 1988 decision (and in the Oslo DOP) that constituted the turning point in the conflict and made breakthrough possible. But Abu Mazen was able to go beyond Arafat's declarative acknowledgement. He did so by means of accommodation of the Israeli attachment to Jerusalem – the Temple Mount, which for Israelis was the symbolic embodiment of the state's legitimacy. Abu Mazen, and Olmert, were each willing to go half way on this sensitive, previously deal-breaking issue by allowing (at least implicitly) that no one country would have sovereignty over the holy places.

The transformation – the breakthroughs and near-breakthrough that did occur in the Arab–Israel conflict – were due to many factors, but most of all to an evolution or series of changes that occurred in Israel. Other changes, first of all in Israel's adversaries, but also in the region and beyond, clearly contributed; they were even vital. Nonetheless, the few successes could not have occurred if Israeli leaders had not come to perceive the threats to Israel somewhat differently over the years. Holding onto the occupied territories appeared to carry the danger of repeated bloodshed – in the earlier period, with regard only to Sinai, but later with regard to uprisings (Intifadas) and rocket attacks (in the north as well as the south) challenging the public's resilience. In time, the so-called demographic threat to the Jewish but also democratic nature of Israel implied a choice, ultimately, between apartheid or a bi-national state in the whole area (as distinct from a state meant to be the fulfillment of Jewish national self-determination within the smaller 1949–1967 borders). These threats to Israel were not necessarily the considerations that guided the general public; but if these were not uppermost in the general consciousness, the perception of the conflict or the means of dealing with it did undergo an evolution among the public. The Palestinians were eventually acknowledged as a people, in time the two-state solution was generally assumed to be the best option, and the future borders of the Palestinian state were understood to be the 1967 lines subject only to the practical (albeit supremely difficult) matter of the numbers of settlers to be evacuated. Like the issue of the settlements, so too the future status of East Jerusalem was placed on the negotiating table, also to be subject to practical rather than ideological, emotional, or even religious criteria. Even third-party involvement in security matters became acceptable, as security was no longer perceived in terms of territory and solutions no longer perceived in terms of ideology or religion. In pragmatic terms, peace agreements began to be perceived as a safeguard against fear and mistrust, at least insofar as changes in the region and beyond suggested the need – or chances – for pragmatism. Louis Kriesberg in his analysis of transformation of intractable conflict might call this an identity change, similar to that which occurred in South Africa. But the change in Israelis' identity was neither total nor irreversible.[2] The failures that also occurred, especially the failure after the initial breakthrough of Oslo and the merely partial breakthrough of Annapolis, left their marks. They served to preserve Israelis' sense of victimhood and restore mistrust, with the result that alongside the acceptance of the two-state solution, the mantra of impossibility, "no partner," much akin to Golda Meir's "they'll never accept us," came to dominate. And with this came the revival of right-wing and religious ideologies: a belief in ultra-nationalism, a sense of exclusive entitlement to all the land, and a reliance on military might. The result for today's Israel is a struggle between ideology/religion, on the one hand, and pragmatism, on the other, with adherents on each side believing that they are the ones who understand Israel's true interests. While past failures suggest that even the pragmatists' solutions are unattainable, the breakthroughs suggest, nonetheless, that there are solutions out there, and given certain circumstances, they *are* attainable if there is a political will.

Notes

1 And again for a few months during late 2010–2011, via American mediation rather than the Turks, who were no longer interested in aiding Israel. *Yedioth Aharonoth*, 12 October 2012; see also *New York Times*, 13 October 2012; *Haaretz*, 14, 15 October 2012.
2 See, Neta Oren, "Israeli Identity Formation and the Arab–Israeli Conflict in Election Platforms, 1969–2006," *Journal of Peace Research*, 47(2), 2010: 193–204.

Bibliography

Books and articles

Abbas, Mahmoud (Abu Mazen), *Through Secret Channels: The Road to Oslo: Senior PLO Leader Abu Mazen's Revealing Story of the Negotiations with Israel* (Reading, UK: Garnet, 1995).

Abrams, Elliott, *Tested by Zion: The Bush Administration and the Israeli–Palestinian Conflict* (New York, NY: Cambridge University Press, 2013).

Aggestam, Karin, "Mediating Asymmetrical Conflict," *Mediterranean Politics*, 7(1), 2002: 69–91.

Albright, Madeleine, *Madam Secretary: A Memoir* (New York, NY: Harper Collins, 2003).

Alon, Yigal, *Be-ḥatirah Le-shalom* [*In Search of Peace*] (Tel Aviv: Hakibbutz Hameuchad, 1989) [Hebrew].

Al-Muallem, Walid, "Interview: Fresh Light on the Syrian–Israeli Peace Negotiations," *Journal of Palestine Studies*, 26(2), 1997: 81–94.

Andrew, Christopher and Vasilij Mitrochin, *The World Was Going Our Way: The KGB and the Battle for the Third World* (New York, NY: Basic Books, 2005).

Arian, Asher, "Israel and the Peace Process: Security and Political Attitudes in 1993," Memorandum 39, JCSS, Tel Aviv University, 1993.

——, *Security Threatened: Surveying Israeli Opinion on Peace and War* (Cambridge, MA: Cambridge University Press, 1995).

——, "Israel Security Opinion," Memorandum No. 46, JCSS, Tel Aviv University, 1996.

——, "Israeli Public Opinion on National Security," Memorandum No. 49, JCSS, Tel Aviv University, 1998.

——, *Israeli Public Opinion on National Security 1999* (Tel Aviv: Jaffee Center for Center for Strategic Studies (JCSS)–Tel-Aviv University, 1999).

——, "Israeli Public Opinion on National Security," Memorandum No. 56, JCSS, Tel Aviv University, 2000.

——, "Israeli Public Opinion on National Security," Memorandum No. 60, JCSS, Tel Aviv University, 2001.

Arieli, Shaul, *Zekhut Ha-ḥashivah* [*The Right to Think*] (Tel-Aviv: Touch Print, 2010) [Hebrew].

——, *Gevul Benenu U-venekhem* [*A Border Between Us and Them*] (Tel Aviv: Aliyat Hagag-Yedioth Aharonot-Sifre Hemed, 2013) [Hebrew].

Ashton, Nigel, *King Hussein of Jordan: A Political Life* (New Haven, CT: Yale University Press, 2008).

Bibliography 219

Auerbach, Jerold, *Are We One? Jewish Identity in the United States and Israel* (New Brunswick, NJ: Rutgers University Press, 2001).

Avner, Yehuda, *The Prime Ministers: An Intimate Narrative of Israeli Leadership* (Jerusalem: Toby Press, 2010).

Azoulai-Katz, Orly, *Ha-ish She-lo Yada' Le-natze'ah: Shimon Peres Be-malkodet Sisyphus* [*The Man Who Did Not Know How to Win: Shimon Peres in the Sisyphus Trap*] (Tel Aviv: Yedioth Sfarim, 1996) [Hebrew].

Baker, James, Lee Hamilton et al., *The Iraq Study Group Report* (New York, NY: Vintage, 2006).

Ball, George, "Israeli–American Relations," *Foreign Affairs*, 58(2), 1979: 231–256.

Barghouti, Mustafa, "Generous to Whom," *al Ahram* weekly online, 10–16 May 2001, no. 533 (www.weekly.ahram.org).

Bar-Joseph, Uri, *The Watchman Fell Asleep: The Surprise of Yom Kippur and Its Sources* (Albany, NY: SUNY Press, 2005).

——, "Last Chance to Avoid War: Sadat's Peace Initiative of 1973 and Its Failure," *Journal of Contemporary History*, 41(3), 2006: 545–556.

Bar-On, Mordechai, *Shalom Achshav: Le-diyukna Shel Tnu'ah* [*Peace Now: Portrait of a Movement*] (Tel Aviv: Hakibbutz Hameuchad, 1985) [Hebrew].

Bar-Siman-Tov, Yaacov, *Israel and the Peace Process 1977–1982: In Search of Legitimacy for Peace* (Albany, NY: SUNY Press, 1994).

——, "Peace Policy as Domestic and as Foreign Policy: The Israeli Case," in Sasson Sofer (Ed.), *Peacemaking in a Divided Society, Israel after Rabin* (London: Frank Cass, 2001): 27–54.

Bar-Tal, Daniel, "Why Does Fear Override Hope in Societies Engulfed by Intractable Conflict, as It Does in the Israeli Society?," *Political Psychology*, 22(3), 2001: 601–627.

——, "From Intractable Conflict through Conflict Resolution to Reconciliation: Psychological Analysis," *Political Psychology* 21(2), 2002: 351–365.

Bar-Tal, Daniel and Itzhak Shnell (Eds), *The Impacts of Lasting Occupation: Lessons from Israeli Society* (New York, NY: Oxford University Press, 2013).

Bar-Tal, Daniel, Eran Halperin, and Neta Oren, "Socio-Psychological Barriers to Peace Making: The Case of the Israeli Jewish Society," *Social Issues and Policy Review*, 4(1), 2010: 63–109.

Bar-Tal, Daniel, Keren Sharvit, Eran Halperin, and Anat Zafran, "Ethos of Conflict: The Concept and Its Measurement," *Peace and Conflict: Journal of Peace Psychology*, 18(1), 2012: 40–61.

Bartov, Hanoch, *Dado: 48 Shana Ve-'od 20 Yom* [*Dado: 48 Years and 20 Days More*] (Tel Aviv, Sifriat Maariv, 2002) [Hebrew].

Beilin, Yossi, *Touching Peace: From the Oslo Accord to a Final Agreement* (London: Weidenfeld and Nicolson, 1999).

——, *The Path to Geneva: The Quest for a Permanent Agreement, 1996–2004* (New York, NY: RDV Books/Akashic Books, 2004).

Ben-Ami, Shlomo, *Scars of War, Wounds of Peace: The Israeli–Arab Tragedy* (New York, NY: Oxford University Press, 2006).

Ben-Eliezer, Uri, *Old Conflict, New War: Israel's Politics toward the Palestinians* (London: Palgrave Macmillan, 2012).

Ben-Porat, Guy, "'Dollar Diplomacy': Globalization, Identity Change and Peace in Israel," *Nationalism and Ethnic Politics*, 12(3–4), 2006: 455–479.

Ben-Porat, Yeshayahu, *Sihot 'im Yossi Beilin* [*Conversations with Yossi Beilin*] (Tel Aviv: Hakibbutz Hameuchad, 1996).

Birnbaum, Ben, "The End of the Two-State Solution," *The New Republic*, 11 March 2013a.

——, "It's Just a Matter of Time," *The New Republic*, 19 March 2013b.

Boutros-Ghali, Boutros, *Egypt's Road to Jerusalem: A Diplomat's Story of the Struggle for Peace in the Middle East* (New York, NY: Random House, 1997).

Brookhyser, Jason, "The Syrian Turn: Israeli–Syrian Peace and the New Moment in U.S. Grand Strategy," *American Diplomat*, August 2007, http://www.unc.edu/depts/diplomat/item/2007/0709/broo/brookhyser_syria.html.

Bush, George, *Decision Points* (New York, NY: Crown Publishers, 2010).

CAMERA, "1967: Reunification of Jerusalem," (CAMERA Committee for the Accuracy of Reporting on the Middle East in America), http://www.sixdaywar.org/content/ReunificationJerusalem.asp.

Carter, Jimmy. *Keeping Faith: Memoirs of a President* (Fayetteville, AK: University of Arkansas Press, 1995).

Center for Democracy and Community Development, *Promoting the Arab Peace Initiative as a Basis for a Comprehensive Middle Eastern Peace Project*, July 2012.

Clinton, Bill, *My Life: The Presidential Years* (New York, NY: Vintage Books, 2005).

Cobban, Helena, *The Israeli–Syrian Peace Talks: 1991–1996 and Beyond* (Washington, DC: United States Institute of Peace, 1999).

Cohen, Akiva, and Gadi Wolfsfeld (Eds), *Framing the Intifada: People and Media* (Norwood: Ablex Pub. Corp, 1993).

Coleman, Peter, "Paradigmatic Framing of Protracted, Intractable Conflict: Toward a Meta-Framework – II," *Peace and Conflict: Journal of Peace Psychology*, 10(3), 2004: 197–235.

——, "Conflict, Complexity, and Change: A Meta-Framework for Addressing Protracted, Intractable Conflicts – III," *Peace and Conflict: Journal of Peace Psychology*, 12(4), 2006: 325–348.

——, *The Five Percent: Finding Solutions to Seemingly Impossible Conflicts* (New York, NY: PBS, 2011).

Corbin, Jane, *Gaza First: The Secret Norway Channel to Peace between Israel and the PLO* (London: Bloomsbury, 1994).

Corr, Edwin, Joseph Ginat, and Shaul Gabbay (Eds), *The Search for Israeli–Arab Peace: Learning from the Past and Building Trust, Studies in Peace Politics in the Middle East* (Brighton, UK: Sussex Academic Press, 2007).

Crocker, Chester, Fen Osler Hampson, and Pamela Aall (Eds), *Grasping the Nettle: Analyzing Cases of Intractable Conflict* (Washington, DC: US Institute of Peace Press, 2005).

Darby, John, and Roger MacGinty (Eds.), *The Management of Peace Processes* (Basingstoke, UK: Palgrave Macmillan, 2000).

Dayan, Moshe, *Breakthrough: A Personal Account of the Egypt–Israel Peace Negotiations* (London: Weidenfeld and Nicholson, 1981).

Dayton, Bruce and Louis Kriesberg (Eds), *Conflict Transformation and Peacebuilding: Moving from Violence to Sustainable Peace* (New York, NY: Routledge, 2009).

Diab, M. Zuhair, "Have Syria and Israel Opted for Peace?," *Middle East Policy* 3(2), 1994: 77–90.

Edelist, Ran and Ron Maiberg, *Ehud Barak: Milhamto Ba-shedim* [*Ehud Barak: His Battle with Ghosts*] (Tel Aviv: Kinneret Zmora-Bitan Dvir, 2003) [Hebrew].

Ellman, Miriam, Oded Haklai, and Hendrik Spruyt, *Democracy and Conflict Resolution: The Dilemmas of Israeli Peacemaking* (Syracuse, NY: Syracuse University Press, 2013).

Erakat, Saeb, "The Political Situation in Light of Developments with the U.S. Administration and the Government and Hamas's Continued Coup d'État," *Journal of Palestine Studies*, 49(3), 2010: 197–201.
Fahmy, Ismail, *Negotiating for Peace in the Middle East* (London: Croom-Helm, 1983).
Fawcett, Louise (Ed.), *International Relations of the Middle East* (New York, NY: Oxford University Press, 2009).
Gans, Haim, *A Just Zionism: On the Morality of the Jewish State* (Oxford, UK: Oxford University Press, 2008).
Gazit, Mordechai, "Egypt and Israel – Was There a Peace Opportunity Missed in 1971?," *Journal of Contemporary History*, 32(1), 1997: 97–115.
Gazit, Shlomo, "The Peace with Egypt: President Sadat's Visit Through 1977 Israeli Eyes", in Edwin Corr, Joseph Ginat, Shaul Gabbay (Eds), *The Search for Israeli–Arab Peace: Learning from the Past and Building Trust* (Brighton, UK: Sussex Academic Press, 2007a): 95–106.
——, "Israel–Egypt: What Went Wrong? Nothing," in Edwin Corr, Joseph Ginat, and Shaul Gabbay (Eds), *The Search for Israeli–Arab Peace* (Brighton, UK: Sussex Academic Press, 2007b): 130–135.
Golan, Galia, *Yom Kippur and After: The Soviet Union and the Middle East Crisis* (Cambridge, MA: Cambridge University Press, 1977).
——, *The Soviet Union and the Palestinian Liberation Movement* (New York, NY: Praeger Publishers, 1980).
——, *Soviet Policies in the Middle East: From World War II to Gorbachev* (Cambridge, MA: Cambridge University Press, 1990).
——, "Israel and Palestinian Statehood," in Winston Van Horne (Ed.), *Global Convulsions: Race, Ethnicity, and Nationalism at the End of the Twentieth Century* (Albany, NY: SUNY Press, 1997), 169–188.
——, "Soviet Foreign Policy and the Gulf War: The Role of Domestic Factors," in Patrick Morgan and Keith Nelson (Eds), *Re-Viewing the Cold War: Domestic Factors and Foreign Policy in the East-West Confrontation* (New York, NY: Praeger Publishers, 2000), 179–202.
——, *Israel and Palestine: Peace Plans and Proposals from Oslo to Disengagement* (Princeton, NJ: Markus Wiener Publishers, 2007).
——, "Asymmetry in Cross-Conflict Collaboration: Is there a Gender Factor?," *Peace and Conflict Studies*, 18(2), 2011: 164–191.
Golan, Matti, *The Secret Conversations of Henry Kissinger: Step-by-Step Diplomacy in the Middle East* (New York, NY: Quadrangle, 1976).
Gordon, Neve, *Israel's Occupation* (Berkley, CA: University of California Press, 2008).
Halevy, Ephraim, *Man in the Shadows* (New York, NY: St. Martin's Press, 2008).
Hanieh, Akram, "The Camp David Papers," *Journal of Palestine Studies*, 30(2), 2001: 75–97.
Hardin, Russell, "Trusting Persons, Trusting Institutions," in Richard Zeckhauser (Ed.), *Strategy and Choice* (Cambridge, MA: MIT University Press, 1991): 185–209.
Herzog, Michael, *Minding the Gaps: Territorial Issues in Israeli-Palestinian Peacemaking*, Policy Focus, 116, Washington Institute for Near East Policy, 2011.
Hof, Frederic, *Mapping Peace between Syria and Israel, Special Report, 219*, United States Institute of Peace, 2009.
Indyk, Martin, *Innocent Abroad: An Intimate Account of American Peace Diplomacy in the Middle East* (New York, NY: Simon and Schuster, 2009).

INSS, "The Israeli Palestinian Negotiation File," Response of the Government of Israel to the Ideas Raised by President Clinton Regarding the Outline of a Framework Agreement on Permanent Status, 5 June 2001, 2013.

Issacharoff, Avi, "Exclusive: 'I Am Still Waiting for Abbas to Call,'" 24 May 2013 (www.thetower.org).

Jervis, Robert, *Perception and Misperception in International Politics* (Princeton, NJ: Princeton University Press, 1976).

Khalaf, Salah (Abu Iyad), "Lowering the Sword," *Foreign Policy*, 87 (Spring), 1990: 92–112.

Kipnis, Yigal, *1973, Ha-derekh La-milhamah [1973: The Road to War]* (Tel Aviv: Kinneret Zmora-Bitan Dvir, 2012) [Hebrew].

Kissinger, Henry, *The White House Years* (Boston, MA: Little, Brown, 1979).

Klar, Yechiel, Noa Schori-Eyal, and Yonat Klar, "The 'Never Again' State of Israel: The Emergence of the Holocaust as a Core Feature of Israeli Identity and its Four Incongruent Voices," *Journal of Social Issues*, 69(1), 2013: 125–143.

Krebs, Ronald, "Can War Be an Engine of Liberalism?," Unpublished paper for APSA, September 2011.

Kriesberg, Louis, "Nature, Dynamics and Phases of Intractability," in Chester Crocker, Fen Osler Hampson, and Pamela Aall (Eds), *Grasping the Nettle: Analyzing Cases of Intractable Conflict* (Washington, DC: US Institute of Peace Press, 2005): 65–98.

——, "Changing Conflict Asymmetries Constructively," *Dynamics of Asymmetric Conflict*, 2(1), 2009: 4–22.

Kriesberg, Louis and Bruce Dayton, *Constructive Conflicts: From Escalation to Resolution* (Maryland: Rowman and Littlefield, 2011).

Kuriansky, Judy (Ed.), *Beyond Bullets and Bombs: Grassroots Peacebuilding between Palestinians and Israelis* (Westport, CT: Praeger, 2007).

Kurtzer, Daniel, Scott Lasensky, William Quandt, Steven Spiegel, and Shibley Telhami, *The Peace Puzzle: America's Quest for Arab–Israeli Peace* (Ithaca, NY: Cornell University Press, 2013).

Kydd, Andrew, *Trust and Mistrust in International Relations* (Princeton, NJ: Princeton University Press, 2005).

Larson, Deborah, "Trust and Missed Opportunities in International Relations," *Political Psychology*, 18(3), 1997: 701–734.

Leon, Dan, "Israeli Public Opinion Polls on the Peace Process," *Palestine–Israel Journal*, 2(1), 1995: 56–57.

Levinsohn, Hanna and Elihu Katz, "The Intifada Is Not a War: Jewish Public Opinion on the Israel–Arab Conflict," in Akiva Cohen and Gadi Wolfsfeld (Eds), *Framing the Intifada: People and Media* (Norwood, NJ: Ablex Publishing Corporation, 1993): 53–61.

Lieberfeld, Daniel, *Talking with the Enemy: Negotiation and Threat Perception in South Africa and Israel/Palestine* (Westport, CT: Praeger, 1999).

Liel, Alon, "Syria Comes to Annapolis," *Palestine–Israel Journal*, 14(4), 2007: 17–20.

Lukacs, Yehuda, *Israel, Jordon, and the Peace Process* (New York, NY: Syracuse University Press, 1999).

Magal, Tamir, Neta Oren, Daniel Bar-Tal, and Eran Halperin, "Psychological Legitimization – Views of the Israeli Occupation by Jews in Israel: Data and Implications," in Daniel Bar-Tal, and Itzhak Shnell (Eds), *The Impacts of Lasting Occupation: Lessons from Israeli Society* (New York, NY: Oxford University Press, 2013): 122–185.

Makovsky, David, *Making Peace with the PLO: The Rabin Government's Road to the Oslo Accord* (Boulder, CO: Westview Press, 1996).
——, *Olmert's Unilateral Option: An Early Assessment*, Washington Institute for Near East Policy, Policy Focus no. 55, May 2006.
Malley, Robert and Hussein Agha, "Camp David: The Tragedy of Errors," *New York Review of Books*, 9 August 2001
——, "Camp David and After: An Exchange," *The New York Review of Books*, 49(10), 2002: 46–49.
Maoz, Moshe, *Syria and Israel: From War to Peacemaking* (Oxford: Oxford University Press, 1995).
——, (Ed.), *Ha-golan Ben Milhama Ve-shalom* [*The Golan between War and Peace*] (Or Yehuda: Hed Artzi, 1999) [Hebrew].
Ma'oz, Moshe, Robert Rothstein, and Khalil Shikaki (Eds), *The Israeli–Palestinian Peace Process: Oslo and the Lessons of Failure: Perspectives, Predicaments and Prospects* (Brighton, UK: Sussex Academic Press, 2002).
McCarthy, William, "The Role of Power in Getting to Yes," in John Breslin and Jeffrey Rubin (Eds), *Negotiation Theory and Practice* (Cambridge, MA: Harvard Program on Negotiation, Pon Books, 1991).
Meir, Golda, *My Life* (New York, NY: GP Putnam's Sons, 1975).
Meital, Yoram, *Peace in Tatters: Israel, Palestine, and the Middle East* (Boulder, CO: Lynne Rienner Publishers, 2006).
Miller, Aaron, *The Much Too Promised Land: America's Elusive Search for Arab–Israeli Peace* (New York, NY: Bantam, 2008).
Moore, J. (Ed.), *The Arab–Israeli Conflict, Readings and Documents* (Princeton, NJ: Princeton University Press, 1977).
Morgan, Patrick and Keith Nelson (Eds), *Re-Viewing the Cold War: Domestic Factors and Foreign Policy in the East-West Confrontation* (New York, NY: Praeger Publishers, 2000).
Morris, Benny, *Righteous Victims: A History of the Zionist-Arab Conflict, 1881–1999* (New York, NY: Alfred A. Knopf, 1999).
Mouallem, Walid, "Light on the Syrian–Israeli Peace Negotiations: An Interview with Ambassador Walid Mouallem," *Journal of Palestine Studies*, 26(2), 1997: 83
Muasher, Marwan, *The Arab Center: The Promise of Moderation* (New Haven, CT: Yale University Press, 2008).
Mutawi, Samir A., *Jordan in the 1967 War* (Cambridge, MA: Cambridge University Press, 1987).
Naor, Arieh, *Greater Israel: Theology and Policy* (Haifa: University of Haifa Press and Zmora-Bitan, 2001).
Naor, Arye, *Begin Ba-shilton: 'edut Ishit* [*Begin in Power: Personal Evidence*] (Tel Aviv: Yedioth Sfarim, 1993) [Hebrew].
Nets-Zehngut, Rafi and Daniel Bar-Tal, "The Intractable Israeli–Palestinian Conflict and Possible Pathways to Peace," in Judy Kuriansky (Ed.), *Beyond Bullets and Bombs: Grassroots Peacebuilding between Palestinians and Israelis* (Westport, CT: Praeger, 2007): 3–13.
Neuberger, Benyamin, *Mediniyut Hutz Shel Yisrael: Kovetz Mismakhim 1*, [*Foreign Policy of Israel: Collection of Documents 1*] (Tel Aviv: The Open University, 2004) [Hebrew].
Nevo, Joseph (Ed.), *Shkheinim Be-mavokh: Yahasei Yisrael–Yarden Lifnei Heskem Ha-shalom Ve-aharav* [*Neighbors in a Bind: Israel–Jordan Relations before the Peace Agreement*] (Tel Aviv: Yitzak Rabin Center, 2004) [Hebrew].

Newman, Edward and Oliver Richmond (Eds.), *Challenges to Peacebuilding: Managing Spoilers during Conflict Resolution* (Tokyo: UN University Press, 2006).
Oren, Neta, "Israeli Identity Formation and the Arab–Israeli Conflict in Election Platforms, 1969–2006," *Journal of Peace Research*, 47(2), 2010: 193–204.
Pedatzur, Reuven, *Nitzahon Ha-mevukhah: Mediniyut Memshelet Eskhol Ba-shetahim Le-ahar Milhemet Sheshet Ha-yamim* [*Embarrassing Victory: The Eshklol Government Policy in the Territories after the Six Day War*] (Ramat Efal: Yad Tabenkin, 1996) [Hebrew].
Peres, Shimon, *David's Sling* (London: Weidenfeld and Nicolson, 1970).
——, *The New Middle East* (New York, NY: Henry Holt, 1993).
——, *Battling for Peace: A Memoir* (New York, NY: Random House, 1995).
Peri, Yoram, *The Rabin Memoirs*, new edition (Berkeley, CA: University of California Press, 1996).
PLO, *Meetings of President Mahmoud Abbas with Jewish Leaders*, undated.
PLO Negotiation Affairs Department, "Camp David Peace Proposal of July 2000," www.nad-plo.org.
Primakov, Yevgeny, *Russia and the Arabs: Behind the Scenes in the Middle East from the Cold War to the Present* (New York, NY: Basic Books, 2009).
Pruitt, Dean, "Ripeness Theory and the Oslo Talks," *International Negotiation* 2(2), 1997: 237–250.
Pundak, Ron, "From Oslo to Taba: What Went Wrong?" *Survival* 43(3), 2001: 31–45.
Quandt, William, *Camp David: Peacemaking and Politics* (Washington, DC: The Brookings Institution, 1986).
——, *Peace Process: American Diplomacy and the Arab–Israeli Conflict since 1967* (Washington, DC: The Brookings Institution, 1993).
Queen Noor, *Leap of Faith* (London: Weidenfeld and Nicholson, 2003).
Qurie, Ahmed (Abu Ala), *From Oslo to Jerusalem: The Palestinian Story of the Secret Negotiations* (London: IB Tauris, 2006).
Rabin, Leah, *Rabin: Our Life, His Legacy* (New York, NY: GP Putnam's Sons, 1997).
Rabin, Yitzhak, *Pinkas Sherut* [*Service Diary*] (Tel Aviv: Sifriat Maariv, 1979) [Hebrew].
——, "Nitzul Pesek Ha-zman," ["*Exploiting the Time-out*"], *Politika*, 44(1), 1992: 28–29 [Hebrew].
——, *Rodef Shalom: Ne'ume Ha-shalom Shel Rosh Ha-memshalah Yitzhak Rabin* [*Peace-seeker: Peace Speeches of Prime Minister Yitzhak Rabin*] (Tel Aviv: Zmora-Bitan, 1995) [Hebrew].
——, *The Rabin Memoirs* (Berkeley, CA: University of California Press, 1996).
Rabinovich, Itamar, *The Brink of Peace: The Israeli-Syrian Negotiations* (Princeton, NJ: Princeton University Press, 1998).
Raz, Avi, *The Bride and the Dowry: Israel, Jordan, and the Palestinians in the Aftermath of the June 1967 War* (New Haven: Yale University, 2012).
——, "The Generous Peace Offer that Was Never Offered: The Israeli Cabinet Resolution of June 19, 1967," *Diplomatic History*, 37(1), 2013: 85–108.
Rice, Condoleezza, *No Higher Honor: A Memoir of My Years in Washington* (New York, NY: Crown, 2011).
Richmond, Oliver, "The Linkage between Devious Objectives and Spoiling Behaviour in Peace Processes," in Edward Newman and Oliver Richmond (Eds), *Challenges to Peacebuilding: Managing Spoilers during Conflict Resolution* (Tokyo: UN University Press, 2006): 59–77.

Bibliography 225

Rosler, Nimrod, *Political Context, Social Challenges, and Leadership: Rhetorical Expressions of Psycho-social Roles of Leaders in Intractable Conflict and its Resolution Process – The Israeli–Palestinian Case*, PhD thesis, Hebrew University of Jerusalem, 2012.

Ross, Dennis, *The Missing Peace: The Inside Story of the Fight for Middle East Peace* (New York, NY: Farrar, Straus and Giroux, 2005).

Rouhana, Nadim and Daniel Bar-Tal, "Psychological Dynamics of Intractable Ethnonational Conflicts: The Israeli–Palestinian Case," *American Psychologist*, 53(7), 1998: 761–770.

Rubinstein, Elyakim, *Darkei Shalom* [Paths of Peace] (Tel Aviv: Ministry of Defense, 1992) [Hebrew].

Sadat, Anwar, *In Search of Identity: An Autobiography* (New York, NY: Harper & Row, 1978).

Sagie, Uri, *Orot Ba-'arafel* [*Lights in the Fog*] (Tel Aviv: Yedioth Sfarim, 1998) [Hebrew].

——, *Ha-yad She-kaf'ah* [*The Hand that Froze*] (Tel Aviv: Yedioth Sfarim, 2011) [Hebrew].

Said, Edward, *Peace and Its Discontents: Essays on Palestine in the Middle East Peace Process* (New York, NY: Vintage Books, 1996).

Savir, Uri, *The Process* (New York, NY: Vintage Books, 1998).

Seale, Patrick, "The Syria–Israel Negotiations: Who is Telling the Truth?" *Journal of Palestine Studies*, 29(2), 2000: 65–77.

Segev, Tom, *1967: Israel, the War, and the Year that Transformed the Middle East* (New York, NY: Metropolitan Books, 2007).

Sela, Avraham, *The Decline of the Arab Israeli Conflict: Middle East Politics and the Quest for Regional Order* (Albany, NY: SUNY University Press, 1998).

Sella, Amnon, "Custodians and Redeemers: Israeli Leaders' Perceptions of Peace, 1967–79," in Ian Lustick (Ed.), *Arab–Israeli Relations*, VII (New York, NY: Garlan, 1994): 248–263.

Shamir, Jacob and Michal Shamir, *The Anatomy of Public Opinion* (Ann Arbor, MI: University of Michigan Press, 2000).

——, *The Dynamics of Israeli Public Opinion on Peace and the Territories*, Tami Steinmetz Center for Peace Research, Tel Aviv University, 1993.

Shamir, Michal, and Asher Arian, "Competing Values and Policy Choices: Israeli Public Opinion on Foreign and Security Affairs," *British Journal of Political Science*, 24(2), 1994: 249–271.

Shamir, Michal and Tammy Sagiv-Schifter, "Conflict, Identity, and Tolerance: Israel in the Al-Aqsa Intifada," *Political Psychology*, 27(4), 2006: 569–595.

Shamir, Shimon and Bruce Maddy-Weitzman (Eds), *The Camp David Summit: What Went Wrong?* (Brighton, UK: Sussex Academic Press, 2005).

Shamir, Yitzhak, *Summing Up: An Autobiography* (Boston, MA: Little, Brown and Company, 1994).

Shapira, Avraham (Ed.), *Siah Lohamim* [*Soldiers' Conversations*] (Kevutzat Haverim Tze'irim Meha-tenu'ah Ha-kibutzit, 1968) [Hebrew].

Sher, Gilead, *Within Reach: The Israeli–Palestinian Peace Negotiations, 1999–2001* (London: Routledge, 2006).

——, *Be-merhak Negi'ah* [*Within Reach*] (Tel Aviv: Yedioth Sfarim, 2001) [Hebrew].

Shifris, Amos, *Yisrael Galili* [Yisrael Galili] (Ramat Efal: Yad Tabenkin, 2010) [Hebrew].

Shikaki, Khalil, "Ending the Conflict: Can the Parties Afford It?" in Moshe Ma'oz, Robert Rothstein, and Khalil Shikaki (Eds), *The Israeli–Palestinian Peace Process: Oslo and the Lessons of Failure: Perspectives, Predicaments and Prospects* (Brighton, UK: Sussex Academic Press, 2002): 37–46.

Shindler, Colin, *Israel, Likud and the Zionist Dream: Power, Politics and Ideology from Begin to Netanyahu* (New York, NY: I. B. Tauris, 1995).

Shlaim, Avi, "The Rise and Fall of the All-Palestine Government in Gaza", *Journal of Palestine Studies*, 20(1), 1990: 37–53.

——, *Lion of Jordan: The Life of King Hussein in War and Peace* (London: Penguin, 2007).

——, "The Rise and Fall of the Oslo Peace Process," in Louise Fawcett (Ed.), *International Relations of the Middle East* (New York, NY: Oxford University Press, 2009).

Silver, Eric, *Begin: A Biography* (London: Weidenfeld and Nicolson, 1984).

Spiegel, Steven, *The Other Arab–Israeli Conflict: Making America's Middle East Policy, from Truman to Reagan* (Chicago, IL: University of Chicago Press, 1985).

Stedman, Stephen, "Spoiler Problems in Peace Processes," in Paul Stern and Daniel Druckman (Eds), *International Conflict Resolution after the Cold War* (Washington, DC: National Academy Press, 2000): 178–224.

Stein, Kenneth, *Heroic Diplomacy: Sadat, Kissinger, Carter, Begin and the Quest for Arab-Israeli Peace* (New York, NY: Routledge, 1999).

Stern, Paul and Daniel Druckman (Eds), *International Conflict Resolution after the Cold War* (Washington, DC: National Academies Press, 2000).

Swisher, Clayton and Ghada Karmi, *The Palestine Papers: The End of the Road?* (London: Hesperus Press, 2011).

Tessler, Mark, "The Intifada and Political Discourse in Israel," *Journal of Palestine Studies*, 19(2), 1990: 43–61.

——, *A History of the Israeli–Palestinian Conflict* (Bloomington, IN: Indiana University Press, 1994).

Tira, Ron, *'Itzuv Mediniyut Yisrael Kelape Suryah [Fashioning Israeli Policy toward Syria]* (Tel Aviv: Yedioth Sfarim, 2000) [Hebrew].

Tovy, Jacob, "Negotiating the Palestinian Refugees," *Middle East Quarterly*, 10(2), 2003: 39–50.

Tzoref, Hagai, *Levi Eshkol: Rosh Ha-memshalah Ha-shelishi: Mivhar Te'udot Mi-pirkei Ha-yav – 1895–1969 [Levi Eshkol: The Third Prime Minister: Selection of Documents from His Life]* (Jerusalem: State Archive, 2002) [Hebrew].

US Senate and US House of Representatives, Committee on Foreign Relations and Committee on Foreign Affairs, "Codification of Policy Prohibiting Negotiations with the Palestine Liberation Organization," *Legislation on Foreign Relations Through 1987*, 1 (Washington, DC: U.S. Government Printing Office, March 1988).

Vallacher, Robin, Peter Coleman, Andrzej Nowak, and Lan Bui-Wrzosinska, "Rethinking Intractable Conflict: The Perspective of Dynamical Systems," *American Psychologist*, 65(4), 2010: 262–278.

Vinogradov, Vladimir, *Diplomatiia: Liudi I Sobitiia. Iz zapisok posla [Diplomacy: People and Events: From the Ambassador's Notes]* (Moskva: Rosspen, 1998) [Russian].

Walter, Barbara, "The Critical Barrier to Civil War Settlement," *International Organization*, 51(3), 1997: 335–364.

Weizman, Ezer, *The Battle for Peace* (New York, NY: Bantam Books, 1981).

Whetten, Lawrence, *The Canal War: Four-Power Conflict in the Middle East*, (Cambridge, MA: MIT Press, 1974).
Ya'ari, Aviezer, "Ha-golan Be-seder Ha-'adifuyot Shel 'Asad – 1974–94" [The Golan in Asad's Priorities] in Ma'oz, Moshe (Ed.), *Ha-golan Ben Milhama Ve-shalom* [*The Golan between War and Peace*] (Or Yehuda: Hed Artzi, 1999): 43–50 [Hebrew].
Yanai, Nathan, *Moshe Dayan: 'Al Tahalikh Ha-shalom Ve-'atida Shel Yisrael* [*Moshe Dayan: On the Peace Process and the Future of Israel*] (Tel Aviv: Ministry of Defense, 1988) [Hebrew].
Yatom, Dani, *Shutaf Sod: Mi-sayeret Matkal Ve-'ad Ha-mosad* [*Party to the Secret: From the Elite Unit to the Mossad*] (Tel Aviv: Yedioth Sfarim, 2009) [Hebrew].
Zartman, William and Rubin, Jeffrey (Eds), *Power and Negotiation* (Ann Arbor, MI: University of Michigan Press, 2000).
Zeckhauser, Richard J. (Ed.), *Strategy and Choice* (Cambridge, MA: MIT University Press, 1991).
Zittrain Eisenberg, Laura and Neil Caplan, *Negotiating Arab–Israeli Peace: Patterns, Problems, Possibilities* (Bloomington, IN: Indiana University Press, 2010).

Archives and official sites

Israel State Archives
Israel Knesset
Beit Berl (Labor Party Archive)
Yad Tabenkin Archives, Ramat Efal
Israel Ministry of Foreign Affairs (www.mfa.gov.il/)
Israel Central Bureau of Statistics (www.cbs.go.il/)
Office of the Prime Minister (Israel) (www.pmo.gov.il/PMO/Archive)
United States Department of State, Office of the Historian, Foreign Relations of the United States (www.history.state.gov/historical)
The White House (www.whitehouse.gov/)
The American Presidency Project (www.presidency.ucsb.edu)
National Archives and Records Administration (United States) (www.archives.gov/)
Hashemite Kingdom of Jordan (www.kinghussein.gov.jo/speeches_letters.html)
PLO Negotiations Department (http://www.nad-plo.org)
Anwar Sadat Archives (University of Maryland) (http://sadat.umd.edu/archives/speeches.htm)

Index

Abbas, Mahmoud *see* Mazen, Abu
Abdulla bin al-Hussein (King Abdulla I) 34
Abdullah, Crown Prince 170, 215
Abington, Ed 129
Abrams, Elliott 173, 182, 183, 184, 191
Abu Dis 148, 161n11, 185–6
Abu Tor 181
Achille Lauro 100
Agha, Hussein 152
Agranat Commission 42, 47
"Agreement on the Gaza Strip and Jericho" 106
Ahdut Avoda 18, 62
Ahdut Hatorah 145
AIPAC 84
airspace (access to) 146, 148, 157, 182
Ala, Abu 120, 128, 144, 154, 159, 178–9, 189
Al Aksa mosque 17
Albright, Madeleine 144, 146
Alon, Yigal 23, 95
Alon Plans 13, 14–15, 23, 94, 99
American Israel Public Affairs Committee (AIPAC) 134
American Jewish Conference of Presidents 173
American policy 10, 23, 34–42, 45–6, 60–1, 79, 103, 151, 170, 213
Amman 100
Ankara 187–8, 214
Annapolis Process 6, 166, 171, 173, 174, 176, 177, 184, 189, 191, 195–6, 204–10, 214, 216, 217
Aqaba 109
Arab–Israeli conflict 1, 4, 17, 42, 172; efforts at resolving 5, 6, 35, 57–61, 119, 170, 211
Arab–Israeli war (1948) 6

Arab League 22, 38, 95, 170, 174
Arab Peace Initiative (API) 169–70, 174, 177, 181, 195, 211, 214, 215
Arabs 15–16, 33, 34, 36, 38, 45, 47, 57, 95, 111, 127, 135, 150, 167, 189, 193, 201
Arab Spring 215
Arab states 10, 13, 38–9, 42, 57, 59, 118, 122–3, 170, 172, 174, 176, 208, 210, 21
Arab world 22, 44, 59, 99, 105, 181
Arafat, Yasser 9n22, 68, 100, 105, 118–21, 124, 129, 130, 132, 142, 144, 145, 146, 148, 149–51, 155–7, 159, 166, 169, 206, 208, 213, 214, 215
Arava border 110, 111, 112
Arens, Moshe 48
Ariel 168, 179, 180, 189
Armistice Lines (1949) 6, 7, 10
arms control 58
Asfour, Hassan 144
Ashton, Nigel 13
Assad, Bashar al- 81, 86, 174, 176, 177, 187–8, 194, 206, 214, 215
Assad, Hafez al- 57–8, 60, 64, 66, 67–70, 72–86, 107, 111, 154, 207, 208
"Auschwitz lines" 24

Ba'al Hazor 183
Baker, James 58, 60, 172, 175
Barak, Aharon 45
Barak, Ehud 70, 77–86, 126, 143–57, 159–60, 166, 171, 178, 182, 185, 186, 187, 190, 192, 202–9, 214
Bar-Joseph, Uri 33
Bar Lev line 42
Bar-tal, Daniel 2, 4
Begin, Menachem 11, 18, 20, 40–50, 67, 78, 103, 111, 112, 124, 153, 185, 202, 204, 206–13, 215

Index

Beilin, Yossi 101, 120
Beitar (Ilit) 135
Ben Aharon, Yosef 71
Ben-Ami, Shlomo 129, 144–5, 152, 153–4, 156
Ben Gurion, David 18, 126, 155, 171, 203
Bethlehem 131
Boutros Ghali, Boutros 45
Brandt, Willy 35
breakthroughs (to peaceful resolution) 1, 5, 8, 10, 57, 59, 73, 95, 109, 118–19, 127, 143, 189, 195–6, 201, 203, 204, 205, 210, 211, 216, 217; concepts of 33, 68; near 6, 8, 193, 210, 216
Brezhnev, Leonid 35
British, the 6, 22
British Mandate *see* Palestine Mandate
Brzezinski, Zbigniew 44
Bush, George 57, 88n26, 128, 160, 175
Bush, George W. 160, 168–75, 178, 183–4, 188, 190, 191

Cairo 106, 210
Camp David 74; 1978 talks at 19, 41, 45, 47–50, 103, 113, 119, 120, 202, 203, 208, 211, 213, 215; 2000 talks at 5, 144, 145–7, 149–60, 166, 168, 171, 202, 204, 206–9, 211, 213, 214
Carter, Jimmy 41, 44–7, 61, 213
cease-fires 10, 64, 172; August 1970 29
Ceausescu, Nicolai 40–1
Center Party, the 143, 153
Chamberlain, Neville 132
Cheney, Dick 175, 191
Christopher, Warren 64, 66–7, 70, 77, 80, 106, 107, 127
citizen diplomacy 4
Clinton, Bill 61, 63, 69–70, 72, 76, 77, 80–3, 85–6, 105, 107, 108, 112, 113, 127, 128, 129, 135, 145, 147, 148, 149, 151, 152, 154, 157–60, 180, 207, 208, 209, 213
Clinton Parameters 157–9, 188, 208
Cold War 59
Coleman, Peter 1, 2, 4, 5
Common Agenda 108
conflict 3, 5; and coercion 1; costs of 3; ethno-national 1; institutionalization of 1; intensity of 2; intractable 1, 2, 4, 5, 15, 49, 217; and means 1; transformation of 3, 5, 217
conflict resolution 1, 4, 5–6
conflict resolution repertoires 4
Cyprus 4

Daoudi, Riad 79
Dayan, Moshe 13, 14, 17, 19, 30, 33, 34, 39, 40, 46, 95
Dayan, Uzi 127
Dead Sea 101, 109, 135
decision-making 3, 23, 40, 46, 212
Declaration of Principles (DOP) (Oslo) 120, 121, 122, 124–8, 130, 132, 216
dehumanization (of adversary) 2, 130, 136
de-legitimization (of adversary) 2
demilitarization 14, 18, 20, 23, 45, 70, 135, 147, 154, 164, 167, 168, 186
demilitarized zone(s) 20, 21, 30, 38, 179
Democratic Party for Change (DASH) 43, 48
demography 3, 11, 18, 20, 123, 135, 155, 156, 167, 181, 193, 209, 210, 220, 226
diaspora 4, 39, 71, 72, 76, 100, 106, 107, 108, 113, 121, 134, 173, 191, 201, 207, 213; Palestinian 137n15, 156
diplomatic relations 64, 69, 83, 105, 182, 187
disengagement of forces (1974) 29

early warning stations 36–8, 45, 48, 70–2, 77, 80, 111, 146, 148, 153–4, 147, 182, 186
Eban, Abba 14, 21, 23, 24, 32, 95
Efrat 135
Egypt 6–7, 10–11, 14, 20–4, 29–36, 38–9, 42–4, 49, 57, 60, 65, 69, 85, 95, 98–9, 111, 129, 131, 171, 183, 195, 201–4, 207–9, 211, 213; economy of 30
Egypt 1975–1979 (talks/agreement) 5, 29, 46, 143
el Baz, Osama 45
Eldar, Akiva 84–5, 182
electromagnetic communications spectrum 182
enemy, the 3–4, 15–16, 31, 82, 130, 136, 186, 189
environment 58
Eran, Oded 155
Erdogan, Recep Tayyip 187
Erekat, Saeb 182, 183, 184
Eretz Israel 11, 21, 43, 45, 46, 50, 118, 203, 210 *see also* "Greater Israel"
Eshkol, Levi 13, 19, 20, 185, 202, 203, 206, 207
Ethos of Conflict 2, 4–5
Ettinger, Yoram 71, 84
Europe 154

Index

European Parliament 184
European Union (EU) 77, 174, 195

F-4 aircraft 29
failure(s) (of peacemaking efforts) 3, 5–6, 8, 11, 23, 24, 29, 30, 35, 42, 45, 80, 82, 95, 101, 143, 145, 146, 149, 156, 159, 160, 166, 201, 204, 211–13, 217; causes of 1, 3, 4–5, 11, 15, 18, 63, 76, 78–9, 81–6, 96, 98, 99, 103, 129–36, 144, 149–53, 156–7, 160, 185, 188, 189, 191, 202–9, 214
Fatah 9n22, 16, 100, 145, 167, 173, 194
Fayyad, Selim 173
Ford, Gerald 36, 38, 58, 98
Framework Agreement (Camp David) 41, 45, 48, 146, 149
Friedman, Tom 170
"frozen" beliefs 2

Gahal Party 11, 18
Galili, Israel 33
Gaza 7, 8, 20, 29, 31, 41, 43, 45, 50, 95, 101, 103, 130, 131, 135, 140n74, 142, 143, 147, 152, 157, 166–7, 170–3, 179, 180, 181, 189, 195, 203, 204
Gazit, Mordecai 33
Geneva 69–70, 72, 80–1, 86, 118
Geneva Conference (1973/1974) 36, 37, 41, 44, 94, 119–20, 207
Geneva Initiative 166
Gidi 31, 36
Ginossar, Yossi 152
Givat Zeev 134
Glassboro meeting 11
globalization 3, 122, 135
global norms 4
Golan (Heights) 7, 20, 21, 23, 35, 43, 57–63, 67, 68, 71, 73–8, 80, 82, 83, 84, 86, 99, 110, 152, 187, 193, 194, 195
Gorbachev, Mikhail 57, 102, 119
grass roots activism 4
"Greater Israel" 11, 23, 47, 102, 103, 171
"green line, the" 8, 47, 133, 168, 179
grievances 1–5, 209
Gulf crisis 119
Gulf War 58, 104, 106, 107, 123, 128, 135, 210, 211, 213
Gur, Motta 19
Gush Emunim 39, 49, 95
Gush Etzion 101, 103, 135, 168, 203

Haber, Eitan 60, 107
Hadash 189

Halevy, Ephraim 105–6, 111
Hamas 71, 121, 126, 132, 133, 136, 142, 166, 167, 168, 171–4, 177, 194, 208
Hamilton, Lee 172, 175
Haram al-Sharif 142, 146, 148–9, 151, 156, 157, 180, 208
Har Eval 183
Har Homa 181
Hariri, Rafic 175
Hashemite Kingdom 6
Hassan bin Talal (Prince) 109
Hebron 110, 131, 142, 158
Hermon, the 77, 80, 81, 177
Herut 11, 18, 49
Herzl, Theodor 82
Herzog, Yaacov 15
Hirshfeld, Yair 120
history 2, 4, 16, 19, 45, 109, 216; Jewish 24, 46
Hizballah 64, 71, 75, 172, 177, 187, 193
Holocaust, the 4, 15, 25n6, 26n22, 28n55
Holocaust, second 11
Holst, Johan Jorgen 120
holy sites 19, 106, 178, 215, 216
Hussein bin Talal (King Hussein) 10, 13–15, 18, 22, 24, 34, 38, 94–113, 119, 124, 129, 142, 154, 206, 207, 208, 213, 215, 216

identities 1, 217; monolithic 1; national 4, 15
identity issues 1, 16, 18, 125, 160, 201
ideology 2, 5, 24, 44, 45, 48, 49, 59, 77, 78, 103, 125, 131, 132, 154–5, 189, 201, 203, 204, 210, 217
immigration 3
individualism 122, 135, 211
Indonesia 174
Indyk, Martin 68, 80, 83, 85, 105, 106, 107, 128, 129, 150, 151
infrastructure 178, 185, 212; of terrorism 169
Interim Accord/Agreement: 1975 29, 35, 37, 38, 39, 41, 43, 48, 57, 58, 99, 100; 1996 71–2, 121
international forces 183
Intifada 59, 103, 104, 118, 120, 121–2, 124, 129, 135, 159–60, 168, 190, 210, 216; second/Al-Aksa 159, 166, 171, 190, 193, 205, 210, 211
Iran 60, 61, 81, 119, 166, 170, 176, 177, 187, 193, 211
Iran–Contra scandal 103

Iraq 16, 57, 60, 61, 81, 95, 107, 110, 119, 123, 135, 175
Iraq–Iran war 100
Iraq Study Group 172, 175–6
Iraq War (2003) 166, 172
Islam 149, 211
Islamic Conference 170
Islamic Jihad 71, 126, 132, 133, 208
Islamism 59, 104, 123, 132, 166, 167
Ismail, Hafez 31, 34
Israel 4, 6, 10–17, 22–3, 29–50, 57–86, 94–114, 118–36, 142–50, 166, 169–96, 201–8; Biblical 11, 16, 20, 43, 48; borders of 6, 12–14, 21, 22, 24, 29, 31, 33–4, 38, 40, 42, 57, 58, 65–6, 70, 72, 77, 79–82, 84, 94–5, 99, 108–10, 130–1, 133, 134–5, 146, 148, 154–5, 159, 167, 169–71, 177, 179–80, 183, 186–90, 209, 216–17; economy of 76, 122; existence of 6, 38, 44, 150, 160, 201; expansion of 18; Jewish character of 28n56, 123, 148, 150, 171, 216; and the Jewish people 15–16, 18, 19; left wing in 11–12, 23, 61, 193; legitimacy of 6, 15, 19, 22, 33, 44, 49, 118, 125, 133, 136, 167, 195, 201, 209, 211, 216; military superiority of 10, 16; national unity government of 11, 19, 21, 43–4; and the Palestinians 8, 12–13, 17, 32, 35, 41, 48, 59, 60–1, 67, 69–70, 73, 75, 76, 79, 81, 99–100, 105, 107, 109, 118–20, 122–3, 130–6, 143–60, 166, 169–86, 188–96, 201–8; right wing in 11, 18, 23, 40, 48, 61, 78, 127, 145–6, 153, 154, 155, 160, 167, 169, 174, 194, 204, 217; security of 6, 15, 16, 18, 22, 31–2, 40, 45, 48, 49, 57, 59, 63, 72, 76, 78, 81, 95, 99, 108, 110, 124, 125, 128, 131, 136, 142, 144, 154, 155, 159, 185, 186, 191, 193, 202, 203, 215; security within 122, 131, 133, 135, 151; and "siege mentality" 125–6
Israel b'Aliyah 83, 84, 143, 146
Israel Beiteinu 189
Israel Defense Forces (IDF) 24n6, 42, 47, 63, 70, 71, 124, 125, 127, 130, 131, 143, 154, 159, 166, 172, 178, 190, 216
Israel–Egypt peace agreement 6, 35, 40, 47, 49, 57
Israeli citizenship 11–12
Israeli–Egyptian disengagement agreement 98
Israeli government 8, 11, 17, 18, 20, 22, 30, 39, 43, 65, 68, 76–7, 95–6, 99, 101, 134, 143, 144, 153, 156, 168, 169, 185, 189–90, 204, 209; differences within 11–12, 23, 48, 62, 83–4, 99, 102, 127, 145, 189–90, 195, 211
Israeli independence struggle 48
Israeli law 12, 62, 71
Israel–Jordan peace agreement 6, 109–14
Israeli settlements 23, 41, 45, 47–9, 61, 63, 68, 83–4, 130–2, 146, 148, 153, 154–5, 166–9, 179–80, 194, 212, 217
Israeli shipping 20, 31
Israeli–Syrian armistice agreement (1949) 65
'Israel proper' 8, 168

Jabel Mukaber 185–6
Jarring, Gunnar 30–1, 40n1
Javits, Jacob 40
Jericho 94, 121, 140n74
Jericho Plan 94, 95, 97
Jerusalem 6, 12, 14–19, 23, 33, 41, 43, 44, 45, 60, 95, 97, 101, 103, 108, 109, 112, 119, 120, 127, 132, 134, 144, 145, 146, 150, 153, 155–8, 168–71, 176–81, 185–6, 190, 194, 203–4, 208, 214, 215; Armenian quarter of 149; division of 155, 156; East 6, 7, 12–13, 14, 17, 18, 21, 23, 99, 106, 109, 118, 120, 131, 146, 148, 149, 150, 152, 155, 169, 180, 184, 203, 206, 209, 217; expansion of 12; Israeli sovereignty over 18–19, 41; Old City of 17, 19, 146, 148, 149, 159, 178; West 12, 17, 135, 149
Johnson, Lyndon 10, 13, 22, 207
Jones, James 182
Jordan 5, 6, 10, 12–18, 20–3, 34, 41, 58, 70, 94–114, 120, 123, 124, 127, 135, 143, 146, 169, 170, 178, 180, 183, 186, 190, 195, 201, 202–3, 205, 207–8, 213–15; Hashemite regime in 105
Jordanian Legion 17
"Jordanian option, the" 18
Jordanians 12, 18, 70, 94, 96, 99, 102, 105, 109, 113, 169
Jordan Rift Valley 12, 14, 16, 20, 23, 94, 95, 99, 101, 109, 134–5, 146, 147, 150, 153, 154, 157, 159, 168, 182, 183, 185, 190, 209
Jordan River 6, 12, 43, 80, 81, 95, 110, 131, 134, 147, 159, 168, 176, 182, 185, 186, 190, 203, 209; east bank of 16, 18 *see also* West Bank
Judea 43, 45, 48, 95, 120, 135

Kadima 167, 179, 185, 189
Katz, Shmuel 48
Kelman, Herb 1
Khartoum summit 14, 22, 32, 202
kibbutz movement 62, 105, 108–9
Kissinger, Henry 24, 32, 34–40, 44, 97–8, 100
Knesset 17, 39, 41, 44, 47, 48–9, 59, 62, 70, 72, 83, 84, 95, 112, 123, 124, 125, 127, 132, 134, 135, 145, 167, 169, 185, 189–90, 204, 211, 215
Kohanovski, Moshe 84
Krebs, Ronald 3
Kriesberg, Louis 1–5, 217
Kuneitra 35
Kurtzer, Dan 127
Kuwait, Iraqi invasion of 57, 119

Labor Alignment 16, 18, 95, 97
Labor Party 16, 17–18, 35, 43, 44, 49, 60, 62, 71–5, 83, 95, 97, 100–4, 120, 122, 124, 127, 133–6, 143, 152, 155, 159, 168, 171, 189, 203, 209–10
Lake Kinneret 65, 80, 81, 82, 86, 176, 209
land (as issue or for bargaining) 6–8, 10, 16, 18–19, 24, 43–4, 49, 77, 83, 85, 105–6, 108–11, 133, 146, 152, 154, 157, 168, 169, 178, 179, 189, 203, 206, 215–17
"Land of Israel, the" 11, 120
Lang, Nicholas 175
Lauder, Ron 77–9, 82, 84, 204
leadership 4, 13, 63, 76, 85, 86, 97, 99, 103, 113, 125, 126, 192–3, 205–6, 211–12; changes in 3, 41–4, 59, 61, 73, 100, 135, 193, 201, 204, 210
Lebanese civil war 100, 118, 121
Lebanon 50, 64, 71, 79, 80, 81, 83, 84, 100, 118, 166, 170, 172, 175
Letters of Mutual Recognition (Oslo) 120, 121, 124, 125, 128
Levy, David 77, 145
Lieberman, Avigdor 189
Liel, Alon 175
Likud 11, 18, 40, 43–6, 49, 62, 78, 100, 104, 112, 132, 133, 142, 153, 155, 167, 169, 171, 189–90, 192, 210
Lipkin-Shahat, Amnon 127, 129, 146, 155
Livny, Tzipy 178–9, 182, 184, 189–92, 212
London Agreement 1987 100–4, 119
London meetings: 1967 13; 1968 14; 1987 101; 1994 106, 108, 113

Maale Adumim 134
Madrid Conference (1991) 57–8, 84, 104, 119–22, 128, 134, 187–8, 213
Mafdal 18
Majali, Abdelsalam al- 107
Malaysia 174
Malley, Robert 152
Mapai 18, 19
Mapam 95, 97
Mazen, Abu 166, 167, 173, 178, 180–1, 183–5, 188–95, 204, 206, 208, 212, 214, 215–16
media 48, 122, 160; Israeli 70, 80, 84–5, 98, 104, 130, 185, 187; Syrian 80
Meir, Golda 29–34, 41–2, 46, 67, 82, 94–5, 97, 98, 185, 201, 202, 203, 205, 207, 217
Meretz 127, 143, 159, 189
messianism 19, 24
Miller, Aaron David 128, 150, 151
Mitla 31, 36
Mordecai, Yitzhak 78
Moritanos, Miguel 77
Morocco 40, 44, 137n11, 213
Mossad 33, 105, 176
Mouallem, Walid 71, 74, 75, 175, 176
Muasher, Marwan 170
Muqata 181

Nablus 151
Nakba Day 145
Nasser, Gamal 22, 29–30, 51n12
nationalism 4, 18–20, 24, 131–2, 167, 189, 201, 203, 204; religious 19, 20, 133, 189, 201; ultra- 217
National Religious Party (NRP) 18, 48, 49, 83, 84, 95, 143, 146, 153
North Atlantic Treaty Organization (NATO) 11, 182, 214
Netanyahu, Binyamin 75, 77–9, 82, 84, 112, 132, 136, 142, 143, 144, 185, 189, 195, 204, 205, 209
"new world order" 59
9/11 166, 170
1956 war 10
1967 war 6, 8, 10–11, 19–22, 24, 31, 42, 97, 134, 201, 202
Nixon, Richard 24, 32, 34, 207
Nobel Peace Prize 132
"non-paper" (on Aims and Principles of the Security Arrangements) 71–2, 77
Noor, Queen of Jordan 105
Northern Ireland 4
Norway 120–1, 213
nuclearization 60, 81, 104, 119, 177, 211

Occupied Territories 8, 11, 13, 43, 58–9, 70, 118, 121, 122, 123, 130, 133, 135, 136, 143, 189, 193, 204, 216
oil embargo 36
oil fields 36
Olmert, Aliza 171
Olmert, Ehud 167, 171–96, 202, 204–7, 209–16
One Israel 143
Oslo 1993–1996 (talks) 5, 64, 68, 70, 71, 74, 106, 107, 113, 120–1, 126–8, 152, 195, 202, 206, 208, 215, 216
Oslo Accords 59, 68–9, 71–3, 78, 79, 89n65, 104–5, 109, 112, 118, 120, 121, 122, 124–9, 142, 146, 156, 160, 203, 204, 213; failure of 129–36, 143–4, 205, 211; monitoring of 131
Oslo–Camp David 1996–2000 (talks) 5
Oslo Declaration of Principles 104, 107, 108, 111, 112, 120, 122, 194, 204
Ottoman Empire 6
Oz, Amos 48, 133

Pakistan 6, 174
Palestine 6; historic 21, 152; partition of 6
Palestine Liberation Organization (PLO) 8, 13, 22, 36, 40, 44, 61, 64, 89n65, 94, 95–6, 98, 100–1, 104, 105, 106, 109, 113, 118–20, 123–5, 128, 132–4, 145, 146, 155, 166, 167, 201, 208, 212, 216; split in 100
Palestine Mandate 6, 7, 20, 118, 152
Palestine National Council (PNC) 100, 130, 142
Palestinian Authority 126, 130, 131, 146, 166, 168, 171, 173, 181, 195
Palestinian autonomy 13, 41, 124, 132, 148
Palestinian Covenant (Charter) 124, 126, 130, 142
Palestinian "homeland" 44, 152
Palestinian issue 6–8, 32, 58–60, 64, 69, 78, 101, 105, 123–4, 172, 206, 207, 211, 213; and two-state solution 104, 118, 123, 141n91, 160, 169, 171, 177, 194, 196n18, 201–2, 208, 217
Palestinian rights 22, 41, 44, 101, 136
Palestinians 6, 13, 20, 45, 95, 100, 120, 128, 129, 145, 169–74; and collective punishment 132; and Israel 8, 12–13, 17, 32, 35, 41, 48, 59, 60–1, 67, 69–70, 73, 75, 76, 79, 81, 99–100, 105, 107, 109, 118–20, 122–3, 130–6, 143–60, 166, 169–86, 188–96, 201–8

Palestinian state 8, 13, 23, 103, 118, 120, 124, 129, 145, 148, 154, 157, 168, 169, 173, 182, 186, 203
Partition Plan (1947) 6–7, 203
patriotism 2, 19, 24
peace 38, 39, 45, 47, 59, 63, 70, 72, 94, 111, 133, 154, 170, 215; as a goal 2, 5, 10, 11, 14, 16, 20, 22, 23, 57, 59, 60, 73, 84, 88n38, 108, 123, 125, 143, 178, 186–7, 191, 202, 208, 210
peace agreements 10, 16, 19, 20, 29, 30, 34, 35, 42, 62, 67–8, 95, 100, 106, 122, 133, 166, 170, 175, 193, 203, 209; bilateral 6, 30
peace education 4
peace groups 3, 146
peace initiatives: 1971 30–1, 35, 42; 1973 30–5, 42; 1989 119
peace journalism 4
peacekeepers 58, 71, 72, 76, 111
peacemaking efforts 3, 8, 58, 107, 192, 201, 203 see also failure(s) (of peacemaking efforts)
Peace Now 119
peace process 5, 59, 124, 125, 126, 132, 133–4, 143, 171, 172–3, 206
Pelosi, Nancy 176
people-to-people endeavors 125
Peres, Shimon 37, 49, 62, 73–6, 78, 84, 86, 97, 100–3, 105, 107, 108, 113, 119, 120, 126, 129, 132, 135, 136, 155, 203, 204, 205, 209, 212
power shifts 4
pragmatism 28n56, 43, 126, 172, 174, 193, 203, 205, 212, 216, 217
prisoner releases 130, 142, 143
proximity talks 31–2
psychology 2, 4, 24, 44, 47, 49, 63, 85, 106, 132, 135, 154, 201, 215; Jewish 46; political 2
public opinion 3, 201; Israeli 11, 19, 21, 23, 24, 34, 44, 63, 68–9, 73–7, 83, 85, 86, 97, 99, 106, 112, 121, 122, 129, 132, 133, 135–6, 138n22, 150, 153, 155, 159–60, 176, 177, 187, 192–3, 205, 211, 214, 217; Palestinian 145, 150
Pugwash Conferences 175
Pundak, Ron 120

Quandt, William 46
Quartet (US, UN, Russia, and EU) 167, 169, 171

Index

Rabat 38, 98
Rabin, Leah 59, 123
Rabin, Yitzhak 31, 32, 34, 35–43, 48, 57, 59–73, 75–9, 81–4, 86, 95–101, 104–13, 119, 120, 122–36, 143, 150, 152–5, 157, 168, 176, 185, 187, 192, 195, 201–7, 209–12
Rabinovich, Itamar 60–5, 67–9, 72, 75, 106
"Rabin pocket" 77, 79, 80
Ramallah 131
Rashid, Mahmoud 150
Reagan, Ronald 103
Reagan Plan 102, 103
recession 3
reciprocity 2
refugees 6, 8, 13, 20, 33, 58, 108, 112, 147–8, 157, 178, 181–2, 194; and right of return 146, 148, 150, 156–7, 159–60, 169–70, 191
religion 2, 4, 16, 18–19, 45, 48, 78, 109, 131, 133, 189, 201, 204, 217
Rhodes formula 29
Rice, Condoleeza 172–3, 176, 178, 179, 184, 190, 191, 192, 195
Road Map (April 2003) 169, 171, 173, 190
rocket attacks 171, 186, 189, 210, 216
Rogers, William 34–5
Rogers Plan, the 31–2
Ross, Dennis 60, 61, 62, 64–8, 70, 73–4, 76, 79, 80, 82, 106, 107, 108, 127–9, 134, 145
Rothchild, Danny 127
Rubinstein, Elyakim 46, 48, 84, 108
Rumania 40, 44, 213
Rusk, Dean 21

Sabra and Chatila massacre 121
Sadat, Anwar 30–3, 35–6, 38, 40–2, 44–7, 62, 98, 119, 127, 192, 202–3, 206–9, 211, 214, 215, 216
Saddam Hussein 57, 61, 84, 106, 119, 123
Sagie, Uri 60, 63, 67, 79, 81, 82, 84–6, 146, 205
SAM 3 missiles 32
Samaria 43, 45, 48, 95, 120, 135
Saudi Arabia 61, 123, 169, 170, 172, 174, 178, 180, 211
Savir, Uri 73–6, 120, 126, 128–9
Schultz, George 103, 119
Scud attacks 60, 122, 123, 135, 210
Seale, Patrick 73
Sea of Galilee 7, 65
Second Lebanon War 172, 175, 177, 187, 193, 210
secular Israelis 16–17, 19, 155, 203
security barrier 167–8, 185
self-determination 8; Jewish 17, 216
self-image, collective 2
Shamir, Yaacov 194
Shamir, Yitzhak 48, 49, 57, 58, 59, 61, 100–4, 119, 120, 128, 135, 185, 210
Shara, Farouk al- 79, 80, 82, 85, 175
Sharm el-Sheikh 20, 21, 30, 31, 33, 34, 40, 42, 176
Sharm el-Sheikh Memorandum 144
Sharon, Ariel 45, 49, 78, 112, 159, 160, 166–71, 175, 185, 209–10
Shas 62, 83, 84, 127, 143, 145, 146, 189–90
Shepherdstown 79, 80, 82, 83, 86, 187, 202
Sher, Gilead 144, 145, 154, 156
Shikaki, Khalil 194
Shinui 83
Shlaim, Avi 100, 106, 109
Silwan 181
Sinai Desert 7, 20–3, 29, 30–1, 34, 37–8, 41, 43, 45, 47, 48, 50, 152, 210, 216
Singer, Yoel 120
Six Day War *see* 1967 war
social norms 2
South Africa 217
Soviet Union 8, 10–11, 13, 21, 29, 30–3, 35–6, 38, 41, 57–8, 98, 102, 103, 104, 113, 119, 175; collapse of 59, 122, 210–11
spoilers 3, 4, 48, 62, 71, 73, 78, 83, 85, 95, 112, 125, 132, 133, 136, 154, 160, 178, 190–2, 201, 204–5, 211; devious 3; greedy 3; Islamic 208; limited 3; management of 3, 4; punishment of 4; total 3; types of 3
Stand With Us 179
State Department (US) 14, 32, 34, 61, 134, 191
Stedman, Stephen 3
Stockholm 144, 162n19
Sudan 181
Suez Canal 23, 30, 42–3
suicide bombings 171
Suleiman, Ibrahim 175
symbolism 16, 19, 44, 94, 103, 106, 148, 150, 155, 160, 216
Syria 5–7, 20, 21, 22, 33, 35, 36, 38, 39, 43, 57–86, 94, 95, 99, 100, 104–7, 109–11, 113, 119, 122, 123, 127, 128, 134, 143, 144, 145, 152, 153, 156, 170, 174–6, 185–8, 191–6, 201–8, 213–15

Taba 157, 159
Tel Aviv 48, 60, 119
Temple Mount 19, 142, 146, 148, 149, 151, 155, 156, 159, 180, 186, 193, 204
Temporary International Presence in Hebron (TIPH) 131
terrorism 20, 35, 75, 76, 100–1, 112, 118, 123, 124, 126, 128, 132, 133, 134, 136, 141n83, 142, 167–8, 170, 171, 176, 182, 186, 205
Third Way 83
"three no's" (of Khartoum) 22, 32, 202
Tourgeman, Shalom 172, 183
tourism 64, 69, 74, 103
track two endeavors 4
trade 64, 67, 68, 69, 74, 80, 83
Transjordan 6
trauma, past 2
"trip wire doctrine" 70
trust 110–11, 125, 201, 215; absence of 2–3, 15–16, 24, 31–2, 34, 38, 40, 42, 44–6, 49–50, 63, 67–8, 70, 72, 76–7, 82, 86, 132–4, 136, 150–2, 160, 201–4, 209, 211, 217
Tunisia 80, 83, 118, 137n11, 213
Turbowitz, Yoram 172, 175, 182, 183
Turkey 174, 177, 187, 213, 214

unilateralism 166–8, 171–2, 174, 189
United Arab Republic (UAR) 23
United Nations (UN) 6, 23, 44, 169, 174
UN General Assembly (UNGA) 169, 184; Resolution 181 of 6, 118; Resolution 194 of 147–8, 169–70
United States (US) 11, 13–14, 16, 21–3, 29, 30, 33, 36, 49, 57, 59, 64, 65–76, 79–80, 82–6, 94, 98–108, 113, 118, 120–1, 123, 127–9, 134, 142–4, 148, 149, 151–2, 157, 167–9, 171–82, 189–93, 195, 202, 204, 206–8, 213–14; and arms supply to Israel 32, 83, 86, 99
United States Institute of Peace 172
UN peace-keepers 30, 41
UN Security Council (UNSC) 19, 184, 188; Resolution 242 of 8, 14, 22, 29, 30–1, 36, 40, 41, 43–4, 46–7, 58, 65, 73, 77, 101, 202, 209, 216; Resolution 338 of 73, 101; Resolution 1397 of 169

US Congress 72, 76, 100–1, 103, 106, 107, 108, 113, 134, 168, 172, 176, 184, 207, 213
US–Israeli relations 10, 68, 207
US–Soviet relations 10–11

Vance, Cyrus 46
victimhood, sense of 11, 16, 125, 132, 135–6, 153, 201, 217
victimization, sense of 2
Vietnam 23
violence 3; culture of 1–2

War of Attrition 29, 32
war-weariness 3, 122, 135
Washington (US administration) 10, 13, 21, 31, 32, 41, 57–8, 61, 67, 71, 97–8, 103, 113, 123, 128, 129, 134, 176, 177, 194, 213, 214
Washington Declaration 111–12
Washington talks: 1992 59, 121; 1999 79, 84
water 6, 58, 67, 82, 103, 108, 109, 111
weapons development 3
weapons of mass destruction 104, 211
Weisglass, Dov 185
Weizman, Ezer 45, 46
West Bank 6, 8, 11–19, 21, 23, 41, 43–6, 48, 50, 58, 61, 78, 89n65, 94–7, 99, 101–4, 109–10, 112, 113, 119, 121, 124, 130, 132, 137n3, 142, 143, 147, 148, 152, 155, 166–8, 170, 171, 173, 178–81, 183, 189, 195, 202, 206, 210, 215
Western Wall 19
World War I 6
Wye Plantation 74, 79, 142, 144, 145

Yahdut Hatorah 143
Yanai, Shlomo 154, 155
Yatom, Dani 79, 82, 83, 84, 155
Yom Kippur War (1973) 35, 36, 40, 42–3, 47, 94–5, 201, 210

Zakeim, Dov 175
Zartman, William 4, 210
Zeira, Eli 33
zero-sum relationship/conflict 1, 6, 8
Zionism 82, 155

eBooks
from Taylor & Francis
Helping you to choose the right eBooks for your Library

Add to your library's digital collection today with Taylor & Francis eBooks. We have over 45,000 eBooks in the Humanities, Social Sciences, Behavioural Sciences, Built Environment and Law, from leading imprints, including Routledge, Focal Press and Psychology Press.

Choose from a range of subject packages or create your own!

Benefits for you
- Free MARC records
- COUNTER-compliant usage statistics
- Flexible purchase and pricing options
- 70% approx of our eBooks are now DRM-free.

Benefits for your user
- Off-site, anytime access via Athens or referring URL
- Print or copy pages or chapters
- Full content search
- Bookmark, highlight and annotate text
- Access to thousands of pages of quality research at the click of a button.

ORDER YOUR FREE INSTITUTIONAL TRIAL TODAY

Free Trials Available

We offer free trials to qualifying academic, corporate and government customers.

eCollections
Choose from 20 different subject eCollections, including:

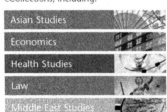

- Asian Studies
- Economics
- Health Studies
- Law
- Middle East Studies

eFocus
We have 16 cutting-edge interdisciplinary collections, including:

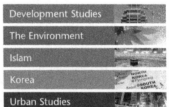

- Development Studies
- The Environment
- Islam
- Korea
- Urban Studies

For more information, pricing enquiries or to order a free trial, please contact your local sales team:

UK/Rest of World: **online.sales@tandf.co.uk**
USA/Canada/Latin America: **e-reference@taylorandfrancis.com**
East/Southeast Asia: **martin.jack@tandf.com.sg**
India: **journalsales@tandfindia.com**

www.tandfebooks.com

CPSIA information can be obtained
at www.ICGtesting.com
Printed in the USA
BVHW01*0354240218
508883BV00008B/38/P